Treatise on Painting

Grotesque heads representing various aspects of human expression.
Windsor 12495.

# TREATISE ON PAINTING

[CODEX URBINAS LATINUS 1270]

## By LEONARDO DA VINCI

TRANSLATED AND ANNOTATED BY

A. PHILIP McMAHON

WITH AN INTRODUCTION BY

LUDWIG H. HEYDENREICH

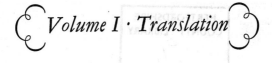

*Volume I · Translation*

PRINCETON, NEW JERSEY

PRINCETON UNIVERSITY PRESS

1956

Printed in the United States of America by
Princeton University Press, Princeton, New Jersey

Illustrations and facsimile by
The Meriden Gravure Company

# PREFACE

THIS first translation into English of the Codex Urbinas 1270 was the major effort of Philip McMahon's last eight years and the culmination of a life of scholarship. At the time of his death in 1947 a literal translation of the Treatise had been completed. In addition, a concordance, working bibliography, and notes were ready.

In the years of our marriage I had ample occasion to see my husband's dedication to teaching and scholarship and the scrupulous care with which he prepared his manuscripts, of which this was to be the major effort. Although he always carried a full teaching schedule and, for many years, had also been chairman of the department of Art History at New York University's Washington Square College, Philip always had a book or an article in preparation. With the exception of the translation of this Treatise, everything my husband had written had been published when he died. The task of bringing this work to publication remained. This involved editing the translation, compiling a bibliography, assembling notes and illustrations, and writing an introduction. Dr. Elmer Belt enlisted the interest of Dr. Ludwig Heydenreich, who has provided an illuminating introduction, which sets Leonardo's Treatise in its appropriate place in the history of art and evaluates its importance. The extensive and scholarly bibliography was compiled by Kate Trauman Steinitz from the working bibliography which my husband had prepared.

It would be difficult for me to give adequate thanks to all those who aided in the task of bringing this work to publication. Among those to whom I turned, William M. Ivins, Charles Rufus Morey, Walter W. S. Cook, Martin Weinberger, Lionello Venturi, Wilhelm Valentiner, and Irma Richter were tremendously helpful. I am also greatly indebted to Henry H. Wiggins of the Columbia University Press, who gave the manuscript deep study and thoughtful analysis, and to New York University for lending me essential books from the Washington Square Library and the School of Fine Arts. I cannot thank Dr. Belt and Mrs. Steinitz enough for their assistance, antedating their help to me by many years during which they were in continuous correspondence with my husband and furnished him with many invaluable aids. I have also been immensely helped by my friend Herbert Weissberger, on whose counsel and support I have leaned.

The editorial work was undertaken primarily by Marie F. Rodell and myself, and there is no way in which I can express the debt of gratitude which I owe to Mrs. Rodell for the hundreds of hours of intensive effort which she has invested in this undertaking, which could not have been realized without her collaboration and encouragement. When we began this monumental task we were faced with the necessity of deciding whether the translation, which was literal and therefore often confusing, should be edited in the interest of readability or should follow the Trattato word for word. Since the Princeton University Press wisely decided to include in the publication the reproduction of the Codex Urbinas itself, affording the reader an opportunity for comparison and reference, we decided to modify the translation only where essential for purposes of clarity. Since neither Mrs. Rodell nor I are scholars in the field of the history of art, we approached the task with deference, and made only those editorial revisions which seemed absolutely necessary.

The index to this work was prepared by Francesco M. Bianco, who also helped me in the final stages of the editorial work.

For the errors which I know must still exist in this translation and which doubtless would not have occurred had my husband been able to finish this book, I beg the reader's indulgence.

AUDREY F. MCMAHON

The illustrations reproduced from the drawings at Windsor Castle are included by gracious permission of Her Majesty The Queen. Those from the *Institut de France* have been made available through the courtesy of M. Tremblot de la Croix, Conservateur en Chef, Bibliothèque de l'Institut de France. Appreciation is due to the Elmer Belt Library of Vinciana for invaluable assistance in the securing of photographs.

# CONTENTS

## *VOLUME I*

## *Codex Urbinas Latinus 1270*
## in translation

Painting is Science 3. Basic Principles of Painting as
Science 4. Painting is Natural Philosophy 5. Vision
is the Most Accurate Sense and its Loss the Most Severe
Damage 6. Painting, Astronomy, and Geometry 8.
Is Painting a Mechanical Art? 8. A Comparison of
Painting and Poetry 12. A Comparison of Vision and
Hearing 14. Arguments on Behalf of Painting in
Comparison with Poetry 20. Painting is Superior to
Music 25. Comparison of Painting with Poetry and
Music 28. Inferiority of Sculpture to Painting 32.
Sculpture is a Mechanical Art 35. A Comparison of
Painting and Sculpture 40.

Training of the Painter in Youth 45. Exercise of the
Imagination and the Memory 47. Science and Practice
47. Advice to Painters 49. Judging Works of Art 54.
How Painters are often Misled 55. Universality and
Versatility 57. Origin and Division of Painting 61.
Relative Importance of the Divisions of Painting 62.
Line Drawing 64. Aids in the Practice of Drawing 65.
Life Drawing 66. Light Suitable for Painting 69.
Light and Shadow Should be Consistent with the Loca-
tion of Figures 71. Objects and their Backgrounds 73.

## PART III    OF THE VARIOUS STATES AND MOVEMENTS OF THE HUMAN BODY

## VOLUME II

Introductory Note

### Codex Urbinas Latinus 1270
### in facsimile

# INTRODUCTION

## BY LUDWIG H. HEYDENREICH

### TRANSLATED BY DORA JANE JANSON

## The Codex Urbinas Latinus 1270 And Its Copies

T HE Codex Urbinas Latinus 1270 in the Vatican Library, which contains the earliest known compilation of Leonardo's *Treatise on Painting*, stems from the collection of the Dukes of Urbino.[1] This famous library, founded by Federigo da Montefeltro in 1472, was left to the Roman Curia in 1626 along with the rest of the ducal domain, upon the death of the last of the line, Francesco Maria della Rovere. Unknown, or at least ignored, the volume remained in the Papal library until Guglielmo Manzi brought it to light again in 1817, and published it for the first time.[2]

How and when the Codex came to Urbino remains a mystery, as, for that matter, does the rest of its history. Nevertheless it is possible to establish upon the basis of textual and stylistic clues that it was written about 1550 under the supervision of Francesco Melzi, Leonardo's friend and pupil, and that it represents a careful compilation of texts taken from Leonardo's original manuscripts which Francesco Melzi had inherited.[3] The appearance of the Codex, its extent, and the nature of its illustrations are discussed in the Introductory Note to the facsimile volume and need not be repeated here.

In the text proper, we can discern the hands of two collab-

[1] The best survey of the history of Leonardo's *Treatise on Painting* is given by Irma Richter in the introduction of the second edition of Jean Paul Richter, *The Literary Work of Leonardo da Vinci*, 1939 (see Bibliography, List D). It is also surveyed in Jordan, *Untersuchungen über das Malerbuch*, 1873, pp. 272ff.; G. Uzielli, *Ricerche*, Florence 1872 and Rome 1884 (Bibliography, List A3); and Heinrich Ludwig, *Das Buch von der Malerei*, 1882 (Bibliography, List A2), II, 383ff. and III 1ff.

[2] *Trattato della Pittura* . . . curata da Guglielmo Manzi, 1817 (Bibliography, List A2).

[3] Francesco Melzi (1473-1570), a nobleman of Milan, stayed with Leonardo in Rome, and afterwards in France (1513-1519). Leonardo designated him the executor of his last will and bequeathed him his library, manuscripts, and scientific instruments. Cf. Luca Beltrami, *Documenti* (Bibliography, List E1), Document 244 (last will) and Document 245; Richter, *op.cit.*, I, p. 6, n. 6.

orators: the scribe who copied specific, prescribed portions of Leonardo's manuscripts, and the editor, who went over the copy making corrections and indications for the transposition of various portions. There are also signs that Francesco Melzi took part in the project, inasmuch as his name appears upon three of the un-filled pages, indicating perhaps that the missing sections were those that he intended to edit himself.[4]

The proof that the book was compiled from Leonardo's orig-inal manuscripts rests upon two points: first, the transcriber makes more than one specific mention of the difficulties he en-countered as a result of Leonardo's left-handed mirror script[5]; second, the Codex ends with a list of eighteen original Leo-nardine manuscripts from which the compilation was made, each of these with its own identifying symbol.[6]

All of these circumstances indicate that the compilation was undertaken in the presence of Francesco Melzi and with his help—indeed, in all probability, at his behest and in his own house. The manuscripts which he had inherited from Leonardo were anxiously guarded with loving care in his Villa Vaprio d'Adda in the environs of Milan. Through the indifference of his heirs, the manuscripts were dispersed soon after his death in 1570. Some were given away, some stolen; some were lost, while others were cut up so that only clippings (mostly draw-ings) remain. Many a long odyssey preceded their arrival in the places where we find them today: Milan, Turin, London, Wind-sor, and Paris.[7]

The fact that less than half of the chapters in the Codex Ur-binas can be found among the still extant Leonardine manu-

[4] On fol. 78v, 79 and 102v. Only the first of these is reproduced in fac-simile since the second and third were otherwise blank. It may be possible that Hand 2 is identical with Francesco Melzi. The handwriting of the latter, dis-covered by G. Calvi on various sheets of Leonardo's literary legacy, is very similar to that of Hand 2, but the scarcity of examples of Melzi's writing does not admit of definite graphological conclusion. Melzi's handwriting is reproduced in G. Calvi, *I Manoscritti di Leonardo da Vinci* (Bibliography, List A3), pp. 255ff., figs. 54 and 57.

[5] Cf. McM. 53 and n. 25.

[6] Folios 330v and 331 of the Codex Urbinas list the original signed Leonardo manuscripts from which the Codex was compiled. The scribe has given each a symbol and has noted marginally on the Codex the source of his text.

[7] Cf. Uzielli, *op.cit.*; Richter, *op.cit.*, II, 400.

scripts proves that substantial parts of Leonardo's literary legacy have been lost. Thus, the Codex Urbinas becomes the primary source for those lost texts, since the possibility of interpolations from some other source may safely be dismissed.[8]

This brings us to the following conclusions: 1519, the year of Leonardo's death, and 1570, the year of Melzi's death, serve as the termini for dating the Codex Urbinas. However this span of time can be further narrowed since the style of the drawings would indicate a date near the middle of the century.

The manuscript was to be preparatory to an edition of Leonardo's *Treatise on Painting*, as conceived and interpreted by Melzi and his assistant. From the layout of the Codex we gain a keen understanding of the method followed in making the compilation. To begin with, the empty volume was divided into eight parts, which were presumably intended to encompass eight major divisions of the *Treatise on Painting* as planned by Leonardo. Each of his notebooks was gone over, and the various excerpts distributed among the eight subdivisions, according to content. In this almost mechanical process of collecting it is hardly surprising to find that repetitions, such as occur in the originals, crop up here too.[9] On the other hand there are a number of passages in the preserved originals which, according to their content, should have found a place in the *Treatise on Painting*. Since they are missing in the Codex Urbinas, however, we may postulate that the transcription as planned was to have been more all-embracing than the existing versions. The numerous blank pages, on which the missing passages would have appeared, are evidence of the premature abandonment of the work, part of which Melzi had probably reserved for himself.[10] The final version would have been based on this preliminary compilation of material, had it ever been completed. From the copious corrections that we find in the text, and from the related mar-

[8] The coherence of the compilation, and the numerous marginal notes of the copyists, referring in almost every case to the original manuscripts of Leonardo, are proof of the great responsibility which the compilers felt to be vested in them. The stylistic unity of the texts is added testimony to the authorship of Leonardo da Vinci.

[9] Cf. the marginal notes of the compilers on fols. 28v, 85, 124, 127v, 149, 157v.

[10] See Volume II, Introductory Note.

ginal notes, it is evident that a great deal of condensation and regrouping was envisaged.[11]

Even though it was never finished, the Codex Urbinas, evaluated upon its own merits, is of great importance: it is the only transcription taken from Leonardo's original manuscripts, and it was made by men who had known him personally and who still lived under the direct influence of his thinking. It contains many excerpts from Leonardo's lost texts, and all in all, forms the most complete collection of Leonardo's studies for the *Treatise on Painting* that has come down to us.

The Codex Urbinas is the archetype of all versions of the *Treatise on Painting*, written or printed, that were available before Manzi's rediscovery of the volume itself. The numerous other handwritten versions of the Treatise (some fifty have come to my attention, but I believe that the number could easily be doubled if a search were made)[12] have one thing in common: none of them contains more material than the Codex but all of them follow the same abbreviated version of the Urbinas text, and differ among each other only in unimportant details. None of them includes the first part of the Codex Urbinas, the so-called *Paragone*: they all begin with the second part, the *Precetti del Pittore*.[13] In the copies, this second part has been shortened by more than 50 chapters, and the third part by more than 70. Of the fourth part, which in the Codex Urbinas contains 15 chapters, only 7 appear in the copies. The fifth, the sixth and the seventh parts are missing entirely, and of the eighth part we find only one or two chapters. This makes a total of between 365 and 375 chapters in the copies as against 1,008 in the McMahon arrangement.[14]

These abridged versions may be classified into three groups: Type A, best represented by the Codex Barberinus 832 in the

[11] Cf. the marginal notes of fols. 28v, 53v, 85 (McM. 53, 283), H. 280.

[12] Cf. Bibliography, List A1.

[13] In these manuscripts the phrase *Parte Seconda* is sometimes written together with the title *Precetti del Pittore*, which proves that the archetype of those copies must have been the Codex Urbinas.

[14] The difference in the number of chapters, which vary between 365 and 375 results from the fact that in the copies some short texts separated in the Codex Urbinas are contracted into one chapter or vice versa.

Vatican Library, is closest to the Codex Urbinas.[15] Here we find
the same general layout: the individual chapters retain their titles
and are not numbered. Type B omits the titles in the text, sub-
stituting consecutive numeration of the chapters, and appending
an index wherein the missing titles appear as indications of the
content of each chapter. This type is later than Type A, and
derived from it.[16] Type C follows Type B for the most part; however, in editing, use was evidently made of the Type A group;
moreover certain corrections of the text give grounds for belief
that some of Leonardo's original manuscripts were consulted.
Type C consists of the group of manuscripts which were prepared for the famous first publication of the *Treatise* by Du
Fresne in 1651.

The story of how this *Editio Princeps* came into being is
known; here we shall give only a summary of the most important facts.[17] The idea of publishing Leonardo's *Treatise on Painting* was conceived in the fourth decade of the seventeenth century, in the circle that surrounded Cardinal Francesco Barberini
in Rome. His secretary, Cassiano del Pozzo (1588-1657), was a
friend of Nicolas Poussin, and it was he who persuaded the
latter to do the illustrations for the project. The manuscripts
which they worked from (the Codex Barberinus 832 Type A,
and another, not specifically identifiable, of Type B—perhaps the
Codex Corsinianus in Rome) were compared with Leonardo's
originals, or such of these as were available at the time in the
collection of Count Galeazzo Arconati in Milan. An extensive correspondence between Arconati and Pozzo reveals the enthusiasm
with which the work was undertaken.[18] A whole series of manuscripts exists relating to this preparation of the first edition: of
these, the most important are Ms. H 228 in the Biblioteca Ambrosiana in Milan; the manuscript formerly in the collection of
Comtesse de Béhague, in Paris and inherited by her nephew,

---

[15] The Codex Barberinus is the best example of the abbreviated version, and
is one of the earliest copies (end of the sixteenth century). Cf. Ludwig, *op.cit.*,
III, 18, and Amelia Clelia Pierantoni, *Studi sul Libro della Pittura di Leonardo
da Vinci* (Bibliography, List A1).

[16] Cf. Bibliography, List A1.          [17] Cf. Richter, *op.cit.*, p. 8.

[18] Enrico Carusi, "Per il *Trattato della Pittura*," p. 433 ff. (Bibliography, List
A3); *Sulla redazione abbreviata* (Bibliography, List A1).

Marquis Hubert de Ganay; and a manuscript in The Hermitage
in Leningrad. Poussin delivered the drawings, which were probably copied in his workshop too, so that it is impossible to say
with certainty which of the three sets of illustrations in the above-
mentioned manuscripts is closest to the master's own hand.[19]
These illustrations were later altered in the most arbitrary manner by the engravers of the copper plates, especially by Errard,
who inserted entire landscape backgrounds. This tampering made
Poussin exceedingly angry, as his famous letter testifies. In 1640
in Rome, Pozzo entrusted a completed manuscript, with Poussin's illustrations, to Paul Fréart, Sieur de Chantelou, who took
it with him to Paris where he was to arrange for the printing.
However he got around to it only after ten years, at which time
it was brought out by Raphael Trichet Du Fresne.[20]

From this final version, which appeared in the same year in
French translation, all subsequent editions are derived, up to the
rediscovery of the Codex Urbinas.[21] The sole exception is the
edition of 1792 by Fontani, in Florence; this one was based on
the Codex Riccardianus in Florence, a manuscript of Type B. It
dates from about the middle of the seventeenth century and is
adorned with splendid drawings by Stefano della Bella, which
come closer to Leonardo's originals than any of the other illustrations with the exception of those in the Codex Urbinas. The

[19] The illustrations of the Codex H 228 are very spontaneously drawn and of
good quality, so that possibly they were done by Poussin himself, or under his
direction in his workshop. The same can be said of the illustrations in the manuscript Béhague, now in the possession of the Marquis de Ganay-Béhague, Paris.
This manuscript was probably a copy brought to Paris by M. de Chantelou. The
illustrations in the manuscript at the Hermitage, Leningrad, known only through
rather mediocre reproductions in a short Russian essay, seem to be of the same
quality as those in the manuscripts mentioned above. The opinion that it is
impossible to determine which of these series of illustrations is closer to those of
Poussin is shared by Walter Friedlaender. Special studies by Kate T. Steinitz
have appeared in the *Art Quarterly*, Spring 1953, and in the Communications du
Congrès du Val de Loire 1953 (Bibliography, List A3).

[20] Raphael Trichet du Fresne, *Trattato della Pittura di Leonardo da Vinci*
(Bibliography, List A2). Poussin's criticism in a letter to the engraver Abraham
Bosse, published in Nicolas Poussin, *Correspondance*, Paris 1911, pp. 420-421.
Concerning Poussin's illustrations, cf. Hautecoeur, *Bulletin d'histoire de l'art Fran-
çais*, 1913 (Bibliography, List A2). F. S. Bassoli in "Racc. Vinciana," XVII, 1954,
pp. 157ff.

[21] Bibliography, List A2.

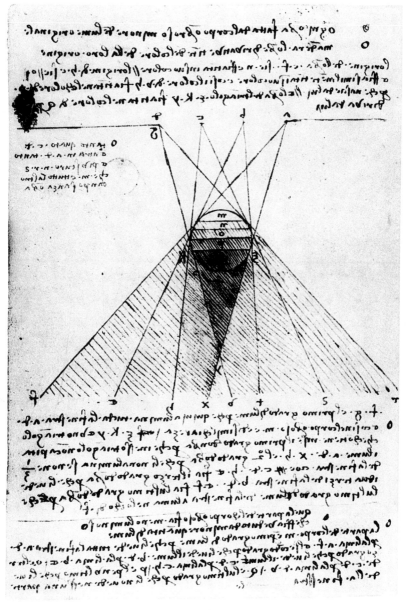

1. Diagram showing gradation of light and shadow. BN 2038, fol. 13v, Institut de France. Cf. Codex Urbinas, fol. 213.

Sketch demonstrating how light from one source falls on a face, and diagrams and notes on the action of light. Windsor 12604. Cf. Codex Urbinas, fol. 219.

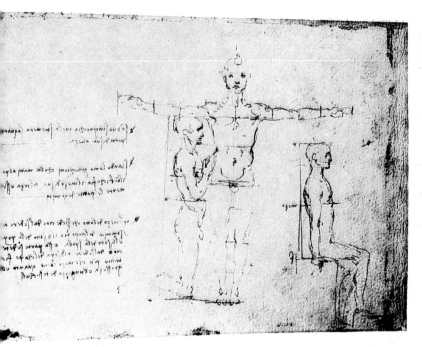

. Studies of proportion. Windsor 19132. The sheet is marked with the sign φ, which shows that it was intended for inclusion in the Codex Urbinas.

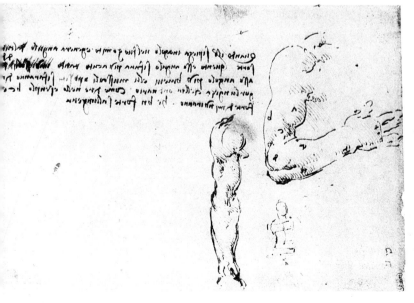

Anatomical sketches of left arm, and study of a torso squared for proportion.
Windsor 12614.

5. A study in perspective, showing how to "draw a figure on a wall 12 braccia high which shall appear 12 braccia high."

6. Figures drawn with plumbline.

7. Sketch of a man swinging a club, to show concentration of force opposite the point to be struck. Codex Atlanticus, Cf. des Vinci, fol. 282.

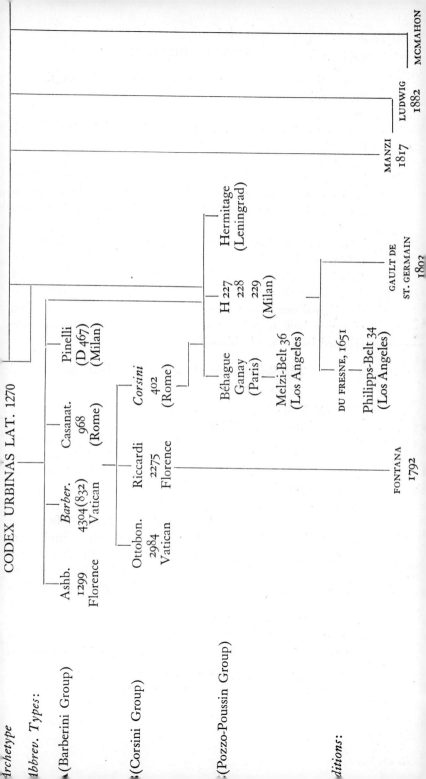

composition of the text however is already based upon the Du Fresne edition.[22]

Thus we find that all the printed editions, including that of Fontani, contain only a sharply curtailed version of the Leonardine manuscripts including 375 chapters since the Codex Urbinas remained unknown until 1817. I have included a chart of the most important manuscripts and printed editions up to that time, in order to clarify the relationship between the various types.

Now that we have established the importance of the Codex Urbinas as the archetype of all other versions of the *Treatise on Painting* which have come down to us, there remains the task of determining the relationship of this first of the compilations to the original manuscripts; and more especially, insofar as possible, of seeing how well it accords with the treatise project as envisioned by Leonardo himself.

### The Relationship of the Codex Urbinas to Leonardo's Original Treatise Plan

Dr. McMahon's exceptional contribution in preparing this edition of the Codex Urbinas consists of finding out which of the chapters can be traced to Leonardo's original manuscripts, insofar as the latter are preserved. This information may be found in the Concordance. Although there have been other scholars similarly occupied (notably the late Monsignor Enrico Carusi in Rome, who devoted his life to the preparation of a critical edition of Leonardo's *Treatise on Painting* from the original texts; and Amelia Clelia Pierantoni, whose studies are worthy of mention),[23] Dr. McMahon's edition is the first to offer a systematic concordance of the Codex Urbinas' chapters with Leonardo's own texts. This enables us to determine exactly which of the latter have been lost, and no longer exist except in the Codex Urbinas and its derivatives.

Furthermore, it is easier now, with the help of the facsimile publications of the complete surviving writings of Leonardo, to

[22] *Trattato della Pittura. . .* di Stefano della Bella (Bibliography, List A2).
[23] Enrico Carusi, *op.cit.*, Amelia Clelia Pierantoni, *op.cit.* (Bibliography, List A3).

determine how much material pertinent to the *Treatise on Painting* as he envisioned it, has been left out of the Codex Urbinas.[24]

These considerations bring us to the crucial problem, which is to endeavor to determine to what degree the material compiled in the Codex Urbinas gives a true reflection of Leonardo's own conception of the *Treatise on Painting*; and whether it is possible for us to obtain a more exact picture of that conception. Having posed this question we find ourselves embroiled in the confused and confusing problems of Leonardo's literary output.

Leonardo repeatedly asserts in his own notes that he intended to write a book on painting. With the exception of a few partial abstracts, such as *On the Flight of Birds*, and the *Ludi Geometrici*, the entire collection of manuscripts, fruits of a lifetime of work, was directed toward the goal of three large publications: *The Book on Painting, The Book on Mechanics*, and *The Book on Anatomy*. In his notes Leonardo makes frequent reference to these as clearly separate entities. In his *Anatomy* he alludes to his *Mechanics*, and vice versa; and similarly, in that por-

---

[24] A. C. Pierantoni, *op.cit.*, gives the number of texts which belong to Leonardo's preparatory studies for the *Treatise on Painting*. Also in Richter, *op.cit.*, I, 112 and in McCurdy, *The Notebooks of Leonardo da Vinci*, 1938, Vol. II, Ch. 28-34 (Bibliography, List D) a great deal of material is brought together from the original manuscripts, some of which is not to be found in the Codex Urbinas. Recently C. Gould in *The Burlington Magazine*, 1947, pp. 239ff. for the first time deciphers the notes on the drawing from the collection at Windsor (W. 12412) which give a fascinating description of the beds of rivers seen through the water, and which were undoubtedly also intended for the *Treatise*.

In addition to these meticulous works of scholarship, the task still remains of excerpting systematically Leonardo's original manuscripts for the purpose of bringing together a complete collection which would include every passage referring to the *Treatise on Painting*. This fatiguing work has to be done in the same way as the stupendous corpus of Leonardo's studies on mechanics by Arturo Uccelli, *Leonardo da Vinci, I libri de meccanica*, and the no less admirable corpus of Leonardo's studies on flight by Giacomelli, *Gli scritti di Leonardo da Vinci sul volo* (Bibliography, List C1).

Since 1919 the project of a complete edition of Leonardo's studies for the *Treatise on Painting* has occupied the minds of scholars internationally; many plans have been announced, but the work has not yet begun. There was hope that it might have been started in the Quincentennial year 1952. Cf. *Per il quarto Centenario della morte di Leonardo da Vinci*, and L. H. Heydenreich in *Rinascita*, pp. 161ff. (Bibliography, List A3), and *Kunstchronik* IV (1951), pp. 255ff.

tion of the *Anatomy* which deals with the eye, he makes a reference to *The Book on Painting*: "Make the rainbow in the last
book 'On Painting.' But first make the book of the colours produced by the mixture of the other colours so that by means of
these colours used by painters you may be able to prove the
genesis of the colours of the rainbow. . . ." (Quad. II, 6r).[25]

Again, in another note on optical experiments: "The surface
of each body takes part of the colour of whatever is set against
it. The colours of the objects in light are reproduced on each
other's surface at different spots according to the varieties in the
positions of these objects . . . and the rest will be set forth in the
Book on Painting. In that book it will be demonstrated, by trans-
mitting the images of the bodies and colours of the things illuminated by the sun through a small round hole in a dark place
onto a smooth surface which in itself is white. . . ."[26]

In addition to such allusions to the *Treatise on Painting* in
connection with other fields of study, the Codex Urbinas itself
contains several of Leonardo's indications for the over-all plan
of his book. In one place he says that the work is "woven together of these functions [i.e., of the eye], reminding the painter
according to what rules and in what fashion he should reproduce
with his art all of these things, the work of nature and the beauties of the world."[27] In another place he gives tables of contents,
which we shall discuss later in greater detail.[28]

We can no longer ascertain with exactitude how much of this
plan had taken decisive shape during Leonardo's lifetime, and
was known to his contemporaries. Although we have a whole

[25] *Dell'Anatomia Fogli A 10.* "Arrange it so that the book of the elements of
mechanics, with examples, shall precede the demonstration of the movement and
force of man and of other animals, and by means of these you will be able to
prove all your propositions." *Quaderni d'Anatomia, I.1* "On machines. Why
nature cannot give the power of movement to animals without mechanical instruments, as is shown by me in this book on the works of movement which nature has created in the animals. And for this reason I have drawn up the rules
of the four powers of nature without which nothing through her can give local
movement to these animals" (i.e., movement, weight, force, and percussion). Cf.
furthermore the notes on Ms.E. 19v and 20 (McCurdy I, 194ff.).

[26] Cod. Atl. 181. r.a.

[27] McM. 427.

[28] Cf. L. H. Heydenreich, "Quellenkritische Untersuchungen," Leonardo
Malereitraktat, in *Kunstchronik*, IV (1951), pp. 255ff.

series of contemporaneous references to Leonardo's *Treatise on Painting*, none of these permits us to come to an unequivocal conclusion as to its form and contents. On the contrary, if we compare these quotations one with another, we are left with a disparate, indeed contradictory impression. The earliest mention is to be found in the *Divina Proportione* of the famous mathematician, Luca Pacioli. In his dedication of the book to Ludovico Sforza he writes as follows about Leonardo: "After he had already finished with all diligence the worthy books on painting and human movement. . . ."[29]

Next Cellini relates, in his *Discorsi sopra l'Architettura*, that *ca.* 1540 he acquired from an impoverished nobleman a small book, copied from Leonardo, on the three great arts, "Scultura, Pittura, e Architettura"; that it contained "the most beautiful discourse on perspective ever composed"; and that he later lent the book to the architect, Sebastiano Serlio, who used it, insofar as he was capable of understanding it, for his own treatise on architecture.[30]

The manuscripts in Francesco Melzi's possession were known to Vasari also. He mentions especially the writings on anatomy, and marvels at Leonardo's versatility: "Whoever reads these notes of Leonardo will be amazed to find how well that divine spirit has reasoned of the arts, the muscles, the nerves and veins, with the greatest diligence in all things." Then he continues: "N. N. a painter of Milan also possesses some writings of Leonardo written in the same characters, using his left hand in reversed writing, which treat of painting and of the methods of design and colour. Not long ago he came to Florence wishing to have the work printed. He afterwards went to Rome to put it in hand, but I do not know with what result."[31]

Finally, Lomazzo notes in his *Trattato della Pittura* (1584) "In the same way Leonardo discoursed and argued in one of his

[29] Luca Pacioli, *De Divina Proportione*, editio princeps, 1509 and 1896, II, 33 (Bibliography, List E2).

[30] Benvenuto Cellini, *I Trattati dell'oreficia*, 1857, De L'Architettura, pp. 225ff. (Bibliography, List A3).

[31] Giorgio Vasari, *Le vite . . .* , Florence 1568 (Bibliography, List E2), here quoted from the English translation in *Leonardo da Vinci*, Phaidon Press, Oxford and London, 1945, p. 10.

books which I read some years ago. This book was written with
the left hand at the request of Ludovico Sforza, Duke of Milan. . . ."[32]

Pacioli's statement is usually interpreted as meaning that Leonardo's *Treatise on Painting* was essentially complete in 1498.
Upon scrutiny of Leonardo's manuscripts up to that date, however, it becomes plain that a large part of the notes for the *Treatise on Painting* was written considerably later than 1498.[33] Thus,
Pacioli's words can only have reference to a more or less completed fractional version that he had seen. It is my belief that
this can be identified as Codex 2038 of the Bibliothèque Nationale
in Paris, since it not only contains the themes mentioned by
Pacioli, but also dates from between 1490 and 1495.[34]

Cellini's manuscript probably represented a compilation of excerpts from Leonardo similar in type to the so-called Codex
Huygens in the Morgan Library, which has been expertly edited
by Panofsky.[35] Leonardo's notes received greater attention during
the sixteenth century than is generally supposed; although the
numerous early copies have never been the object of systematic
research, a perusal of them discloses wide variation in the selection of subject matter from the originals, which shows that
they were studied by people of many different sorts and of
diverse interests.[36] The loss of the Cellini-owned manuscript is

[32] G. P. Lomazzo, *Trattato dell'Arte de la Pittura*, Milan 1584 (Bibliography,
List E2) here quoted from Luca Beltrami, *op.cit.* Document 263: 25 (Bibliography, List E1).

[33] Cf. note 53.          [34] For this date cf. Richter, *op.cit.*, I, 108.

[35] Erwin Panofsky, *The Codex Huygens*, London 1940 (Bibliography, List
B2 Proportion).

[36] The Codex Huygens was compiled before 1570, the year of Melzi's death,
after which the rapid dispersal of Leonardo's manuscripts made the compiling of such a work impossible. Cellini's manuscript, bought in 1541, must
of course have been written before that date. The copies of Wenzel Hollar, the
drawings of the Codex Vallardi, reproduced in Panofsky, *The Codex Huygens*,
fig. 108, and finally the existence of hundreds of single copies, not only from
artistic but from scientific drawings (cf. Heydenreich, *I disegni di Leonardo da
Vinci nella Galleria dell'Accademia di Venezia*, Folio, Florence 1949) prove that
Leonardo's manuscripts were fairly well known in the sixteenth century. A systematic study of the various groups of copies after Leonardo would give us valuable
information about the interest which Leonardo attracted in the Cinquecento both
as artist and as scientist. In the seventeenth century the study of Leonardo is very
obvious, as the various compilations of his *Treatise on Painting*, of his studies
on water, and of the other aspects of his scientific work amply prove.

particularly regrettable, since the highly praised essay on perspective that it contained would doubtless have helped to decide how far Leonardo had progressed with his book on perspective, a matter which must remain undetermined in view of the paucity of notes on this subject that have come down in the remaining original manuscripts.[37]

The texts referred to by Vasari and Lomazzo—there is a possibility that they are one and the same[38]—must be regarded as lost. Lomazzo's words, "written for Ludovico Sforza," point to the conclusion that the text he knew was dedicated to the Duke, and hence must have been written before the latter's fall in 1499.

These source accounts do not give a precise picture of Leonardo's treatise as a whole; all of them are based merely upon an acquaintance with some fractional manuscript or other, if not upon copies.

This fact enhances the importance of the Codex Urbinas as a source document, especially in any attempt to reconstruct Leonardo's original treatise plan. As we have pointed out, the compilation of these passages, nearly two thirds of which stem from manuscripts since lost, is indubitably traceable to Francesco Melzi, who probably intended to organize the treatise exactly as he thought Leonardo had conceived it. In this task of reconstruction he had the following aids: 1) the recollection of Leonardo's spoken opinions, which the latter must often have shared with his friend and favorite pupil; 2) the written references contained in Leonardo's notes; and 3) the literary tradition for treatises of this sort that was prevalent before and during Leonardo's lifetime. It is possible for us to verify only points 2 and 3.

Two plans for the organization of the treatise are to be found among Leonardo's notes; these, however, are so vaguely formulated that they would not suffice as working outlines. In the

---

[37] For Leonardo's studies of perspective, most of which are collected in Richter, *op.cit.*, I, cf. Panofsky, *Perspektive als Symbolische Form*, 1927, pp. 258ff. especially pp. 287 and 324: *idem*, Dürer's *Kunsttheorie, vornehmlich in ihrem Verhaeltnis zu den Italienern*, Berlin 1915 (*passim*); *idem*, *Codex Huygens*, pp. 90ff.; W. M. Ivins, Jr., *On Rationalization of Sight*, 1938; and John White, "Developments in Renaissance Perspective" 1949-1951, p. 40 (Bibliography, List B2 Perspective).

[38] I suppose that the manuscript presented to Vasari was the same as that mentioned later by Lomazzo. Probably it was also the Ms. 2038 in Paris.

chapter "On the mixture of colors" (McM. 178), he says that this subject is to be placed between the theory and the practice of painting, from which one may draw the conclusion that the treatise was to be divided into two principal parts, the one on theory and the other on practice. In the second instance Leonardo speaks of the ten categories of visual perception: light and dark, color, volume, shape, locale, nearness and distance, motion and rest (McM. 427), and says that he will weave these ten categories together in his work. However, since he indicates concomitantly that the study of light and shade should form *one* book, he thereby abandons the ten-partition plan, so that it seems preferable to regard the latter merely as an enumeration of the problems that his book would cover and not as a specific sequence of chapters. In this general sense, the ten useful functions of the eye are frequently alluded to in the first book, the *Paragone*.[39] From other passages we gather that the treatise was to have included a book on perspective; one on shadows; and another on movement.[40]

The arrangement of the Codex Urbinas reflects relatively little of the above-cited elements. Of its eight principal parts, as can be seen by a glance at the Table of Contents for this translation, only portions of the second, the third with the fourth included as appendix, and the fifth, can be related to Leonardo's scheme. Parts VI to VIII inclusive must at best be understood as subheadings under the broader categories of "figure" and "situation."[41] By examining the treatises of this kind that antedate Leonardo we may judge whether or not the first part and the beginning of the second can be fitted into some kind of scheme that goes beyond those discussed in his own original manuscripts.

Although there is no direct reference in Leonardo's writings to the four most important treatises on painting that preceded his, demonstrably he knew all of them, either directly or indirectly: Cennino Cennini's (*ca.* 1400); Leone Battista Alberti's

---

[39] Cf. McM. 19, 51, and *passim*.

[40] Quotations from the *Book on Perspective* in the Codex Urbinas text: McM. 174, 195, 524, 966, 1006, 1007. From the *Book on Light and Shade*: McM. 435, 478, 617, 630, 710. From the *Book on Movement*, McM. 312, 331, 394.

[41] "Figure" means every object: "situation" means locale (i.e. the relation of the object to space and time).

(1435); Averlino Filarete's (*ca.* 1460); and Piero della Francesca's (*ca.* 1485).[42] We cannot be sure that he saw Cennini's in the original version, but it is certain that he was familiar with Filarete's big treatise, which made extensive use, albeit without acknowledgement, of Cennini's book on painting.[43] Leonardo made use of the Filarete book, which existed in a large and splendidly decorated manuscript in the Sforza library, for his own architectural studies.[44] Therefore he must have known the sections dealing with the art of drawing and painting also (in books 22-24), which are largely derived from Cennini. In addition to Cennini, Filarete is here indebted to Alberti, whose treatise he imitated, in crude and debased form, in every train of thought.[45]

That Leonardo knew Alberti's then famous and widely accessible treatise in the original is certain. The astonishing parallelism of many of their ideas; their critical analyses by means of various theorems; and especially the significant furthering and enriching of the subject as a whole, testify amply to this.[46]

[42] Cennino Cennini, *Libro dell'Arte*, editio Milanesi, Florence, Le Monnier 1859 (English translation by Christiana Herringham, London, 1899). Leone Battista Alberti, *De Pittura libri II* (written in 1435) editio princeps, Basel 1540; first critical modern edition: H. Janitschek, L. B. Alberti, *Kleinere kunsttheoretische Schriften*, Vienna 1877 (Bibliography, List A3). A good modern edition by L. Malli, Florence 1950. Antonio Filarete, *De Architettura libri XXV* (written between 1451 and 1461). There is no printed edition, although an incomplete version was done by W. von Oettingen, *Antonio Averlino Filarete's Tractat ueber die Baukunst nebst seinen Buechern ueber die Zeichenkunst*, Quellenschriften N.F. III, Vienna 1896. Piero della Francesca, *De Prospectiva Pinghiendi* (written about 1485), first edition by C. Winterberg, Strassburg 1899, and recently a new and good edition, presented by Giusta Nicco Fasola in *Raccolta di Fonti per la Storia dell'-Arte*, v, Florence 1942 (Bibliography, List A3). For all four treatises, see the historical and critical statements in Schlosser, *op.cit.*
Cennini and Filarete are not especially mentioned in Leonardo's manuscripts. Concerning his acquaintance with the books of Alberti and Piero della Francesca, see notes 45 and 47.

[43] Books XXII-XXIV of Filarete's *Treatise on Architecture* are dedicated to the art of drawing and painting, with many technical remarks taken from Cennini.

[44] Among the architectural drawings of Leonardo there are some which have reference to illustrations found in Filarete's treatise. See L. H. Heydenreich, *Die Sakralbau-Studien Leonardo da Vinci*, Leipzig 1929.

[45] Alberti is often quoted and enthusiastically praised by Filarete. His book on painting furnished the basis for Filarete's treatment in *Arte del disegno*.

[46] See the splendid essay by Sir Kenneth Clark, *Leone Battista Alberti on Painting*, Annual Italian Lecture of the British Academy, 1944 (Bibliography, List A3). Alberti is twice mentioned by Leonardo, in connection with the speed of ships (Ms.F, folio 82 and Ms.G, folio 54. McCurdy, I, 561, and II, 170).

Leonardo was doubtless familiar with Piero della Francesca's treatise. Even if it might have escaped his notice earlier, he could not have failed to be introduced to it by Luca Pacioli, who was active in Milan between 1497 and 1499, and who worked in close collaboration with Leonardo. Pacioli refers to Piero in his works as his venerable and revered teacher, and makes specific mention of the latter's *De Prospectiva Pingendi*.[47]

In all of these treatises, painting is founded on three basic studies: the representation of line, of surface, and of solid bodies. The categories are systematically developed in the second book of Alberti's treatise; Filarete takes them over from him, almost exactly, while Piero della Francesca makes use of them, though only in principle, in the introduction to his *Prospectiva*. The formula obviously goes back to the Middle Ages and echoes of this older form are still to be found in Cennini's book.[48] Under the heading of *Circumscriptio*, this traditional scheme discusses all the elements of linear representation; under *Compositio*, we find the directions for gathering the individual elements, as learned in the former category, into a planimetric surface composition. This chapter also included directions for the representation of men and objects; proportion, measurements, and movement—even descriptions of entire pictorial scenes. Finally, under *Ricevimento del lume* there are instructions for endowing these elements with the appearance of plastic, corporeal reality by means of light, shadow, and color.

Cennini's treatment of painting as a purely practical matter is

[47] The name Piero della Francesca "Maestro de Borgo" is written by Leonardo in a list among his personal records in the Codex Br.M., folio 190v (McCurdy, II, 588). We find the name of Luca Pacioli on another sheet (Codex Atl. 120. McCurdy II, 583), where Leonardo writes: "Learn how to multiply roots from Messer Luca." Luca Pacioli, who eulogizes Leonardo in the dedication to Lodovico Sforza in his *Divina Proportione, op.cit.* (cf. note 29), left Milan together with Leonardo in 1499. Both went to Venice where Leonardo drew the figures of the five regular bodies for Pacioli's *De Cinque Corporibus Regolaris*. On the collaboration between Pacioli and Leonardo, see Schlosser, *op.cit.*, and L. Olschki, *Geschichte der neusprachlichen wissenschaftlichen Literatur in Italien*, Heidelberg 1919, pp. 151ff. (Bibliography, List B3 Other Sciences.)

[48] The exact terms used by Alberti, Filarete, and Piero are: Alberti "circonscrizione, componimento, ricevimento dei lumi"; Filarete "disegno stati e movimenti, luce e colore"; Piero "disegno, commensuratio, colorare."

also in accord with medieval tradition. His recipes are aligned according to the various individual techniques: drawing, fresco, oil painting, etc. These practical recipes are interspersed with directions for the representation of various pictorial themes, and in the resultant conglomeration the three subdivisions, as described above, are discernible only as basic premises. In contrast to him, the Renaissance authors beginning with Alberti make a significant innovation in that they divide their material into a theoretical and a practical part.[49] The *Theory* of painting, which is expounded before the *Practice*, deals with the principal achievements of this period: the knowledge of mathematical perspective, which puts painting on a scientific basis. The tripartition along Euclidian lines, into line, surface, and bodies makes its appearance in the chapter on *Theory* in connection with the explanation of optical phenomena. It forms the framework of the second chapter dealing with *Practice*.[50]

This main theme, the doctrine of painting subdivided into theory and practice, is accompanied by two minor themes: an apologia, or definition of painting, in which its position as one of the *Artes Liberales* (hence as a "science" according to the medieval classification of human activities) is proved; and secondly, a moralistic and aesthetic chapter on general "rules of life" (*precetti*) for the painter, wherein specific mention may be made of the cultivation of the painter's talents, his powers of observation and imagination.

Let us now compare the construction of Leonardo's treatise, insofar as it can be determined from his own expressions on the subject and the Codex Urbinas, with these treatises of the early Renaissance. We find that all themes treated by his predecessors reappear in Leonardo; and furthermore, that there is an aston-

[49] Cf. Panofsky's concise exposition of the development from the practical instruction in the medieval treatises to the focusing on the theory of art in the Renaissance treatises, and the significance of perspective (*Codex Huygens, op.cit.*, pp. 90ff.).

[50] In the disposition of the geometrical constructions ("linea superfici piani—superfici composti," i.e. corpi) we find one of the first allusions to this tripartition. Later, in the same book, Alberti speaks of the three "cose mediante le quali li superfici appariscono a chi le reguarda disforme e varie: la positione del ragio centrico, la distanza del radio centrico ed il ricevimento dei lumi."

ishing similarity of arrangement, especially in the division of the subject into a theoretical and a practical part.[51]

Perspective, subdivided under the headings of linear-, color-, and aerial-perspective, would have been included in the first part. Here too, the chapter on light and shade would have found its place, and presumably also his twice-mentioned discussion of color theory.[52] Part 2 would have encompassed drawing and color in their practical application; and following this would have come the important sections on the human figure (proportion and anatomy), and its movements (bodily and psychic). Both parts would naturally have included, as they do in Alberti, rules for composition and other similar advice. Again, as in Alberti, we may assume that the section on drapery would have been included under the discussion on movement.

After these rules and suggestions for the representation of the human being, Leonardo, by a concatenation of thought thoroughly characteristic of him, intended to add a book on the representation of nature. This was the great central theme of his art as it was of his research. In it, his studies of atmosphere, clouds, water, air and wind, the morphology of plants, and the structure of the earth, would have coalesced into a view of the cosmos and the forces that govern its configuration.

Like his predecessors, Leonardo would have opened his treatise with an exposition of the essential nature of painting, a definition of art as science in connection with the *Paragone*, which establishes the preeminence of painting over the other arts, especially poetry and sculpture. Whether the *Precetti* (the rules by which the artist should regulate his life) were intended to follow the introduction, as they do in the Codex Urbinas, or to conclude the work, as they do in Alberti's treatise, cannot be determined; but this is a matter of minor importance.

The existing sources tell us nothing more about Leonardo's general scheme. This is not surprising since it is highly doubtful that he himself had a definitive and detailed plan in mind. This may be deduced from a chronological examination of the ma-

[51] A systematic study of the reciprocal relationships among the main treatises of the Renaissance and their influence on Leonardo is in preparation.

[52] *Quaderni d'Anatomia*, ii, 6, and *Treatise*, McM. 178.

terial intended for the *Treatise on Painting*, insofar as it can be studied in his original notes. In checking these for dates, we find that they were written over a span of years from 1490 to 1513, i.e., throughout the major part of his active life, and well into old age.[53] In this same period of time, Leonardo's scientific studies underwent a most extraordinary development, as can be seen by comparing the plan for the *Anatomy* as it first appears in 1490, with its counterpart of 1513; or by noting the change in the very formulation of the problems in his hydrodynamical and aerodynamical studies.[54] In this light, it is not too much to suppose that the *Treatise on Painting* also had assumed a different form and content in the mind of the aged Leonardo, from the plan in Codex 2038, conceived when he was forty. If we read the passages in this same original manuscript written *ca.* 1495 that deal with a battle or a storm, and compare them with his description of The Deluge (1513), we cannot fail to be impressed by the change in his observation and evaluation of natural phenomena, and by the pervasive transformation that had taken place in his entire mode of thinking; for, whereas in the earlier work, the forms of nature

[53] The notes made by Leonardo on the *Treatise on Painting* are spread over most of his manuscripts, and all of them can be dated fairly exactly. To help in fixing the dates of those single texts incorporated in the Codex Urbinas which can be identified in Leonardo's original manuscripts, note this outline of chronological order:

1490-1500: Mss. A, B, C, D, H, I. Ashburnham 2037, 2038; SKM II, III; also *Anatomia Fogli B*, Codex Trivulzio.
1500-1513: Mss. L (1502), K (1504-09), Codex Leicester (1504-10), SKM I (1505), F and Codex Br.M. (1508-13), *Anatomia Fogli A* (1510-13).
1513-1517: Mss. E, G, *Quaderni d'Anatomia* III, IV.

In the Codex Urbinas these original texts are distributed among the eight parts as follows:

Part I: Ms. Ashburnham 2038 and *Quaderni d'Anatomia* IV.
Part II: Codex Trivulzio, Ms. Ashburnham 2038, Mss. L, F, E, G.
Part III: Mss. A, H, E, G, L, Codex Leicester.
Part IV: Ms. Ashburnham I, 2037.
Part V: Mss. C, K, E, G, F. Codex Br.M.
Part VI: Mss. E, F, G.
Part VII: Mss. SKM II, Codex Br.M.

In addition, there are many texts taken from the Codex Atlanticus, an intermingling of texts from 1480-1519, so that the single notes should be dated individually in relation to the text involved.

[54] Cf. L. H. Heydenreich, *Leonardo da Vinci*, New York, 1953, pp. 136ff., 51-154; Giacomelli, *op.cit.*

are described according to their outer appearance, or introduced
into a pictorial composition merely as manifestations of certain
motions or emotions (e.g. agitated draperies, puffs of dust behind
a horse's hoofs, etc.), his later works all present the phenomena,
observed and recorded, under a new aspect of "forms symbolizing
cosmic energies," wherein the law and order of nature are revealed.[55]

Now let us turn back to the Codex Urbinas and try to decide
how much of Leonardo's original project it preserves. Although
itself incomplete and not fully articulated, it encompasses such
substantial segments of Leonardo's program that it gives us a
broader understanding of his plan. The introductory part on the
essential nature of painting contains an extensive collection of raw
material.[56] In the theoretical section, on the other hand, the division dealing with mathematical perspective is so fragmentary
that a question arises as to whether this entire portion has, in
reality, been lost in the original, or whether it was intentionally
neglected by Leonardo; in view of the existence of the treatises
by Alberti and Piero della Francesca, it may well be that Leonardo
felt it unnecessary to treat the subject systematically again.[57] If
this were the case, then Melzi would purposely have avoided the
inclusion of the many isolated notes that deal with all manner
of matters pertinent to mathematics, from the principles of Euclidian geometry, to drawings of perspectival constructions; and
would rather have limited himself to the compilation of notes
relating to light and color perspective. The latter are presented

[55] Cf. L. H. Heydenreich, *Leonardo da Vinci*, New York, 1953, pp. 120, 150.
[56] The material compiled in the Codex Urbinas is full of repetitions both in
the main themes, and in the various ideas expressed in them. There is no doubt
that Leonardo intended to give final shape to his *Paragone*, with much reduction
in quantity and with a clearer and much more carefully selected argumentation.
[57] There are many clearly apparent indications but no documentary evidence for
this hypothesis. Authorities, from Winterberg to Olschki, Schlosser, and even
G. Nicco Fasola have noted that "Luca Pacioli mentioned that Leonardo, after
having seen Piero's treatise, abandoned work on his book on the same theme.
Yet no direct mention of this is to be found in the works of Luca Pacioli, either
in *Divina Proportione*, or in *De Cinque Corporibus Regolaris*. The vague statement was first made by Winterberg in his introduction to his edition of Piero's
work, where he may have remembered wrongly some passage in Luca's *Divina
Proportione*, which he had edited a decade earlier.

ɔoth forcefully and explicitly in the Codex Urbinas; the part on ight and shade is particularly extensive.

The subjects of drawing and color, scattered throughout the econd half, are rather sparse. These problems were apparently neglected to a large extent by Leonardo himself, for even in the original manuscripts we find relatively little material that could ɔe used to piece out the Codex Urbinas where painting technique s concerned. As we shall have further occasion to observe, the ntire subject of color is one which did not greatly interest Leonardo, at least not in its technical aspects.[58]

The book on the human figure, which was to have included the tudies in proportion and anatomy, is fragmentary also. But it s precisely this portion of the Codex Urbinas that contains the greatest number of those empty pages marked "Meltius" indicating that Melzi himself either wished to complete them or was upposed to have done so.[59] To anyone familiar with the awesome ɔundance of Leonardo's anatomical studies, Melzi's failure will e perfectly understandable. The mere sorting of the notes into ɪose which might rightfully be included in the painting treatise, against those which were destined for the *Treatise on Anatomy*, resents a huge problem, upon which, or so it seems to us, even .elzi's zeal foundered.[60] The best complement to this portion of e Codex Urbinas is the material compiled by Richter which

[58] See note 74.  [59] Cf. Volume II, Introductory Note.
[60] The interdependence of the artistic and scientific elements in his anatomical ɪdies is indicated by Leonardo da Vinci himself in some notes, e.g. "This ɪonstration is as necessary for good draughtsmen as the derivation from Latin rds is to good grammarians; for anyone must needs depict the movements and ɪons of the muscles and figures badly, unless he knows which are the muscles t are the cause of these movements." (*Anatomia Fogli* B 4v) and: "Different scles become apparent in the different movements of animals, and other scles become hidden in this diversity of movement; and concerning this it is essary to write a long treatise for the purpose of recognizing the places that e been injured by wounds and also for the convenience of sculptors and ɪters." (*ibid.*, 20). Cf. S. Esche, *Das anatomische Werk Leonardos*, Basel, 1954. he twofold orientation of Leonardo's study of anatomy is also documented by wings such as Windsor 12640, where Leonardo, while making a preliminary ch for his painting on the Battle of Anghiari, becomes inspired by an anaɪical problem, and in the accompanying notes describes the functioning of the ɪlder muscles in an almost scientific way. Leonardo's tendency to stylize his wings for his own specific purposes often makes them almost impossible to ɪify as either completely artistic or scientific.

brings together the more important of the studies on proportion as well as some on anatomy-for-artists that can, quite certainly be related to the *Treatise on Painting*.[61] Moreover, the Codex Huygens, as Panofsky has convincingly demonstrated, offers us some insight into the broad scope of Leonardo's original plan for this portion.[62]

Greatest in quantity as well as in significance, is the collection of material for the next part, on movement. This has always elicited the most interest, and exerted the most influence, from the time of Leonardo's direct followers on through the art theory and practice of the seventeenth century, and finally down to the Classical and other Revival styles of the nineteenth century.[63] Of all the parts, it is also the most profusely illustrated; the change that these illustrations have undergone in the countless copies both drawn and printed, that are descended from them, form a problem which is, in itself, of great interest to art history. It demonstrates, for example, that elementary questions such as how to represent movement, are common to all styles, no matter how heterogeneous. For proof one need only compare Poussin's classicizing copies of the Leonardo or Codex Urbinas originals with the Baroque versions of the same made by Stefano della Bella for the Fontani edition.

The material included in the sixth, seventh, and eighth parts of the Codex Urbinas, as well as some of the notes in Part V, were undoubtedly originally to have found their place in the book on Nature. This portion of Leonardo's treatise, as he conceived it, would have embraced the essentials of his entire cosmology, to the degree that this knowledge lends itself to the painter's task. Many of these passages are among his most powerful, both as to their thought content and the creative language in which they are couched. To those in the Codex Urbinas might be added a large number from the original manuscripts, which were never transcribed; some of the most significant of these may be found in Richter's and McCurdy's splendid Leonardo anthologies.[64]

---

[61] Cf. Richter, *op.cit.*, I, 243ff.    [62] Panofsky, *Codex Huygens*, p. 1

[63] Leonardo's theory on human movements is analyzed and characterized by Panofsky, *Codex Huygens*, pp. 122ff. with special reference to its influence on Dürer on the one hand, and on the other to its manneristic extension by Lomazzo.

[64] McCurdy, *op.cit.*, II, 227ff.; Richter, *op.cit.*, I, *passim*.

This part of the *Treatise on Painting* must, at one time, have included several magnificent color illustrations by Leonardo; there are two specific references to these in the Codex Urbinas.[65] Like most of Leonardo's other watercolor paintings, which are frequently mentioned in the sources, these have been lost. Only a few examples of that technique are preserved but bear no relation to the treatise. However, we reproduce some drawings of Leonardo's, which are closely connected with the Treatise, and may have been preparatory studies for those lost colored illustrations (figs. 11, 12).[66]

The second half of the Codex Urbinas contains a wealth of material relating to the *Precetti*. These too are masterpieces of expression as well as thought, especially the parable of The Mirror, which is an impressive piece of prose poetry.

The influence of Leonardo's treatise on painting was both strong and constant, even while its contents were available only in abridged versions, preceding Manzi's rediscovery and publication of the Codex Urbinas. Beginning with Du Fresne's *Editio Princeps*, the stream of printed editions of the work has continued uninterrupted to the present day. Thus it is fitting that the introduction to this latest edition should conclude with an examination of Leonardo's realm of thought as it is expressed in the treatise with the purpose of finding out what makes it of special and lasting significance.

Even in the fragmentary state in which it has come down to us, Leonardo's *Treatise on Painting* is the most thoroughgoing of all similar Renaissance works in scope as well as content.[67] Three features which are basic to Leonardo's scientific method and which find vent and application in all of his studies distinguish his treatise from the others: first, Leonardo's astounding powers of observation which enabled him to perceive phenomena that were entirely outside the limits of artistic problems, and belonged within the sphere of scientific study; second, his equation of seeing with comprehending, which led Leonardo to the conclusion

[65] McM. 552 and 280-281.
[66] The group of maps, some allegorical drawings, and a drawing of a country-house, all in Windsor Castle. See Kenneth Clark, *Catalogue of the Drawings of Leonardo da Vinci at Windsor Castle*, London 1939 (Bibliography, List E4).
[67] Cf. Schlosser, *op.cit.*, pp. 150-163.

that sight is the natural medium for the collection of scientific data, while graphic reproduction is its perfect means of dissemination; finally, the constant interrelating of theory and practice, i.e., of experimental data and practical application, so that, to quote Leonardo, "sometimes the effects are deduced from the causes, and sometimes the causes from the effects."[68] All of these led inevitably to the bursting of the traditional treatise pattern; Leonardo's book on painting had, properly speaking, grown into an encyclopedia of visually transmissible science. To this is due its great and unique historical value; but also, it must be admitted, the unfortunate fact that he was never able to bring it to a state of final completion.

Leonardo made use of all the principal themes of earlier treatises, in order to transform and utilize them according to his own concepts. In his introduction he takes the old idea of defining the position of painting in relation to the other sciences, and changes it into an apodictical demonstration. He is on the side of the newly awakening experimental approach to science, as against the old scholastic view, which classified all knowledge gained through experience as "mechanical," and as "scientific" only such knowledge as arises out of the mind or spirit. Against the latter he argues: "But to me it seems that those sciences are vain and full of errors which are not born of experience, mother of all certainty, and which do not end in recorded experience. . . . But the true sciences are those which become known through the senses, by experience, and which put to silence the tongues of the contentious. They do not feed those who investigate them on a dream but always, based on true and verified first principles, proceed to the end in orderly fashion and with true consequences. This is seen in the elementary principles of mathematics which deal with number and measure and are called arithmetic and geometry, and which treat with utmost truth of discontinuous and continuous quantity. . . . The scientific and true principles of painting, first determining what a shadowed body is, and what

[68] Codex Atlanticus, 203r. The passage is taken almost literally from John Peckham's *Perspectiva Communis* of the thirteenth century. See Solmi, *Leonardo da Vinci, Frammenti Letterari*, Florence 1908, pp. 91 and 407, note 101 (Bibliography, List D).

primary and derivative shadows are, and what is illumination, i.e. darkness, light, color, body, form, location, distance, nearness, motion and rest, are principles which are comprehended by the mind alone without manual participation. This is the pure science of painting which is in the mind of those who reflect upon it. From it is born creative action which is of much more value than the reflection or science just mentioned." (McM. 19)

Leonardo considers sight to be the most refined, as well as the most reliable of the five senses, and concludes from this that painting, being the sphere which makes fullest use of this faculty, is therefore also the best transmitter of knowledge: "That science is most useful the results of which are most communicable, and, conversely, that is less useful which is less communicable. Painting makes its end result communicable to all the generations of the world because it depends on the visual faculty; not reaching understanding through the ear. . . . Thus painting does not have need of interpreters for different languages as does literature and at once satisfies mankind, no differently than do things produced by nature." (McM. 17)

Thus in Leonardo's opinion, the qualities of truthfulness and directness of statement confirm the primacy of painting among the sciences; it was his further conviction that the sensory impression that painting makes is more penetrating, and more conducive to knowledge than that produced by the disembodied word. Lastly, Leonardo concerns himself with the truth of representation, which he considers to be the result of objectively correct knowledge. Although the debate in the *Paragone* (an early work dating from his forties) is often dialectic in tenor, and makes use of some well-worn literary and metaphorical devices which do nothing to lend it either conviction or force,[69] it nevertheless contains some ideas of revolutionary import. In the contest between poetry and painting (McM. 32) he concedes that painting, like poetry, must

[69] Leonardo's texts for more than half of the chapters found in the Codex Urbinas concerning the *Paragone* are lost, and only a small group is to be found in the Ms. Ashburnham 2038 (written between 1490 and 1495). We must take into consideration that Leonardo's opposition to poetry was directed, and for very good reasons, against the very mediocre poetry produced by the court poets of his time. Furthermore, it is important also to take into consideration the fact that he takes issue only with the content, and never with the form, of poetry.

borrow from the other sciences, such as rhetoric, philosophy, and theology, in order to do justice to an important subject; but he contends that painting is less dependent upon these than poetry which lives exclusively upon borrowing, and that this is the weakest part of painting anyway. Here we find the first, still somewhat literary formulation of his thesis that the true task of painting is to represent nature directly. This thesis was so boldly implemented by the mature Leonardo that the original "literary" subject becomes merely an excuse for representing the phenomena of the universe, to the point where a reversal of the significance of form and content takes place: in his series of drawings of The Deluge, the myth of the end of the world serves only as the welcome motive for the representation of Leonardo's own ideas of the self-dissolution of the cosmos. These develop out of his scientific observations on the ultimate consequences of natural laws and forces[70] quite apart from any iconographic tradition of the theme.

The equation of painting and natural science, meaning the utilization of the artist's perceptual powers in the service of scientific knowledge, appears in another early intimation. "If poetry includes moral philosophy, painting deals with natural philosophy." (McM. 30).

Therefore the value of the *Paragone* lies less in its establishment of painting as the highest of the arts—for as we have seen, Leonardo was only following a traditional argument in doing this—than in the flashes of a far bolder theme which appear from time to time in this disputation, i.e., that painting is the most perfect instrument for the transmission of scientific knowledge. This basic idea is traceable in his treatment of all the material that pertains to the treatise, and it explains the constant interpenetration of theoretical and practical discussions. In the texts that belong to the theoretical half of the book, many of the postulates are based upon examples taken from actual observation, just as in the practical division, that is, suggestions for the representation of specific pictorial themes, the theoretical principles of the first part are constantly referred to. The basic rules of color perspective, in particular the definition of the blue of the sky, may well be

[70] Cf. Heydenreich, *Leonardo da Vinci*, 1953, pp. 157ff.

8. Studies of human movements, as described in Codex Urbinas, fol. 111 ff.
Windsor 12644.

9. The edge of a copse of trees. Windsor 12431. The drawing seems to be an
illustration of Leonardo's note: *Della trasformazione delle piante in se*, Codex
Urbinas fol. 265v.

10. A volcanic eruption and a tree uprooted by a storm. Windsor 12404. These drawings are not by Leonardo, but are copies intended as illustrations for the *Treatise*. The sketch on the left corresponds almost exactly to a lost drawing by Leonardo described in a marginal note, Codex Urbinas, fol. 149v.

11. The Deluge. Windsor 12380. The didactic style of Leonardo's notes on the drawing proves the close connection of this drawing with Leonardo's description of *Il Diluvio* on Windsor 12665, which belongs to his latest preparatory studies for the *Treatise*.

12. A rainstorm breaking over a town in a valley. Windsor 12409. This famous drawing seems to be a preparatory study for Leonardo's lost illustration, *tocca d'aquarella*, for his note *Del principio d'una pioggia* which is mentioned in Codex Urbinas, fol. 158.

13. Stratified rocks suggesting the "anatomy of the earth" (Kenneth Clark, *Catalogue of Windsor Drawings,*

chosen to illustrate this. These rules make their appearance throughout the book, and in the most diverse contexts; they naturally have their place in the chapter on color perspective; but in addition they are mentioned in the sections on anatomy (McM. 848), on the composition of historical scenes (McM. 282), and in the description of landscapes (McM. 966).[71]

Leonardo does not set forth a theory in Alberti's sense. Schlosser has made an excellent analysis of the degree to which Leonardo adopted the principal ideas of Renaissance art theory, and in so doing, was led to the astonishing observation that the classical art of antiquity, the idol of that period, played a very minor role in Leonardo's scheme.[72] To him, nature alone was the authoritative teacher. He looks upon mathematical perspective with a distinctly critical eye, pointing out that it is insufficient—indeed misleading—unless supplemented by a knowledge of aerial and color perspective.[73] This is an interesting indication of the differences between mathematical and physiological vision. For the same reason he warns against exaggerated reliance upon mechanical aids for proportion (McM. 48), whose usefulness he would limit to the pedagogical (McM. 118 and 119). His discussions of aerial and color perspective are all the more intensive for this; he collected a most awe-inspiring mass of observations on individual phenomena in their most varied aspects, whether for use in the book on light and shade, or the section on color, or merely as practical suggestions for the representation of natural forms or landscape conformations. He has the least to say on the subject of color; a typical Tuscan, he classifies it under *rilievo*, and at one point even denies its independent artistic value (McM. 108). Upon closer examination however, this seeming prejudice is found to apply mainly to "tinting" in the narrow sense, and to be directed against the primitive color treatment of the Tuscan school.[74] That

[71] Other quotations: Part II: McM. 148, 221, 226, 244; Part III: McM. 507, 523; Part IV: McM. 578, 579, 741; Part V: McM. 675ff., 824, 955 and *passim*; Part VI: McM. 935, 936, 952, 960.

[72] Schlosser, *Materialen zur Quellenkunde der Kunstgeschichte*, p. 163.

[73] Cf. McM. 528 and 822; Ms.E. folio 15v, 16r. (McCurdy, *op.cit.*, II, 372.)

[74] Cf. Schlosser, *op.cit.*, p. 159. In the technique of colors, Leonardo was too great an experimenter, particularly concerning painting on walls—and with negative results, as the fate of his pictures demonstrates. So his experience in this field was not as good as he himself may have felt it to be.

his own sensitivity to color was of the subtlest order cannot be doubted: were the products of his brush not enough to prove it so, the extraordinarily perceptive discussions of color and tonal values in connection with color perspective, or of the harmony of color values in connection with the practical section on colors, would leave small doubt. Many of these problems as analyzed by Leonardo, anticipate the solutions that were found in the color-created forms of the Venetian school. His famous "Sfumato" must be regarded as the synthesis of light and color perspective: it is a brilliant conciliation of *clair-obscur* and color value, and his discussion of the subject in the treatise defines the problem for the first time. It continued to be one of the chief problems of setting down forms on a painted surface, right through the *Plein-air* and *Pointilliste* schools of the nineteenth century.

Leonardo's section on the representation of the human body and its movements is likewise an extended and intensified continuation of the theme as it had been treated by his predecessors, Alberti in particular. He turns his mind to the development of an entire new concept of movement, based on the laws of mechanics;[75] he regarded anatomy as an independent field of science, and used the results, obtained through scientific investigation, in formulating his anatomy-for-artists.[76] He discusses the relatedness of physical movement and psychic emotion, between gesture and expression, and in the process always lays stress upon the things that give to a representation truth, conviction, meaning, and measure. It is not surprising, therefore, to find that this portion of his treatise was capable of becoming the canon of the academicians, whose teachings remained consistent from Poussin far into the nineteenth century. In this section, too, we find a spontaneity of language which is as affecting today as it ever was.

Lastly, great significance must be attached to the ethical and moral observations which Leonardo, in his *Precetti*, formulates as rules for the artist to live by. What he has to say about the education and knowledge of the painter, his deportment and dignity, and, above all, his truthfulness and self-criticism, belongs among the finest of his utterances. Furthermore it illuminates the

[75] Heydenreich, *Leonardo da Vinci*, 1953, pp. 103ff.
[76] Cf. *Dell'Anatomia A*, folio 10. Panofsky, *Codex Huygens, passim*.

purity of his own personality, whose very impersonality manifests itself in his aloofness from other human beings and in the love that he expends on all objects of his research. The most beautiful and lucid of these statements is, perhaps, his paraphrasing of the use of the mirror to verify the painter's work; in this he takes a practical rule and turns it into an ethical precept.[77]

"The painter should be solitary and consider what he sees, discussing it with himself, selecting the most excellent parts of the appearance of what he sees, acting as the mirror which transmutes itself into as many colors as exist in the things placed before it. And if he does this he will be like a second nature." (McM. 72)

The supreme significance of Leonardo's *Treatise on Painting*, and the strong influence that it has exercised upon the artistic concepts of the following eras, continuing into our own time, is mainly owing to his specific capacity of visualization: it characterizes his method of unearthing and communicating all those experiences, that he, one of the greatest artists, had gained from his practical work. No greater man has ever undertaken to speak as a painter to other painters; and none has ever equaled him in wealth of ideas and information, and in his considered expression of them.

The unusual, and in fact unique feature of Leonardo's system of teaching, is his completely new correlation of word and image. In the treatise as he originally conceived it we may assume that this correlation might have been even more striking; however, the scope of its intent is recognizable in the Codex Urbinas.

Alberti, in his treatise, consciously deviates from the formula of the medieval pattern and recipe books:[78] to the practical workshop knowledge of the latter he opposes a theory determined by systematic thought; one that establishes principles without regard to concrete artistic practice. Perspective, alone, as the mathematically scientific foundation of painting, is demonstrated, albeit without stressing its application. The latter was done by Piero della Francesca who made use of drawing—and this is both

[77] Cf. McM. 211, for the use of the mirror as an instrument of technical control.

[78] Cf. Panofsky, *Codex Huygens*, pp. 110-111.

characteristic and important—as an aid to demonstration.[79] In his treatise the perspectival constructions described in the text are brought to view, thus taking up once again the principle of the medieval pattern book, inasmuch as it too gives graphic examples of various types of representation,[80] although in a totally new sense. He no longer gives typical examples which provide a basic scheme for all cases, but individual examples dependent upon the unique combination of optical and perspectival circumstances. What all of these individual instances have in common is the method of perspectival construction that demonstrates the rule by which any given scene is analyzed as a variant of the same basic act of seeing.

Leonardo takes over Piero's idea of didactic illustration and applies it to all of the fields that are the concern of artistic representation. His illustrations for the book on light and shade place all the variables of the phenomenon in a paradigmatic scheme based upon optical principles, so that the painter is enabled to recognize every individual variant of the phenomenon.

The illustrations for his book on proportion are similarly systematically developed: taking its point of departure from an ideal canon of the human figure and its proportions, which are never fully realized in any one individual, he expounds the endless variability of these relationships, in order to make it possible to define each individual example in the light of its deviations from the ideal norm.[81] In this connection, Leonardo's recommendation that one take special notice of faces that are memorable because of some "landmark," such as the shape of the nose, is very characteristic. In some, he offers a system, abetted by illustrations, for determining what is individual about any individual.

The principle of visualization, i.e., of giving graphic representation to processes which are governed by set laws, is developed to the full in his book on movement. Here we find a prodigious illustrated catalogue of the factors that regulate movement, from

[79] Piero's drawings are now available in the new edition of his work by G. Nicco Fasola, *op.cit.* where they are completely reproduced.

[80] Compare Villard de Honnecourt's examples, particularly on folio 18-19 (H. R. Hahnloser, *Villard de Honnecourt*, Vienna 1935).

[81] Panofsky, *Codex Huygens*, pp. 122ff.

the most seemingly insignificant bending of a finger, to the most
vehement motion of an entire body; their purpose is to enable
the painter to recognize, and therefore represent, each and all
of them correctly. Leonardo also makes a thorough examination
and explanation of the connection between movement and expression. This collaboration of graphic illustration with textual
elucidation, to lay bare the basic types of human movements and
expressions (cf. the masterly formulations in McM. 404, 405, 409),
provides a method of learning whose impact is damaged neither
by the passage of time nor changes of style.

Leonardo also intended to make full use of this collaboration
of word and image, of linguistic explanation and pictorial representation, in his book on nature. The extremely graphic drawings for passages on the growth of trees and plants give us at
least an inkling of the illustrative material that was prepared, but
not used in the Codex Urbinas. We can only guess at the reason
for this omission. It may be that copying the illustrations for
The Rainstorm or The Deluge both of which are mentioned
by the transcriber (footnotes to McM. 471, 552), was beyond his
powers, since they represent artistic creations which would require the understanding services of a copyist who is himself an
artist of no mean power; or it may be that the original drawings
were to have been inserted once the book had been put into final
shape.[82] Several reproductions of the illustrations which were,
beyond doubt, intended for this section of the original treatise,
are included in this volume. They clearly reveal how varied and
far-reaching was Leonardo's conception of illustration. The finished sketch of a rainstorm (Fig. 12) to be used for the landscape background of a painting possesses a pictorial value and an
effect of its own; there are other preparatory drawings, which
analyze the individual forces that have simultaneously materialized
in the various forms in the rainstorm picture. There is the one of
the boulder (Fig. 13), whose strata show the general forces of
nature which account, also, for this particular shape;[83] the super-

[82] Cf. Quaderni d'Anatomia II, f.6.

[83] Compare the absolute contrast between the way Cennini recommends painting a mountain using a stone as a model, with Leonardo's drawing of a rock
which, with its traces of erosion, represents the structure of a whole mountain.

lative drawing of The Deluge (Fig. 14) is annotated by a marginal text explaining the mechanical principles involved in the catastrophe, and also by schematic stylizations which illustrate a shower of rain, a cloud formation and a whirlpool or whirlwind. Pictures such as that of The Last Judgment, or The Deluge series, are made up of pictorial formulae like these; whatever the title, the subject itself becomes an artistic interpretation of scientific phenomena, and is totally subordinated to the main theme: the representation of nature as cosmos.[84]

Leonardo's *Treatise on Painting*, then, represents a unique combination of theory and practice, a fusion of the thought legacy of the Middle Ages with Renaissance ideas, welded into a completely new didactic method. Whereas the medieval pattern books consisted of typical examples which could be used as references for the ever-recurrent compositions that the artists of the Middle Ages were asked to paint, Leonardo's illustrations are demonstrations of "basic categories," each proved by relative laws. These help to verify the individual phenomenon, so that it can be represented with objective correctness. Thus every variation of individual forms and processes in nature, whether these be human, nonhuman, or purely functional can be determined exactly.

This synthesis of scientific observation and artistic representation is the *Leitmotiv* of Leonardo's doctrine. The *Treatise on Painting* is an exhortation to the painter to make use of *saper vedere,* that gift which, according to Leonardo's conviction, the painter possesses above all other men, predestining him to the service of science. Doubly blessed with the gift of seeing and with the faculty of reproducing what he sees, the artist is enabled in the course of his activity to obtain exact knowledge, and to communicate this to all the generations of the world. This proud but exacting consciousness is the crown of Leonardo's conception of art, as defined in his *Treatise on Painting*.

The treatise originated at the significant moment in history when art and science met in the task—important to both—of gaining "objective experience." But Leonardo feels that art is superior even to science. He maintains (McM. 15) that the mathe-

[84] Cf. Heydenreich, *op.cit.,* Chapter Kosmologie.

matical sciences "do not encompass anything but the investigation of continuous and discontinuous quantity. They are not concerned with quality, the beauty of nature's creations, and the harmony of the world." In our time of disintegrating worlds, both physical and sensory, his words echo as though they were an exhortation to us: painting shows not only truth, but the beauty of our world; and the harmony that is beyond regulated order.

# Book on Painting

BY

Leonardo da Vinci

Florentine painter and sculptor

# EDITORIAL NOTE

The headings in the translation are of three kinds. In addition to the part and chapter headings, both of which appear in the Codex, headings have been added by the translator to subdivide each of the eight parts into groups of chapters which show some affinity in subject matter. These last, which are bracketed in the text, together with the part headings have provided a convenient Table of Contents for the translation.

Since the notes written in the margins and between the lines on the original manuscript are not always legible in facsimile, they are reproduced both in Italian and in translation in the footnotes. The errors, inconsistencies, and contractions are preserved with the exception of the contractions for *che* and *per*, which, for typographical reasons, are written out.

The chapters in this translation of the Codex total 1,008 as against 944 in Ludwig's translation into German. This is the result of the fact that chapters have been incorporated or subdivided according to the judgment of the translator.

# PART ONE

## PARAGONE: OF POETRY AND PAINTING

### [PAINTING IS SCIENCE]

**1.** *Whether or not painting is a science.*[1] Science is that mental *1* analysis which has its origin in ultimate principles, beyond which nothing in nature can be found which is part of that science. For example, continuous quantity, that is, the science of geometry, beginning with the surface of bodies, is found to have an origin in line, which is the boundary of surface. We are not satisfied with this because we know that the line ends in the point, and the point is that than which nothing can be smaller. Therefore, the point is the first principle of geometry, and nothing in nature or the human mind can be the origin of the point.

If you say that the creation of a point is due to the contact of the very fine point of a stylus with a surface, this is not true. We say that this contact is a surface, surrounding its center, and within the center is the location of the point. The point itself is not part of the substance of the surface. Neither it, nor all the points in the universe together, could they be united, would be capable of composing any part of a surface. For the sake of argument, if you were to conceive of a whole composed of a thousand points, on dividing any part of that quantity of a thousand, that part, it might well be said, would be equal to its whole. This is shown by zero or nought, the tenth figure of/arithmetic, in which *1v* nought is represented by o. Placed after one, it will mean ten, and placed twice after one, it will mean a hundred, and so it increases tenfold the number to which it is added to infinity. But in itself its value is nought, and all the noughts in the universe are equal to a single nought in substance and value.

No human investigation can be termed true science if it is not capable of mathematical demonstration. If you say that the sciences which begin and end in the mind are true, this is not

---

[1] Hand 3 has added to the heading: Sarebbe meglio dire a questo Cap^to: Che cosa sia sciẽtia. (It would be better to call this chapter: What is science.) In a marginal note, Hand 2 has corrected the reading "ualitudine" and replaced it by "ualore." On the first page of the MS there are many corrections of the scribe's spelling; on later pages the writing improves and corrections are fewer.

conceded, but is denied for many reasons, and foremost among these is the fact that the test of experience is absent from these exercises of the mind, and without these there is no assurance of certainty.

[BASIC PRINCIPLES OF PAINTING AS SCIENCE]

*2 and illus.*   2. *Basis of the science of painting.* The plane surface has its complete image in another plane surface which is the object opposite it. This is proved as follows: let R S be the first plane surface, and O Q be the second plane surface placed opposite the first. I say that the image of the first surface R S is wholly on the surface O Q, and wholly at O, and Q, and P, because R S is the base of the angle at O, and of the angle at P, and thus of an infinity of angles produced on O Q.

*1v*   3. *Of the first principle of the science of painting.* The first principle of the science of painting is the point, then comes the line, then the surface, and then the body bounded by a given surface. This refers to the representation of a body, because in fact, painting does not extend beyond the surface which represents a body in the form of a visible object.[2]

*2*   4. *Of the second principle of painting.* The second principle of painting is the shadow of the body which it represents. We shall give the principles of this shadow, and proceed to show how shadow gives sculptural relief to the surface.

*2*   5. *What does the science of painting include?* The science of painting includes all the colors of surfaces, and the forms of the bodies bounded by them, as well as their nearness and distance, including the proper degrees of diminution, according to degrees of distance. This science is the mother of perspective, or visual lines.

[2] Hand 3 has added at the bottom of the page: Questo Cap^to del p° principio della sciētia della pittura ed li tre altri ch° lo seue (?) haueuano piu conuenēte loco nella 2^a Parte di questo libro dietro il Cap^to come Fu la p^a Pittura, qual è a' carte 49 F 2. (This chapter on the first principle of the science of painting and the three others that follow would have a more suitable place in the second part of this book after the chapter, "How the first picture originated," which is on folio 49v.) Cf. McM. 98.

Perspective is divided into three parts. The first part includes only the outlines of bodies, the second includes the diminution of colors at varying distances, and the third loss of/distinctness[3] *2v* of bodies at various distances.

The first, which includes only the outlines of bodies, is called design, or the configuration of a body. Thence there arises another science, which includes shadow and light, or brightness and darkness, a science capable of great development. The science of visual lines has given birth to the science of astronomy, which is simple perspective, since it is all visual lines and sections of pyramids.

### [PAINTING IS NATURAL PHILOSOPHY]

6. *How he who disparages painting loves neither philosophy nor* *4v* *nature*. If you disparage painting, which alone can portray faithfully all the visible works of nature, you certainly disparage a discovery which considers all manner of forms with subtle and philosophic attention: the sea, places on land, plants, animals, grass, flowers, all of which are surrounded by shadow and light. Truly this is a science and the legitimate daughter of nature, since painting is born of nature. To speak more accurately, we would say the grandchild of nature, for all visible things are born of nature, and/painting is born of these. Therefore, we *5* rightly call painting the grandchild of nature and related to God.

7. Painting is proved to be philosophy because it treats of the *4* motion of bodies and the rapidity of their actions, and philosophy also includes motion.

8. Painting is therefore philosophy because philosophy treats of *4* the increase and decrease of motion, as shown in a preceding proposition, and we shall now state the converse of that proposition, and say: a thing seen by the eye acquires more size, distinctness, and color, as the space lying between it and the eye decreases.[4]

---

[3] Urb. 2v reads "congiontione," in error. Ludwig suggests "cognitione."

[4] At the end of this section, Hand 3 has observed: Vorebbe sequitare il *2* terzetto che segue che dice Si Proua la Pittura. (Should follow the second group of three lines which says: Painting is proved.)

*4* 9. All the sciences which end in words die as soon as they are born, except for their manual phase; that is the actual writing, which is the mechanical part.

[VISION IS THE MOST ACCURATE SENSE
AND ITS LOSS THE MOST SEVERE DAMAGE]

*4* 10. *How painting encompasses the surfaces, forms, and colors of natural bodies, but philosophy includes only their natural properties.*[5] Painting encompasses the surfaces, colors, and forms of anything created by nature, and philosophy penetrates those same bodies, considering their properties, but is not satisfied with the truth as shown by the painter, which embraces the primary truth of bodies, for the eye is less deceived.

*4v* 11. *How sight is less deceived than any other sense, in the perception of luminosity, transparency, and uniform media.*[6] The eye, at the proper distances and with the proper media, is less deceived in its functioning than any other sense, because it sees along straight lines that compose a pyramid based on the object and leading to the eye, and this I propose to prove.

The ear is greatly deceived with regard to the location and distance of objects, because sounds do not reach it along straight lines but along tortuous and reflected lines often causing distant objects to seem nearer than those close at hand, owing to the paths they have traversed, although an echo reaches the ear only along straight lines.

The sense of smell is less certain still as to where the cause of an odor may be located. Only taste and touch, which come into direct contact with the object, have accurate perception of that contact.

*12v-13* 12. *Of the eye.* The eye,/by which the beauty of the world is reflected for those who behold it, is of such great excellence, that he who consents to lose it deprives himself of the representation of all the works of nature. Because it views these works by means

---

[5] Hand 1 has added to the heading: questo cap°. sta unito cō quello di sopra e' fatto tutt'uno. (This chapter is joined with the one above [McM. 14] and made all one.)

[6] The "et" before "mezzi" in the heading seems to be an error.

of the eyes, the soul is content in the human prison of the body; by means of the eyes the soul represents to itself all the manifestations of nature. But he who loses his eyes leaves the soul in a dark prison, in which all hope is lost of again seeing the sun which is the light of the world. How many are they who abhor the shades of night, even though these do not last! What would they do if that darkness were a life-long companion?

Certainly there is no one who would not prefer to lose the senses of hearing and smell rather than lose his sight. The loss of hearing means the loss of all the sciences expressed in words, and one so chooses only that he may not lose the beauty of the world, which consists of those outer aspects, accidental as well as natural, which are reflected in the human eye.

13. *Which is the more damaging to a man, to lose his sight or* 7 *his hearing?* Greater damage is suffered by living creatures by loss of sight than by loss of hearing, and this is true for several reasons. First: food, necessary to all living creatures and that by which they are nourished, is found through sight; second, the beauty of created objects, especially those that arouse love, is comprehended through sight. He who is born blind cannot grasp this beauty through hearing for he never knew what the beauty of anything was. Hearing he still has, by means of which he understands only human speech and sounds, including the names of all objects to which a name is given. One can really live happily without knowledge of these names, as we see in the case of those born deaf or dumb, who understand and make themselves understood through drawing, in which most of the dumb delight, and which compensates them for the loss of words.

If you should say that vision impedes the exact and subtle understanding by which sciences dealing with divinity are penetrated, and that such an impediment induced a philosopher to deprive himself of vision, the answer is: vision, as the master of the senses, does its duty in offering an impediment to the confused and untruthful discourses which are not sciences. These are always disputed with loud shouting and gestures of the hands, and hearing also should oppose them, for it is the most offended, since it seeks harmony in which all/the senses combine. If a 7v certain philosopher took out his eyes to remove the impediment to his discourses, you may take it that his action was consistent with his brain and his discourses, which were all insensate. Could he not have closed his eyes when he entered into such a frenzy, and have kept them shut tight until his fury had ended? But the man was mad, and so was his discourse, and the most stupid thing of all was to destroy his eyes.

### [PAINTING, ASTRONOMY, AND GEOMETRY]

*3v* 14. *How painting embraces all the surfaces of bodies and includes them.*[7] Painting includes only the surface of bodies, and the perspective of painting includes the increase and the decrease in the size and colors of bodies. An object that is moved *4* away from the eye/loses as much size and color as it gains distance.

*7v* 15. *How the science of astronomy is born of the eye, because it was created by the eye.*[8] There is no part of astronomy which is not a product of visual lines and of perspective, daughter of painting, because the painter is he who, through the requirements of his art, has brought forth that perspective, and astronomy cannot be executed without lines, within which are enclosed all the different shapes of bodies created by nature, and without which the art of geometry is blind.

The geometer reduces every surface surrounded by lines to the shape of a square and the volume of every object to the shape of a cube, and arithmetic does likewise with its square and cube roots; these two sciences do not encompass anything but the investigation of continuous and discontinuous quantity. They are not concerned with quality, the beauty of nature's creations and the harmony of the world.

### [IS PAINTING A MECHANICAL ART?]

*18* 16. If you say that sciences which are not mechanical are of the mind, I say that painting is of the mind, for, as music and geometry treat of the proportions of continuous quantities, while

[7] Hand 3 has added to the heading the words: et come ell'e' filosofia (and how it is philosophy).

[8] Ludwig's transcription of this heading is inaccurate.

arithmetic treats of the discontinuous, painting treats of all continuous quantities as well as the proportions of shadow and light, and the variations of distance in perspective.

17. *What science is most useful and of what does its utility consist?* That science is most useful the results of which are most communicable, and, conversely, that is less useful which is less communicable. *2v*

Painting makes its end result communicable to all the generations of the world, because it depends on the visual faculty; not reaching the understanding through the ear, it does not proceed in the same way that impressions of vision[9] do.

Thus painting does not have need of interpreters for different languages as does literature and at once satisfies mankind, no differently than do things produced by nature; and not mankind alone, but other living creatures also. This was shown by a painting, representing the father of a family, which was caressed not only by the little children when still in swaddling clothes, but likewise by the dog and the cat of the household, a marvelous thing and an extraordinary spectacle to behold.

Painting presents the works of nature to the senses with more truth and certainty than do words or letters./But letters present words with greater truth than does painting. Let us state that science to be more admirable which represents the works of nature, than that which represents the works of workers, that is, the works of men. Words, in the case of poetry and such creations are the work of men and are made known by means of the human tongue. *3*

18. *Of imitable sciences.* The imitable[10] sciences are those in which the disciple becomes the equal of his master, and produces his results similarly. These are useful to the imitator but are not as excellent as are those which cannot be left as an inheritance, as can other things. *3*

Among the latter painting is foremost. It cannot be taught to those who are not naturally fitted for it, as can mathe-

[9] So in the original but the word should, in the context, be "hearing."

[10] Hand 1 had first written "inimittabili" and then corrected it. Hand 3 has added in the margin: e come la Pittura e' inimittabile. Pero e' scientia (and how painting is inimitable, therefore it is a science).

matics, where the disciple absorbs as much as the teacher reads to him. It cannot be copied as can words and phrases, where the copy is worth as much as the original. It cannot be cast, as sculpture can, where the cast is worth as much as the original, insofar as the excellence of the work is concerned. It does not have an infinity of progeny as does the printing of books. Painting alone remains noble, it alone honors its author and remains precious and unique, never bringing forth children equal to itself. Such rarity makes it more excellent than those things which are made public widely.

For do we not see the greatest kings of the Orient going about veiled and covered, in the belief that they diminish their prestige by divulging their presences and showing themselves publicly? Do we not see paintings that represent deities in their divinity always covered with draperies/of very great price? When they are uncovered, great ecclesiastical solemnities are first celebrated, with many chants and sounds of music. And when a picture is unveiled, a great multitude assembles there and the people immediately throw themselves upon the ground adoring and praying to Him whom the painting depicts and praying for the return of health and for eternal salvation, just as though the living divinity were actually present.

This does not happen in the case of science or other human endeavor. If you say that this is not due to the merit of the painter but to the object painted the reply is: in that case the mind of men could be satisfied by staying in bed and it would not demand that men go on pilgrimages as it does continually. But if these pilgrimages continue what is it that causes them since they are not caused by actual necessity? Certainly you will admit that it is the painted image that causes them, something which all the writings about the subject could not do but which the image can accomplish by representing the appearance and the power of the Deity. Therefore it appears that God loves painting and loves him who loves and cherishes it, and He delights to be adored in it rather than in any other form representing Him, wherefore He grants grace and the gifts of health, according to the belief of those who assemble to view His image.

*3v*

19. *Which science is mechanical and which is not?* That knowl- *19*
edge, they say, is mechanical which is born of experience, and
that is scientific which is born and ends in the mind, and that is
semi-mechanical which is born of science and ends in manual
activity. But to me it seems that those sciences are vain and full
of errors which are not born of experience, mother of all certainty, and which do not end in recorded experience, that is,
where the origin, or middle, or end is not made known to any
of the five senses. [If we doubt the certainty of that which comes
to us by means of the senses, how much more ought we to doubt
those things which rebel against the senses, such as the essence
of God, the soul, and such matters, about which there are always
dispute and contention. Truly it always happens that where
reason is lacking, loud protesting takes its place, but this does
not occur in the case of certainties.

For this reason, where there is loud protesting true knowledge
is absent, since truth has one end only and when this is made
public, controversy is destroyed forever; but if the controversy
should again arise, there is lying and confused knowledge, and
certainty is not reborn.][11]

But the true sciences are those which become known through
the senses, by experience, and which put to silence the tongues
of the contentious. They do not feed those who investigate them,
on a dream, but always/based on true and verified first principles, *19v*
proceed to the end in orderly fashion and with true consequences.
This is seen in the elementary principles of mathematics which
deal with number and measure and are called arithmetic and
geometry, and which treat with utmost truth of discontinuous
and continuous quantity. It will not be argued here that two
three's make more or less than six, nor that the sum of the
angles of a triangle is less than two right angles, for all such
arguments are destroyed and rest in eternal silence, and the results
of mathematics are enjoyed in peace by those who are devoted to
this science, which cannot be said of the lying sciences of the mind.

If you say that such exact and known sciences are of the me-

[11] This passage in brackets in the text was crossed out on 19, and the edition
published in Rome, 1817, also omitted part of this passage, probably in order
not to incur the disapproval of the censor.

chanical sort, for they cannot achieve their ends except manually,
I shall say the same of all the arts that go through the hands of
writers, who are designers of a sort, and design is a part of painting. Astronomy and the other sciences proceed by means of manual activities, but originate in the mind as does painting, which
is first in the mind of him who reflects on it but painting cannot
achieve perfection without manual participation. The scientific
and true principles of painting, first determining what a shadowed
body is, and what primary and derivative shadows are, and what
is illumination, i.e. darkness, light, color, body, form, location,
distance, nearness, motion and rest, are principles which are
comprehended by the mind alone without manual participation.
This is the pure science of painting which is in the mind of those
who reflect upon it. From it is born creative action, which is of
much more value than the reflection or science just mentioned.

[A COMPARISON OF PAINTING AND POETRY]

28  20. *Of painting and poetry*. To represent words, poetry surpasses painting; and to represent facts, painting surpasses poetry.
There is the same relation between facts and words that there is
between painting and poetry, because facts are subject to the eye
and words are subject to the ear, so that the senses have the same
relation to one another as the objects within their scope, and
thus I judge that painting is superior to poetry. But because those
who practice it do not know how to justify it in words, it has
remained for a long time without advocates. It does not speak,
but in itself shows what it is and its end result is factual, while
poetry results in words, with which it praises itself enthusiastically.[12]

[12] After the end of this section, the scribe has written on 28v: Questo capitolo
de Pittura et poesia e ritrovato doppo l'auer scritto tutto'l libro. pero mi pare
starebbe bene s'ei seguissi dietro il cap. quale scientia e' meccanica et quale nō
e' meccanica, a car. 19. f. 1. (This chapter on painting and poetry was found
after having written this whole book. It seems to me that it would be well if it
followed the chapter, Which science is mechanical and which is not, on folio
19r.) Cf. McM.-19. With darker ink another hand has added: piu tosto dietro
al cap. arguitione del poeta contra'l pittore a car. 14. f. 2. ouero dietro al seguente
(rather, after the chapter, Argument of the poet against the painter on folio 14v,
or after the following). McM.-32.

21. *Exposition of difference between painting and poetry*. The 1v
same relation exists between the imagination of a thing and its
actuality, as between a shadow and a body casting a shadow, and
there is this same relation between poetry and painting. Poetry
places things before the imagination in words, while painting
really places the objects before the eye, and the eye accepts the
likenesses as though they were real. Poetry offers things without
this likeness and they do not make an impression by way of
visual impact as does painting.

22. *The painter argues with the poet*. Lover, what poet can put 7v
before you in words the true image of your adored one with as
much truth as the painter? Which poet is he who, with more
truth than the painter, will show you the location of rivers,
woods, valleys and fields, where past/pleasures are represented? 8

If you say that painting is in itself mute poetry, when there is
nobody there to tell you what it represents, do you not see that
your book[13] of poetry is even worse off? Even if there is a man
there who speaks for it, nothing is seen of the thing of which
he speaks, such as is seen when he speaks of paintings. Paintings,
if they show actions consistent with the mental attitudes of those
depicted, will be understood as though they spoke.

23. *Comparison between poetry and painting*. The imagination 5v
does not see as well as does the eye, because the eye receives
the images or likenesses/of objects, transmits them to the impres- 6
sionable mind, and this in turn sends them to the community of
senses, where they are judged. But imagination does not go beyond the senses, except to refer to memory, and there it stops
and dies, if the thing imagined is not of much value. Poetry is
recovered in the poet's imaginative mind, who represents the
same things as the painter, and because of this he aspires to be
the equal[14] of the painter. But in truth he is far from being the
equal of the painter, as has been shown above. In the case of

---

[13] Hand 3 has, in the margin, added: che la copositione del poeta (that the
composition of the poet), to explain "tuo libro" (your book). The same editor
corrects the scribe's "egli" to read "ella," and "lui" to read "lei."

[14] Hand 3 has substituted in the text: "ugualiarsi" for "equipararsi," and
"lontano" for "rimoto."

such a representation, we may say that there is the same relationship between the sciences of painting and poetry that there is between a body and its derivative shadow. There is an even closer relationship, for at least the shadow of such a body achieves sensory perception through the eye, but in the absence of the function of the eye the image of that body does not become known to the senses, but remains where it originates. What a difference there is between imagining a light while the eye is in darkness and seeing it in actuality without that darkness!

*6v* 24. The subjects included in painting are, beyond comparison, more various than those included in words, because the painter will create an infinite number of things which words cannot even name, since there are no words appropriate to them. Do you not see that if the painter wishes to represent animals, or devils in hell, with what an abundance of discoveries his mind teems?

*19v-20* 25. *Why painting is not numbered among the sciences.*/Since writers have not had any knowledge of the science of painting, they have been unable to describe its degrees and parts, and since painting itself does not display its achievements in words, through ignorance it has been left behind the sciences already mentioned, but it is not on that account lacking in divinity.

Truly, it is with reason that they have not ennobled it, because it ennobles itself without the help of others' tongues, just as the wonders of nature do. If painters have not written about it and reduced it to a science, this is not the fault of painting, and it is not therefore the less noble, since few painters make a profession of letters, for their life is not long enough to encompass that.

Should we say that the properties of herbs, stones, and trees are not in them for the reason that men have not known them? Certainly not, and we say that those herbs remain noble in themselves, without the help of human tongues or letters.[15]

[A COMPARISON OF VISION AND HEARING]

*17v* 26. That is more worthy which satisfies the better sense. Therefore, painting which satisfies the sense of sight is more noble than

[15] At the end of this section the scribe wrote: Fine (End) referring to the end of the comparison of poetry and painting, as arranged in Urbinas 1270.

music, which satisfies only hearing. That is more noble which has longer life, and thus music, which is ended as soon as it is born, is less worthy than painting which becomes everlasting when glazed.

That which in itself contains the greater scope and variety is to be called the more excellent, and therefore painting is to be placed before all other activities because it contains all forms that are and those that are not to be found in nature, and it is more to be magnified and exalted than is music, which concerns only the voice.

By means of painting likenesses of the gods are made; with its aid divine service is rendered, adorned by music as a servant; it gives lovers portraits of the objects of their loves; it preserves beauties which time and nature make fugitive; by means of it we preserve the appearance of famous men, and if you say that music is made everlasting by writing it, we are doing the same here for painting by writing about it. Therefore, since you have placed music among the liberal arts, you must also include paint- *18* ing, or take away music. If you/say that low men practice paint- ing, I say that music also is ruined by those who do not know it.[16]

27. Who is there who would not wish to lose the senses of hear- *6v* ing, smell, and touch, before losing sight? For he who loses his sight/is like one expelled from the world, when he does not see *7* it any more, nor anything in it. And such a life is a sister to death.

28. *Reply of King Mathias to a poet who competed with a* *14v* *painter*. On the birthday of King Mathias a poet brought him a work that he had written in honor of the day, declaring that the king was born to benefit the world. A painter presented him with a portrait of his beloved. The king hastily closed the poet's book, turned to the painting, and fixed his gaze upon it with great admiration.

The poet, then, with much indignation said: "O King, read, read, and you will find something of greater substance than a mute picture."

---

[16] At the end of this section the scribe has written: mancaui pi quel ch'io veggio. (A piece is missing here, as I see it.)

The king, hearing himself reproached for gazing at mute things, said: "Poet, be still, for you do not know what you are saying. This painting serves a better sense than does your work, which is for blind men. Give me something that I can see and touch and not only hear, and do not blame my choice in having put your work under my elbow, but this work of the painter I hold with my two hands, offering it to my eyes, because my hands of their own accord have taken it to serve the sense which is more noble than that of hearing. I myself judge that there is the same relation between the science of the painter and that of the poet, that there is between the senses to which they appeal. Do you not know that the soul is composed of harmony and harmony is not/engendered except in the moments when the proportion of things is seen or heard? Do you not see that in your science there is no proportion created at any given moment, but that one part is born of another in succession, and the next one is not born until the preceding one dies? For this reason I judge that your creation is much inferior to that of the painter: because no harmonious proportion is composed by yours. It does not content the mind of the hearer or observer as does the proportion of most beautiful features, composing the divine beauties of this face before me, which, shown to me as a whole, give me so much pleasure with their divine proportion that I judge there is nothing on earth made by man that could please me more."

If asked which he would rather select, to be in perpetual darkness or to be willing to lose his hearing, no man's judgment is so senseless that he would not at once reply he would sooner lose his hearing, together with the sense of smell, rather than to be blind. For whoever loses his sight loses the beauty of the world and all the forms of created things, and the deaf man loses only the sound made by the motion of air under percussion, which is the least thing in the world.

You say that a science becomes nobler, the worthier its subject, and for this reason a false fancy of the essence of God is more valuable than the imagination of a thing less worthy; in reply to your statement I shall say that painting, which includes only the works of God, is more worthy than poetry, which includes only lying fictions about human actions.

/With justified lamentation, painting complains that she has *15v*
been driven from the number of the liberal arts, although she is
a true daughter of nature and appeals to the noblest of senses.
Hence, writers, it is wrong to have left her outside the number of
the seven liberal arts, since painting gives heed not only to the
works of nature but to an infinite number of things that nature
never created.

29. *Difference between painting and poetry.*/Painting is a poetry *9-9v*
that is seen and not heard, and poetry is a painting which is
heard and not seen. So then, these two poetries, or, if you will,
two paintings, have exchanged the senses by which they reach
the intellect, because if both be painting, they ought to reach
understanding through the most noble sense, that is, the eye; but
if both one and the other are poetry, they should reach it through
the less noble one, which is the ear.

Let us submit painting to the judgment of him who is born
deaf, and poetry will be judged by one who is born blind. If a
painting represents the actions appropriate in every situation to
the mental attitudes of the figures in it, doubtless he who is born
deaf will understand the actions and intentions of the actors. But
he who is born blind will never understand what the poet relates, those things which do honor to poetry, such noble parts as
the representation of gestures, the composition of narratives, the
description of places adorned and delightful—transparent waters
through which are seen the green depths of their courses, waves
that play over meadows and small stones with grass, mingling
with playful fish and similar details. These could as well be told
to a stone as to a man born blind, because he has never seen anything of what composes the beauty of the world: that is, light,
darkness, color, body, form, location, distance, nearness, motion,
and rest, which are the ten ornaments of nature.

But the deaf man, having lost the less noble sense, even
though/he has at the same time lost speech, because of never *10*
having heard speech, and thus can never learn any language, will
understand every physical condition of human bodies better than
one who speaks and hears but does not see, and likewise he will
know the works of painters and what is represented in paintings
and what is appropriate to such representations.

*8* 30. *How painting goes beyond all the works of man because of the subtle reflections that pertain to it.*[17] The eye, which is called the window of the soul, is the principal way through which the mind can most copiously and magnificently consider the infinite works of nature, and the ear is second to it, becoming noble through hearing about things that the eye has beheld. If you historians, poets, or mathematicians had not seen these things with the eye, you would hardly be able to report them in writing. And if you, poet, represent a narrative with a painting of the pen, the painter with a brush will more easily make it satisfying and less tedious to comprehend.

If you call painting mute poetry, poetry can also be called blind painting. Now think, which is the more damaging affliction, that of the blind man or that of the mute?

If the poet is as free as the painter in his inventions, his representations do not give as much satisfaction to men as do paint-
*8v* ings, because if poetry includes the representation of forms,/actions, and locations by words, the painter is moved by the real likenesses of forms to reproduce those forms. Now consider, which is nearer to a man, the man's name or the likeness of that man? A man's name changes in various countries, but his form is not changed except by death. If the poet serves the senses by way of the ear, the painter does so by way of the eye, a worthier sense.

I ask no more than that a good painter represent the fury of a battle and the poet write a description of it, and the two descriptions be placed together before the public. You will see where the witnesses stop more often, where they pay more attention, where more praise is given, and which satisfies more fully. Certainly the painting, being by far more useful and beautiful, will please more. Place the name of God somewhere in writing, and place a representation of His form opposite, and you will see which will be the more revered.

[17] Ludwig has transcribed the "sotile" of the heading to read "sottili." The heading does not indicate the nature of the contents of this section. It may be a preliminary version. The latter part of the text has been corrected by an early editor, making it still more difficult to understand. Cf. notes: Ludwig, *Quellenschriften*, XVII, 193; Richter, *Literary Works*, I, 56-58.

Painting in itself includes all the forms of nature, but you, poet, have nothing but their names, which are not universal, as are their forms. If you have the effects of the manifestations, we painters have the manifestation of the effects.

Take the case of a poet who describes to a lover the beauties of his lady, and take that of the painter who represents her, and you will see which way nature inclines the lover who judges between the two.

Certainly the matter should be decided by the test of experience. You have placed painting among the mechanical arts, but certainly if painters were as ready as you are to praise their own work in writing, I believe they would not have to endure the burden of such low repute. If you call painting mechanical because it is initially the work of the hand, as the hands delineate that which is found in the imagination, you writers also inscribe manually with the pen/that which is found in your minds. If 9 you say it is mechanical because it is executed for a price, who falls into this error, if error it can be called, oftener than you do? If you lecture in classrooms, do you not go where you are best paid? Do you do any work without some payment? To be sure I do not say this to condemn such actions, for any labor expects reward. The poet may say: I will create a story which will signify great things; the painter will do the same, as did Apelles when he produced his *Calumny*.

If you say that poetry is more durable, I will reply that the works of coppersmiths are still more so, that time conserves them better than your works or ours, but nevertheless they rely little on the imagination. Painting, by using enamel colors on copper can be made much more enduring.

Because of our art we can be called the grandchildren of God. If poetry includes moral philosophy, painting deals with natural philosophy. If poetry describes the functioning of the mind, what does painting consider, except the mind working through bodily motion? If poetry terrifies people with infernal inventions, painting does likewise with its representations. Let a poet represent a beauty or a frightful thing, an object horrible and ugly such as a monster, in competition with a painter, and let the painter work in his own way, transmuting forms as he pleases, and the painter will satisfy the more. Are there not paintings to be seen so like the object that they represent that they have deceived men and animals?

[ARGUMENTS ON BEHALF OF PAINTING IN COMPARISON WITH POETRY]

5 31. *Of the poet and the painter*.[18] Painting serves a more worthy sense than poetry does, and represents the forms of nature's works with more truth than does the poet. The works of nature are of much more value than are words, which are works of man, because there is the same relation between the works of men and those of nature that there is between man and God. Hence it is more valuable to copy objects of nature and effect true likenesses, than to copy with words the deeds and words of men.

5v    If you, poet,/wish to describe the works of nature according to your own profession, simulating various places and the forms of varying objects, you will be surpassed by the painter with his infinitely greater power. You may wish to clothe yourself with sciences belonging to others, apart from poetry, but these are not really yours; as, for example, astronomy, rhetoric, theology, philosophy, geometry, arithmetic, and the like. If you do so, you are then no longer a poet, you have transformed yourself, and you are not the man of whom we speak. Now, do you not see that if you wish to approach nature, you arrive there by means of sciences developed by others, which they have based on the effects of nature? But the painter without the help of scientists or other intermediaries, arrives immediately at the representation of those works of nature.

By means of painting, lovers are impelled toward the portraits of the beloved, and speak to the paintings that portray the appearance of the beloved; by it people are moved to beseech the portraits of the Gods making fervent vows, but this is not brought about by looking at the works of poets, who represent the same Gods with words. Painting even deceives animals, for I have seen a picture that deceived a dog because of the likeness to its master; likewise I have seen dogs bark and try to bite painted dogs, and a monkey that did an infinite number of foolish things

18 Hand 3 has added to the heading: sara meglio dire Come la Pittura serue a' piu degno sēso che la poesia (it would be better to say, How painting serves a more worthy sense than poetry).

with another painted monkey. I have seen flying swallows light
on painted iron bars before the windows of buildings.[19]

32. *Argument of the poet against the painter.* You say: Painter, 14
your art is adored; do not impute such power to yourself but
to the thing that the painting represents. Here the painter replies: Poet, make yourself an imitator also; why do you not represent things in words in such a way that your writings, containing
those words, will also be adored?

But nature has favored the painter more than the poet, and the
works of the favorite ought properly to be more honored than
those of him who is not in favor.

Therefore, let us praise him who with words satisfies the ear
and him/who with painting satisfies and contents the sight, but 14v
much less him of the words, for these are accidental, created by a
lesser author than the works of nature which the painter portrays.

33. *Dispute between the poet and the painter and what difference* 13
*there is between poetry and painting.* The poet says that his
science consists of invention and measure, invention of subject
and measure of verses, and that this is the basis of poetry, which
is later clothed with all the sciences. To this the painter replies
that there are the same requirements in the science of painting;
that is, invention and measure, invention concerning the subject
which he must represent and measure concerning the objects
painted, so that they shall not be disproportionate, but/painting is 13v
not embraced by these three sciences, and the others are in large
part affected by painting. For example, astronomy cannot function
without perspective, which is a principal element of painting. (I
mean mathematical astronomy and do not speak of false divina-
tion or popular astrology. Let him who makes a living from
fools by means of it forgive me.)

The poet says that he describes a thing that represents another
in verses full of beautiful sentences. The painter says that he has
the power to do the same and in this respect he also is a poet.

If the poet says that he can inflame men with love, a principal
concern of all kinds of living creatures, the painter has the power

[19] At the end of this section, Hand 3 has added: tutte operationi del pittore
marauigliosissime (all most admirable productions of the painter).

to do likewise, the more so in that he places before the lover the very effigy of the beloved, and the lover often kisses and speaks to the picture, which he would not do were the same beauties placed before him by the writer. The painter goes even further in affecting the minds of men, by inducing them to love and to fall in love with a painting that does not represent any living woman.

It once happened that I made a picture representing a divine subject, and it was bought by a man who fell in love with her. He wished to remove the emblems of divinity in order to be able to kiss the picture without scruples. But finally conscience overcame his sighs of desire and he was obliged to remove the painting from his house.

Now you, poet, describe a beauty without describing anything alive and try to arouse men's desire therewith. If you say: I shall describe hell or paradise, and other delights or horrors, the painter will surpass you because he will place before you things that, although silent, will tell you of delights, or will terrify you 14 and move your spirit to/flight, for painting moves the senses more quickly than does poetry.

If you say that with words you will stir up a people to tears or to laughter, I say that it is not you, the poet, who move them, but it is the orator, and oratory is another science, and is not poetry. The painter will move to laughter but not to tears, for tears are a greater disturbance of the emotions than laughter. A painter once made a picture which made everybody who saw it yawn and yawn repeatedly as long as they kept their eyes on the picture, which represented a man who was also yawning. Others have represented lust and sensuality in such a way that they excited beholders to the same excesses, which poetry cannot accomplish.

If you, poet, describe the figure of some deities, the writing will not be held in the same veneration as the painted deity, because vows and various prayers will continually be made to the painting. To it will throng many generations from many provinces and from over the eastern seas, and they will demand help from the painting and not from what is written.

**34.** *Conclusion of the dispute between the poet and the painter.* *15v*
Since we have concluded that poetry is in utmost degree compre-
hensible by the blind as is painting by the deaf, we shall say that
painting is proportionately more valuable than poetry as painting
serves a better and more noble sense than does poetry. Its nobility
is proved to be three times as great as that of three other senses,
since the loss of hearing, taste, and touch, have been chosen deliberately rather than the loss of the sense of sight.

Whoever loses sight, loses the beautiful view of the world and
is as one who is shut alive in a tomb wherein he can move and
live. Now, do you not see that the eye embraces the beauties of
all the world? It is the master of astronomy, it makes cosmog-
raphy, it advises and corrects all human arts, it carries men to
different parts of the world, it is the prince of mathematics, its
sciences are most certain, it has measured the heights and the
dimensions of the stars, it has found the elements and their locations. It has predicted future events through/the course of the *16*
stars, it has created architecture, and perspective, and divine
painting. Painting, most excellent above all other things created
by God, what praises are there to express your nobility? What
peoples, what tongues, can describe your scope?

The eye is the window of the human body through which the
soul views and enjoys the beauties of the world. Because of it
the soul in its human prison is content, and without it this human
prison is its torment. Through it human industry has discovered
fire, by which the eye has regained what darkness first took away.
It has adorned nature with agriculture and pleasant gardens.

But what need is there for me to carry my discourse to such
heights and lengths? What is there which is not accomplished by
the eye? It carries men from the east to the west, it has discovered navigation, it surpasses nature in dealing with things that
are simply natural and finite, for the works which our hands do
at the command of our eyes are infinite, as the painter shows in
his representation of the infinite number of forms of animals,
herbs, plants, and places.[20]

[20] At the end of this section, on Urb. 16, the scribe has written: Fine in
quanto di poesia e' pittura. (End, with respect to poetry and painting.)

5 35. *How the painter is master of all sorts of people and of all things.*[21] If the painter wishes to see beauties which will make him fall in love with them, he is a lord capable of creating them, and if he wishes to see monstrous things that frighten, or those that are grotesque and laughable, or those that arouse real compassion, he is their lord and their creator. If he wishes to create desert places, or fresh and shady places in warm weather, he depicts them, as also warm places in cold weather. If he wishes valleys, he makes them also; if he wishes from the high crests of mountains to disclose a great countryside and if, after that, he wishes to see the horizon of the sea, he is their lord, and so too if he wishes to see high mountains from deep valleys, or from high mountains to see low valleys and seashores. Indeed, whatever exists in the universe through essence, presence, or imagination, he has it first in his mind and then in his hands, and these are of such excellence that within a given space of time they have created a proportioned harmony reflecting things in nature as seen in a single glance.

6 36. If you, poet, describe a bloody battle, will it be with the air dark and murky, in the midst of frightful and death-dealing arms, mixed with the thick dust that defiles the atmosphere and the frightened flight of miserable men afraid of a horrible death? In this case, the painter will surpass you because your pen will be worn out before you describe fully what the painter with his medium can represent at once. Your tongue will be paralyzed with thirst and your body with sleep and hunger, before you depict with words what the painter will show you in a moment.

6v    In the picture/there is lacking only the soul of the objects represented, and in each body that part which can be shown in a single aspect is given entirely. It would be a long and tedious task for poetry to relate all the movements of those who take part in a war, with the limbs and their ornaments, which painting places before you, finished with great conciseness and with accuracy.

[21] Hand 3 has added to the heading, in the margin: Il pittore e' S° di tutto le cose che possono cadere in pensiero allomo percioche se egli ha desidero di . . . (The painter is lord of all things that can occur to a man's mind, if he wishes to . . .). This sentence was apparently suggested to precede "to see beauties that will . . ." as the opening of this section.

In this display there is nothing lacking except the noise of arms, the shouts of terrifying victors, the cries and plaints of the frightened, again things which the poet cannot represent to the sense of hearing.

We shall say, then, that poetry is a science that functions particularly for the blind, and painting does the same for the deaf. But painting remains the more valuable, as it serves the better sense.

37. *Difference between poetry and painting.* Painting makes an *10v* immediate presentation to you of the view which the artist has created, giving as much pleasure to the greatest of senses as anything created by nature. The poet who reports the same occurrences through hearing, a lesser sense, gives the ear no more pleasure than if one heard a common report. Now see what a difference there is between hearing a thing related, which, over a period of time gives pleasure to the ear, and seeing it instantaneously with that speed with which things in nature are seen. Moreover, the poet's creations are read over long intervals of time, and frequently they are not understood and need various commentaries,/but rarely do the commentators understand what *11* was in the poet's mind. Many times readers do not read more than a small part of these works, for lack of time. But the work of the painter is immediately understood by those who look at it.

38. The only true office of the poet is to represent the words of *6v* people talking together; only these represent things in a natural way through the sense of hearing, because these are natural things in themselves, and are created by the human voice. In all other matters, the poet is surpassed by the painter.

[PAINTING IS SUPERIOR TO MUSIC]

39. *How music must be called a sister, a younger sister, of paint-* 16 *ing.* Music is to be termed the sister of painting, for it is subject to the sense of hearing, a sense second to the eye. It composes harmony with the conjunction of proportioned parts sounded at the same time. It is obliged to be born and to die in one or a number of harmonic rhythms,/rhythms that surround the pro- *16v* portion of its parts, and create a harmony which is not composed

otherwise than is the line which surrounds the forms from which human beauty is derived.

But painting excels and lords it over music, because it does not die immediately after its creation, as does unfortunate music. Thus it remains in being and shows you as alive what is in fact only an inanimate representation.

Marvelous science of painting! You preserve alive the ephemeral beauties of mortals, which through you become more permanent than the works of nature, which vary continually with time, leading them to expected old age. Such a science bears the same relation to divine nature as its works do to the works of nature, and therefore it is adored.

*10* 40. *What difference there is between painting and poetry.* "Painting is mute poetry and poetry is blind painting," both imitating nature as far as possible within their capacities, and through both moral customs can be shown, as Apelles did with his *Calumny.*

But from painting which serves the eye, a more noble sense than the ear, a harmonious proportion results. For example, many different voices joined together at one time result in a harmonious proportion, which so delights the sense of hearing that those who hear it remain stupefied with admiration and only half alive; yet much greater is the effect of the proportionate beauties of an angelic face in a painting, from whose proportion there results ordered harmony, affecting the eye in the same space of time that music does the ear.

If such a harmony of beauties is shown to the lover of the woman whose beauty it imitates, without a doubt he will remain stupefied with admiration and with an incomparable joy, for sight is superior to all the other senses.

But poetry produces no comparable grace for it has to combine *10v* the representation of perfect beauty/with the representation of each particular part of which, in painting, the harmony just mentioned is composed. It is as though in music one were made to hear each voice separately at a different time, and from this no accord could be composed, or if we wished to show a face part by part, continually covering up the parts already shown. This would be an exhibition in which forgetfulness would disallow any harmonious proportion to be composed, because the eye would not embrace the parts all at the same time with its visual power. The same thing happens to the beauties of anything represented by the poet, from which the memory receives no harmony, since each part is spoken separately at different times.

41. *Conclusion of the dispute among poet, painter, and musician.* **18** There is the same difference between the representation of bodily things by the painter and by the poet, as between dismembered and whole bodies. The poet, in describing the beauty or ugliness of a body, will describe it to you part by part and at different times, but the painter will make you see it all at the same time. The poet cannot give you in words the true shape of the parts of which the whole is composed, as can the painter, who places it before you with the same truthfulness that is in nature.

The same thing happens to the poet as to the musician who sings alone a song composed for four singers, singing first the soprano, then the tenor, continuing with the contralto, and finally the bass part. From this performance there results no grace of harmonious proportion, set in harmonious rhythms.

A poet does likewise in the case of a beautiful face, which he shows you feature by feature, but when he does so you will never be satisfied with its beauty which alone consists in the divine/ *18v* proportion of those features assembled together. Only at one and the same time do they compose that divine harmony from a commingling of features, which often enslaves him who sees it.

Music, also, with its harmonious rhythm produces smooth melodies composed of various voices. The poet is deprived of their harmonious distinction, and although poetry reaches the seat of judgment through the sense of hearing, as is the case with music, the poet cannot describe the harmony of music, since he has not the power to say different things at one time. The harmonious proportion of painting, composed of different parts at one time, does have this power, and its sweetness is judged simultaneously as a whole and in detail. It is judged as a whole with respect to the intent of the composition, in detail with respect to the intent of the parts which compose that whole. For this reason, the poet remains far behind the painter in the representation of bodily things, and far behind the musician in the representation of invisible things.

But if the poet borrows the help of the other sciences, he can appear at the fairs, as do the merchants who bring various things made by many inventors. The poet does this when he borrows from the sciences of others, such as the orator's, the philosopher's, the astronomer's, the cosmographer's and the like, whose sciences are wholly separate from that of the poet. Therefore, he is a broker who gathers together the talents of different persons, to bring a sale to conclusion. If you would discover the true office of the poet, you will find that it is nothing other than that of a

18v man who gathers together things stolen from other sciences,/with which he makes a lying composition, or if you would call it by a more honorable name, a fictitious composition. In this freedom to indulge in imagination the poet has placed himself on a par with the painter, although this is the weakest aspect of painting.

[COMPARISON OF PAINTING WITH POETRY AND MUSIC]

11 42. *Of the difference and similarity of painting and poetry.*
Painting presents its essence in an instant to the power of sight through the same medium by which man's receptive capacity is aware of natural objects. At the same time the harmonious proportion of the parts pleases the senses. Poetry makes the same report, though through a less worthy medium than the eye, and carries to the receptive capacity the shape of things named, with greater confusion and tardiness than does the eye, which is a true intermediary between the object and the receptive capacity. The eye reports with utmost truthfulness the true surfaces and shapes of that which is presented to it. From this arises the harmonious proportion that with sweet accord pleases the senses. It does so in the same way that the proportion of different voices pleases the sense of hearing, which is still less worthy than that of the eye, because as soon as harmony, which pleases the ear, is born it dies, and its death is as rapid as its birth. This cannot happen with

11v the sense of vision, since, if you represent to the eye a human beauty composed of proportioned, beautiful parts, those beauties are not so mortal nor will they disappear so rapidly as music.

A painting has great permanence and it allows you to see and consider it. It is not reborn as music is, when the playing is repeated, nor does it bore you. It fills you with love for it and makes all the senses, as well as the eye, desire to possess it; it seems that all the senses vie with the eye in enjoyment. The mouth would like to swallow it bodily, the ear takes pleasure in hearing of its beauties, the sense of touch would absorb it through all its pores, the nose also would inhale the air which continually emanates from it.

The beauty of such harmony is destroyed by time in a few years, unless it happens that the beauty has been depicted by the painter, so that time will long preserve it. The eye, insofar as its function is concerned, takes as true pleasure in such a painted beauty as it would in the living beauty. The satisfaction of touch is lacking, but at the same time it becomes an older brother, and although it will have known desire, this will not impede reason in considering the divine beauty.

In this case, by re-creating, painting supplies in large part what the poet's description cannot supply. Although the poet would here rival the painter, he does not realize that his words, mentioning the parts of the beauty, are divided by time, one from another. Forgetfulness intervenes and divides the proportion into its elements, but since the poet is unable to name it he cannot compose its harmonious proportion,/which is derived from di- 12 vine proportion. The poet cannot describe a beauty in words during the time which is taken up by reflection on the beauty in painting. He sins against nature in attempting to tell the ear what ought to be told to the eye, in letting music function here, and in not putting in its place the science of painting, true reproducer of the natural forms of all things.

What moves you, man, to abandon your home in town and leave relatives and friends, going to country places over mountains and up valleys, if not the natural beauty of the world which, if you consider well, you know you enjoy with the sense of sight alone? If the poet in these circumstances would also call himself a painter, why not accept the poet's description of those places and stay at home, escaping the excessive heat of the sun? Would this not be more useful to you and less fatiguing? You would stay in a cool house, without moving, and in no danger of falling ill. But your soul would not be able to enjoy the benefit of the eyes, the windows of its dwelling, and would not receive the visual images of pleasant places. It would not be able actually to see shady valleys watered by twisting streams, would not be able to see various flowers, which make a harmony for the eye with their colors, and so with all the other things that can be presented to the eye.

But if the painter during the cold and harsh weather of winter, places before you the same painted landscapes, and others, where you have had pleasure beside some spring, you can see yourself as a lover, with your beloved, in the flowered meadows, beneath
*12v* the sweet shade of trees/growing green. Would you not receive quite a different pleasure than you would from hearing such an effect described by a poet?

Here the poet replies and acknowledges these arguments, but says he surpasses the painter. He makes men speak and converse of varying fantasies in which things that do not exist are simulated. He will move men to take up arms; he will describe the sun, the stars, the arts, and everything.

To this the reply is: none of these things of which he speaks belongs to his real profession, for if he would speak and orate, he must be convinced that in this he is vanquished by the orator, and if he speaks of astronomy, he has filched it from the astronomer, if he speaks of philosophy he has taken it from the philosopher. Indeed, poetry has no basis of its own and deserves no more credit than does a merchant who collects goods produced by various artisans.

But the divine science of painting considers the works, human as well as divine, which are encompassed by surfaces, that is, the lines that are the boundaries of bodies, and with these she commands the sculptor to achieve the perfection of his statues. By means of her basic principle, that is, design, she teaches the architect to make his edifice so that it will be agreeable to the eye, and teaches the composers of variously shaped vases, as well as goldsmiths, weavers, and embroiderers. She has discovered the characters by which different languages are expressed, has given numerals to the arithmetician, has taught us how to represent the figures of geometry; she teaches masters of perspective and astronomy, machinists, and engineers.

43. *The musician speaks with the painter.*[22] The musician says *16v* that his science is to be placed on a par with that of the painter, because his science is the sum total of many parts, of which the listener may contemplate all the graces in as many harmonious rhythms as there are rhythms in which music is born and dies, and with those rhythms its grace delights the soul which resides in the body of him who contemplates it.

But the painter to this answers that the body, composed as it is of human limbs, does not in itself give pleasure in harmonious rhythms wherein its beauty must change, exchanging one concept for another, nor does it have to be born and die in those rhythms; but painting makes this beauty permanent for many years, and it is of such excellence that it preserves that harmony of proportioned limbs/which nature with all its strength could not do. How many *17* paintings have preserved the likeness of a divine beauty of which nature's example has been destroyed by time or death, and the work of the painter has thus become of greater value than that of nature, his teacher.

44. *The painter gives the degrees of things presented to the eye* *17* *as the musician gives the degrees of the voices presented to the ear.* Although things placed before the eye touch one another at arm's length, nevertheless I shall apply my rule of intervals of twenty braccia between them, as does the musician with his voices, who, although the voices may be united and connected, places each voice at short intervals, calling them first, second, third, fourth, and fifth, and thus he has given names to the various ways of raising and lowering the voice, from degree to degree.

If you, musician, say that painting is mechanical because it is produced through exercise of the hands, while music is produced with the mouth, which is a human organ, though in this instance it is not acting on behalf of the sense of taste, then note that the hand of the painter is not functioning on behalf of the sense of

[22] Hand 1 had written: Parla il pittore col musico. (The painter speaks with the musician.) But Hand 3 had crossed out "il pittore" and added "col Pittore" at the end of the heading.

touch. Less important, also, are words than facts. But you, writers on the sciences, when you write what is in your minds do you not copy with the hand as does the painter?

If you say that music is composed of proportion, I have employed proportion in painting, as you will see.

[INFERIORITY OF SCULPTURE TO PAINTING]

*17*  45. [23]After painting comes sculpture, a very valuable art but it is
*17v* not produced by minds of such excellence as is painting./In the two principal problems, perspective and shadow and light, with which the painter has to deal in his art, painting is most difficult, whereas sculpture is aided in these by nature. Sculpture, also, does not duplicate the colors which the painter strives to find. In sculpture shadows come about naturally with lights.

*27*  46. *How sculpture is indebted to light but painting is not.* If sculpture is lighted from below, it will seem monstrous and strange, but this does not happen with painting which carries all its elements within itself.

*23*  47. *How sculpture requires less intelligence than painting and how many aspects of nature are lacking in it.* Applying myself no less to sculpture than to painting, and practicing both in the same degree, it seems to me that with little change of bias I can judge which demands more of the mind, and which presents greater difficulty and is more perfect than the other.

First, sculpture is subject to a specific illumination from above, but painting carries with it everywhere a light and shade of its own. Light and shade are the important things in sculpture, but in these the sculptor is aided by nature, in bringing out relief which exists in nature. The painter, by the conditions of his art, creates relief artificially and according to reason in the places where it would exist in nature.

The sculptor cannot diversify his work by using different kinds of color; painting is not deficient in any respect.

The perspectives of sculptors do not seem true at all; those of

[23] Hand 3 has written at the foot of fol. 17: Questo da a. a' b. uole essere posto tra li doi cap[11] c. et de che seguitano. (From a. to b. this should be placed between the two chapters c. and d. which follow.)

the painter encompass aerial perspective and seem to extend hundreds of miles beyond his work.

Sculptors cannot represent transparent or luminous bodies, nor lines of reflected light, nor shining bodies, such as mirrors and other objects that reflect light, nor mists, nor murky weather, nor an infinite number of things which are not mentioned in order not to be tiresome.

What sculpture possesses is that ordinarily it resists time better, although painting made on thick copper, covered with white enamel, then painted upon with colors of enamel, returned to the fire and fused, is more durable than sculpture.

The sculptor can say that when he makes a mistake, it is not easy for him to remedy it./But it is a weak argument to try to *23v* prove that an irremediable oversight makes a work more worthy. I will say of such a master that it is more difficult to repair his mind if he makes errors, than to repair the work spoiled by him.[24]

There is no comparison between the mental effort, amount of skill, and analysis required in painting and that required in sculpture. In sculpture there is no difficulty with perspective, because of the limitations of the material, and not because of the artificer. If the sculptor says that he cannot replace the material taken away from the stone that covers his work as the painter can replace parts of his work, the reply here is that he who takes away too much, understands too little and is not a master, for if he has control of the measurements of his work he will not remove what he ought not, and so we shall say that such a defect is in the master and not in his material.

But painting is a marvelous artifice, based on most subtle observations, of which sculpture is wholly devoid since it involves only brief analysis.

The reply to the sculptor who says that his science is more permanent than painting is that the permanence belongs to the material of which sculpture is composed and not to the sculptor. The sculptor ought not to claim this as his glory, but leave it to nature which created the material.

---

[24] In the margin at this point in MS, there is this note by the scribe: il resto del cap. e' a' car. 28. Fac. 1 al segno W (the rest of the chapter is on folio 28 recto at the place marked W). Cf. McM. 53.

*23v* 48. *Of the sculptor and the painter.* The sculptor's art brings greater fatigue to its creator than that of the painter; it is mechanical and less tiring, however, to the mind. Compared with *24* painting, it requires little thought,/because the sculptor is always taking away material, and the painter is always adding it. Furthermore the sculptor constantly takes away a single material, and the painter constantly adds colors of different materials.

The sculptor attends only to the contours that encompass the sculptured material, while the painter attends to the same outlines and in addition he attends to shadow and light, color and foreshortening, matters in which the sculptor is continually helped by nature. Shadow and light, and perspective, are subjects which the painter must learn by force of mind, identifying himself with nature, while the sculptor always finds these matters determined by fact.

If you say that there is any sculptor who understands what the painter knows, I reply to you that when the sculptor understands the details of painting, he is a painter, and when he does not, he is simply a sculptor. But the painter always needs to understand sculpture or nature in which there is relief which creates light and dark and foreshortening. Many return to nature because they are not trained in the theory of shade and light and perspective, and therefore portray the natural, because only by copying it can they apply these concepts without science or reasoning about nature under such specific conditions.

Of these, there are some who look at the things produced by nature through sheets of glass, or other transparent material such as veils. They trace outlines on the surface of the transparent medium, and according to the rules of proportion they surround these with profiles, and sometimes increasing them within the profiles, they fill them with light and dark, observing the location, quantity, and shape of the shadows and lights.

*24v* This is to be approved in the case of those who know how/to paint from imagination creating the effects of nature, but use these methods only to relieve themselves somewhat of fatigue, and in order not to be lacking in any particular in the true imitation of that which ought to be made precisely like nature.

But this invention is to be condemned in those who do not

know how to paint without it, nor how to reason about nature with their minds, for such laziness is destructive to their talent, nor do they ever learn how to produce good work without this aid. They are always poor and mean in every invention and in narrative composition, which is the final aim of this science, as will be shown in the proper place.

### [SCULPTURE IS A MECHANICAL ART]

49. *Beginning discussion of sculpture and whether or not it is a* 20 *science.* Sculpture is not a science but a most mechanical art, for it brings sweat and bodily fatigue to him who works at it. For such an artist the mere measure of the limbs, and the nature of movements and poses is sufficient. In this way he brings his work to an end, displaying to the eye what it is, and it gives the observer no cause for admiration, as does painting, which, by virtue of science, shows on a flat surface great stretches of land-scape, with distant horizons.

50. *Comparison of painting and sculpture.* Painting is produced 25v by the use of greater mental analysis than is sculpture and with greater skill, for sculpture is nothing more than it seems. It is a body in relief, surrounded by air, covered with shadowy and bright surfaces, as are natural bodies. It is carried out by two agents, that is by nature and by man, but the greater skill is that of nature, since if it did not help the work with shadows more or less dark and with lights more or less bright, the work would be all one color, either bright or dark, like a plane surface.

Furthermore, there is in addition the aid of perspective which, with its foreshortening, helps to make the muscular surfaces of bodies stand out at several points, one muscle covering another to a greater or lesser extent.

Here the sculptor answers and says: If I had not made those muscles, perspective would not foreshorten them for me. To this the reply is: If/it were not for the aid of the light and dark, you 26 would not be able to make those muscles, because you could not see them.

The sculptor says that it is he who makes the light and dark appear by removing parts of the material being carved. The reply is: that it is not he and not the art, but nature, that makes the shadow, and if he carved in darkness, he would not see anything, because in the dark there are no differences. Nor would he see differences if fog surrounded the material of the sculpture, so that it was equally lighted, and he could see nothing but the outlines of the material within the boundaries of the fog around it.

I ask you, sculptor, why you do not perfect your works in the open country, surrounded by the uniform and universal light of the air; and why you work indoors with a specific light, which descends from above to illuminate your work? If you make shadows at will when taking away material, why do you not do the same in sculpture carved in a universal light as you do when you carve in a specific light? Certainly you deceive yourself and it is another master that makes those shadows and lights for which you, as a servant, prepare the material on which that master impresses those accents of light and shadow. Therefore do not glory in the work of another. For you the lengths and thicknesses of the limbs of any body and their proportions suffice, and this is your art. The rest, which is the entity, is created by nature, a greater master than you.

The sculptor says that he will carve bas relief and by means of perspective he will show that which is not so in fact. The reply is that perspective is an element of painting, as was shown before.

20-20v  51. *Difference between painting and sculpture.*/I do not find any difference between painting and sculpture except that the sculptor pursues his work with greater physical fatigue than the painter, and the painter pursues his work with greater mental fatigue. This is proved to be true, for the sculptor in producing his work does so by the force of his arm, striking the marble or other stone to remove the covering beyond the figure enclosed within it. This is a most mechanical exercise accompanied many times with a great deal of sweat, which combines with dust and turns into mud. The sculptor's face is covered with paste and all powdered with marble dust, so that he looks like a baker, and he is covered with minute chips, so that he looks as though he had been out in the snow. His house is dirty and filled with chips and dust of stones. In speaking of excellent painters and sculptors we may say that just the opposite happens to the painter, since the well-dressed painter sits at great ease in front of his work, and moves a very light brush, which bears attractive colors, and he is adorned with such garments as he pleases. His dwelling is full of fine paintings and is clean and often filled with music, or the sound of different beautiful works being read, which are often heard with great pleasure, unmixed with the pounding of hammers or other noises.

Furthermore, the sculptor in carrying out his work has to make many contours for each figure in the round, so that that figure will look well from all sides. These contours are produced by the meeting of high and low areas of the stone, which he cannot place accurately unless he retires and views it in profile, that is, when the boundaries of concave areas and those in relief are seen in silhouette against the air/that touches them. But truly this *21* does not add to the labor of the sculptor, considering that he, as well as the painter, has true knowledge of all the outlines of things seen from any side whatever, a knowledge that is always within the reach of the painter as well as the sculptor.

But the sculptor, having to remove stone where he wishes to leave intervals between muscles, and to leave it where he desires to show those muscles in relief, cannot create them with the right shapes, beyond getting their length and breadth, unless he leans across the stone, bending over and raising himself up in such a way that he sees the true height of the muscles and the true depth of intervals between them. These are judged by the sculptor who must place himself in that position, and thus the contours are corrected, otherwise he could never make the contours or the form of his sculpture well.

They say this is a mental fatigue for the sculptor, although his fatigue is only physical. So far as his mind or judgment is concerned, he has only to correct in profile the portions where the muscles project too high. This is the proper and ordinary way for the sculptor to bring his work to completion, and is ordinarily carried out with true knowledge of the contours of the figure from every side.

The sculptor says that if he takes off too much of the outer portion of his material, he cannot add to it later as can the painter.

The reply to this is that if his art were perfect, through knowledge of the measurements, he would have removed just enough and not too much of the covering material. Excessive removal of material arises from his ignorance, which makes him remove more or less than he should.

But I am not really speaking of such as these, for they are not
*21v* masters but wasters/of marble. Masters do not depend on the judgment of the eye, because it is deceptive, as is proved when one wishes to divide a line into two equal parts by means of the judgment of the eye, and there experience shows it often to be deceptive. Because of this uncertainty good judges always fear what the ignorant do not, and therefore they are continually guided by knowledge of the measurement of each dimension, length, and breadth of the limbs, and when they do thus, they do not remove more than they should.

The painter has ten different subjects to consider in carrying his work to completion: light, shadow, color, body, form, location, distance, nearness, motion, and rest. The sculptor has to consider only body, form, location, motion, and rest. He does not need to be concerned about darkness or light, because nature itself creates these for his sculpture, and about color there is no concern at all. He concerns himself moderately about distance and nearness. He employs linear perspective but not that of color, although at different distances from the eye, color, and clarity in the contours and forms of figures vary.

Therefore sculpture has fewer matters to consider and consequently is less fatiguing to the mind than is painting.

*26v* 52. *Apologia of the sculptor.* The sculptor says that if he removes more marble than he should, he cannot correct his error, as can the painter. The reply to this is that he who removes more than he should is not a master, because master is the name for one who has true knowledge of his art.

The sculptor replies that when he is at work on the marble and a crack appears, it is the crack and not he, the master, who is responsible for such a mishap. The answer is that the sculptor in this case is like the painter whose panel splits and annoys him, while he is painting.

The sculptor says that he cannot make one figure without making an infinite number of them because of the infinite contours that continuous quantities have. The reply is that the infinite outlines of the figure are reduced to two half figures; one half from the middle to the back, and the other half from the middle to the front, and if they are well proportioned they compose a figure in the round. Since these halves have the proper relief in all their parts, they will answer by themselves, without further skill, for all the infinite shapes the sculptor says he has made. The same thing could be said by one who makes a vase on the potter's wheel, since he also can show his vase from an infinite number of points of view.

But what can the sculptor do if the accidents of nature do not continually rescue him in all necessary and opportune situations? This aid which is brightness and darkness and which the painter calls light and shade never disappoints. The painter creates it by himself with very great thought, and provides it with the same quantity, quality, and proportion, with which nature aids sculpture, without mental exertion on the part of the sculptor./ 27 It is nature also that aids that artisan with the proper diminutions, which perspective produces by itself without mental analysis by the sculptor, but the painter needs the knowledge, and he acquires it by mental effort.

The sculptor will say that he creates works that are more enduring than the painter's. The reply here is that this is to the credit of the material carved and not to the credit of the sculptor who carves it. If the painter paints on terracotta with glazes, his work will be even more durable than sculpture.

53. [25]We know that he who is experienced will not make similar 28 errors, but observing good rules, he will proceed by removing as little at a time as will enable him to carry out his work well.

The sculptor also, if he works in clay or wax, can remove and add material, and when his work is done it is easily cast in

---

[25] The first six lines on folio 28 is a note which may be translated: Note that the following half chapter comes after the other half which begins on folio 23 of the present book and is divided on folio 23v at the sign W, and ends thus: THE WORK spoiled by him, an error which occurred because of the writing, which is left-handed, and because it was written on another page facing it.

bronze, and this is the final and the most permanent form of sculpture. That which is made of marble only is subject to destruction, but bronze is not.

Painting made on copper has the advantages of both painting and sculpture in bronze, for in painting on copper, as has been said, it is possible to remove and add material, and in the case of bronze sculpture it is also possible to remove or add material. If bronze sculpture is durable, painting on copper with glazes is more durable. Bronze remains black and brown, but this kind of painting is full of varied, pleasant colors, in infinite range. As this has been mentioned above, nothing more need be said about it, in order not to prove tiresome.

If somebody speaks of panel painting, in this case I would side with sculpture and say that as painting is more beautiful, more imaginative, and more inclusive, so sculpture is more durable, but it has no other advantage. Sculpture, with little effort, shows in fact what in painting is only appearance. But what a miraculous thing that appearance is: it makes intangible things appear tangible, flat things appear in relief, things near appear 28v distant. Indeed, painting is/equipped with infinite resources that sculpture does not employ.[26]

[A COMPARISON OF PAINTING AND SCULPTURE]

27 54. *The difference between painting and sculpture.* The first marvel that appears in painting is that it appears to be detached from the wall or other flat surface, and deceives those of subtle judgment as it is really not separated from the surface of the wall. In comparison with this, the sculptor creates his works so that they appear as they are. And this is the reason that the painter needs to understand the shadows that go with lights. The sculptor does not need this knowledge, because nature aids his works, as it does all other objects which are all of the same color when the light is gone, and are of different colors when the light is returned, being changed by means of the intervention of brightness or darkness.

27v      The painter's second task is to evaluate with care/the true

[26] At the end of the text of this section Hand 3 has added above the line: delle quali māca la scultura (which sculpture does not have).

qualities and quantities of shadows and lights. Nature provides these for the sculptor.

The third thing is perspective, which is the most subtle discovery in mathematical studies, for by means of lines it causes to appear distant that which is near, and large that which is small. Sculpture is aided by nature in this case, which accomplishes its end without any artifice of the sculptor.

55. *Comparison of painting and sculpture.* Painting is a matter 24v of greater mental analysis, of greater skill, and more marvelous than sculpture, since it compels the mind of the painter to transform itself into the very mind of nature, to become an interpreter between nature and art. It explains the causes of nature's manifestations as compelled by its laws: in what ways the images of objects before the eye come together in the pupil of the eye; which, among objects equal in size, looks larger to the eye; which, among equal colors will look more or less dark or more or less bright; which, among things at the same depth, looks more or less low; which, among those objects placed at/equal 25 height, will look more or less high, and why, among objects placed at various distances, one will appear less clear than the other.

This art comprises and includes within itself all visible things such as colors and their diminution which the poverty of sculpture cannot include. Painting represents transparent objects but the sculptor will show you the shapes of natural objects without artifice. The painter will show you things at different distances with variation of color due to the air lying between the objects and the eye; he shows you mists through which visual images penetrate with difficulty; he shows you rain which discloses behind it clouds with mountains and valleys; he shows the dust which discloses within it and beyond it the combatants who stirred it up; he shows streams of greater or lesser density; he shows fish playing between the surface of the water and its bottom; he shows the polished pebbles of various colors lying on the washed sand at the bottom of rivers, surrounded by green plants; he shows the stars at various heights above us, and thus he achieves innumerable effects which sculpture cannot attain.

The sculptor says that bas-relief is a kind of painting. This may be accepted in part, insofar as design is concerned, because it shares in perspective. But with regard to shadows and lights, it is a false statement both for sculpture and for painting, because the shadows in bas-relief are supplied by nature in all relief, as are the shadows in foreshortening, and they do not have the darkness of painting or of sculpture in the round. This art is a mixture of painting and sculpture.

*21v* 56. *The painter and the sculptor.* The sculptor says that his art is more worthy than painting, because his work is more enduring, for it has less to fear from humidity, as well as fire, heat, and cold, than does painting.

The reply is that this does not make the sculptor more worthy, because this permanence comes from the material and not from *22* the artist. The same kind of permanence can also be found in/ painting when it is done in enamel on metals, or terracottas, which are fired in a furnace and then polished with various instruments that give a smooth and lustrous surface. These can be seen in several places in France and Italy, and most of all in Florence among the della Robbia family, who have discovered a way to carry out every kind of great work in painting on terracotta covered with glaze. It is true that this sort of painting is subject to knocks and breaks, as is also sculpture in marble, but not to destruction by melting as are figures in bronze. With regard to durability it is equal to sculpture and surpasses it with regard to beauty, since in it are combined the two perspectives, but in sculpture in the round there is no perspective except that found in nature.

In making a figure in the round, the sculptor makes only two forms, and not an infinite number for the infinite number of points of view from which it can be seen; one of these forms is seen from in front and the other from in back. This is proved to be so, for if you make a figure in bas-relief which is seen from in front, you will never say that you have put more of the work on display than a painter would do with a figure made from the same point of vantage and the same thing happens with a figure seen from the back.

But bas-relief requires incomparably greater thought than that which is wholly in relief and somewhat approaches painting in concept, because it is indebted to perspective. Work wholly in relief is not troubled at all about this problem, because it employs the simple measures that it finds in life, and therefore the painter/ *22v* learns sculpture more quickly than the sculptor does painting.

But to return to the claim of what is called bas-relief, I say that it requires less physical fatigue than work wholly in relief, but far more study, since it requires consideration of the proportion of the distances which lie between the first and the second planes of bodies and those from the second to the third and so forth in succession. If these are being considered by you, master in perspective, you will find no bas-relief which is not full of errors, with regard to the greater or lesser relief required by the parts of the body, in relation to their distance from or proximity to the eye. There is never any error in total relief because nature helps the sculptor, and therefore he who works in total relief is freed of this great difficulty.

There exists a basic enemy of the sculptor who works in the round as well as in bas-relief. His works are worth little if the light in which they are seen is not adjusted so that it is similar to that of the place in which it was made. If the light is from below, the works will appear distorted, and this will be so most of all in bas-relief, because of shadows cast in a direction opposite to that intended, almost eliminating recognition of the work. This cannot happen to the painter who, after having placed the limbs of his figures properly, turns to two functions of nature which are very great, which are the two perspectives, and also to the third great factor which is the brightness and darkness in shadows and lights, of which the sculptor is ignorant and in which he is aided by nature in the way in which it aids other visible things, natural as well as artificial.

57. *Parallel of painting and sculpture.* Sculpture lacks the beauty *25* of colors, lacks/the perspective of colors, lacks the perspective and *25v* indistinctness of the outlines of objects distant from the eye, for it records the outlines of things nearby in the same way it does those that are distant. It cannot show the air lying between the

distant object and the eye, enveloping that object in greater amount than is the case with a nearby object. It cannot represent bodies that shine or are transparent, such as veiled figures which show the nude flesh beneath the veils covering them, and it cannot show the minute pebbles of various colors beneath the surface of transparent waters.

4 58. Whoever condemns painting, condemns nature, for the works of the painter represent the works of nature, and he who condemns either lacks feeling.

# PART TWO

## OF RULES FOR THE PAINTER

[TRAINING OF THE PAINTER IN YOUTH]

59. *What the student should learn first.* The young man should first learn perspective, then the proportions of all objects. Next, copy work after the hand of a good master, to gain the habit of drawing parts of the body well; and then work from nature, to confirm the lessons learned. View for a time works from the hands of various masters. Then form the habit of putting into practice and working what has been learned.[1]

60. *What rule should be given to boys who paint?*[2] We know clearly that vision is one of the swiftest actions there is, and in an instant sees infinite forms; nevertheless, it understands only one thing at a time. Suppose that you, reader, glance at all this written page, and you will quickly judge that it is full of various letters, but in this time you will not know what letters they are, nor what they would say. Hence you need to proceed word by word, line by line, if you would have an understanding of these letters. Just so, if you wish to mount to the top of an edifice it is advisable to go up step by step, otherwise it would be impossible to reach the top. So I say to you, whom nature turns to this art, if you wish to acquire knowledge of the forms of things, you will begin with their details, and not go on to the second phase until you have the first well fixed in memory and know it through practice. For if you do otherwise, you will be wasting your time, or rather, you will prolong your study a good deal. Remember first/to acquire diligence, rather than speed.

[1] At the end of this section, as applicable either to it or to the section that follows, Hand 3 has written: Sara meglio dire Del studio de' giouani. (It will be better to say, Of the study of young men.)

[2] At the end of the preceding section, but with reference to this, Hand 3 has written: Sara meglio dire Regola co'la quale s'haño da gouernare quelli che uogliono imparare la pittura. (It will be better to say, Rule by which those who wish to learn painting must be guided.)

*34* 61. *Rules for the painter.*[3] The painter ought first to train his own hand by copying drawings from the hands of good masters, and when this has been done under the guidance of his teacher, he should represent objects well in relief, according to those principles which will be stated about the representation of objects in relief.

*31* 62. *What study the young should follow.*[4] Young men who wish to perfect themselves in the sciences that portray all the forms of the works of nature, should in their study be concerned with drawing, together with the shadow and light appropriate to the place wherein such forms are located.

*37* 63. *That diligence should be learned before quick execution.*[5] Designer, when you would study well and profitably, go slowly with your drawing; distinguish among the lights to see which and how many have the finest degree of brightness; and likewise distinguish which among the shadows are those that are darker than the rest; in what way they mingle with one another; observe their quantity, compare them with one another. With respect to the outlines, note in what direction they turn; and with regard to lines, what portion twists toward one side or the other, and where it is more or less clear and therefore broad or fine. Finally, see that your shadows and lights are united, without heavy strokes or marks, as is the case with smoke. When you have trained your hand and judgment to this diligence, you will see facility in practice come quickly, even before you are aware of it.

*31v* 64. *Characteristics of the youth disposed toward painting.* Many are the young men who have a desire for and love of drawing, but have not the capacity for it, and this is to be recognized in

---

[3] Hand 3 has added: Sara meglio dire a questo cap¹º Del modo del studiare. (It will be better to call this chapter, Of the way to study.)

[4] Hand 3 has added to the title: Stara meglio dire, Del studio de giouani. (It will be better to say: Of young men's study.)

[5] Hand 3 has added: Sara meglio dire Modo di far buon principio nella Pittura e d'imparar pᵃ la deligētia che la prattica. (It will be better to say: Way to make a good beginning in painting, and to learn diligence first rather than facility.)

boys who are without diligence and never finish their works with shading.

### [EXERCISE OF THE IMAGINATION AND THE MEMORY]

65. *Of studying when you awake or before you go to sleep in* 36 *bed in the dark.* I have also proved for myself that it is of no little advantage, when you are in bed in the dark, to exercise the imagination, recalling the outlines of forms you have already studied, or other noteworthy things comprehended by subtle reflection, and this is really an admirable thing to do, useful for fixing these things in the memory.

66. *How to memorize well.*[6] When you wish to remember well 37v something you have studied, do this: when you have drawn the same object so many times that you seem to have it in your memory, try to execute it without the model. Trace your model on a thin, smooth glass, and place it upon the drawing you have made without a model, and note well where the tracing does not coincide with your drawing. Where you find that you have made errors, resolve not to repeat your mistakes. Return to the model and draw the wrong part again so many times that you will have committed its image to the mind. If, in order to trace an object, you cannot find a smooth glass, take a sheet of very fine parchment, oil it well and then dry it. When you have used this for one drawing, you can remove the drawing with a sponge and make a second.

### [SCIENCE AND PRACTICE]

67. *How to study.*[7] First study science, and then follow the prac- 32 tice born of that science.

68. [8]The painter ought to study methodically and not leave any- 32 thing without fixing it in memory, observing what difference there is between the limbs of animals and their joints.

---

[6] Hand 3 has added to the heading: quello si desegna (what is drawn).
[7] Hand 3 has inserted as an improvement on the heading: Quello che P^r si de' studiare o' la pratica o' la scientia. (What should be studied first, practice or theory.)
[8] Hand 3 has added a proposed heading: Studio del pittore giouane. (Study of the young painter.)

32 69. *How should a young man proceed in his study?* The mind
of the painter ought to be as continually concerned with as many
orderly analyses as there are forms of notable objects appearing
before him. He should stop and note them, reducing his observations to rules, taking into consideration the place and the surroundings, and the lights and shadows.

39v 70. *Of the error of those who practice without science.*[9] Those
who fall in love with practice without science are like pilots who
board a ship without rudder or compass, who are never certain
where they are going.

Practice ought always to be built on sound theory; perspective
is the guide and the path to this theory, and without it nothing
is done well in painting.

32 71. *What should the mind of the painter be like?* The painter's
mind should be like a mirror, which transforms itself into the
color of the thing that it has as its object, and is filled with as
many likenesses as there are things placed before it. Therefore,
painter, knowing that you cannot be good, if you are not a versatile master in reproducing through your art all the kinds of
forms that nature produces—which you will not know how to
do if you do not see and represent them in your mind—as you go
through fields, exercise your judgment of various objects, noting
first this thing and then that, making a collection of various objects, selected and harvested from among those less good. Do
not do as some painters who, tired with exercising the imagination, leave their work and take exercise, walking for recreation.
32v Being still tired mentally,/they do not pay attention to a variety
of things. But often on meeting friends or relatives, and being
greeted, they neither see nor hear them, and are considered ill-
disposed.[10]

[9] In the heading, Hand 1 first wrote "diligentia" but later struck out the first
five letters of this word and wrote "sci" above, to give "scientia." In the margin,
Hand 3 has added: Errore di quelli ch' amano[?] piu la pratica che la teorica.
(Error of those who love facility rather than theory.)

[10] The last word in this section, according to Urb. 32v is "scontrastino," or
"scontrassino." Hand 3 has added the suggestion: that it would be good for this
passage to follow that one marked with a symbol. Cf. McM. 13 and 27, where
such marks are found in Urb. 7 and 6v respectively. Could either of these be
the passages that Hand 3 had in mind? It is more probable that he meant the

72. The painter should be solitary and consider what he sees, dis- *33v*
cussing it with himself, selecting the most excellent parts of the
appearance of what he sees, acting as the mirror which transmutes itself into as many colors as exist in the things placed before
it. And if he does this he will be like a second nature.

[ADVICE TO PAINTERS]

73. *Whether or not it is better to draw in the company of others.* 37
I declare and affirm that it is much better for many reasons for
a student to draw in company than alone. First, because if you
are inadequate, you will be ashamed to be seen among the number of men drawing, and this mortification is a motive for studying well. Secondly, a sound envy will stimulate you to become
one of the number who are praised more than you, and the praise
of others will spur you on. Another reason is that you will get
something from the way in which they draw, who do this better
than you. If you are better than the others, you will benefit by
despising their defects,/while the praise of others will increase *37v*
your efficacy.

74. *Of the life of the painter in his study.* In order that the well- *31v*
being of the body may not harm that of the mind, the painter
or designer ought to be solitary, and should be so most of all,
when he is intent on those reflections and considerations that,
continually appearing before the eyes, give material to the memory to be well stored. If you are alone, you will be all yours. If
you are accompanied by a single companion, you will be half
yours, and so much less, the greater the inconsiderateness of his
behavior. If you are with more people, you will fall deeper into
similar inconvenience. And if you say, I will do things my own
way, I will draw apart from them, the better to reflect on the
forms of natural things, I reply, this cannot easily be done, because you cannot work in such a way that you will not lend an
ear to their chatter. Two masters cannot be served. You will do
ill in the duty of companionship, and worse will be the effect on
your reflections on art. And if you say, I will draw so far apart

second page of the next folio, for on Urb. 33v there is a passage marked with the
same sign. (Cf. McM. 72.)

that their words cannot reach and annoy me, I reply to you, that you will be taken for a fool, for you see, acting this way, you would also be alone.

36v  75. *Of the games that designers should play.* Designers, when you wish to gain some useful entertainment from games, you must always do things that are beneficial to your profession; that is, by making your eye a good judge, in estimating the true breadth and length of objects. To accustom your mind to such matters, let one of you draw a straight line at random on a wall, and each of you, at a distance of ten braccia, hold a thin blade or a straw in hand, and cut it. Then let each one go up to the model to measure it with his estimated length. He who most closely approaches the length of the model is the superior and victor, and gains from all the prize which was agreed upon by you in advance. Again, you ought to take foreshortened measures; that is, take a spear or a pole, and look beyond it a certain distance. Relying on his own judgment, each one should estimate how
37  many/times that measure will go into that distance. And again, see who will best draw a line a braccio long; let it be tested with a drawn-out thread. Such games give the eye an opportunity to gain good judgment of distance, which is a primary requirement in painting.

35v  76. *Way to augment and stimulate the mind toward various discoveries.* I shall not fail to include among these precepts a new discovery, an aid to reflection, which, although it seems a small thing and almost laughable, nevertheless is very useful in stimulating the mind to various discoveries. This is: look at walls splashed with a number of stains or stones of various mixed colors. If you have to invent some scene, you can see there resemblances to a number of landscapes, adorned in various ways with mountains, rivers, rocks, trees, great plains, valleys and hills. Moreover, you can see various battles, and rapid actions of figures, strange expressions on faces, costumes, and an infinite number of things, which you can reduce to good, integrated form. This happens thus on walls and varicolored stones, as in the sound of bells, in whose pealing you can find every name and word you can imagine.

Do not despise my opinion, when I remind you that it should
not be hard for you to stop sometimes and look into the stains
of walls, or the ashes of a fire, or clouds, or mud, or like things,
in which, if you consider them well, you will find really marvelous ideas. The mind of the painter is stimulated to new discoveries, the composition of battles of animals and men, various compositions of landscapes and monstrous things, such as devils and
similar creations, which may bring you honor, because the mind
is stimulated to new inventions by obscure things. But be sure
that you first know how to make all the parts of the objects that
you wish to represent, such as the limbs of animals, and the elements of landscape, that is, rocks, plants, and such things.

77. *Of imitating other painters.*[11] I say to the painter that nobody    *39v*
ought ever to imitate another's manner, because he will be called
a grandson and not a son of nature, with respect to art. Since
natural things exist in such great abundance, we wish and we
ought to resort to nature rather than to those masters who have
learned from her. This I say, not for those who by means of art
desire to attain riches, but for those who from this art desire
fame and honor.

78. *Of the painter and his rules.*[12] I remind you, painter, that    *34*
when, through your own judgment or another's warning, you
discover some error in your works, you should correct it, so that
when you show the work you do not with it show what you are
made of. And do not make excuses to yourself,/persuading your-    *34v*
self that you will be able to redeem your disgrace in your next
creation, because painting does not die as soon as it is created,
as does music, but will for a long time testify to your ignorance.
If you say that in making corrections you lose time, which, if
you spent it on another work, would make you much money,
you must know that the money we make over and above our

[11] Hand 3 has added: Sara meglio dire Come il Pittore nõ debbe imitare la
maniera d'alcun altro Pittore. (It will be better to say: How the painter ought
not to imitate the manner of any other painter.)

[12] Hand 3 has added, apparently as an alternative to this heading: Preccetto
Che si de' correggiere l'opera conoscendoui errore pa che la si dia fuora in
publico per finita. (Rule: that one should correct one's work, when errors are
found in it, before it is placed before the public as finished.)

cost of living is not of much worth. If you want money in abundance, you will end by not enjoying it, for it is not yours, and all the treasure which is not used is ours in the same way, and whatever you earn that does not serve your living is in the hands of others without satisfaction to you.

But if you will study and go over your works well, according to the treatise on the two perspectives, you will leave works which will give you more honor than the money would, because money is esteemed only for its own sake, and not for the sake of him who possesses it, who always arouses envy; and whose strong-box becomes an attraction to thieves, and then he loses his fame of being a rich man as well as his life. There remains the fame of the treasure and not that of the treasurer. How much greater is the glory of the virtue of mortals than of their treasures? How many emperors and how many princes have passed away, of whom there now remains no memory? They sought only estates and riches to leave as testimonials to their fame. How many were they who lived in poverty, as to money, to become rich in virtue? And such a desire has been more successful for the virtuous than for the rich, in the same measure that virtue surpasses wealth. Do you not see that the treasure in itself does not give praise to him who has accumulated it, after his life is done, as science does, which always trumpets in testimony to the fame of her creator, because she is the daughter of him who created her and not a stepdaughter like money.

If you say that you can satisfy your desire for gluttony and 35 lewdness/by means of that treasure and not by means of virtue, think about others who have served only the foul desires of the body, like other ugly animals; what fame of theirs remains?

If you excuse yourself because you do not have time to study and make yourself truly noble, because you have to struggle to meet your needs, blame nobody but yourself, because striving for virtue is food for both the soul and the body. How many philosophers, born rich, have separated themselves from their treasures, in order not to be cursed with them!

If you excuse yourself because of the children whom you have to feed, a little is enough for them, but see to it that virtues be their food, which is faithful wealth and does not leave us except with life itself.

If you say that you want first to acquire a capital of money that will be an endowment for your old age, I say to you the pursuit of virtue will never fail, nor let you grow old and leave you the receptacle of dreams and vain hopes.[18]

79. *Of the sad illusion of those who have themselves falsely called* 38 *painters.* There is a certain generation of painters, who because they have studied little, must live by the beauty of gold and azure, and who with extreme stupidity profess that they do not use good materials in their work for a miserable payment, but they would know how to do as well as anybody else, if they were well paid. Now, look at these stupid people! Do they not know that they ought to keep some good work and say: This is good work, and this is medium, and this is ordinary; and show that they have work at every price?

80. *Of those who blame him who designs on feast days and in-* 38v *vestigates the works of God.* Among the number of fools there is a certain sect, called hypocrites, who continually endeavor to deceive themselves and others, but others more than themselves. /Yet in truth they deceive themselves more than they do others. 39 And they blame painters who, on feast days, study such things as pertain to the true understanding of all the forms of nature's works, and solicitously contrive to acquire an understanding of those forms so far as is possible.

But let such censors be still, for this is the way to understand the Creator of so many admirable things, and this is the way to love such a great Inventor. In truth, great love is born of great knowledge of the thing that is loved, and if you do not know it, you can love it little or not at all. If you love Him for the good that you expect, and not because of His supreme goodness, you act like the dog who wags his tail, fawns, and leaps toward him who may give the dog a bone. But if he knew the goodness of such a man and that goodness were directed to him, he would love the man even more.

[18] On 35, lines 14-15, the scribe wrote "il richo cettaculo," which Ludwig corrected to read "il ricettaculo" (receptacle).

[JUDGING WORKS OF ART]

*32v* 81. *Of the painter's judgment.* It is a bad master whose work is in advance of his judgment, but he goes on toward the perfection of his art whose work is surpassed by his judgment.

*34* 82. [14]That painter who doubts not, attains little. When the work surpasses the judgment of the painter, the painter attains little, but when his judgment surpasses his work, the work never ceases to improve, if avarice does not intervene.

*38* 83. *How the painter should be disposed to listen to everybody's judgment while he is at work.* Certainly while a man is painting, he ought not to reject the advice of anybody, because we know clearly that a man, even if he is not a painter, will have knowledge of the form of another man, and will judge well, if he is humpbacked, or if he has a shoulder too high or low, if he has a large mouth, or nose, or other defects. If we know that men can truly judge the works of nature, how much more should we be ready to admit that they can judge our errors, because we know how much a man deceives himself in his work, and if you do not see this in yourself, consider it in others, and profit by others' errors.

*38v*      Be disposed to listen/with patience to another's opinion. Consider it well and think over well whether he who blames you has reason or not to blame you; and if he has, correct your error; but if you find that he has not, look as though you had not heard him; or if he is a man whom you respect, make him see by means of argument that he is mistaken.

*35* 84. There is nothing that deceives us more than our own judgment, when it gives an opinion on our productions. It is good in judging the works of enemies, but not those of friends, for hate and love are two of the most powerful emotional conditions that there are in living beings. Therefore, painter, be disposed to hear none the less willingly what your enemies say of your work, than what your friends say of it. Hate is more powerful than love, since hate ruins and destroys love. If he is a true friend, he is your other self, and contrary to an enemy. But the friend could

---

[14] Hand 3 has added a heading: Preccetto (Rule).

be deceived. There is a third kind of judgment which is moved by envy and brings forth flattery, praising the beginning of good works, that the lie might blind the painter.

[HOW PAINTERS ARE OFTEN MISLED]

85. *Of the self-deception experienced in judging parts of the body.* 43v
The painter who has clumsy hands will make those in his works like his own, and the same will happen with any part of the body, unless long study prevents it. Therefore, painter, consider well the most ugly part that you have in your person and in your study remedy it carefully, for if you are brutal in appearance your figures will seem similar and without talent, and likewise every part of your body, good or bad, will be manifest in like part in your figures.

86. *Of the greatest defect of painters.* It is an extreme defect when 44
painters repeat the same movements, and the same faces and manners of drapery in the same narrative painting and make the greater part of the faces resemble that of their master, which is something at which I have often wondered. For I have known some, who in all their figures seem to have portrayed themselves from life, and in these figures are seen the motions and manners of their creator. If he is quick in his speech and/in his move- 44v
ments, his figures are similar in their quickness; and if the master is pious his figures seem the same with their necks bent; and if the master is good for little, his figures seem idleness itself por-trayed to the life; and if the master is disproportioned, his figures are the same; and if he is mad, it is shown amply in his narrative paintings where the figures are incoherent and do not attend to what they are doing, so that one looks here, and the other there, as if they were dreaming. Thus each condition in painting fol-lows the painter.

Having often considered the cause of this defect, it seems to me one must conclude that the soul which rules and directs each body is really that which forms our judgment before it is our own judgment. Thus it has developed the whole shape of a man, as it has deemed to be best with long, or short, or flat nose, and defi-nitely assigned his height and shape. This judgment is so powerful that it moves the painter's arm and makes him copy himself, since it seems to that soul that this is the true way to construct a man, and whoever does not do so, commits an error. If it finds somebody who resembles the body that it has composed, it likes that person and often falls in love. For this reason, many fall in love and marry women who look like themselves, and often the children who are born of such parents resemble their progenitors.

44v  87. *Precepts: the painter should not deceive himself in selecting the figure that he considers normal.* The painter ought to make
45  his figure according to the rule of a natural body,/which is commonly thought to be praiseworthy in its proportion. Furthermore, he should measure himself and ascertain in what part his person varies much or little from that already termed praiseworthy, and when he has secured this knowledge, he protects himself through all his study from falling into the same faults in the figures created by him, which are found in his person. You must know that you have to fight to the last against this bad habit, since it is a defect that was born at the same time as your judgment. For the soul, the master of your body, is that which is your own judgment, and readily delights in things made like that which she created in composing your body. Thence it happens that there is no figure of a woman so ugly as not to find a lover, if she is not monstrous. By all means remember the defects that are in your person, and defend yourself against them in the figures you compose.

46v  88. *How errors are not noticed in small objects as they are in large.* In objects of minute form the extent of an error is not so easily comprehended as in large ones, and the reason is that if this small object is made to resemble a man or other living creature, the parts, because of their great diminution, cannot be carried out by the maker with that proper detail which would be suitable. Hence it remains unfinished, and not being finished, its errors cannot be determined.

As an example: look at a man at a distance of three hundred braccia and judge carefully whether he is handsome or ugly, whether he is deformed, or of common quality; you will see that with greatest exertion you cannot persuade yourself to give a judgment. The reason is that at such a distance, the man diminishes to such an extent that the quality of the details cannot be determined. If you want to see clearly the diminution of that man, hold a finger one span from the eye, and raise or lower your finger, until the tip stops at the feet of the figure at which you are looking, and you will perceive an incredible diminution. For this reason we are often uncertain of the form of a friend at a distance.

89. *Rule of the painter*.[15] Painter, if you would exert yourself to *33v* please the prime painters, you will make your paintings good, because they alone can judge your work truly. But if you would please those who are not masters, your paintings will have few foreshortenings, and little relief, or quick movement. On this account you will be lacking in that respect in which painting is considered an excellent art, that is, to make appear in relief that which is not at all in relief. And here the painter surpasses the sculptor, who does not give us things that are marvelous in themselves, when his work is three-dimensional, since there it is done by nature, but the painter achieves this by means of his art.

90. *Of shunning the calumnies and varying judgments of those* *46* *who practice painting.* If you would shun the blame which painters give to all those whose opinions on various aspects of the art do not agree with their own, it is necessary to practice the art in several modes so that you conform to some extent with each judgment which passes on the painter's works. Of this mention will be made below.

### [UNIVERSALITY AND VERSATILITY]

91. [16]That painter is not praiseworthy who executes only one *31v* thing well, such as a nude, a head, draperies, animals, landscapes, or similar details; for that is not a great talent which, devoted to a single object only and always at work on it, executes it well.

---

[15] Hand 3 has added to the heading: che si dè dilettare di piacere alli piu eccti Pittori (that one should delight in pleasing the most excellent painters).

[16] Although this section did not originally have a separate heading, Hand 3 later wrote in Preccetto (Rule).

32v   **92. *Statement of rules of the painter*.**[17] I have always observed that among all those who profess to portray faces from life, he who gives the best resemblance is the worst composer of action paintings. This arises from a fact manifest to him who does a thing well, that nature has disposed him to do that thing rather than some other, and therefore he has loved it more, and the greater love has made him more diligent, and all the love that is given to one part of painting is lacking in the rest, because he has brought together all his delight in that one thing, abandoning the universal for the particular. Since the power of such a talent has been reduced to a small range, it has no power of expansion, and this talent is like the concave mirror, which, after catching the sun's rays, reflects that quantity with greater expansion, but with a cooler temperature. When it reflects them all in a smaller space, then those rays are of immense warmth, but concentrated in a small space. That is what those painters do when they love no other part of painting save the human face, and it is even worse that they do not recognize any other part in the art, which they esteem or concerning which they have any judgment. Their

33   own paintings being without/movement, because they themselves are languid and of little motion, they criticize that which has greater and more ready movements than are represented by them, saying that they appear possessed and like masters of a Moorish dance. It is true that one ought to observe decorum, and that movements should be indicative of the motions of the mover's mind. If it is a case of representing one who should show timid reverence, he should not be represented with such audacity and presumption that the effect appear one of desperation, or of command—as I saw, some days since, in the picture of an angel who, while he was making The Annunciation, appeared to be chasing Our Lady out of her room, with movements which displayed such offensiveness as one might show to a most vile enemy, and Our Lady seemed as if she, in despair, would throw herself from a window. Bear it in mind, not to fall into any such defects.

    About this I will not make an excuse to anybody, if anybody would believe what I say to him; because each one who works

---

[17] Hand 3 has added to the heading: intorno all esser uniuersale (about being universal), and then crossed out these words.

in this way condemns himself, but thinks he is doing well. This you will recognize in those who engage in practice without ever taking advice from the works of nature, try only to do well enough, and for a soldo more wages a day would rather sew shoes than paint. But of these I do not speak further, because I do not accept them into the art, which is the daughter of nature.

But to speak of painters and their judgments, I say that he who agitates his figures too much, finds that he who moves them agreeably makes figures that are asleep; and he who moves them little, finds that one who creates them with a due and agreeable movement depicts them as if they were possessed.

Therefore the painter ought to consider the manners of/men *33v* who talk with one another, coldly or warmly, and listen to the subject matter of which they speak, and see if their actions are appropriate to the matter of which they speak.

93. *Precepts of the painter*.[18] He is not versatile who does not *33v* love equally all things that are contained in painting. For example, if one does not like landscape, he esteems it a matter of brief and simple investigation, as when our Botticelli said, that such study was vain, because by merely throwing a sponge full of diverse colors at a wall, it left a stain on that wall, where a fine landscape was seen. It is really true that various inventions are seen in such a stain. I say that a man should look into it, and find heads of men, diverse animals, battles, rocks, seas, clouds, woods, and similar things, and note how like it is to the sound of bells, in which you can hear what you like. But although those stains give you inventions they will not teach you to finish any detail. This painter of whom I have spoken makes very dull landscapes.

94. *On being universal*.[19] You, painter, to be versatile and please *34* different judges, will paint your picture so that in one composition there will be things of great darkness and of great softness in the shadows, always making clear the reasons for such shadows and softness.

[18] Hand 3 has added: del essere uniuersale (of being universal, or versatile).
[19] Hand 1 had first written: Del esser' uniuersale nelle sue opere (On being universal in his works), but Hand 3 crossed out the last three words of this heading.

37v  95. *That a painter is not praiseworthy unless he is versatile.* Of some it may clearly be said that they deceive themselves when they call him a good master who paints only a head or a figure well. Surely it is not a great feat that he who studies a single thing his whole lifetime should reach some degree of perfection. But since we know that painting embraces and includes all the things that nature produces, and also the accidental actions of men and ultimately whatever can be comprehended by the eyes, he seems to me a poor master who can execute only a figure well.

Now, do you not see how many and what kind of acts are done by men? Do you not see how many different animals there are,
38  and also trees, plants, and flowers,/how great is the variety of mountainous places and plains, springs, rivers, cities, public and private edifices, instruments meet for human use, how various are the kinds of dress, and ornaments, and arts? All these things have to be of equal effectiveness and excellence, when used by him whom you call a good painter.

39  96. *Of being versatile.* For a man who knows how, it is an easy thing to become versatile, for all terrestrial animals have a certain resemblance in their parts, that is, their muscles, sinews, and bones, and these do not vary, except in length or in breadth, as
39v  will be shown in the/book on anatomy. Then there are the aquatic animals, which are of great variety, and concerning which I will not persuade the painter to make any rule, since they are of almost infinite variety, as are the insects.

39  97. *Of the variety of figures.*[20] The painter ought to try to be versatile, because he is wanting in merit who does one thing well and the other badly, as many are who only study the measurements and proportions of the nude, and do not analyze its variety, for a man may be well proportioned and be fat and short, or tall and thin, or average. And he who takes no account of these differences makes his figures as if they had been turned out by a stamp, so that they all seem sisters. Such a thing merits grave reproof.

[20] Hand 3 has added to the heading: che si dè cercare d'essere vniuersale (that one ought to seek to be universal).

[ORIGIN AND DIVISION OF PAINTING]

98. *How the first picture originated.*[21] The first picture was of 49v
only one line, which circumscribed the shadow of a man cast by
the sun on a wall.

99. *Of the first eight parts into which painting is divided.* Dark- 50
ness, light, body, form, location, distance and proximity. There
can be added to these two others, which are motion and rest,
since it is necessary to represent them in the movements of the
objects that are represented in painting.

100. *How painting is divided into five parts.* There are five parts 50
in painting, which are: surface, form, color, shadow and light,
proximity and distance, or increase and diminution with distance,
which are the two perspectives, as in the diminution of quantity
and distinctness of objects seen at a great distance; and then the
perspective of color which determines what color first diminishes, and what remains the same at an equal distance.

101. *Of painting and its division.*[22] Painting is divided into two 45v
principal parts: of which the first is form, that is, line which de-
lineates the forms of bodies and their details; the second is the
color contained within these boundaries.

102. [23]Painting is divided into two principal parts: that is, out- 50
line, which surrounds the forms of the objects depicted—and
which are termed drawing—and the second which is called
shadow. But this drawing is of such excellence that it not only
investigates the works of nature, but infinitely more than those
that nature produces. This demands of the sculptor that he finish
his images with knowledge, and it assigns their perfect end to all
the manual arts, although they be infinite. And for this reason
we conclude that design is not only a science but a deity whose
name should be duly commemorated,/a deity which repeats all 50v
the visible works of God the highest.

[21] Hand 3 has inserted, before the heading: à che modo fusse (in what way
was).

[22] Hand 3 has added, after the heading: Diuisione della pittura in due parti
principali. (Division of painting into two principal parts.)

[23] Hand 3 has inserted a heading: In due parti principali si diuide la Pittura.
(Painting is divided into two principal parts.)

*50v* 103. *Of the parts of painting.*[24] The first task of painting is that the objects it presents should appear in relief, and that through the use of the three perspectives, the backgrounds surrounding them with their several distances should appear to be contained within the wall on which the painting is created. These perspectives are diminution of the forms of objects, diminution of their magnitudes, and diminution of their colors. The first of these three perspectives originates in the eye; the other two derive from the air lying between the eye and the objects seen by the eye. The second task of painting is to create actions and varied postures appropriate to the figures, so that the men do not look like brothers.

*45v* 104. *Proportion of parts of the body.* The proportion of the parts of the body is divided into two parts also which are quality and movement. By quality is implied that in addition to the measurements corresponding to the whole, you should not mix the limbs of young people with those of the aged, nor those of the fat with those of the lean, and beyond this you should not give men feminine attributes, nor mix graceful limbs with clumsy ones. By movement is understood that the attitudes or movements of the old should not be made with the same vivacity which would be suitable to the movement of a young man, nor that of a small child like that of a young man, nor that of a woman like that of a man. Do not represent actions that do not become him who embodies them; that is, in depicting a man of great vigor, make his motions manifest this, and do likewise for the man of little force, employing ineffective and foolish motions, which threaten ruin to the body that produces them.

*45v* 105. *Form and its division.* The form of bodies is divided into two parts also, which are proportion of the parts each to the other, which ought to correspond to the whole, and the motion appropriate to the state of mind of the living thing that moves.

[RELATIVE IMPORTANCE OF THE DIVISIONS OF PAINTING]

*47v* 106. *Which requires greater consideration and is more useful: the lights and shadows of bodies or their contours?* Greater analysis

[24] Hand 3 has struck out the word "della" in the heading, and inserted: et qualità della (and qualities of).

and/ability are required to depict the outlines of bodies than 48
shadows and light, because the outlines of parts of the body that
are not pliable are immutable and always the same, while the
location and quantity and quality of shadows are infinite.

107. *Which is more difficult: shadow and light, or good design?* 48
I say that thing is more difficult which is restrained within a
boundary than that which is free. Shadows have certain boundaries, and the works of him who ignores them will be without
relief. This relief is the most important element in and the soul
of painting. Design is free, for although you will see an infinite
number of faces, each will be different; one will have a long nose,
and another a short one. Therefore, the painter can also take this
freedom, and where there is freedom there is no rule.

108. *Which is of greater importance: that the form should abound* 48
*in beautiful colors, or display high relief?* Only painting presents
a marvel to those who contemplate it, because it makes that which
is not so seem to be in relief and to project from the walls; but
colors honor only those who manufacture them, for in them
there is no cause for wonder except their beauty, and their beauty
is not to the credit of the painter, but of him who has made them.
A subject can be dressed in ugly colors and still astound those
who contemplate it, because of the illusion of relief.

109. Note in your drawing, how among the shadows some are 40
indistinguishable as to darkness and form, and this is proved by
the third proposition[25] which states: rounded surfaces have as
many different degrees of darkness and brightness as there are
differences of darkness and brightness to be found in the object
opposite.

110. *Levels of painting.* What is beautiful is not always good. I 72v
say this in reference to those painters who so love the beauty of
colors that, not without great regret, they give their paintings
very weak and almost imperceptible shadows, not esteeming the

---

[25] Leonardo's references such as the one in the present section to "the third"
(la terza), because of the disorder of his surviving manuscripts and the loss of
many others, cannot be verified. It is not even clear whether he refers to an
existing work or to a plan or outline that he had in mind. Similar references to
numbered books and propositions occur in many sections.

relief. In this error they are like good speakers whose words are
without any sense whatever.

48  111. *Which is of greater importance: movement originating from
the mental conditions of living creatures, or their shadows and
lights?* The most important things that can be found in the
analysis of painting are the movements appropriate to the states
of mind of each living creature, such as desire, contempt, anger,
pity, and the like.

[LINE DRAWING]

39v  112. *Program of representation.*[26] First copy drawings by a good
master made from nature and not a drawing made by way of
practice without reference to nature. Then draw from an object
in relief, together with the drawing copied from that relief, and
then from a good model in nature, and this is the one to use.

43  113. *To represent a nude or other object from nature.* Habitually
hold in hand a line with a lead weight hanging from it, to be
able to see the inclination of things from the perpendicular.

40  114. *Of representing an object.*[27] When you are drawing or beginning a line, be sure to look over the whole body that you are
representing, for anything that meets the direction of the line you
are beginning.

50v  115. *Of pictures in outline.*[28] The contours of any object should
be considered with the most careful attention, observing how they
twist like a serpent. These serpentine curves are to be studied to
see whether they turn as parts of a round curvature or are of an
angular concavity.

[26] Hand 3 has struck out the word "ritrare" and added, instead, the word
"disegnare." He then adds: ordine che de' tenere nel disegnare chi uol imparar
la Pittura (order which he who desires to learn painting must observe in de-
signing).

[27] Hand 3 has placed the word "ordine" before "Del" in the heading, struck
out "una," replacing it by "qualōche," and then adding: ordine di bon imparare
a' rittrare qualōche cosa, so that the heading, with additions, would read: ordine
del ritrar qualōche cosa (program of representing anything. Program for learning
well how to represent anything).

[28] Hand 3 has written before the heading: Considerationi d'hauersi nel stabilire
le figure. (Considerations to be had in mind while establishing shapes.)

[AIDS IN THE PRACTICE OF DRAWING]

116. *Of the representation of relief.*[29] He who draws from a relief  *41*
should take a position such that the eye of the figure portrayed
is on a level with the eye of him who makes the portrait. This
should also be done with a head which you have to represent
from nature, because the shapes of persons whom you meet on
the street always have their eyes on a level with yours, and if you
make them either too high or too low, you will see that your
portrait is not a likeness.

117. *Of representation.*[30] When you have to draw from nature,  *39v*
stand at a distance three times the size of the object you draw.

118. *How to draw a site correctly.*[31] Have a sheet of glass as  *41*
large as a half-sheet of royal folio paper, and place it firmly in
front of your eyes; that is, between the eye and the thing that
you draw. Then place yourself at a distance of two-thirds of a
braccio from your eye to the glass, and hold your head with an
instrument in such a way that you cannot move your head in
the least. Then close/or cover one eye, and with a brush or with  *41v*
a pencil of red chalk draw on the glass what appears beyond it.
Then trace this on transparent paper from the glass, and transfer
it to good paper and paint it if you like, while employing aerial
perspective well.

119. *To learn to draw from a well-posed figure.* If you wish to  *42v*
become really accustomed to correct and good poses of figures,
divide a frame or stretcher by threads into squares inside, and
fasten it between your eye and the nude that you draw, and make
those same squares lightly on the paper on which you wish to
draw that nude. Then place a round drop of wax in a part of the
network where it will serve as a mark which you will always

[29] The words: finto o' di natturale (imitated or natural) have been added to
the heading later, apparently by Hand 1.

[30] Hand 3 has added: di natturale (from nature), to the heading. He continues: questo uole dināzi al ca¹º. su la seguēte facia segnato ∅ (this should go
before the chapter on the following page marked ∅). Cf. McM. 129, Urb. 40.

[31] Urb. 41 reads "coretto" in the heading, but some editions, including that
of Borzelli, read "vetro."

find when you are looking at the nude, covering the pit of the throat, or, if the back is turned, it may cover a vertebra in the neck. And these vertical threads will show you all the parts of the body which in each attitude are to be found beneath the pit of the throat, below the points of the shoulders, below the nipples, the flanks and other parts of the body, and the transverse lines of the network will show you how much higher one side of the body is than the other when it rests on one leg, and so with the flanks, the knees, and the feet.

But always fasten the network with reference to a perpendicular line in such a way that all the parts of the network which the nude takes up, your nude in the drawing will also occupy in the network drawn on paper. The squares of the drawing may be as much smaller than those of the network of threads as you wish your figure to be smaller than nature. Then remember, in the figures that you make, the rule of how the parts of the body meet, as the network of threads showed it to you.

This frame should be three and a half braccia high, and three braccia wide, seven braccia away from you, and one braccio from the nude model.

*43* 120. *Proportions and divisions of the figure.* Divide the head into twelve degrees, and divide each degree into twelve points, and each point into twelve minutes, and each minute into seconds, and the seconds into half-seconds.

[LIFE DRAWING]

*41* 121. *Of drawing the nude.* When you represent the nude, always draw it as a whole, and then finish that part which seems to you the best, then work it in with the other limbs. Otherwise you would get a habit of never putting the limbs together well.

Never make the head turn in the same direction as the chest, nor let the arm go together with the leg, and if the head is turned toward the right shoulder, make the parts on the left lower than those on the right, and if you make the body with the chest projecting, make it so that with the head turning to the left side, those parts on the right side are higher than those on the left.

**122.** *When one should consider the selection of material.* Winter   *42v-43*
evenings should be used by young men to study the things prepared during the summer; that is, to bring together all the nudes
made during the summer, and make a selection of the best limbs
and bodies among them, employing them in practice and commit-
ting them to memory.

**123.** *Of attitudes.* Later in the next summer, you will select some-   *43*
body who is in good condition, and was not brought up in tight-
fitting doublets, so that his person has not become stiff, and make
him go through some agile and graceful motions. If he does not
show his muscles well within the contours of his limbs, it matters not at all; it is enough for you to have good attitudes from
him, and correct the limbs to conform to those you studied during the winter.

**124.** *How it is necessary for the painter to know the inner struc-*   *43v*
*ture of man.* The painter who knows the sinews, muscles, and
tendons, will know very well, when a limb moves,/how many   *44*
and which sinews are the reason for it, and which muscle, by
swelling, is the reason for the contraction of the sinew, and which
sinews, changed into very thin cartilage, surround and contain
the muscle. Thus in varying and comprehensive ways he will
display the diverse muscles through the various attitudes of his
figures, and not, as many do, show the same muscles prominent
in the arm, backs, breasts, and legs in different actions of their
figures. These are things that ought not to be included among
small errors.

**125.** *On posing figures.* By as much as the part D A of the nude   *59 and*
figure decreases because of the pose, by that much the opposite   *illus.*
side increases. That is, by so much as the part D A diminishes,
the opposite part B C increases in length. The position of the
navel does not change its height, nor does that of the male organ.

This lowering comes about because when the figure rests on
one foot, that foot becomes the center of the weight placed above.
Under these circumstances, the middle point between the shoulders moves over above it, departing from the perpendicular line
which passes through the middle of the surfaces of the body, and

this line twists its upper end to above the weighted foot. The transverse horizontal lines, obliged to make equal angles, make their ends lower on that side on which the figure rests, as appears in the lower sketch A B C.

*48v*  126. *Precepts of the painter.* Painter-anatomist, take care that excessive indication of bones, tendons, and muscles does not make of you a wooden painter through a desire that your nudes should display all their emotions. When you wish to remedy this defect, see in what manner the muscles in old or lean men cover or rather clothe their bones; and furthermore note the regular way in which the same muscles fill up the spaces on the surfaces which occur between them; and which are the muscles that never lose their prominence in any degree of fatness; and which are the muscles whose attachments lose their prominence with any slight plumpness. Often several muscles become one with increasing fatness, and often on becoming lean or old a single muscle becomes several. In this discussion will be set forth, in the proper place, all the details, especially in the case of the spaces placed between the joints of each part of the body.

Again, you will not fail to observe the variations that the muscles already mentioned produce around the joints of the limbs of any living creature, through diversity of the movements of
*49* each limb; for on occasion, at the side of the joint,/indications of the muscles are completely lost because of the increase or lack of flesh of which such muscles are composed.

*49* 127. *Memorandum by the author to himself.* Describe which are the muscles and which the tendons that, through various movements of each limb, become obvious, or hidden, or do neither one nor the other. Remember that such action as this is most important and necessary for painters and sculptors who profess to be masters.

Do the same for a boy from his birth to the time of his decrepitude, through all the stages of life, such as infancy, childhood, adolescence and young manhood.

And in all describe the changes of the limbs and their joints, and which grow fat or lean.

[LIGHT SUITABLE FOR PAINTING]

128. *Of the kind of light.* A large, high and not too powerful light  43v
is the one that will render the details of bodies very agreeable.

129. *How the light should be high in drawing from nature.* The  40
light for drawing from nature should be from the north, in order
not to have it vary, and if you draw with the light from the
south, keep the window screened, so that even with the sun shining all day, it will not vary. The height of the light should be
such that each body casts a shadow on the ground as long as
its height.

130. *Of painting.*[32] Do not make definite or finite the shadows  50v
which you can distinguish with difficulty and the edges of which
you cannot recognize. Thus, with your judgment uncertain on
these matters, transfer them to your work, but do not make them
finished or definite, for, if you do, your work will look wooden.

131. *Way to represent a relief at night.* Place a sheet of paper that  43
is not too transparent between the relief and the light and thus
you will have something good to draw.

132. *Of representing the shadow of bodies by the light of a candle*  41v
*or oil lamp.* At night place in front of this light a frame on which
paper, made transparent or not, has been stretched, but use only
one whole sheet of chancellery size. You will see the shadows appear smoky, that is, not sharp at the edges, and the light, where
it is not cut off by the paper, will illuminate the paper on which
you are drawing.

133. *How the painter should place himself with respect to the*  43
*light and relief.* Let A B be the window, M the central point of
the light. I say that in/whatever position the painter places him-  43v and
self, he will be well situated, provided his eye is between the  *illus.*
shaded and the illuminated part of the body that he is drawing.
You will find that place by putting yourself between the point M
and the division between the shadow and the light made on the
body drawn.

[32] Hand 3 has added to the heading: Cioè dell'ombre. (That is, of shadows.)

*51* 134. *How to select an atmosphere to make faces attractive.* If you
have a courtyard that you can cover when you wish with a linen
awning, this light is good; or when you wish to make somebody's
portrait, do so in bad weather or at twilight, placing the sitter
with his shoulders against one of the walls of your courtyard. In
the streets at twilight note the faces of men and women when
the weather is bad, how much attractiveness and softness is seen
in them. Therefore, painter, have a courtyard made suitable with
walls stained black and a roof projecting somewhat over the wall,
and it should be ten braccia wide and twenty braccia long and
ten high, and when you do not cover the courtyard with the awning, make your portrait at twilight, or when there are clouds or
mist. This is a perfect atmosphere.

*47v* 135. *What method of painting it is best to employ to make objects stand out.* Figures illuminated by a specific light show
greater relief than those which are illuminated by a general light,
since specific light causes reflections which make forms stand out
from their backgrounds. These reflections originate from the
lights of a figure which are reflected into the shadow of that
which is in front of it, and illuminate it in part. But a figure
placed before a single light in a large, dark place, does not receive reflected light, and then only the illuminated side is seen.
This method is to be used only in the representation of night
with a small single light.

*40v* 136. *Of the quality of light in which to represent relief, natural
or simulated.* Light cut off too obviously by shadows is condemned severely by painters. Therefore to avoid such unpleasant-
ness, if you portray bodies in the open country, you will not paint
their forms as though illuminated by the sun, but pretend that
there is some sort of mistiness or transparent cloud placed be-
*41* tween/the object and the sun. As the figure is not sharply illuminated by the sun, the edges of the shadows will not be sharp
against the edges of the lights.

*41v* 137. *Under what conditions a face is to be represented to give it
grace through shadow and light.* A very high degree of grace in
the shadow and lights is added to the faces of those who sit in

the doorways of rooms that are dark, where the eyes of the observer see the shadowed part of such a face obscured by the
shadows of that room, and see the illuminated part of that face
with added/brightness which the brilliance of the air gives it. *42*
Through this increase in the shadows and lights the face is given
great relief; on the illuminated side the shadows are almost indistinguishable and on the shadowed side the lights also are almost indistinguishable. The face acquires a great deal of grace
from such a representation with its increase of shadows and
lights.

138. *Whether the light should be in front or come from the side* *55*
*of the figure, and which lends more attractiveness.* When the
light falls from in front on faces placed between dark side walls,
this gives the faces great relief, especially when this light is also
above the face. This relief occurs because the nearer side of the
face is illuminated by the general light of the air before it, so that
this side in the light has shadows that are almost imperceptible.
Then come the sides of the face, darkened by the side walls of
the street, which darken the face the more its sides are placed
between them. Furthermore, it follows that because the light descends from above, it leaves entirely without light those parts of
the face to which/protection is given by parts projecting from it, *55v*
as the eyebrows do, which take away the light from the sockets
of the eyes; the nose takes light away from the mouth, the chin
from the throat, and other protruding parts act similarly.

[LIGHT AND SHADOW SHOULD BE CONSISTENT
WITH THE LOCATION OF FIGURES]

139. *How to represent landscapes.* Landscapes should be repre- *41v*
sented in such a manner that the trees are half illuminated and
half in shadow, but it is better to paint them when the sun is
covered by clouds, for then the trees are illuminated by the universal light of the sky and by the universal shadow of the earth.
And their parts are darker, the closer those parts are to the middle
of the tree and to the earth.

140. *What lights should be selected for drawing the shapes of* *40*
*bodies?* When delineating the contours of any body you are

obliged to take the light in which you represent those contours;
that is, if you portray them as being in the country, they are surrounded by a great quantity of light, when the sun is not covered.
If these contours are exposed to the sun, their shadows will be
very dark in comparison with the illuminated parts, and these
will be shadows with definite edges, the original as well as the
derivative. These shadows will be in little accord with the lights,
because the azure of the air illuminates one side, giving it a tinge

40v of itself/—this is manifested sufficiently in white things—and
that side which is illuminated by the sun takes on the color of
the sun. This you will observe very readily when the sun sinks
to the horizon among reddened clouds, for those clouds are tinged
with the color that illuminates them. The red of the clouds with
the red of the sun, reddens that which is illuminated by them.
The side of bodies which does not face that redness remains the
color of the air, and whoever sees such bodies judges them to be
of two colors. You cannot avoid showing the causes of such shadows and lights, and making the shadows and lights take on the
color of their causes. If you do not, your work is vain and false.

   If the form you portray is in a dark house and you see it from
outside, the shadows of that figure will be dark and smoky when
you stand in line with the light. Such a figure is graceful and
does honor to him who represents it because its soft and smoky
shadows give it great relief, especially in that part where you do
not see the obscurity of the room, for there the shadows are almost indistinguishable. The reason will be set forth in its proper
place.

42 141. *How to represent shadow, both simple and compound.* Do
not draw a figure indoors under a specific light as if it were in
the general illumination of the country without sunshine, because
in the country there is simple shadow, and the specific light from
a window or the sun makes a compound shadow, that is, one
mixed with reflections.

45 142. *Defect of painters who depict an object in relief indoors in
one light and then place it in the country or elsewhere where
there is another light.* It is a great and frequent error of some
painters to paint an object in relief indoors, working under a

specific light, and then place it in relief in their composition as though it were in the general light of the open air of the country, where the air embraces and illuminates equally all sides of things seen. Thus they make dark shadows where there cannot be a shadow, or if there is, it is so light that it cannot be distinguished, and they also show reflected lights where it is impossible for these to be/seen.

*45v*

143. *Of the light in which to represent the flesh tones of faces or nudes.* The room in which flesh tones are painted should be open to the air, with walls of flesh color. Portraits should be made in summer when clouds cover the sun; or, to be sure, you can make the south wall so high that the rays of the sun do not reach the northern wall, and reflected rays will not spoil the shadows.

*42*

144.[33] To draw objects in relief, painters should stain the surface of the paper with a tint that is medium dark and then put on the darkest shadows, and finally the principal lights in little spots, which are those first lost to the eye at a short distance.

*69v*

[OBJECTS AND THEIR BACKGROUNDS]

145. *Of the backgrounds of painted objects.* It is of the greatest importance to consider the backgrounds against which opaque bodies stand, clothed in shadows and lights, because their illuminated sides/should be shown against dark backgrounds, and the dark sides against light backgrounds, as I have shown in part in the margin.

*71v*

*72 and illus.*

146. *Of the backgrounds of the figures of bodies in painting.* The background surrounding the form of any painted thing should be darker than the illuminated side of that form, and brighter than the shadowed side.

*74*

147. *Of objects placed against a light background and why this practice is useful in painting.* When a shadowed body edges on a background that is bright and illuminated in color, then it necessarily appears detached and removed from that background.

This happens because bodies with a curved surface are neces-

*75*

[33] Hand 3 has added: Modo per ritrare di rileuo et preparare la carta per questo. (Way to draw from relief and to prepare paper for this.)

75v and illus. sarily in shadow on the side opposite to the one struck by luminous rays, since that side is devoid of such rays./On this account it differs much from the background. And the illuminated side loses some of its original brightness where its edge meets the illuminated background, since between the background and the original light of that body, there is interposed an edge of the body, which is darker than the background or the light on that body.

71 148. *Of backgrounds which are suitable for shadows and lights.* Backgrounds suitable to the edges of any color, whether illuminated or shadowed, will be those which are the most different so that one may be distinguished from the other. That is, a dark color should not border upon another dark color, but on a very different one, which would be white or partaking of white; and in like manner the color white should never border upon a white color, but, as far as possible, upon a dark color or one tending toward dark.

71v 149. *Of the backgrounds of figures.* Of two objects of equal brightness, that one will seem less bright which is seen against a background brighter than itself, and that one will seem whiter which is located against a darker background. Flesh tone will seem pale against a red background, and a flesh tone will seem reddish when seen against a yellow background. Similarly other colors will be judged to be what they are not because of their background.

71 150. *How to solve the problem when white borders on white or dark on dark.* When a white body borders on a white background, then the whites will be equal or not; and if they are equal, then that which is nearer you should be made some-71v what/darker where it comes in contact with the white background; and if the background is less white than the color which it serves as a background, then that which is located against a background will detach itself from it by reason of its contrast, without the aid of a dark border.

66v 151. *Of colors which vary in their nature through contrast with their backgrounds.* No border of uniform color shows that it is the same color as the interior of the area which it surrounds unless it borders on a ground of color similar to it.

This is seen clearly when black borders on white or white on black, in which cases each color shows more distinctly where there is proximity to the one in contrast to it than it does in the center of its own area.

152. *To cause forms to detach themselves from their backgrounds.* 54
The form of any body will seem to be in greater relief and more detached from the backgrounds when the borders between the form and the background are of the greatest possible contrast of bright or dark color. This will be shown in its proper place. In the colors a lessening of brightness in the whites and of darkness in the dark colors should be observed.

153. *Backgrounds.* Of the backgrounds of forms, that is light 75v against dark, and dark against light: white against black, or black against white seem more powerful, one because of the other, and thus opposites always appear more powerful because of one another.

154. *Of the nature of colors in the background behind white.* A 71v white object looks whiter when it is against a dark background, and darker when it is against a whiter background. Falling snow teaches us this, for when we see it against the background of the air, it seems dark to us, and when we see it against the background of an open window, through which the dark shadows of an interior are seen, then the snow appears very white.

155. Snow that falls near us seems to us to move quickly, and 71v that which is far away seems to move slowly; snow near at hand seems of a continuous quantity, like white cords, and that which is distant seems to be discontinuous.

156. *Shun profiles, that is, sharp edges for objects.*/Do not make 46-46v the contours of your forms of a color other than that of their own background, which bounds them; that is, you must not make dark outlines between the background and the form depicted.

[REFLECTED LIGHTS]

*55v*  157. *Of reverberation.* Reflections of light are caused by bodies of a bright kind, with a smooth, semi-opaque surface, which, struck by the light as if it were a ball striking, makes the light rebound to the first object.

*55v*  158. *Where there cannot be any luminous reverberation.* The surfaces of all dense bodies are covered with different kinds of lights and shadows. The lights are of two kinds: one is called original, the other derivative. I call that original which comes from the flame of fire, from the light of the sun, or from the air. Derivative light is reflected light.

But, returning to the definition just given, I say that luminous reflection is not given off by that side of a body which faces other bodies in shadow, such as dark places, meadows with grass of unequal heights, forests either green or dry. In these, although every branch turns toward the original light and is covered by the quality of that light, nevertheless there are so many shadows made by each individual branch and so many shadows cast by one branch on another that the whole results in obscurity and the light in such a place amounts to nothing. Hence, such bodies cannot give objects opposite them any reflected light.

*74v*  159. *Of the color of lights, incident and reflected.*[34] When there is a body which casts shadows between two lights, the lights will either be of equal strength, or they will be unequal. If they are unequal they can differ in the brightness they throw upon the object, which may be equally or unequally brilliant. If they are equal they will be so when they are at an equal distance and they will be unequal when they are at unequal distances. At equal distances they differ in two other ways, that is, the object will be less illuminated by equal lights in respect to brilliance and distance. When lights are equal in strength and in distance from the object opposite them, the following is true: the object situated at an equal distance between two lights equal in color and in brilliance may be illuminated by those lights in two ways: that

---

[34] The text of this section has been mutilated and the meaning in places is now uncertain.

is, equally or unequally on every side. This object will be equally illuminated by the lights, when the space which surrounds the two lights is of equal color and darkness or brightness. It will be unequally illuminated/when the spaces around the two lights *75* differ in darkness.

160. *What part of a reflected light will be the brightest?* That *56v and* part of the reflected light will be the most luminous which re- *illus.* ceives the light from the luminous body at angles most nearly equal, as occurs in percussion. This is proved as follows: let the luminous body be N, and A B be the side of the illuminated body, from which light rebounds through all the concavity opposite, which is in shadow. Let the light which is reflected at E, strike at equal angles, but on the base from which it is reflected the angles are not equal, for the angle E A B is more obtuse than the angle E B A. The angle A F B, however, although it is one of the angles which are less nearly equal to one another, than the angle E, on the base A B, the angles (F A B and F B A) are more nearly equal to each other than that at E. Therefore, there is more light at F than at E. It is also brighter, because it is nearer to that which illuminates it, according to the sixth proposition which states: that side of the shadowed body will be most illuminated which is closest to the luminous source.

161. *Of double and triple reflected lights.*[35] Doubled reflected *57 and* lights are stronger than simple ones, and the shadows found *illus.* between them and those which fall directly are of little density. Let A be the luminous source, B C a wall which receives light from that luminous body, and D R E and N S O the sides of two spherical bodies which are illuminated by direct light. Let N P M and D H E be the sides of those bodies illuminated by reflected lights. D H E is the simple reflected light, N P M a doubled one. The simple reflected light means one which is exposed to only one luminous body, a double reflected light is one exposed to two luminous bodies. The simple reflected light D H E is made by the illuminated B G,[36] the doubled reflected

[35] The text in this section appears to be mutilated and the lettering of the diagram as presented on Urb. 57 requires revision.
[36] B A in the text.

light N P M is composed of the illuminated B K and of the illuminated D R E. Its shadow is not very deep, being placed between the direct light N and the reflected light N P.

*58v* 162. *Of the color of reflected lights.* All the colors of reflected lights are less brilliant than those of direct light. The brilliance of direct light and of reflected light is in the same relation as are the causes of their luminosity.

*56* 163. *Of the reflections of light that surround shadow.* The reflected lights from the illuminated sides rebound to the shadows opposite, more or less relieving their obscurity, depending on how near or far they are, and how bright. This theory has been put into practice by many, but there are many others who avoid it, and each side laughs at the other. But if you would avoid the calumnies of both, employ both practices where they are necessary. Be sure to make the causes clear, so the obvious reason for the reflected lights and their colors, and also the obvious reason why things do not reflect may be seen. Thus you will not be entirely blamed nor praised by judges, who, if they are not completely ignorant, will necessarily praise you on the whole, one as well as the other.

[REFLECTED LIGHT AND COLOR]

*57v-58* 164. *Where reflected light is most seen.*/Between reflected lights of uniform shape, size, and strength, that side will appear stronger or less strong which borders on a darker or less dark ground.

*57* 165. *Where reflected lights are most readily perceived.* The reflected light most clearly apparent will be that which is seen against a background of greatest darkness, and that will be less perceptible which is seen against a brighter background. This comes about because when objects of differing degrees of darkness are placed in contrast to one another, the less dark will make that which is darker seem darker still, and when objects of different degrees of whiteness are placed in contrast, the whiter will make the other appear less white than it is.

*56* 166. *Where reflected lights are of greater or less brightness.* Reflected lights are of greater or lesser clarity, depending on whether they are seen against backgrounds of greater or lesser darkness.

This happens because, if the background is darker than the reflected light, then the reflected light will be very clear because of the great contrast between them. But if the reflected light is seen against a background that is brighter than it, then the reflected light will appear/dark compared with the brightness by *56v* which it is surrounded, and so the reflected light will be imperceptible.

167. *Of reflected lights.*/Reflected lights take on more of the color *55v-56* of the place where they are created than of the color of that which creates them, when the place where they are created has a more polished surface than has that which creates them.

168. *How reflected lights are very rarely of the color of the body* *57v and* *at the point where they meet it.* Very rarely are reflected lights of *illus.* the same color as the body where they merge with it. Let the sphere D F G E be yellow, and the object which reflects upon it be B C, which is blue. I say, that the side of the sphere which is struck by such a reflection will be tinged with the color green, when B C is illuminated by the air and the sun.

169. *How no reflected light is simple but is mingled with the* *57v and* *visual images of the other colors.* No color that is reflected on *illus.* the surface of another body will tinge that surface with only its own color, but it will mingle with the concurrence of the other reflected colors which rebound on the same place.

Let A be the color yellow which is reflected on the side of the sphere C O E, and on the same place there is reflected the color blue, or B. I say that this mixed reflection of yellow and blue will strike the sphere with a concurrence of colors. If the sphere is white, the color green will result, because it is proved that yellow and blue mixed together compose a very beautiful green.

170. *Reflection of light.* That reflected light will be of most *58* broken color which is generated by objects of differing colors.

171. *Which side of the body will be tinged most with the color* *69* *of the object opposite?* The surface of any body will take on most

intensely the color of the object nearest it. This occurs because the object nearby takes on the greatest number of visual images, and these, coming to the surface of a body, would alter the surface of that body more than they would do if they were distant. When these visual images cover the original color of such an opaque body, they display their own nature more completely.

58  172. *Of reflected lights.*

1. The surface of bodies will assume more of the color of objects reflecting their own likenesses on it, when the angles of reflection are most nearly equal.

2. Of the colors of objects which reflect their likenesses on the surface of bodies placed opposite them at equal angles, that will be the strongest which reflects its ray by the shortest line.

3. Of the colors of objects which are reflected at equal angles and at an equal distance on the surface of bodies placed opposite them, that will be the strongest which is of the brightest color.

4. That object reflects its color most intensely on the opposite body, which has around it no colors other than those of its own kind.

58v  173. *Of the edges of reflected lights against their background.* The juxtaposition of reflected lights with a background lighter than the reflected light is the reason why such a reflected light is hardly perceptible, but if the reflection borders on a background darker than it, then that reflected light will be perceptible, and will make itself all the more apparent, the darker the background is, and vice versa.[37]

56v  174. *Of the reflected colors of flesh.* When flesh receives light from other flesh, its reflected lights are redder and of more excellent flesh tone than any other part of the flesh that a man has, and this happens according to the third proposition of the second book, which states: the surface of every opaque body will take on the color of its opposite object, and it will do so the more, the closer the object is to it, and the less the more removed it is. It will also do so the more the larger it is, because, since it is

[37] At the end of this section, Hand 1 has written: Fine de reflessi. (End of reflected lights.)

large, it intercepts the images of the surrounding objects,/which *57*
are often of different colors, and adulterate the first close visual
images when the bodies are small. But nevertheless a small, close
color will tinge a reflected light more than one that is large but
farther away, according to the sixth proposition of perspective,
which states: large objects can be so far away that they seem
much smaller than small objects near at hand.

175. *Of reflection.* That color which is closest to the reflected *58*
light will tinge it most, and vice versa.

   Therefore, painter, in practice color the faces of your figures
by reflected lights from those parts of the garments which are/ *58v*
closest to the parts of the flesh, but do not separate those parts
too emphatically from the rest of the face if there is no need
for it.

### [HARMONY AND CONTRAST OF COLOR]

176. *Of the colors that result from the mixture of other colors,* *75v*
*which are called secondary.* The simple colors are six, of which
the first is white, although some philosophers do not accept white
or black in the number of colors, because one is the origin of all
colors and the other is their absence. But as painters cannot do
without them, we include them in the number of the others, and
say/that in this order white is the first among the simple, and *76*
yellow is second, green is third, blue is fourth, red is fifth, and
black is the sixth.

   White we shall name for light without which no color can
be seen; yellow for the earth; green for water; blue for air; red
for fire; and black for darkness, which is stronger than the element of fire, for there is no question of density in black through
which the rays of the sun can possibly penetrate, and in consequence, illuminate.

   If you wish quickly to see all the varieties of composite colors,
take pieces of colored glass and through them look at all the
colors of the countryside which you can see beyond them. There
you will see that all the colors of objects which are seen beyond
the glass, are mixed with the color of that glass, and you will
see which color is strengthened or impaired by such a mixture.

For example, if the glass is yellow, I say that the visual images of objects which pass through that color to the eye can be impaired as well as improved. Deterioration will take place with blue, black, and white more than in the case of all the others, and improvement will occur in the case of yellow and green more than in that of all the others. Thus with the eye you will review mixtures of color which are infinite in number, and in this way you will make a choice of colors for innovations of mixed and composite colors. You will do the same with two glasses of different colors held before the eye, and thus continue by yourself.

76-76v 177. *Of colors.*/Blue and green are not in themselves simple colors, because blue is composed of light and darkness, as in the case of the air; that is, it is composed of most perfect black and purest white.

Green is composed of a simple and a compound color, that is, it is composed of blue and yellow.

68 178. *Of the mixture of colors, one with another, which extends to infinity.* Although the mixture of colors with one another extends to infinity, I will not fail to say a little about it, putting 68v down first some simple colors,/and with each one of them, I will mix each of the others, one with one, then two with two, and three with three, following thus through the whole number of colors.

Then I will begin again to mix the colors, two with two, then three with two, and then four, continuing to the end with these first two colors. Next I shall put down three of them, and to these three add three more, and then six, and continue thus. Later, I shall continue these mixtures in all their proportions.

I call those simple colors which are not composite, nor can they be compounded by means of a mixture of other colors.

Black and white are not commonly included among the colors, because one is darkness and the other is light, that is, one is absence of color and the other is the origin of color. But I do not wish for that reason to leave them out, because they are the principal ones used in painting, as painting is composed of shadows and lights, that is, of lightness and darkness.

After black and white come blue and yellow, then green, lion-

colored or tawny, or, if you wish, ochre, then the color of black-
berries and red. These are the eight colors and there are no more
in nature. With these I commence the mixtures, first black with
white, then black with yellow, and black and red; afterwards,
yellow and black, yellow and red, but because here I lack paper,
I shall leave the details to be discussed at length in my work on
this subject, which will be of great use, as well as very necessary.
This description will be placed between the theory and the practice of painting.

179. *Of the mutation of transparent colors placed upon or super-* 67
*imposed over divers colors with the varying ways in which they*
*veil the first colors.* When a transparent color is placed on another color, it becomes changed by it, there is composed a mixed
color, different from both the simple ones that compose it. This
is seen in smoke coming out of chimneys which, when it is in
contrast to the black of the chimney, appears blue; and when it
rises, in contrast with the blue of the air, it appears gray or reddish. So also scarlet laid upon blue makes violet, and when blue
is put on yellow it makes green, saffron on white makes yellow.
Bright color upon dark makes a blue the more excellent as the
bright and the dark color are themselves the more excellent.

180. *Of colors.*/Among colors of equal perfection the one which 76v-77
will appear most excellent is that which is seen with its direct
contrast. A direct contrast is a pale color with red, black with
white—although neither one of these is a true color—azure blue
and golden yellow, green and red.[38]

181. [39]Every color is more discernible when opposed by its con- 77
trast than by one like itself, as, for example, dark on light, and
light on dark. White which borders on dark produces the result
that at the edges the dark appears blacker and the white appears
purer.

[38] At the end of this section an unidentified hand has added: à questa stella *
segue la seguēte poco ingiù. (After this star * comes the passage that follows
a little below.) Cf. McM. 181.

[39] The unidentified hand has placed an asterisk at the beginning of this section.
Cf. McM. 180.

*75v*   182. *Of colors.* Colors which go together harmoniously are green with red or purple or violet, and yellow with blue.

*62v*   183. Notice now that if you wish to produce an excellent darkness, give it an excellent lightness by way of contrast[40] and thus the excellent lightness will produce the greatest darkness, and the pale area will make the red seem a more fiery red than it would seem in comparison with scarlet. This rule will be more distinctly shown in the proper place.

There remains a second rule that does not aim at making colors in themselves of a supreme beauty which is greater than they naturally are, but at increasing their attractiveness in proximity to one another, as green does to red, and red to green, and mutually adding grace to one another, as does green with blue. And there is a second rule with regard to discordant combinations, such as azure blue with yellow which then becomes lighter, or with white and others similar, which will be spoken of in the proper place.

*72v*   184. *Of the nature of contrasts.* Black garments make the painted flesh tints of human beings whiter than they are, and white garments make the flesh tints dark, and yellow garments make them seem more highly colored, while red garments show them pale.

*62*   185. *Of putting colors together in such a way that each makes the other attractive.*[41] If you wish the proximity of one color to make another which it borders attractive, observe that rule which is seen in the rays of the sun that compose the rainbow, otherwise called the iris. Its colors are caused by the motion of the
*62v* rain, because each little drop changes/in the course of its descent into each one of the colors of that rainbow, as will be set forth in the proper place.

*77*   186. An object seen in dark, thick air, if it be white, will seem larger in shape than it actually is. This occurs because, as I say above, a bright object increases in size against a dark background, for reasons already given.

[40] The MS has "bellezza" in error for "bianchezza."
[41] Above the heading, Hand 1 had first written and then crossed out: Regole da far che le figure. (Rules to make figures.)

[COLOR IN LIGHT AND SHADOW]

187. *How every color that does not shine is more beautiful in* 67
*its illuminated parts than in those shadowed.*/Every color is more 67v
beautiful in the light than in shadow, because light enlivens and
gives a true perception of the quality of color, while shadow
deadens and darkens this same beauty and clouds perception of
the color. If, on the contrary, black is more beautiful in shadow,
the reply is that black is not a true color, and neither is white.

188. *How the beauty of color must be in the lights.* If we see that 67v
the true quality of colors is known through light, it is to be concluded that where there is more light, the true quality of the illuminated color is better seen; and where there is more darkness, the color is tinged with the color of that darkness. Therefore, painter, remember to show true color in the illuminated
parts of your painting.

189. *Of colors.* Color found between the shadowed and the il- 73
luminated parts of shadowed bodies is less beautiful than that
which is entirely illuminated, so that the prime beauty of colors
is to be seen in the principal lights.

190. *What part of a color looks most beautiful in painting?* Here 67
it must be noted in which way a color will look most beautiful
in nature; when it shines, or when it has light, or when it is in
medium shadow, or in the dark, or when it has transparency. It
is necessary to understand what color is here referred to, since
the beauty of different colors is enhanced in different ways.
Black looks most beautiful in the shadows, and white in the light;
and blue, green, and brown in medium shadow; and yellow and
red in the light; gold in reflected light, and lake blue in medium
shadows.

191. *How to make the colors in your paintings vivid and beauti-* 62v
*ful.* For those colors that you wish to be beautiful, first always
prepare a very pure, white ground. This I say with regard to
transparent colors, for a bright ground is not an advantage to
those which are not transparent. An example of this is shown
by colored pieces of glass which, when they are held between the

eye and the luminous air, display great beauty, but which cannot do so when the air behind them is darkened by shadow, or some other obscurity.

70 192. *Of the brightness of landscapes.* The colors of painted land-
70v scapes will never have the vivacity and brightness/of natural landscapes illuminated by the sun, unless the painted landscapes are also illuminated by the sun.

73v 193. *Of colors.* Colors placed in shadow will partake more or less of their natural beauty, depending on whether they are in greater or lesser obscurity.

But if the colors are located in luminous space, then they will look the more beautiful, the greater the brilliance of the source of light.

THE ADVERSARY: The differences of colors in shadow are as numerous as are the differences of color in the things shadowed.

74 REPLY:/Colors placed in shadow will differ less and less as the shadows in which they are situated grow deeper. For this there is the testimony of those who from the squares look inside the doors of shadowed temples, where the paintings covered with different colors all appear enveloped in obscurity.[42]

66 194. *Whether different colors can appear to be of uniform obscurity because of a common shadow.* It is possible for all the different colors with a common shadow to appear to be transmuted into the color of that shadow.

This is shown in the shadows on a cloudy night in which no shape or color of a body is perceived. Since shadow is nothing but the absence of light, either direct or reflected, through which all the shapes and colors of bodies are comprehended, it necessarily follows that when the cause of the light is completely removed, the effect and the perception of the colors and forms of those bodies should be lacking.

66 195. *Why the colors and form of bodies are lost through what seems to be darkness but is not.* There are many places, illumi-

---

[42] Hand 3 has added, at the end of this section, after citing "L° B. car. 18," four times in the margin at different points: Seguita un cap¹° al L° B. a questa car. 18. (Another chapter follows this folio 18 in Book B.)

nated and bright in themselves, which look shadowed and entirely without any differentiation of colors and forms in the things that are found there.

This happens because of the light of the illuminated air, lying between the things seen and the eye, as is seen inside windows that are far from the eye, where only a uniform, very dark obscurity is perceived. But if you then enter into the house, you will see that/it is strongly illuminated inside, and you can quickly dis- *66v* tinguish every minor part of anything that can be found inside that window. This comes about because of a defect of the eye which, overcome by the excessive light of the air, contracts the size of its pupil a good deal and so loses much of its visual power, whereas in dark places the pupil expands and its visual power increases as much as its size increases, as is proved in my second book on perspective.

[THE COLOR OF A BODY AND THE OBJECT OPPOSITE IT]

196. *Of colors.* The light of fire tinges everything with yellow, *74* but this will not appear to be true except through comparison with things illuminated by the air of daylight. This comparison can be made near the end of the day, or just after the dawn, and also/where through an opening in the wall of a dark room, there *74v* falls upon the object a thin beam of light from the air and through another opening a thin beam of light from a candle. In such a situation, the difference can certainly be seen clearly and quickly. But without such a comparison the difference will never be seen, except between colors which are very similar but are recognized to be different, such as white and bright yellow, green and blue. The light which illuminates the blue, having a yellow tinge, produces the same effect as mixing together blue and yellow, which compose a beautiful green. If afterward you mix yellow with the green, it becomes even more beautiful.

197. *How nothing seems its true color if it does not have light* *66v* *from another, similar color.* Nothing ever looks to be its real color, if the light which strikes it is not all of that color.

This assertion is demonstrated in the colors of draperies, where the illuminated sides of folds reflect and give light to the shadowed folds opposite, making them show their true color. The same thing is done with gold leaf when one color gives light to another, and the contrary results when light is taken from another color.

*69* 198. *What part of the surface of bodies appears most beautiful in color?* That surface of an opaque body, which has as its near object a color similar to its own, will seem to be most perfect in color.

*67v and* 199. *What part of a color ought, according to reason, to be the* *illus.* *most beautiful?* Let A be the light, and B illuminated in a straight line by that light, and C which does not face that light, but only the illuminated part, which, we may say, is red. Under such conditions, the light which springs from that side will resemble its source, and will tinge the face C red. If C itself is also red, you will also see that it is much more beautiful than B. If C is yellow, you will see created a color intermediate between red and yellow.

*62v* 200. *Of the colors of the shadows of any color.* The color of the *63* shadow of any color will always take on/the color of its opposite object, and will do so as much more or little as this object is closer or more distant from that shadow, and as it is more or less luminous.

*68v* 201. *Of the surface of every shadowed body.* The surface of every shadowed body takes on the color of the object opposite. Shadowed bodies display this with certainty, for none of these bodies displays its form or color, if the medium between the body and *69* the luminous body is not/illuminated with the same color as the object illuminated. Let us say, then, that the opaque body is yellow and the luminous body is blue; I say that the part illuminated will be green, a green composed of yellow and blue.

*72v* 202. *Of the color of the shadows of any body.* Never will the *73* color of the shadow of any body be a true,/proper shadow, unless the object opposite, which casts the shadow, is of the same color as the body to which the shadow is given.

Let us suppose, for example, that I have a room whose walls are green. I say that if a blue object is seen in such a place, illuminated by the bright blueness of the air, then the illuminated side will be a very beautiful blue. But the shadow of such a beautiful blue will be ugly and not a true shadow of a beautiful blue, because it is spoiled by green, which reverberates in it. It would be worse if the walls were tan.

203. *Of the colors of shadows.* It often happens that the shadows *75 and* of shadowed bodies are not consistent with the colors in the lights; *illus.* the shadows are greenish when the lights are reddish, although the body is only of one color.

This happens when the light is thrown on the object from the east and illuminates it with the color of its brilliance. In the west another object is illuminated with that light, but it is of another color than the first object. The second object's reflected rays of light rebound toward the east and strike with the side of the first object turned toward it, where those rays are cut off and remain fixed with their color and brilliance.

I have often seen a white object with reddish lights and bluish shadows. This happens on snowclad mountains at sunset, when the horizon appears on fire.

[WHITE AND ITS SHADOW]

204. *Why white is not a color.* White is not a color but has the *74* capacity of receiving any color. When it is in high open country, all its shadows are blue. This comes about according to the fourth proposition which states: the surface of every opaque body takes on the color of its opposite object. Therefore, when white is deprived of the light of the sun through the intrusion of some object between the sun and that white, all the white exposed to the sun and the air, and the part which is not turned toward the sun, will be in shadow, taking on the color of the air only. And if this white does not face toward the greenness of the fields as far as the horizon, and does not face the whiteness of the horizon, doubtless that white would seem to be the simple color of the air.

205. *What surface is most receptive to colors?* White is more *69* receptive to any color than the surface of any other body except a mirror.

The proof is given by saying that every empty body is capable of receiving that which bodies which are not empty are incapable of receiving. For that reason we shall say that because white is empty, or if you wish, devoid of color, when it is illuminated with the color of any luminous body it takes on the color of that luminous body. Black would not do so, for black is like a broken vessel, which is deprived of the capacity to contain anything.

63v 206. *Color of the shadow of white.* The shadow of white, exposed to the sun and air, has a shadow derived from blue. This comes about because white has no color in itself but receives any color. This is proved by the fourth proposition of this book, which says: the surface of every body takes on the color of its opposite object, and so it follows that that part of the white surface will take on the color of the air which is opposite it.

63v 207. *What color will create the blackest shadow?* That shadow will be blackest which is created by the whitest surface, and it will have a greater amount of variety than any other surface. This comes about because white is not counted among the colors but receives any color, and its surface takes on more intensely the colors opposed to it than a surface of any other color, and chiefly that of its direct contrary, which is black, or some other dark color from which white is most remote by nature. For this reason it seems that there really is a great difference between its principal shadows and its principal lights.

[REFLECTED LIGHT AND THE COLOR OF SURFACES]

77 208. *Of true color.* The true color of any body whatever is shown in that part which is not covered by any kind of shadow, nor in the case of a polished body by luster.

70 209. *What body will show you its true color most?* That body will show you its true color most whose surface is least polished and smooth.

This is seen in linen cloth and in the leaves of grass and trees which are fuzzy, and where no luster can be created. There, by the nature of things, objects cannot be reflected, so that they must render to the eye only the true color, otherwise they would be affected by the light of a body with an opposite color, such as the redness of the sun when it sets and tinges the clouds with its own color.

210. *Which is the surface that shows its true colors less than* 70
*others?* That surface will show its true color least which is smoothest and most polished.

We see this on the grass of the fields and on the leaves of trees which shine, having a polished and lustrous surface, in which the sun, or the air which the sun illuminates, is reflected, and thus in that lustrous part the grass and leaves lose their natural color.

211. *Of colors mirrored on lustrous objects of varied colors.* A 76
reflected object always takes on the color of the body which reflects it. The mirror is tinged in part with the color reflected in it, and each partakes of the color of the other, as the object reflected is more or less powerful than the color of the mirror. That will appear of the most powerful color in the mirror, which most resembles the color of the mirror.

212. *Of objects reflected in the waters in landscapes, beginning* 71 *and*
*with air.* The only air that gives a semblance of itself on the *illus.*
surface of water will be that whose reflection comes from the surface of the water to the eye at an equal angle, that is to say, the angle of incidence equal to the angle of reflection.

213. *Of the reflection and color of sea water seen from various* 72v
*points of view.* The sea with tossing waves does not have a universal color, but he who sees it from dry land sees its color as dark, and the nearer it is to the horizon the darker it seems; and he sees some bright spots or high lights which move slowly like a flock of white sheep. He who looks at the sea while he is on the high seas, sees it as blue. This comes about because from land the sea seems dark, since there you see the waves which reflect the darkness of the earth, and from the high sea they seem blue, because you see the blue air reflected by the waves.

[TWO GREEN PIGMENTS]

214. *Of the green color made of oxidized copper.* Green made of   67v-68
copper, even when this color is mixed with oil, loses its beauty

like smoke if it is not quickly varnished. It not only goes up in smoke, but if it is washed with a sponge dipped in simple, ordinary water, the copper green will disappear from the panel on which it has been painted, especially in humid weather. This comes about because copper green is made from salt, which dissolves easily in rainy weather, and especially when it is bathed and washed with a sponge.

68  215. *Increasing the beauty of copper green.* If you mix with the copper green some cavalline aloe, the copper green will acquire great beauty, and it would acquire more with saffron if it did not go up in smoke. This cavalline aloe is known to be good when it is dissolved in alcohol, and it dissolves better when it is hot than when it is cold. If you have finished a work with this simple green, and you glaze it thinly with aloe dissolved in water, then the work has a very beautiful color. This aloe can be crushed in oil by itself, and also together with copper green, and with any other color that you wish.

[A SINGLE POINT OF VIEW IN PAINTING]

49v  216. *How a painting should be seen from only one window.*[48] A painting ought to be viewed from a single window, as appears in the case of objects shaped like this O. If you wish to paint a round ball at a height, it is necessary for you to make it long in
50  this way, and stand far enough back so that/foreshortening makes it appear round.

55  217. *Of definite and indistinct objects.* Things sharply outlined should be those seen near at hand, and the indistinct, that is, those with unclear outlines, should be represented as in distant places.

49  218. *Rules of painting.*[44] That object, or rather the shape of that object, will look the most distinct and sharpest at the edges, which

---

[48] In the left margin Hand 3 has written: a carte 2 (?). (On folio 2 [?].)

[44] Hand 3 has added to the heading: Come quella Pittura alla quale si puo auicinare l'occhio di chi la uede, tutte le parti di quella uogliono essere ben finite nei gradi loro. (How the painting which can be closely approached by the eye of the observer ought to be well finished in all its parts according to their degree of distance.)

is/nearest the eye. And for this reason, painter, when under the  *49v*
name of practice you represent the view of a head seen at a short
distance, using vigorous brush-strokes, and rugged, crude touches,
know that you deceive yourself; because at whatever distance you
represent your form, it is always finished, according to the position in which it is placed, and this is also so when, although at
a great distance, it loses the sharpness of its edges. Do not therefore fail to paint so that a smoky contour can be seen, rather
than contours and profiles that are sharp and hard. Hence, it is
to be concluded that the work to which the eye of the observer
can approach closely should be finished with extreme diligence in
all its parts, and moreover, those in the foreground should be defined against the background with clear, sharp contours, and those
that are more distant should be well finished but with more
smoky edges, that is, edges that are more indistinct, or if you
wish, less clear. In the successively more distant object, observe
what is said above; that is, first the contours are less clear, and
then the parts of the composition, and finally the whole is less
clear both in form and color.

219. *Of representing the sizes of painted objects.*[45]/The repre-  *54-54v*
sentation of the dimensions of objects as they are placed before  *and illus.*
the eye, should be so carried out that forms in the foreground,
when they are small, are as finished as the works of miniature
painters, and as the large ones of other painters. But those of
the miniature painters are made to be seen close at hand, while
those of other painters are made to be seen at a greater distance,
in such a way that the forms reach the eye through angles of
equal dimensions. This comes about because those forms reach
the eye through angles of equal width. This is proved as follows:
let the object be B C, and the eye A, and D E a sheet of glass
through which penetrates the image B C. I say that when the
eye remains fixed at A, the dimensions of the painting made in
imitation of B C should be as much smaller a shape, as the glass
sheet D E is nearer the eye A, and ought to be finished in corresponding degree. If you represent the figure B C on the glass

---

[45] This section is not clear and it has been suggested that it combines several
different sections in one, or is a hasty, preliminary sketch.

sheet D E, your figure should be less finished than the shape
B C, and more finished than the shape N M made on the glass
sheet F G, because if P O were finished as is the natural B C,
the perspective of O P would be false. With regard to the diminution of the figure, that would be well, for B C would be decreased
in P O, but the detail would not be in accord with the distance,
because on examining the perfection of finish in the natural B C,
this B C would appear to be in the position O P. But if you wish
to examine the diminution of O P, this O P seems to be at the
distance B C, and in regard to decrease of finish, on the glass
sheet F G.

*46v* 220. *Why a painting can never appear to have as much relief as
do objects in nature.* Many times painters despair of their ability
to imitate natural appearance, seeing that their paintings do not
*47 and* have/that relief and vividness that things seen in a mirror have,
*illus.* though they claim that they have colors, which in brightness or
darkness far surpass the lights and shadows of objects seen in the
mirror; in this case reproaching their own ignorance and not the
reason for it, because they do not know it.

It is impossible for a painted object to appear in such relief
that it approach the reflections in a mirror, although both are on
a surface, unless it is seen with only one eye. The reason is the
two eyes see one object behind the other, as A and B see, but M
cannot conceal N[46] entirely because the base of the triangle formed
by visual lines is so broad, that the second body is seen after the
first. But if one eye is closed, and one is open, as at S, the body F
will cover R, because the visual line originates in a single point
and has a base for the visual triangle in the first body; hence the
second body of equal size is never seen.

[OBJECTS SEEN AT A DISTANCE]

*77* 221. The medium which lies between the eye and the object seen
transmutes that object into its own color, for example: the blue
air makes distant mountains appear blue; whatever the eye sees
through red glass, looks red; the light which the stars shed about

[46] M and N are interchanged in the manuscript diagram.

them is absorbed by the darkness of the night which lies between the eye and the illumination of those stars.

222. *Diminution of colors through the medium lying between them and the eye.* A visible thing will appear that much less its natural color, the greater the density of the medium lying between it and the eye. 71

223. *Of the perspective of colors in dark places.* In illuminated places where the light diminishes uniformly to the point of darkness, that color will be darkest which is farthest from the eye. 73

[THE PERSPECTIVE OF COLOR]

224. *At what distance from the eye the colors of objects are lost.* The variations of distance at which the colors of objects are lost are as great as are the variations of the times of day, and as great as the variations of density and thinness of the air, through which the visual images of the colors of objects penetrate to the eye. For the present we shall not give any other rule on this. 63v

225. *Whence comes the blue of the air?* The blue of the air comes from the density of the body of illuminated air lying between the upper darkness and the earth./The air in itself has no quality of odor, taste, or color, but takes on the semblances of the things placed beyond it, and the blue will be the more beautiful, the greater the darkness behind it, provided there is not too much space lying between nor a too heavy humidity. Thus it is seen that mountains that have the most shadow are the most beautifully blue at great distances, but where they are most illuminated, they show the color of the mountains themselves rather than the blue given them by the air which lies between them and the eye. 73 / 73v

226. *Common perspective and the diminution of color at a great distance.* The air will take on the color blue the less, the nearer it is to the horizon, and will be the darker the more distant it is from that horizon. 70v and illus.

This is proved by the third proposition of the ninth book which shows that that body will be least illuminated by the sun which is of the thinnest material. Therefore, the elementary fire which envelops the air, and which, because it is rare and thinner than

the air, takes on the darkness which is above it, less than does
the air. In consequence the air, a body not so thin as fire, is more
illuminated by the solar rays which penetrate it, illuminating the
infinity of atoms which pervade it, and it becomes bright to our
eyes. Hence, the visual images of that darkness, penetrating
through the air, make it necessary that the whiteness of the air
seem blue, as is proved by the third proposition of the tenth book.
And the blue seems clearer the denser the air lying between that
darkness and our eyes.

It is as if the eye which beholds it were at P, and looked above
it at the thickness of air P R. Then, lowering the eye somewhat,
it would see the air along the line P S, which would seem brighter
because there is greater density of air along the line P S than along
the line P R. And if the eye is directed toward the horizon, it
will see the air almost wholly devoid of blue, which comes about
71 because the line of vision penetrates/a much greater quantity of
air along the horizontal line P D, than along the oblique P S.
Thus our proposition is proved.

54 227. *How the air should be lighter the lower you depict it.* Because the air is dense near the earth, the more it rises, the thinner it becomes. When the sun is in the east, if you look toward
the west, the southwest, and northwest, you will see that the
dense air receives more light from the sun than the thin air, because the rays encounter more resistance. If the sky in view
ends in low plains, the lowest part of the sky will be seen through
that denser and whiter air. This adulterates the true color, seen
through it as a medium, so that the sky seems whiter than it
does above you, where the visual line passes through a smaller
quantity of air adulterated with heavy vapors. And if you look
toward the east, the air will seem darker the lower down it is,
because in this lower air fewer luminous rays pass through.

69v 228. *Of the gradations in the same color seen at different distances.*
Among colors of the same kind, that one will vary least which
is least removed from the eye. The proof is: that air, which lies
between the eye and the object seen, conceals that object somewhat. If the air between is great in amount, then the object seen

will be strongly tinged with the color of that air, and if that air is thin in amount, then the object will be little obstructed.

229. *At what distance the colors of objects are entirely lost.* The colors of objects are entirely lost at a greater or lesser distance, as the eye and the object seen are at a greater or lower elevation. This is proved by the seventh proposition of this book, which says: the air is more or less dense in the degree that it is nearer to or more distant from the earth. Therefore, if the eye and the object seen are near the earth, the density of the air lying between the eye and the object seen will be thick and will greatly obstruct the color of the object seen by the eye. But if the eye and the object seen by it are distant from the earth, the air will then obstruct the perception of the object but little. 63

230. *Of the way to deal with distant objects in painting.* It is clearly seen that the air which is close to the flatness of the earth is thicker than other air, and the higher it rises the rarer and more transparent it is. The lower parts of large, elevated objects which are distant from you are little seen because you see them along a line of vision that passes through continuous, dense air. The summits of those heights are seen along a line of vision which, although it originates in dense air, nevertheless terminates in air much thinner than in the lower portions. For this reason the farther this line extends from you the more it becomes thinner from point to point in the thin atmosphere. 53v

Therefore, painter, when you depict mountains, paint them so that from hill to hill the lower parts are always/lighter than the summits, and the more distant you make them appear one from the other the lighter the lower parts are to be painted; and the more they rise on high, the more will they show their true shape and color. 54

231. *Of the perspective of colors.* The illumination of the same color placed at various distances and equal elevations is in proportion to the distances which each of these colors has from the eye that sees them. 65 and illus.

The proof is: Let E B C D be the same color. The first, or E, is placed two degrees of distance from the eye at A. The second, or B, is distant four degrees; the third, or C, is at six degrees. The fourth, or D, is at 8 degrees, as is shown by the circles that cut the line, seen above the line A R. Let A R S P be one degree of thin air, and S P E T a denser degree of air. It will follow that the first color E will pass to the eye through one degree of dense air, or E S, and through one degree of less dense air, or S A. The color B will send its image to the eye at A through two degrees of dense air and the color C will send it through three of the dense and three of the less dense degrees; the color D through four of the dense and through four of the less dense degrees.

Thus we have proved that the diminution or loss of colors is in proportion to their distance from the eye that sees them. But this happens only with colors that are at an equal elevation; those which are at unequal elevations do not observe the same rule, because they are in air of different densities which absorb those colors differently.

64 and illus. 232. *Of color which does not display any difference in varying densities of air.* It is possible that a color may not change at different distances, and this happens when the proportion of the density of air and the proportion of the color's distance from the eye is the same but in inverse proportion.

This is proved as follows: let A be the eye, H a color, whatever you wish, placed at a degree of distance distant from the eye in air of four degrees of density. But because the second degree of air above A M N L, has a thinner air by half, it follows that this color which is in it is twice as far removed from the eye as it was at first, and therefore we put it at two degrees away from the eye, i.e. A F and F G, and this will be the color G.

Afterward, raising it to the degree doubly thinner than M A N L, which is the degree O M P N, it will be necessary to place it at the height E, and it will be distant from the eye the whole line A E. This is proved to equal in density of air the distance A G, and it is proved in the following way.

If the distance A G, placed between the eye and the color, is of the same degree of density of air and occupies two degrees, and the color is raised two and a half degrees in distance, this

distance is sufficient to produce the result that the color G, raised
to E, does not vary in strength. This is so because the degree A C
and the degree A F, being the same density of air, are similar
and equal; the degree C D, although it is equal in length to the
degree F G, is not similar/in density of air, because half of it is *64v*
in air twice the density of that above it, where half a degree of
distance absorbs as much color as a whole degree of the air above,
which is twice as thin as the air which bounds it below.

Therefore, calculating first the density of the air and then the
distance, you will see that the colors, although in different locations, have not changed their beauty. We say this because of
the calculation of the density of the air: the color H is placed
in four degrees of density of air, the color G is placed in air with
two degrees of density; color E is found in air of one degree of
density.

Now let us see if the distances are in equal but inverse proportion: color E is found distant from the eye at A two and a
half degrees of distance, G at two degrees, and A H at one degree.

This distance does not correspond with the proportion of density.

It is then necessary to make a third calculation, and it is this
which it is necessary to tell you: the degree A C, as was said
above, is similar and equal to the degree A F, and the half degree C D is similar but not equal to the degree A C, because a
half degree of length is equal to a whole degree of the air above. . . .[47]

Therefore the calculation made satisfies the problem: because
A C equals two degrees of density in the air above, and the half
degree C D is equal to a whole degree of the air above, and one
more is included, that is, B E,[48] which makes four. It follows:
A H has four degrees of density of air, A G also has four, that
is, A F has two, and F G two more, which makes four. A E/ *65*
also has four, for A C has two and one, C B,[49] which is the half
of A C of the same density of air, and a whole one is above in
the thin air, which makes four.

[47] An omission or erasure obscures the following clause.
[48] Emended from "D E" of the MS.
[49] Emended from "C D" of the MS.

Thus, if the distance A E is not twice the distance A G, nor four times the distance A H, it is compensated by C D, half a degree of dense air, which is equal to a whole degree of thinner air which is above.

Thus is concluded our proposition, that the color at H, G, E is not different at different distances.

65v 233. *Of color that does not change in different densities of air.* A color in varying densities of air will not change if it is farther from the eye in the degree that it is in thinner air.

The proposition is proved thus: if the first air at the bottom has four degrees of density and the color is one degree distant from the eye, and the second air above it has three degrees of density, having lost one degree, the result is that the color gains a degree and a third of distance. And when the still higher air has lost two degrees of density, the color gains two degrees of distance, and then the first color is the same as the third. To put it briefly, if the color is raised in air that has lost three degrees of density, and the color is removed three degrees in distance, then you can be certain that the loss of color has made the high color as distant as the lower color is near. If the air has lost three-quarters of the density of the lower air, the color in rising has gained three quarters of the whole distance by which it is removed from the eye. Thus we have proved our proposition.

[APPLICATIONS OF AERIAL PERSPECTIVE]

73 234. *Perspective of colors.* The colors in the foreground should be simple and the degrees of their diminution should be consistent with the degrees of their distance; that is, objects will approximate the size of a point, the nearer they are to the visual center point, and colors will take on more of the color of the horizon the nearer they are to it.

63 235. *Of the differences in colors according to their distance or nearness.* Objects darker than the air will appear less dark, the more distant they are, and objects brighter than the air will appear less bright the more distant they are from the eye.

Objects brighter or darker than the air change their color at a great distance, because the bright grows darker and the dark brighter.

236. *How the painter ought to put the perspective of colors into* 77v
*practice.* If you wish to put into practice this perspective of varying and losing or diminishing the very essence of colors, take points a hundred braccia apart from one another in the country, as for example, trees, houses, men and sites. With respect to the first tree, you will have a glass firmly fixed in position, and also your eye must remain fixed. On this glass you will draw a tree according to the tree's shape. Then move the glass horizontally so that the natural tree will almost border on your drawing, afterward color your/drawing in such a way that in color and shape 78 there will be such likeness between the two, that shutting one eye both trees may appear painted on the glass and at the same distance.

Apply this same rule to the second tree, and to the third, a hundred braccia apart in depth. These drawings will serve you as aids and teachers always when you work at pictures where they are relevant, and they will make the work you are doing recede in a proportionate way.

But I find as a rule that the second tree decreases to four-fifths of the first, when it is twenty braccia away from the first.[50]

237. *Of those who, painting in the country, represent the most* 72
*distant object as the darkest.* There are many painters who, in the open country, paint figures darker the more distant they are from the eye. The fact is to the contrary, unless the object depicted be white, for then there would happen that which is put forward below.

238. *Of aerial perspective.* There is another perspective which we 78 and
call aerial, because through the differences in the air we can per-   *illus.*
ceive the varying distances of various buildings which are cut off at the visual base by a single line. This would be the case if many buildings were seen beyond a wall, so that all of them appeared to be of the same size above the edge of that wall, but in painting

[50] The final part of this section is mutilated; it was probably misunderstood by the scribe.

you wished to make one seem more distant than the other. To do this, it is necessary to represent the air as a little thick. You know that in such air, the farthest things seen in it, such as mountains, seem blue, and almost the color of the air when the sun is in the east, because of the great quantity of air which occurs between your eye and the mountains. Therefore, paint the first building above the wall its true color; the next in distance make less sharp in outline and bluer; another which you wish to place an equal distance away, paint correspondingly bluer still; and one which *78v* you wish to show/as five times more distant, make five times bluer. By this rule, the buildings which are on one line and seem to be of the same size will clearly be understood, so that it will be known which is most distant and which is larger than the other.

[MODIFICATIONS OF AERIAL PERSPECTIVE]

*67v* 239. *Of the visibility of colors.* That which is brightest is most visible from a distance, and the darkest is the contrary.

*69v* 240. *Of the flesh tones of faces.* At a great distance that color is best retained which is greatest in extent.

This proposition is demonstrated to us by the fact that a face appears blurred at a distance, because shadow covers the larger part of it, and there are few lights which are lost at a very brief distance, and the highlights are extremely small. This is the reason that, being the darkest part, the face is or appears to be dark, and tends the more to black when that head has in back of it or on it, something whiter than the face.

*72* 241. *Of the colors of things distant from the eye.* The air which separates the objects from the eye tinges them the more with its own color, the more dense it is. Thus when the air has separated a dark object from the eye with a thickness of two miles, it tinges that object more than would a thickness of one mile.

Here the adversary replies and says: in landscapes trees of the same species are darker at a distance than when they are near, which is not true, if the trees are equal in size and separated by equal spaces. But it is really true, if the first trees are sparsely spaced, and the brightness of the fields which separate them is seen, and the last ones are thickly spaced, as happens on the banks and in the vicinity of rivers, where spaces of bright fields are not seen, but are all joined together, casting shadow upon one another.

It also happens that the shadowy part of trees is much greater than the luminous part, and because the visual images which the tree sends from itself to the eye become mixed at a long distance, the dark color/which is found in greater quantity maintains its *72v* image more than the less dark part, and so the mixture carries the more powerful part the longest distance.

242. *Of colors.* Among colors which are not themselves blue, *73v* that which at a great distance takes on blue most will be that which is nearest to black, and thus, conversely, that will maintain its own color for a long distance which is most unlike black.

Therefore, the green of the fields will transmute itself into blue more than yellow or white will; and so conversely, yellow and white will be transmuted into blue less than green and red.

243. *Of the colors of bodies.* Of bodily colors, that will be seen *76v* at the greater distance which is the most brilliant white, and so that will be seen at the least distance which is darker.

Of bodies of equal whiteness and distance from the eye that one will appear purest which is surrounded by the greatest darkness, and on the contrary that darkness will appear deepest which is seen against the purest whiteness.

244. *Of the color of mountains.* That distant mountain will show *77* itself to be of the most beautiful blue which is darkest in itself, and that will be darkest which is highest and most wooded, because/such woods show the trees from the under side, since they *77v* are very high, and the under part is dark because it is not exposed to the sky. Wild plants in the woods are in themselves darker than those cultivated. Oak, beech, fir, cypress, and pine are much darker than olive trees and those of other fruits.

That brightness, which lies between the eye and blackness, since the air is thinner on the great peak, will make of that black the most beautiful blue, and so conversely.

That tree seems to separate itself least from its background whose contours are on a background of color like its own, and so conversely.

69v 245. *Of verdure seen in the country*. Of verdure of the same kind, that part will be the darkest which belongs to the foliage of
70 trees, and/the brightest will be that of the fields.

77v 246. That part of white will appear purest which is nearest to a border of black, and thus that part will seem less white which is farthest from such darkness.

That part of the black will seem darkest which is nearest to white, and equally that part will seem least dark which is farthest from the white.

70 247. *What verdure will seem bluest?* That verdure will appear to take on most blue which has the darkest shadows, and this is proved by the seventh proposition which states: blue is composed of the bright and the dark viewed at a great distance.

[HUMAN GESTURES]

60v 248. *How a good painter must depict two things: man and his mind*. The good painter has two principal things to paint: that is, man and the intention of his mind. The first is easy, the second difficult, because it has to be represented by gestures and movements of the parts of the body, and this is to be learned from the mute, who make such gestures better than any other sort of men.

60 249. *How to learn the movements of man*. The movements of man should be learned after first gaining a knowledge of the parts of the body and of the whole body engaged in all the motions of the limbs and of their joints. Then observe and sketch briefly, with few lines, the actions of men as they occur accidentally, without their being aware of it. If they become aware of your observation, their minds will be occupied with you, which will make them abandon the energy their actions showed when their minds were wholly intent, as they are when two angry men contend with one another. Each one thinks he is in the right, and with great energy they move their eyebrows, their arms, and other parts, with gestures appropriate to their intentions and

their words. But you cannot accomplish this if you wish them to pretend anger or any other condition, such as laughter, tears, pain, amazement, fear and the like. For this reason be sure to take with you a little book with pages prepared with bone meal, and with a silver point briefly note the movements and actions of the bystanders and their grouping. This will teach you how to compose narrative paintings. When your book is full, put it aside/and keep it for your later use, then take another book and *60v* continue as before. This will be very useful for your method of composition, on which I shall compose a special book, which will come after the analysis of forms and limbs in detail and the differences in their articulations.

250. *Of movements and various opinions about them.*[51] The *46* forms of men must have attitudes appropriate to the activities that they engage in, so that when you see them you will understand what they think or say.

This can be done by copying the motions of the dumb, who speak with movements of their hands and eyes and eyebrows and their whole person, in the desire to express the idea that is in their minds. Do not laugh at me because I propose a teacher without speech to you, who is to teach you an art which he does not know himself, for he will teach you better through facts than will all the other masters through words. Do not despise such advice, for these men are the masters of gesture and understand from afar that which one says, when he fits the motions of his hands to the words he would speak.

This viewpoint has had many opponents and many defenders. You, painter, therefore, follow both sects with moderation, according to the situation, doing what is suitable to the kind of people who speak and the nature of the things of which they speak.

251. *Rules of painting.*[52] The painter who would gain honor from *49* his work ought always to study alacrity in gestures from the

[51] In Italian editions, such as that of Borzelli, "opinioni" has been emended to read "operazioni," in the heading.

[52] Hand 3 has added: Come si de' gouernar (nel dissegnare) depingēdo chi e desideroso di honore. (How he who is desirous of honor should govern himself in painting—in drawing.) "Nel dissegnare" is inserted above "depingēdo."

natural gestures made spontaneously by men, and with the powerful impression of their effects fresh in mind, make brief memoranda of them in his notebooks, and afterward adapt them to his purposes by making a man take the same pose, to see which parts of his body are employed in these actions.

*51v*  252. *How small children should be represented.* Little children when sitting should be represented with quick, awkward, irregular movements, and when they stand up, with timid and fearful movements.

*51v*  253. *How women should be represented.* Women should be represented with modest gestures, the legs close together, the arms gathered together, heads bent and inclined to one side.

*51v*  254. *How old men should be represented.* Old men should be represented with languid, slow movements, the legs bent at the knees when they stand up, the feet parallel but apart from one another. They should have their backs bent, the head inclined forward, and the arms not extending too far from the body.

*52*  255. *How old women should be represented.* Old women should be represented with aggressive, quick, and wild gestures, like infernal furies, and their gestures should appear to be quicker in the arms and head than in the legs.

[THE COMPOSITION OF NARRATIVE PAINTING]

*38v*  256. *How a man engaged on an important work should never trust his memory so much that he will not deign to draw from nature.* Certainly that master who let it be understood that he could remember all the forms and effects of nature, would seem to me to be clothed in great ignorance, inasmuch as these effects are infinite and our memory does not have sufficient capacity to retain them all. Therefore, painter, see to it that the greed for gain does not surpass in you the honor of the art, for the gain of honor is much greater than the honor of wealth. Truly, because of these and other reasons that could be given, attend first to drawing the intention and invention first created in your imagination, in form clear to the eye. Then go on, subtracting or adding enough to satisfy you. Then pose men, dressed or nude, in such a way as you may have determined in your work. And see to it that in proportion and size, subject to perspective, nothing occurs in the work which is not considered, reasonable and in accordance with nature. This is the way to make yourself honored because of your art.

257. *Rule.*[53] The sketching of narrative scenes should be rapid, *34* and the limbs not too detailed; be content with only the position of the limbs, which you can finish at your leisure, when it pleases you.

258. *Of the method of learning to compose figures in narrative* *58v and* *paintings.* When you have learned perspective well and have *illus.* committed to memory all the bodies of things and the parts thereof, you should often take pleasure when you walk for recreation in seeing and considering the attitudes and actions of men in conversation, in quarreling, or laughing, or fighting together, noting their gestures and those of the bystanders who intervene or look on in such cases. Make a note of them with a few lines in your little book which you should always take with you. Its pages should be of colored paper, so that you cannot rub your sketch out, but will have to change from an old page to a new when the old one is filled. For these are not/things to be *59* erased but preserved with great care, because these forms and actions are so infinite in number that the memory is not capable of retaining them, wherefore keep your sketches as your aids and teachers.

259. *Of the composition of narrative paintings.*[54] Composers of *60v* narrative paintings should first seek to arrange the figures in a general way, that is, sketched, but first knowing them well from all sides, including the contractions and expansions of the parts of the body.

Then undertake the description of two men who contend ardently with one another, and this invention should be examined in its different actions and aspects. Then should follow a

[53] Hand 3 has added: intorno allo dissegno del schizzare istore e figure (about drawing sketches of narrative paintings and figures).
[54] Hand 3 has commented, to the right of the heading: in p$^a$ bozza (in a first sketch).

combat of a valiant man with one who is cowardly and timid. These actions and many other conditions of mind should be considered with careful analysis and study.

55 260. *Figures separated from one another should not appear to be joined together.*[55] The colors with which you clothe your forms should be such that they lend attractiveness to one another, and when the color of one is the background of another, let them be so arranged that they do not appear joined and attached to one another, even though they should be of the same kind of color, but let them be different in brightness, as is required by the coming between them of distance and volume of air. Let the clarity of their outlines follow the same rule, making these sharper or less sharp as their proximity or distance requires.

61v 261. *Rules on the composition of narrative paintings.* When you compose narrative paintings, do not separate the parts of your narrative paintings with sharp lines, or that will happen to you which happens to many painters, who want every little stroke of charcoal to stand. These may well acquire riches but not praise for their art, because many are the times when the body of the living creature so represented does not move in a way representative of its thoughts and emotions. But having painted a finished, beautiful, and agreeable arrangement of the limbs, it seems to the artist a damaging thing to alter those limbs, putting

62 them higher or lower,/or farther back or forward. Men such as these do not deserve any praise at all for their knowledge.

Now, have you never considered how poets compose their verses? It does not annoy them, just because they have written beautiful letters, to erase some of their verses, then writing them out again better. Therefore, painter, compose the parts of your figures arbitrarily, then attend first to the movements representative of the mental attitudes of the creatures composing your narrative painting, rather than to the beauty and goodness of the parts of their bodies. Because you must understand that if such an unfinished composition turns out to be consistent with your invention, it will satisfy all the more when afterward it is

[55] Hand 3 has added to the heading: deli colori che vestono le figure (of the colors that clothe the shape).

adorned with the perfection appropriate to all its parts. I have seen clouds and stains on walls, which have given rise to beautiful inventions of different things; although these stains were completely lacking in the perfection of any part, yet they did not lack perfection in their movements or other actions.[56]

262. *Method of composing narrative paintings.* That figure in a *59v* narrative painting will appear in greatest relief which is represented as nearest the eye. This happens by reason of the second proposition of the third book which states: that color displays the greatest perfection which has the least quantity of air lying between it and the eye which perceives it, and therefore the shadows, which show that opaque bodies are in relief, look darker when near than when at a distance, where they are dulled by the air lying between the eye and those shadows. This does not happen with shadows near the eye, which show bodies in greater relief, the darker they are.

263. *Of placing a figure in the first plane of a narrative painting.* *59* You should make the foreground figure of a narrative painting as much smaller than life-size as you represent it braccia away from the ground line, and then make the other figures in relation to it, according to the foregoing rule.

264. *Of representing figures for narrative paintings.* The painter *42* ought always to consider, when he has a wall on which he has to represent a story, the height at which he will locate his figures, and when he draws from nature for this purpose, he ought to take a position with his eye as much below the subject that he is drawing, as the subject placed into the work/will be above the *42v* eye of the observer. Otherwise the work will be reprehensible.

265. *Why depicting rows of figures one above the other is a* *47* *method of working to be avoided.* There is a universal custom followed by those who paint on the walls of chapels which is much to be deplored. They make a composition with its landscape and buildings on one plane, then go higher and make a composition in which they change the point of view, and then

[56] At the end of this section, Hand 1 has written: Fine. Comincia de colori. (End. Beginning of colors.)

paint a third and a fourth, so that one wall has four points of
view. That is utmost stupidity on the part of those masters. We
know that the point of view is placed opposite the eye of the
47v observer of the composition. If you ask: how shall I paint the/life
of a saint divided into many episodes on one and the same wall?
I answer, that you must put the first plane with the point of view
at the height of the eye of the observers of the composition, and
on this plane represent the first episode large in size, and then,
diminishing the figures and buildings on the various hills and
plains progressively, you will make provision for the whole narrative. The rest of the wall, up to the top, paint full of trees of a
size that bears relation to the figures, or fill it with angels if
these should be suitable to the story, or birds, or clouds or such
subjects. Do not exert yourself in any other way, or all your work
will be false.

59v 266. *Of composing narrative paintings.* Remember, painter, when
you depict a single figure, avoid foreshortening it in its parts as
well as the whole, because otherwise you will have to contend
with the ignorance of those who are uneducated in that art. But
in narrative paintings do this wherever you have an opportunity,
and especially in battles, where necessarily there occurs an infinite number of distortions and contortions of those who take
part in such discord or, you might say, most brutal madness.

[CONSIDERATIONS IN NARRATIVE PAINTING]

61v 267. *Of the components of narrative paintings.* The elements of
narrative paintings ought to move those who look at or contemplate them in the same way as him whom the narrative painting represents. That is, if the narrative painting represents terror,
fear, flight, sorrow, weeping, and lamentation; or pleasure, joy,
laughter and similar conditions, the minds of those who view it
ought to make their limbs move so that they seem to find themselves in the same situation which the figures in the narrative
painting represent. If they do not do so, the skill of the painter
is in vain.

61 268. *Of variety in narrative paintings.* The painter takes pleasure
in the abundance and variety of the elements of narrative paint-

ings, and avoids the repetition of any part that occurs in it, so
that novelty and abundance may attract and delight the eye of
the observer. I say that, depending on the scene, a narrative
painting requires a mixture of men of various appearances, ages,
and costumes, and also mixed with women, children, dogs, horses,
buildings, fields, and hills.

269. *Consistency among the parts of narrative paintings*. Do not 61
mix the melancholy, those who weep and lament, with the cheerful and those who laugh, for nature provides that one should be
sad with those who lament, and cheerful with those who laugh,
and their laughter and lamentations and tears should be separated
from one another.

270. *Variety among the people in narrative paintings*. In narra- 59v
tive paintings the men ought to be of many complexions, ages,
flesh tints, attitudes, fatness, leanness, such as heavy, slender,
large, small, corpulent, great, proud, courteous, old, young,
strong and muscular, weak and with few muscles,/cheerful, 60
melancholy; some with their hair curled and some plain, short
and long, with movements quick and common, as well as a
variety of clothing, colors, and whatever else is required in the
narrative painting. It is an extreme defect in the painter to portray the faces so that they look like one another, and the repetition
of gestures is also a great vice.

271. *Of varying the vigor, age, and complexion of bodies in nar-* 61
*rative paintings*. I say also that in narrative paintings one ought
to mingle/direct contraries so that they may afford a great con- 61v
trast to one another, and all the more when they are in close
proximity; that is, the ugly next to the beautiful, the big to the
small, the old to the young, the strong to the weak, all should be
varied as much as possible and close together.

272. *Of history*. In a narrative painting the dignity and decorum 61
of a prince or sage should be evident; it may be shown by sep-
arating him and setting him entirely apart from the tumult of
the crowd.

273. *Of diversifying the expression of faces in narrative paint-* 61
*ings*. It is a common defect of Italian painters that one recog-

nizes the expression and figure of the artist throughout the many figures painted by him. Therefore, to avoid such an error, do not repeat or paint them again, either as a whole, or as parts of figures, so that the face of any one is seen twice in a narrative painting.

44  274. *Of the defect which those masters have who repeat the same expressions in faces.* It is an extreme error of some masters to repeat the same motions in the same compositions, one alongside the other, and likewise the beauty in the faces is always the same, though this is never found repeated in nature. If all the past beauties of equal excellence returned to life, they would be greater in number than those that exist in our age, and since in this age no one precisely resembles another, the same would be true of those beauties.

### [BEAUTY OF THE FACE]

60v  275. *Of not ornamenting the figures in narrative paintings.* In narrative paintings never put so many ornaments on your figures and other objects that they impede the perception of the forms and attitudes of those bodies, for form and attitude are their essentials.

50v  276. *Of the selection of beautiful faces.* It seems to me no small
51  attraction that a painter/give a charming air to his figures. The painter who does not possess this grace by nature can acquire it by casual study in this manner. Look about for the good parts of many beautiful faces, parts considered beautiful by public opinion, rather than by your own preference. You can deceive yourself by selecting faces that are similar to your own, since it often seems that such similarities please us; and if you should be ugly, you would select faces that are not beautiful and you would paint ugly faces, as do many painters, whose painted figures often resemble that of their master. So choose beautiful faces as I tell you and commit them to memory.

51  277. *Of beauty and ugliness.* Beauty and ugliness seem more effective through one another.

278. *Of beauty.* Beauty of face may be equally fine in different 51v persons, but it is never the same in form, and should be made as different as the number of those to whom such beauty belongs.

279. *Of judges of various beauties of equal excellence in various* 51v *bodies.* Although in different bodies there be different beauties of equal attractiveness, different judges of equal intelligence will judge that there is great difference between one and the other among those they prefer.

[DESCRIPTIONS OF STORM, BATTLE, NIGHT, AND FIRE]

280. *Pleasure of the painter.*[57] The divinity which is the science 36 of painting transmutes the painter's mind into a resemblance of the divine mind. With free power it reasons concerning the generation of the diverse natures of the various animals, plants, fruits, landscapes, fields, landslides in the mountains, places fearful and frightful, which bring terror to those who view them; and also pleasant places, soft and delightful with flowery meadows in various colors, swayed by the soft waves of breezes, looking beyond the wind that escapes from them, rivers that descend from the high mountains with the impetus of great deluges, dragging along uprooted plants mixed with stones, roots, earth and foam, carrying away everything that opposes its own ruin.[58] And so it envisages the sea with its storms, which battle and contend with the winds that fight with the sea, and raising itself in proud waves, it falls, destroying the wind that beats against the base of the waves, enclosing and imprisoning it, smashing and dividing it, mixing it with muddy foam. Then the angry sea is relieved of its rage, but sometimes, overcome by the winds, it escapes from the ocean beds, and plunges over the high banks of neighboring/ 36v promontories, where, coming over the summits of mountains, it descends into the valleys opposite. Part dissolves into spray, the booty of the storm; part escapes from the winds falling back into the sea in rain; and part descends, spreading ruin from the high promontories, bearing away all that opposes itself to ruin, and

[57] Hand 3 has placed "del" before "Piacere" in the heading.
[58] An unidentified hand has written in the margin on Urb. 36, the remark: qua mi ricordo della mirabile discritione del Diluuio dello Autore. (Here I recall the admirable description of the Deluge given by the author.)

often it meets another wave coming toward it, and coming to blows, raises itself to heaven, filling the air with confused and foamy mist, which, battered by the winds on the sides of the promontories creates dark clouds that are the prey of the conquering wind.

*52v* 281. *How to represent a storm.* If you wish to represent a storm well, consider and place before your mind the effects of the wind, blowing over the surface of the sea and the earth, as it removes and carries with it those things which are not firmly imbedded in the mass of the earth. In order to represent the storm well first of all paint the clouds, torn and rent, swept along by the course of the wind, together with the sandy powder lifted from the seashores; include branches and leaves, raised by the powerful fury of the wind, scattered through the air, as well as many other light objects. The trees and grass are bent against the earth, seeming almost as if they were trying to follow the course of the winds, with their branches twisted out of their natural direction, their leaves battered and turned upside down. Some of the men there have fallen and, wrapped in their clothing, are almost unrecognizable because of the dust, while those who are still standing are under some tree, hugging it so the wind will not tear them away. Others, with their hands before their eyes because of the dust, are bent down to the earth, and their garments and hair stream in the direction of the wind.

The turbulent and tempestuous sea is filled with whirlpools of foam between the high waves, with the wind raising the thinnest foam, amid the striving air, in the fashion of a thick, enveloping mist. Depict some of the ships in the painting with torn sail, the pieces flapping in the air with some ropes torn apart, some masts broken and gone overboard, the ship cracking up and broken by the tempestuous waves, while men shout and cling to the wreck of the ship.

*53* You will paint the clouds pursued by/impetuous winds, beaten against the high crests of the mountains and enveloped among them, whirling about like waves dashed on the rocks, with the air itself terrifying because of the dark shadows created in the air by dust, mist and thick clouds.

282. *How one ought to represent a battle*. Paint first the smoke 53
of the artillery mixed in the air with the dust raised by the
movement of the horses of the combatants. You arrange these
elements thus: the dust, being earthy and heavy, although it is
easily raised and mixed with the air because of its fineness, nevertheless readily settles down, and the highest elevation is gained
by the part that is finest, so that it will be the least visible and
will seem almost the color of the air. The smoke that mixes with
the dust-filled air, when it has risen to a certain height, will
seem to be a dark cloud, and you will see this smoke more easily
up above than dust. The smoke will take a somewhat blue color,
and the dust will tend to remain its own color. On the side from
which the light comes, this mixture of air, smoke, and dust will
seem much brighter than on the opposite side. As for the combatants, the farther they are within this turbulent scene, the less
will they be seen, and the less difference will there be between
their lights and their shadows.

You will redden the faces and bodies and the air around the
harquebusiers and those near them, and this redness will tend
to be lost, the farther away it is from its cause. The figures that
are between you and the light, if they are distant, will seem dark
against a light background, and their legs will be the less visible
the closer they are to the ground, for the dust there is greater
and heavier.

And if you depict horses running/away from the crowd, paint 53v
them with little clouds of dust as far apart, one from the other,
as are the intervals between the strides made by the horses, and
the cloud that is farthest from that horse is least visible, as well
as high, scattered, and thin, while that which is nearest is most
visible, small, and dense.

The air should be full of arrows pointing in different directions, some rising and others falling, with some in a straight line.
The balls from fire-arms should be followed in their course by
smoke.

You will paint the figures in the foreground with dust in their
hair and eyebrows and on flat surfaces of their bodies that can
carry dust. You will portray the victors running, with their hair

and other light things spread out in the wind and their eyebrows drawn down.[59]

85   283. [60]And put opposite parts of the body forward, that is, if
you push the right foot forward, the left arm must also come
forward. If you depict someone fallen, mark the trace of his fall
on the dust turned to bloody mud, and again in the half liquid
earth make visible the footprints of men and horses that have
passed there. Paint a horse dragging his dead master, and leaving
behind in the dust and mud the trace of the dragged body.
Depict the conquered and beaten pale, their eyebrows raised and
meeting, and the flesh above them creased with pain. The sides
of the noses should have some wrinkles arching from the nostrils
and ending at the beginning of the eyes, the noses pulled high,
causing those wrinkles, the arched lips show the tops of the teeth,
the fingers spread over the face as when shrieking with grief.
One hand protects the frightened eyes, turning the palm toward
the enemy, while the other is on the earth, to hold up the raised
upper body. You will portray others shrieking with their mouths
open and in flight.

Paint many kinds of arms among the feet of the combatants,
such as broken shields, lances, broken swords and other similar
things. Portray dead men, some half covered with dust, others
85v  entirely so. The dust which mixes/with the blood is converted
into red mud; show the blood, in its natural color, running in
a twisted stream from the body to the dust. Others, dying, teeth
grinding, their eyes starting forth, their fists clutching their bodies, and their legs distorted. You might see someone, disarmed
and beaten down by the enemy, turn to that enemy, with bites
and scratches taking a cruel and harsh revenge. You might see a
swift horse with his mane spread in the wind, running among
the enemy and doing much damage with his hoofs. You would

[59] At the end of this section, there is a note by Hand 1: nõ finito. LT e'l segno
della parte che segue a' car. 85. (Not finished. LT is the mark of the part which
follows on folio 85.) Cf. McM. 283.

[60] Before this section, the scribe has written: Qui finisce il capitolo, Come si
debbe figurare una bataglia il quale comincia a carte 53, errore acaduto et scritto
dal autore in due diuersi manere et tinte d'inchiostro, pero segue al segno L.T.
(Here ends the chapter, How one ought to represent a battle, which begins on
folio 53, an error which occurred because the author wrote in two different
manners and colors of ink, and it follows at the sign L.T.) Cf. McM. 282.

see a wounded man, fallen to earth, covering himself with his shield, while the enemy, leaning down, tries to give him the death stroke. You might see many men fallen in a group upon a dead horse.

You would see some of the victors stop fighting and leave the crowd, wiping their eyes with both hands, their cheeks covered with mud, made by the tears from their eyes and the dust. You would see the reserve squadrons waiting, full of hope and suspicion, their eyebrows drawn up, shading their eyes with their hands, looking toward the thick and confused clouds of dust, while attentive to the command of their captain. Likewise, the captain with his baton raised running toward the reserves, showing them in what place they are needed.

And a river, with horses running in it, breaking the surrounding waters into turbulent waves of mingled foam and water, splashing into the air and between the legs and bodies of the horses. And do not leave any open place without footprints full of blood.

284. *How one ought to represent night.* Whatever is entirely 52 devoid of light is all darkness. Since the night is such a condition, and you wish to represent a scene in the darkness, do it with a great fire, for that which is nearest to the fire is more tinged with its color, since that which is nearest to the object opposite takes on more of its nature. By painting the fire tending toward red, you will make all the things illuminated by it also reddish and those which are farther away from the fire will be more tinged by the black color of the night. The figures that are against the fire will seem dark in the brightness of the fire, because the part of what you see is tinged with the darkness of the night and not with the brightness of the fire, and those that are at the sides are half dark and half reddish, and those which can be seen beyond the outlines of the flames will be all illuminated by ruddy light against a dark background. With regard to their actions, show those that are near protecting themselves with their hands and mantles, to guard against the excessive heat, their faces in the contrary direction showing an inclination to move away. A large part of those more distant will protect their eyes with their hands, hurt by the intolerable brilliance.

# PART THREE

## OF THE VARIOUS STATES AND MOVEMENTS OF THE HUMAN BODY[1]

[THE PROPORTIONS OF THE PARTS OF THE BODY]

285. *Of the changes in the measurements of man from his birth* 103
*to the end of his growth.* The shoulders of a man in early infancy are as broad as his face is long; their breadth equals the space from the shoulder to the elbow when the arm is bent, and also equals the space from the thumb to the bent elbow, and the space from the beginning of the male organ to the middle of the knee, as well as the space from the joint of the knee to the joint of the foot.

But when a man has reached his full height, each of these spaces is doubled in length, except for the length of the face, which changes little as does the size of the whole head. For this reason the height of a well proportioned man who has reached full size is ten times the length of his face, and the breadth of his shoulders is twice the length of his face. All the other breadths are twice the length of the face, and the rest will be stated in the general measurements of man.

286. *Of the proportions of the parts of the body.* All parts of any 105
animal exist in relationship to the whole; that is, those short and stocky ought to have each part short and stocky, and those long and thin should have parts that are long and thin, and the medium-sized should also have medium-sized parts. It is my intention to say the same about trees, when they have not been injured by men or winds, because these renew their youth above their older portions, and thus their natural proportion is destroyed.

287. *That every part of the body should in itself be in proportion* 125
*to the whole body.* Make each part of a whole proportionate to the whole, so that when a man has a thick, short figure, his every part is also thus, that is, arms short and thick, broad hands,

---

[1] The latter portion of Part Three contains subjects not related to the human body, although this is given as the theme of this part.

thick fingers with their joints similar, and so also with the rest. I would say the same about animals and plants in general, regarding the diminution or increase of their proportions.

*107v* 288. *Of the composition of limbs of creatures.* Let the parts of living creatures be in accordance with their type.

I say that you should not take the leg of a delicate figure, or the arm, or other limb, and attach it to a figure with a thick chest or neck. And do not mix the limbs of the young with those of the old, nor limbs that are vigorous and muscular with those that are delicate and fine, nor those of males with those of females.

*103v* 289. *Of the difference in measurements of children and men.* I find a great difference in the length of the bones between the joints in men and children; for in a man, from the junction of the shoulder to the elbow, and from the elbow to the point of the thumb, and from one shoulder to the other, is in each case the length of two heads, but in a child it is only one, because nature first creates the size of the seat of the intellect, before that of the vital spirits.

*103* 290. *How children's joints differ in size from those of men./*
*103v* All the joints of little children are thin, and the spaces between them are thick. This happens because the skin over the joints has no other flesh than that which is in the nature of sinew, which connects and binds the bones together, and the fat fleshy part lies between one joint and the other, held between the skin and the bone; but since the bones are thicker at the joints than between them, when a man grows, his flesh loses that superfluity which was between the skin and the bone, on which account the skin clings closer to the bone, and those parts of the body grow thinner. But there is nothing over the joints but cartilaginous and sinewy skin, that cannot dry out, and because it cannot dry out it does not decrease. For these reasons little children are thinner in the joints and thicker between the joints, as is seen in the joints of the fingers, arms, and shoulders which are thin, with deep dimples; but a man, on the contrary, is thick in all his joints, in the fingers, arms and legs, and the places which in little children are hollows, in men are in relief.

291. *Of the general measurements of bodies.* I say that the general *104*
measurements should be observed in the length of figures, and
not in their thickness. Among the praiseworthy and marvelous
things that appear in the works of nature, is the remarkable fact
that none of its works in any species precisely resembles any other
in detail. Therefore, you/imitator of that nature, note and be *104v and*
attentive to the great variations of contours. I would be well *illus.*
pleased to have you avoid monstrous things, such as long legs
with short torsos, narrow chests with long arms. So take the
measurements of length in the joints as constants, and when it
comes to the thicknesses in which they vary greatly, vary them
also.

But if you wish to make your figures on the basis of one and
the same measurement, know that they cannot then be distinguished from one another, which is something never seen in
nature.

[CHANGES IN THE MEASUREMENTS OF THE BODY AS IT MOVES]

292. *Of the changes in the measurements of man through move- 103
ment of his limbs in different directions.*[2] The measurements of
a man change on one side or another, as he bends, diminishing
or increasing more or less on one side as much as they increase or
diminish on the opposite side.

293. *Of man's bending and stretching.* When a man bends to one *113 and*
side, the length of that side diminishes as much as the length of *illus.*
the opposite side increases, to the point where the bent side is one
half as long as the extended side. A special treatise will be written
on this.

294. *Of the motion of animals.* Every living creature with two *124v*
feet, when it moves lowers the side over the raised foot more
than the side over the foot that rests on the ground, but the
upper part of its body does just the contrary. This is seen in the

---

[2] This section begins the Third Part. It is preceded by the statement: Comincia
de i uari accidenti et mouimenti del Huomo, e'prima (Here begins the part on
the various conditions and movements of man, and first . . .) Later, Hand I
crossed out the words from "e'prima" through "aspetti," and proposed to insert,
instead, the words: et proportione di membra (and proportions of members), as
indicated in the margin.

125 hips and/shoulders of a man when he walks, and in birds the same thing happens with the head and the tail.

129v 295. *Of the relation in size of each half of a man to the other half.*
130 /The thickness and breadth of one half of a man will never equal the other, unless the limbs of that half move in the same way.

104v and 296. *Of the measurements of the human body and the flexings*
illus. *of the limbs.* Necessity requires the painter to know the bones that sustain and protect the flesh that rests on them, and the joints that increase or decrease as they bend, on which account the measurement of the extended arm is not the same as that of C, the bent arm.

The arm increases and diminishes by one-eighth of its total length its farthest extension and its bending.

The lengthening and shortening of the arm bone come about through the bone which advances beyond the elbow joint of the arm, which, as can be seen in the figure, A B, increases the length from the shoulder to the elbow, when the angle of the elbow is less than a right angle, and increases the more as that angle diminishes, and diminishes all the more as that angle becomes greater.

105 The space from the shoulder/to the elbow increases more as the angle of the bend of the elbow becomes less than a right angle, and decreases more as that angle becomes greater than a right angle.

121 297. *Of limbs of the body that bend and the function of the flesh that covers them where they bend.* The flesh that covers the joints of bones and other parts near them, increases and diminishes in thickness according to the bending or extending of those parts; that is, it increases on the side inside the angle that is created through the bending of the limbs, but becomes thinner and extended on the side outside the external angle; and in the middle, lying between the convex and concave angles, it shares, more or less, in such increase or decrease, depending on nearness or remoteness to the angles of the bent joints.

104 298. *Of the joints of the shoulders and their increase and decrease.*
The joints of the shoulders and the other flexible parts of the body

ill be discussed in the proper place in the treatise on anatomy,
where will be shown the motions of all the parts of which man
s composed.

99. *Of the joints of the fingers.* The joints of the fingers of the   *103v*
and thicken on every/side when they bend, and the more they   *104*
re bent, the more they thicken, and they also diminish the more
he fingers straighten out. The same thing happens with the
oes, which change more the fleshier they are.

00. *Of the joint of the hand with the arm.* The wrist or joint   *105*
f the arm and the hand decreases when the hand closes, and
ncreases when the hand opens. The arm does the contrary on
ll sides between the elbow and the hand, and this comes about
ecause when the hand opens, the inside muscles distend and
hin the arm between elbow and hand; and when the hand closes,
he inner and the outer muscles shorten and swell, but only the
uter muscles separate from the bone because they are stretched
oy the closing of the hand.

01. *Of the joints of the feet and their increase and decrease.* Only   *105*
he decrease and increase of the joint of the foot or ankle is shown
on the outside in D E F, which increases when the angle of the
oint/becomes more acute, and decreases by as much as the angle   *105v and*
oecomes obtuse, that is, speaking of the front of the joint, A   *illus.*
nd D.[3]

302. *Of limbs that diminish when they are bent, and increase*   *105v*
*when they are extended.* Of the limbs that have flexible joints,
the knee is the only one which grows thinner when bent and
thicker when extended.

303. *Of limbs that become thicker in the joints when they are bent.*   *105v*
All the limbs of man, except his legs, become thicker when bent at
their joints.

304. *Of bending.* Flexible parts of the body lengthen as much on   *113 and*
one side as they shorten on the other. The central outer line of   *illus.*

[3] This and the preceding section are not entirely clear, and the lettering of the
figure is probably incorrect.

the sides of flexible parts that are unbent never increase or diminish in length.

[WHEN MUSCLES ARE EMPHASIZED]

*118v* 305. *Of the lengthening and shortening of muscles.* The muscle at the back of the thigh varies more in its extension and contraction than any other muscle in man; the second is that which composes the buttock; the third that of the back; the fourth that
*119* of/the neck; the fifth that of the shoulders; sixth, that of the abdomen, which originates below the breast and terminates in the pubis. Thus all will be discussed.

*119* 306. *Of the muscle between the chest and pubis.* There is a muscle which begins near the breast and ends at the pubis, which has three functions, since it is divided lengthwise by three ligaments; that is, first there is the upper muscle and then follows a
*119v* tendon as broad as the muscle; next follows/the second muscle lower down, with which the second tendon is connected; finally there follows the third muscle with the third tendon, which is attached to the pubic bone.

These three groups of three muscles with three tendons are produced by nature for the large motion made by a man in bending or extending by means of this muscle, which, if it were in one piece, would cause too much variation when expanded or contracted, as a man bends or stretches. It would be more beautiful in man to have little variation in that muscle in his actions: the muscle has to extend in distance the breadth of nine fingers and then contract as much, but the division of the muscle causes only the width of three fingers to be involved in each muscle, which results in little variation in their shapes and so deforms the beauty of the body only a little.

*109v* 307. *Of placing the parts of the body.* Depict as muscular the parts of the body which endure strain, and portray those which are not exercised without muscles and soft.

*110v* 308. *Of composition of the parts of the bodies of nudes and their functioning.* The muscles of the parts of the nude should show more or less distinctly, according to the greater or lesser strain imposed on them.

309. *Of not including all the muscles of figures unless they are* 116v
*exerting great force.* Do not try to make all the muscles of your
figures apparent/because even if they are in the right places, they 117
do not show very clearly unless the parts in which they are
located are exerting great force or are greatly strained; the muscles
of those parts which are unexercised should not show. If you do
otherwise, you will make something that looks more like a bag
of nuts than a human figure.

310. *Of the limbs of nude men.* Nude men, engaged in various 105v
tiring activities, display their muscles on that side of the body on
which the muscles are at work; and the muscles of the other
parts are more or less prominent according to whether they are
more or less strained.

311. *Of the disposition of limbs in relation to forms.* Thicken the 123
muscles of the limbs when they are being exercised, and make
them correspond to their activity, and keep those smooth which
are not being exercised.

312. *Which are the muscles that disappear in the diverse move-* 116v
*ments of man?* The breasts disappear, or gain greater relief on
raising or lowering the arms, and the same is done by the flesh
in relief, such as the hips when bent outward or inward. The
shoulders, the hips and the neck display greater variations than
any other articulation, because they have the most manifold
motions, and on this a special book will be written.

313. *Of the display or concealment of the muscles of each part* 110v
*in the attitudes of living creatures.* I remind you, painter, that in
the movements which you represent/as being made by your fig- 111
ures, you should make distinct only those muscles which function
in the motion and action of your figure, so that the muscle which
is most exercised in such case is most distinct, and that which is
not exercised at all remains relaxed and soft and little apparent.

On this account I urge you to study the anatomy of the muscles, sinews and bones, without knowledge of which you will do
little. If you draw from life, perhaps the model whom you select
will lack good muscles in the action which you wish him to take.
But you cannot always conveniently find good nude models, nor

can you always draw them. It is better for you and more useful to practice such variety and to keep it in memory.

*119*  314. *Where tendons without muscles are found in man.* Where the arm terminates in the palm of the hand, near the four fingers there is found a tendon without muscle, the largest in man. It originates in the middle of the lower arm bone and terminates in the middle of the other arm bone, and it has a square shape, and is about three fingers broad and half a finger thick. It serves only to keep the two forearm bones together so that they do not separate.

*119*  315. *Of the eight bones which exist in the middle of the tendons in various joints of man.* There are in the joints of man some small pieces of bone which are firmly placed in the middle of tendons that connect certain joints, as in the kneecaps and the shoulder blades, and the instep. These amount to eight in all, since there is one for each shoulder, one for each knee, and two for each foot under the first joint of the big toe, toward the heel. These become very hard with increasing age.

*121v-122*  316. *Of creases in the flesh.*/The flesh is always creased and wrinkled on the side opposite to that which is stretched.

*107*  317. *Of parts of the body.* All parts of the body should exercise that function for which they were destined. In the dead or the
*107v*  sleeping no part should appear alive or awake./A foot that receives the weight of a man's body should lie flat, without play of the toes, unless the weight rests on the heel.

[EXAGGERATED MUSCLES SHOULD BE AVOIDED]

*116*  318. *Quality of nudes.* Never make a slender figure with muscles too greatly in relief, for slender men never have too much flesh on their bones; they are slender through lack of flesh, and where there is little flesh, there cannot be thickness of muscles.

*117v*  319. *That the muscles of nude figures should not be stressed too much.* None of the muscles in nude figures should be stressed too much, because the figures become tiresome and unattractive.

You should know all the muscles of man, but make less marked those on that side where a man does not exert effort.

That part of the body which exerts itself most should be the one that displays its muscles most.

On that side to which the limb turns when it exercises its function, the muscles should be most pronounced.

The muscle itself is usually shown in detail through exercise and in a way not otherwise seen.

320. *Of the quality of parts of the body in relation to age.* In *123* youths you will not look for muscles or tendons, but soft fleshiness, with simple creases and roundness of limbs.

321. *Of muscles.* In youth muscles should not be emphasized, *116v* because these are a sign of mature strength, and in youths there is no effect of time.

Let the play of parts of the body be more or less distinct, as they are more or less exercised.

The muscles of those parts which are exercised with the greatest effort will always be most apparent.

Those muscles will be least in relief which are exercised with least effort.

Muscles which are exercised are always in greater relief and thicker than those which are at rest.

The central inside lines of limbs that bend never retain their natural length.

Thick, broad muscles should be made for the powerful, with limbs that are consistent with such an organism.

322. *Of the composition of the parts of animals.* All the parts of *123v* any living creature should correspond to the age of the whole; that is, the limbs of the young should not be worked out with emphatic muscles, tendons and veins, as some portray them, who, to display clever and great design, spoil the whole by interchanging parts of the body, and the same thing is done by others who, through inability to draw, give old men the limbs of young ones.

323. *Of the harmony of limbs.* I remind you again to pay great *126v* attention to giving the figure limbs that will appear to be suitable to the size of the body, and also to its age; that is, young men with little muscle in their limbs, few veins, and a soft sur-

face rounded and with an agreeable color. Mature men should
*127* be sinewy and full of muscles, while old men should have/skin
full of wrinkles, folds and veins, with conspicuous sinews.

*118* 324. *How nature tries to conceal the bones of animals, insofar as
the arrangement of their parts permits.* Nature tries to conceal
the bones of animals so far as the necessary structure of their
limbs allows, and this occurs more in one body than in another.
It occurs more in bodies where it is not impeded than in those
where it is impeded.

Therefore, in the flower of youth the skin is drawn tight, as
much as possible, provided the body is not fat or corpulent and
has reached its full height. Later through the exercise of the
limbs, the skin is stretched over the bendings of the joints, and
thus, when parts of the body are distended, the skin that has
grown over the joints is wrinkled. Moreover, as they increase
in age muscles become thinner, and the skin that covers them
*118v* grows full of wrinkles,/and becomes slack and separated from
the muscles because it has lost the humors lying between the
muscles and the skin. The ramification of sinews that hold together the skin and the muscles and give them feeling, despoil
parts of the muscles that cover them, and in place of those muscles
they are surrounded by bad humors, and therefore are badly and
inadequately nourished. Because of the weight of the skin and
the abundant bad humors this arrangement of the parts of the
body lengthens and separates the skin from the muscles and the
bones, and produces various sacks full of swellings and wrinkles.

*116* 325. *How muscular men are short and thick.* Muscular men have
thick bones and are short, thick, and lack fat; for the muscles,
because of their growth, are drawn together and leave no room
for the fat which would otherwise lie between them. The muscles in those who are thin, as they are in close contact with one
another and cannot extend, increase in thickness and most of
all in that part which is farthest from the ends, that is, toward
the middle of their breadth and length.

*116* 326. *How fat men do not have thick muscles.* Although fat men
are short and thick in themselves, like the muscular men men-

tioned above, they have soft muscles. Their skin covers a great
deal of fat that is spongy and empty, or full of air, and so these
fat men sustain themselves better in the water than do muscular
men, whose skins are/full, and within whom there is less air. *116v*

327. *Of the muscles of animals.* The concavities between muscles *117 and*
ought not to be such that the skin looks as if it covered two rods *illus.*
in contact, nor two rods separated a little from such contact, with
the skin hanging in an empty space with a long curvature as at
F. It should be like I, placed over the spongy fat between angles,
such as the angle M N O, which originates from the points of
contact of the muscles. So that the skin cannot descend into such
an angle, nature has filled it with a small quantity of spongy fat,
or you might say, with minute vesicles full of air, which condense or become emptier, in accordance with the growth or diminution of the substance of the muscles. It has always greater
curvature than the muscles. . . .[4]

328. *That the nude represented with muscles in full evidence is* *117*
*without motion.* The nude represented with all its muscles clear
and emphasized is without motion, for motion is impossible/un- *117v*
less some of the muscles relax when the opposite muscles pull,
and those which are relaxed lack distinctness, while those which
pull are strongly marked and make themselves apparent.

329. *How it is necessary for the painter to know anatomy.* It is *118v*
a necessary thing for the painter, in order to be good at arrang-
ing parts of the body in attitudes and gestures which can be
represented in the nude, to know the anatomy of the sinews,
bones, muscles, and tendons. He should know their various
movements and force, and which sinew or muscle occasions each
movement, and paint only those distinct and thick, and not the
others, as do many who, in order to appear to be great draughtsmen, make their nudes wooden and without grace, so that they
seem a sack full of nuts rather than the surface of a human being, or indeed, a bundle of radishes rather than muscular nudes.

[4] This section ends in an incomplete clause, which has been crossed out, and
Hand I remarks: ui mancha il fine (the end is lacking).

[BALANCE OF STANDING FIGURES]

*115* 330. *Of balancing the weight about the center of gravity in bodies.* The figure which sustains itself motionless on its feet will automatically place equal weight on opposite sides about its center of gravity.

I say that if the motionless figure is posed on its feet, and an arm is thrust in front of the chest, it will thrust as much natural weight backward as it thrusts natural and accidental weight forward. And I say the same of each part that projects beyond the whole more than is usual.

*129-129v* 331. *Of the balance of a man standing on his feet.*/When a man stands on his feet, he either bears equal weight on each foot or unequal weights on them. If he bears down equally on his feet, it is with his own natural weight combined with added accidental weight, or with simple, natural weight. If it is with natural weight, combined with added accidental weight, then the opposite extremities of his limbs are not equally distant from the poles of the joints of his feet; but if he loads them with simple, natural weight, then the opposite extremities of his limbs will be equally distant from the joint of the foot. A special book will be written about this balance.

*128v and illus.* 332. *The balance of bodies not in motion.* The balance or equilibrium of men is divided into two parts; that is, simple and complex. Simple balance is that of a man on his two motionless legs, above which that man opens his arms at different distances from the center of gravity, or bends while standing on one or both feet; but the center of gravity is always on a perpendicular line through the center of that foot on which the weight rests, and if it rests equally on both feet, then the weight of the man will have its center of gravity on a perpendicular line which divides the space between the centers of his feet.

Complex balance is that of a man who sustains a weight above him by various motions, as in representing Hercules who crushes Antaeus, suspended above the earth between Hercules' chest and arms. Place his figure as far back of the line through the center of his feet as Antaeus' center of gravity lies in front of those feet.

333. *Precept.* The navel is always in the central line of the weight, *160v*
which is in balance above it, and thus takes account of the accidental added weight of a man, as well as his natural weight.
This is shown when the arm is extended, for the fist at its extremity performs the function of the counterpoise at the end of
a steelyard, so that as much weight is necessarily thrown on one
side of the navel as the accidental weight of the fist adds to the
other. It is also suitable that the heel on the side on which the
arm is extended should be raised.

334. *Of the poses of figures.* There should always be variation in *129*
the limbs of posed figures; that is, if one arm goes forward, the
other should be still or go backward, and if the figure poses on
one leg, the shoulder that is above that leg should be lower than
the other. This is the practice of men of sense, who naturally
attend to balancing a man on his feet, so that he does not fall
down; since, when he rests on one foot, the opposite leg does
not sustain that man, and being bent, it is as if it were dead.
It necessarily follows that the weight which is above the legs
should thrust its center of gravity on the joint of the leg that
sustains it.

335. *Of attitudes.* The hollow of the throat lies above the foot *109v*
on which the body rests; when the arm is thrown forward, the
hollow moves to one side of the line of the foot, and if the leg
moves back, the hollow goes forward, and thus it changes with
each attitude.

336. *Of the balance of figures.* If a figure balances on one foot, *113v*
the shoulder on the side on which its weight rests will always be
lower than the other, and the hollow of the throat will be above
the middle of the leg on which the weight rests. The same thing
/will happen along whatever line we view that figure, provided *114*
it is without arms extending very far beyond the figure, or without a weight on its back, in the hand, or on the shoulder, or
extension forward or backward of the leg on which the weight
does not rest.

337. *Of the man who poses on two feet, resting more weight on* *129*
*one foot.* When, because he has long been on his feet, a man

has tired one of the legs on which he stands, he transfers part of his weight to the other leg; but this pose is to be used for the portrayal of advanced old age or for an infant, or for one who really is tired, since it demonstrates fatigue or little strength in the limbs. But one always sees a young man who is healthy and vigorous, resting on one leg, while placing some weight on the other, and he does this when he would begin to move; for without this stance motion is impossible, since motion is created by inequality in the distribution of weight.

115   338. *What are the principal requirements with regard to the figure?* Among the principal and important things that are required in the representation of living creatures, is to place the head well upon the shoulders, the chest upon the hips, and the hips and shoulders upon the feet.

[BALANCE OF STANDING FIGURES]

112v   339. *Of the distribution of man's weight upon his feet.* The weight of a man who rests on only one leg will always be divided equally on each side above the center of gravity and the leg which sustains him.

113   340. *Of equilibrium.* The figure which sustains a weight outside itself and the central line of its mass, must always thrust as much natural or accidental weight on the opposite side, as will bring about a balance of weight about the central line. This line begins at the center of that part of the foot resting on the ground and passes through the whole weight above that part of the foot.

We see that a man who lifts a weight with one arm, naturally thrusts the opposite arm out, and if that is not enough to keep 113v   his balance, he adds as much of his own weight/as necessary, bending sufficiently to resist the added weight. This is seen also in one who is about to fall backward toward one side, for he always thrusts out the arm on the opposite side.

115   341. *Of figures that have to handle or carry weights.* A man never lifts or carries a weight without throwing outside him again as much weight as that which he lifts, and he thrusts it in the direction opposite to that from which he lifts the weight.

342. *Of the man who carries a weight on his shoulders.*/The *112-112v* shoulder sustaining a weight is always higher than the shoulder *and illus.* without a weight, and this is shown by the figure placed in the center, through which passes the central line of all the weight of the man and the weight carried by him. This compound weight, if it were not equally divided above the leg on which it rests, would necessarily fall down. But natural necessity has provided that so much natural weight of a man should be thrust to one side, as there is accidental weight added on the other side. This cannot be done if the man does not bend and if he does not lower the side with the lesser weight enough so that it partakes of the accidental weight carried by him. And this cannot be done if the shoulder with the weight is not raised and the unburdened shoulder is not lowered. This is the expedient which ingenious necessity has found for such an action.

343. *How the whole distribution of a man's weight changes when* *112* *an arm held against the side is extended.* The extension of an arm previously held at the side changes the whole distribution of a man's weight upon the foot which sustains the whole, as is shown by one who, with arms spread, walks a tightrope without any pole.

344. *Of four-footed animals and how they move.* The height of *129v and* the upper part of four-footed animals varies more in those that *illus.* are walking than in those standing still, and does so more or less by as much as those animals are greater or smaller in size. This is caused by the oblique line of the legs that touch the earth, which raise the body of the animal, and when these legs are no longer oblique, they are perpendicular to the earth.

345. *Of the balance of weight on its legs of any motionless animal.* *112v* Loss of motion in any animal that/rests its weight on its feet *113* comes about from loss of inequality between the weights on opposite sides, which are sustained on its feet.

[LOSS OF BALANCE AND MOTION]

346. *Of motion created by the destruction of balance.* Motion is *113v* created by the destruction of balance, that is, of equality of weight, for nothing can move by itself which does not leave its

state of balance, and that thing moves most rapidly which is farthest from its balance.

111v 347. *Of the motion in man and other animals when running.* When a man or other creature moves either rapidly or slowly, that side which is above the leg that sustains the body will always be lower than the opposite side.

112v 348. *Of man in motion.* The center of gravity of a man in motion will be over the center of the leg which rests on the ground.

112 349. *Of man and other animals whose center of gravity is not too remote from their supports when they move slowly.* That animal which moves most slowly will have the center of gravity of its supporting legs nearest the perpendicular line of the center of gravity of its whole body. Conversely, that animal which moves most rapidly will have the center of its supports farthest from its center of gravity.

129v 350. *Of more or less rapid motion from position.* Man or any other animal will move from position with more or less velocity, in proportion as the center of gravity is farther away from or nearer to the center of the sustaining foot.

111v 351. *When, during a man's actions, the difference in the height of his shoulders is greatest.* There will be the greatest difference in height between the shoulders or sides of man or another animal when the whole is in slowest motion. The converse follows; that there will be the least difference in height in those parts of an animal whose whole is in most rapid motion.

This is proved by the ninth proposition of motion from position, where it is stated: every weight presses along the line of its motion. Therefore, when the whole moves toward some point, the part united to it follows the shortest line of the motion of the whole, without itself weighing down the lateral parts of that whole.

OBJECTIONS: The objector says with regard to the first part of the above, that it is not necessary for a man who is standing still or who walks with a slow motion, continually to employ the above-mentioned redistribution of weight of his body over the

center of gravity, which sustains the weight of the whole. There
are many times, he says, when/a man does not employ or observe  *112 and*
any such rule, rather the contrary. Sometimes he bends sideways,  *illus.*
while standing on only one leg, and sometimes he rests part of
his weight on the leg which is not straight, that is, the one which
bends at the knee, as is shown in the two figures B, C.

The reply is that what is not done by the shoulders in figure
C, is done by the hips, as will be shown in the proper place.

352. *Of the motion and course of animals.* That figure will ap-  *138v*
pear swiftest in its course, which is about to fall forward.

353. *Of bodies which move by themselves, either quickly or*  *138v*
*slowly.* A body which moves by itself will be faster, the more
its center of gravity is distant from the center of its support. This
is said with regard to the motion of birds which, without beat-
ing their wings or without favor of the wind, move by themselves, and this happens when their center of gravity is beyond
the center of their support, that is, beyond the middle of the resistance of their wings. If the middle of the wings is behind the
middle or center of gravity of the whole bird, then that bird will
move forward and down. But it will move forward rather than
down to the degree that the center of gravity is distant from the
center of the wings. This makes the descent of the bird very
oblique, and if the center of gravity is near the middle of the/  *139*
wings the descent of the bird will be less oblique.

354. *Of the figure which moves against the wind.* The figure  *137 and*
which moves against the wind along any line of direction at all  *illus.*
never preserves its center of gravity in proper relation to the
center of its support.

355. *Of the movements of man and other animals.* The motions  *111*
of animals are of two kinds, that is, motion in space and contained motion. Motion in space is that of the animal moving from
place to place, and contained motion is that which the animal
makes within itself without change of place.

Motion in space is of three kinds, that is, ascending, descending,
and motion on a level, and to these three are added two qualifi-
cations: that is, slowness and rapidity, and two additional forms

of motion: which are straight and tortuous motion, and then one more, that is, the motion of leaping.

But contained motion is infinite, like the infinite actions in which, not without danger to himself, a man engages.

Motions are of three general kinds; that is, motion in space, simple contained motion, and the third, motion compounded of contained motion and motion in space.

Slowness and rapidity ought not to be counted among motions in space but are incidental conditions of those motions.

*111v* /Compound motions are infinite, and among them are: dancing, fencing, playing, sowing, plowing, and rowing, but rowing is really a simple contained motion, because contained motion made by man in rowing is not combined with man's motion in space, but with the motion of the boat.

[TYPES OF MOVEMENT AND THEIR INFINITE VARIATIONS]

*122* 356. *Of man's simple movement.* That is called simple movement in man when he simply bends forward, or backward, or to the side.

*122* 357. *Of man's compound movement.* That is called a compound movement in man when some purpose requires bending down and to the side at the same time.

Therefore, painter, portray compound movements that are integrated in their composition; that is, if a man makes a compound movement, because the action makes this necessary, do not represent it contrariwise by having him make a simple movement, which will be quite different from that action.

*107* 358. *Of the joints of limbs.* Observe the joints of the parts of the body, and the various ways in which they bend, with regard to how the flesh increases on one side and diminishes on the other. This is to be studied in the necks of animals, as their motions are of three kinds, two of which are simple, and one compounded of the two simple ones. One of the simple motions occurs when either of the shoulders is bent, or the head poised on them is raised or lowered; and the second occurs when the neck bends to the right or the left without curving, but remains straight, while it turns the face toward one of the shoulders; and the third, which is called compound, occurs when the head twists as well as bends, as occurs when the ear is inclined toward one of the shoulders, and the face is turned toward the same side or to the opposite shoulder, with the face turned to the sky.

359. *Of the shoulders.* The principal movements made by the *104* shoulder joints are simple, that is, when the arm joined to a shoulder moves up, down, forward, or backward, although it might be said that such motions are infinite, because if you turn the shoulders to the side of a wall, and trace a circular figure with the arm, you will make all the motions of the shoulder. And because every circle is a continuous quantity, therefore it is a continuous quantity that is made by the motion of the arm. But that motion does not produce a continuous quantity unless that continuation makes it so. Thus the motion of the arm has been through every part of the circle, and since this circle is infinitely divisible, the different positions of the shoulders are also infinite in number.

360. *Of human motion.* When you would represent a man mov- *113v* ing some weight, consider that motions are made along different lines, that is, raising the weight from below upward with a simple motion, as does one who, bending over, lifts the weight which he would raise by straightening himself. When he would drag something after him, or push it in front, or pull it down with a rope that passes through a pulley it is noted that the weight of a man pulls as much as his center of gravity is beyond the center of his support, and to this is added the force exerted by the legs, and by the bent back as it straightens out.

Whenever a man goes down or up or walks in any direction the heel of the foot in back is raised.

361. *Of the same action seen from varied points.* The same action *110v* will appear to be infinitely different because it can be seen from an infinite number of positions which have continuous quantity, and continuous quantity is divisible to infinity. Therefore, infinitely different points show that every human action is in itself infinite.

110v 362. *Of the movements of man and other animals.* The movements of a man in a given action are infinitely varied in themselves. The proof is this: let a man be striking some object. I say that the striking occurs in two directions; either he is raising the implement that is to descend when creating the stroke, or he is making a descending motion. In either case it will not be denied that the motion is made in space and that space is a continuous quantity and that any continuous quantity is infinitely divisible. Therefore it is concluded that every motion of an implement that descends is infinitely variable.

130 and illus. 363. *That it is impossible for any memory to preserve all the aspects and changes of the parts of the body.* It is impossible for any memory to retain all the aspects or changes of any member of any animal whatsoever. This we shall demonstrate by analyzing the movement of a hand.

Because every continuous quantity is infinitely divisible, the motion of the eye which looks at the hand as it moves from A to B, moves through the space A B which is also a continuous quantity and consequently infinitely divisible, and in each part 130v of its motion changes the aspect/and shape of the hand as it is seen, and thus it moves through the whole circle.

The hand which rises in its motion does likewise; that is, it will pass through space, which is a continuous quantity.

## [PUSHING AND PULLING]

128 364. *Of the motion of figures in pushing or pulling.* Pushing and pulling are one and the same motion, for pushing is only an extension of parts of the body and pulling is a contraction of those parts, and to both forces there is added the weight of him who moves against the thing pushed or pulled. There is no other difference except that one pushes and the other pulls. He who pushes standing on his feet has the thing to be moved in front of him, and he who pulls has it in back of him.

Pushing and pulling can be done along different lines in relation to the center of force of him who moves, a center which, with respect to the arms, is in the place where the sinew of the upper arm of the shoulder, that of the breast, and that of the socket alongside the breast, meet with the bone of the upper shoulder.

365. *Of the compound force of a man, and first that of his arms* *120* *will be discussed.* The muscles which move the larger bone of the arm, in extending and retracting the arm, originate one behind the other about the middle/of the bone called assistant *120v and* (ulna). The muscle which extends the arm develops in back and *illus.* the muscle which bends it is in front.

Whether a man is more powerful in pulling or in pushing is proved by the ninth proposition on weights, where it is stated: Of weights of equal power that one appears more powerful which is farther away from the fulcrum of balance. It follows that the muscle H B and the muscle H C, being muscles of equal power, the muscle in front, H C, has more strength than the muscle in back H B, because it is attached to the arm at C, a position more remote from the fulcrum of the elbow at A than is B, which is on the other side of that fulcrum, and so the question is determined. But this is a simple and not a compound force, which is what is to be treated, and we should put this first.

A compound force is that which, when the arms are at work, has a second power added, that of the weight of the person, and of the legs, as in pulling and pushing. To the power of the arms there is added the weight of the person, the force of the back and of the legs, which occurs in the effort to stretch, as would be the case of two men at a column, one of whom pushes the column while the other pulls it.

366. *Which is the greater power in a man, that of pulling or* *120v* *pushing?* A man has much greater power in pulling than in pushing, because in pulling there is added the power of those muscles/of the arms, which are designed only for pulling and *121* not for pushing, for when the arm is straight, the muscles which move the elbow cannot have any further action in pushing, any more than a man would have by leaning his shoulder against the thing which he would remove from its place, an action in which only the sinews which straighten the curved back are employed, with those which straighten the bent leg and are under the thigh and in the calf behind the leg.

Thus it is concluded that in pulling there is added the power of the arms and the powerful force of the back and of the legs, together with the weight of the man, in the way required by his oblique posture; and in pushing, the same things occur without the power of the arms, because pushing with a straight arm, without motion, does no more than would a piece of wood laid between the shoulder and the thing that is pushed.

## [FORCEFUL MOTIONS]

*122* 367. *Of motions appropriate to men's actions.* The motions of your figures should be expressive of the kind of force that it is appropriate to use for different actions; that is, do not make a man display the same strength to lift a stick which would be suitable to lift a rafter. Therefore, make your figures ready to display their strength according to the kinds of loads they handle.

*120 and illus.* 368. *Of the use of force by a man who would strike a great blow.* When a man prepares to make a forceful motion, he bends and twists as much as he can in the direction contrary to that where he wishes the blow to fall, and thus he prepares a force as great as is possible for him, which he then brings together and, with a compound motion, launches upon the thing struck.

*105v and illus.* 369. *Of powerful motions of man's limbs.* That arm will have the more powerful and longer motion which, on moving from its natural position, has the most powerful support from other parts of the body to project it to the position desired. For example, the man first moves his arm back to C, and then carries it to the opposite side by moving his whole body to B.

*128v and illus.* 370. *Why he who drives an iron spear into the ground raises the opposite leg in a curve.* He who would drive or push a spear into the ground raises the leg opposite the arm that is exerted, and that leg bends at the knee, and causes the body to balance on the foot that rests on the ground; and without this bending or twisting of the leg the action could not be effected, nor could he drive the spear in if that leg were not extended.

*128 and illus.* 371. *Of the man who would throw an object away from himself with great energy.* The man who wants to throw a spear or rock or something else with an energetic motion, can be represented in two principal ways: that is, you can represent him when he is preparing to make the motion, or when the motion itself is made. If you represent him beginning the motion, then the inner side of the outstretched foot will be in line with the chest, and will bring the opposite shoulder over the foot on which his weight rests. That is: the right foot will be under his weight, and the left shoulder will be above the tip of the right foot.

372. *That those who are inclined to be fat, increase a good deal* 117v *in strength after their early youth.* Those who put on fat increase a good deal in strength after early youth, since the skin is always drawn over the muscles; but such persons are not too dexterous and agile in their movements; and because their skin is tight, they have great general power infused into all parts of their bodies./From this it comes about that those who lack such 118 a disposition of the skin help themselves by wearing their clothes tight around their bodies, and bind themselves with various bandages so that when their muscles are condensed they may have points at which they can be pressed together and supported.

But when the fat is reduced, many are enfeebled, because the collapse of the skin leaves it slack and wrinkled, and when the muscles do not find support, they cannot condense or make themselves hard; whence they remain of slight strength.

Medium fatness which is not collapsed through sickness results in the skin being drawn over the muscles, and these muscles are little manifest on the surface of bodies.

373. *Of the movements of man.*/The highest and principal part 105v-106 of the art of painting is the invention of the component parts for *and illus.* the composition of a theme.

And the second part is that of movement, where the people represented should be intent on what they are doing. Their actions should be executed with alertness, corresponding to the degrees of their activity, apathetic as well as diligent, and the urgency of ferocity should be extremely expressive, as is expected of one who is moved by that emotion. For example, when a man is to cast darts, stones or something of the sort, the figure should display the utmost concern in his action. Here are two figures in different kinds of action and power. The first in vigor is figure A, the second in movement is B. But A will cast farther the thing thrown by him than will B, because although both display the intent to throw the weight on the same side, A having turned his feet toward it, twists and moves himself from there to the opposite side, where, when he gathers his strength and prepares to throw, he turns with speed and ease to the position where he lets the weight leave his hands. But in this same case, figure B, having his feet turned in the direction contrary to the target at which he would cast the weight, twists himself with great inconvenience, and consequently the effect is weak and the movement is like its cause. The preparation of force in each movement should be carried out with twistings and/bendings of great violence, and the release with ease and facility, so that the action has a good result. If a cross-bow is not drawn with violent intent, the movement of the arrow will amount to little or nothing. Because where there is no release of energy, there is no motion, and where no tension has been acquired, it cannot be released, and thus the bow that has no suspended energy cannot create motion; it must acquire tension, and after acquiring it must release it.

*106v*

Thus the man who does not twist or bend has not acquired power. Therefore, when B has thrown his spear he will find himself twisted and weak on that side on which he has thrown his weapon and he has acquired power enough only to return to the opposite direction.[5]

*123* 374. *Of the eighteen positions of man.* To be still, to move, to run, to be upright, to be supported, to sit, to bend over, to kneel, to lie down, to be suspended, to carry, to be carried, to push, to pull, to strike, to be struck, to make heavy, to lighten.

*121-121v* 375. *Of turning the leg without turning the thigh./*It is impossible to turn the leg from the knee outward, without turning the thigh with an equal motion. This is so because the bone of

[5] This section is damaged.
[6] The word "otto" in the heading is an obvious error for "diciotto," as shown by the heading of the same passage in the autograph MS of Leonardo da Vinci.

the knee joint has contact with the bone of the thigh, and is connected and combined with the bone of the leg in such a way that the joint can move only forward and backward as is required in walking and kneeling, but it can never move laterally from the joint, because the parts which meet and which compose the joint of the knee do not permit this. If this joint were flexible and pliable as is the bone that is part of the shoulder and that which is part of the hip, a man would always have legs as easily turned toward the two sides as they move forward and backward, and his legs would always be twisted. But the joint cannot go beyond the straight line of the leg, and it is pliable only forward and not backward, because, if it bent backward, a man could not rise to his feet from a kneeling position. On rising from a kneeling position on both knees, a man first rests the weight of his body on one of his knees and releases the weight from the other. At that time the other leg feels no weight but its own, so that it easily raises the knee from the ground and places the sole of the foot so that it rests completely on the ground. Then the man places all the weight on this foot, pressing it on the ground, and pressing one hand on the knee, and at the same time extending the other arm, which brings the chest and the head up, and thus he stretches, straightening up the thigh and the chest, and draws himself upright on that foot that rests on the ground, until the other leg is raised.

376. *How there are three movements when a man jumps upward.* 130

When a man jumps upward, the head has three times the velocity of the heel of the foot, before the tip of the foot leaves the ground, and twice the velocity of the hips. This occurs because three angles open at the same time, of which the uppermost is where the trunk joins the thighs in front; the second is where the backs of the thighs join the backs of the legs; and the third is where the fronts of the legs join the bones of the feet.

377. *Of jumping and what helps the jump.* Nature teaches us, 127v and works so that the jumper does not need to reflect, but when he wishes to jump, he simply raises his arms and shoulders energetically. These then move together with a large part of the body

to raise him up until the energy is exhausted, and this energetic movement is accompanied by the sudden stretching of the body bent in a curve of the backbone, and in the joints of the thighs, knees, and feet. This stretching is made obliquely, that is forward and upward, and thus the motion intended for walking forward carries forward the jumping body, and the motion of

*128* rising raises the body and produces a great/arch, increasing the jump.

*127v* 378. *Of a man's rising up from sitting on level ground.* When a man is seated on the floor, the first thing he does in raising himself is to draw a leg toward him and place his hand on the ground on that side on which he wishes to arise, and he thrusts the weight of his body on that arm, and puts his knee to the ground on that side on which he wishes to arise.[7]

*119v and illus.* 379. *Of the farthest twist that a man can make in looking backward.* The farthest that a man can twist is when he shows the back of his heel and the front of his face at the same time. But this is not done without difficulty, unless the leg is bent and the shoulder lowered, as he looks backward. The cause of this twisting will be shown in the books on anatomy, discussing which muscles move first and last.

*119v* 380. *How near one arm can be brought to the other, in back.* When the arms are placed in back, the elbows never come closer

*120 and illus.* together than enough for the longest finger to pass/the elbow of the opposite arm; that is, the closest that the elbows held behind the back can come to one another will be the space from the elbow to the end of the longest finger of the hand. The arms thus placed make a perfect square.

---

[7] At the end of this section, Hand 1 has written: Trovo scritto apresso al capitulo di sopra il suggeitto del suo contrario ma poi nõ ne parla niẽte et e' questo.*
  * Del cadere l'huomo a' sedere in sito piano.
(After the chapter above I find written a heading for a chapter on the opposite action but he says nothing about it. The heading is this*
  * Of a man's falling into a seated position on the flat ground.)
This section is numbered 389 by Ludwig but it is omitted by Borzelli from the text, and placed in a note.

381. *How far the arms can be brought over the chest with the* 120
*elbows over the center of the chest.* The elbows, with the shoulders and upper arms, make an equilateral triangle.

[GRACE AND VARIETY IN FIGURES]

382. *Of the grace of limbs.* The parts of the body should be ar- 114
ranged gracefully with regard to the effect that you wish the
figure to create. If you wish the figure to display attractiveness,
you should make it delicate and elongated, without showing too
many muscles, and those few which you deliberately bring out,
make soft, that is, with little distinctness, and their shadows without tint, and the limbs, especially the arms, relaxed, that is, no
limb in a straight line with the part of the body joined to it. If
the hips, the poles of the human figure, are placed so that the
right hip is higher than the left, you will make the articulation
of the higher shoulder so that a perpendicular line from it would
fall on the uppermost part of the hip. And let the right shoulder
be lower than the left, while the pit of the neck should always be
in line with the middle of the articulation of the foot on which
the weight rests, and the leg on which it does not rest, should
have the knee lower than that of the other and near to the
other leg.

The attitudes of the head and arms are infinite in number and
so I shall not undertake to give any rule for them, but simply
say that they should be easy and agreeable with different inclinations, and the joints that are there should be united intelligently, so that they will not seem to be pieces of wood.

383. *Of the freedom of limbs.* With regard to the freedom of 114
limbs, you will have to/consider that when you would represent 114v
a man who, for some reason, has to turn backward or to the side,
you should not make him move his feet and all the parts of his
body on that side on which he moves his head, but you will work
by dividing that turning among four articulations; that is, those
of the feet, the knees, the hips, and the neck. If he is posed
on the right leg, you will make the knee of the left bend inward,
and the foot will be raised somewhat outward, and the left
shoulder should be somewhat lower than the right, and the nape

of the neck turned in the same direction as the outside of the ankle of the left foot, and the left shoulder should be in a perpendicular line over the point of the right foot. Always use the figure in such a way that wherever the head is turned, the chest is not turned in the same direction, since, for our convenience, nature has made the neck so that it can easily serve us by turning in different directions, wherever the eye wishes to turn, and the other joints are in part obedient to it.

If you depict the man seated, and if his arms sometimes are occupied horizontally with something, make the upper body turn above the joint of the hip.

*106* 384. *Of the attitudes and movements of limbs.* Identical movements should not be repeated in a figure, in the parts of its body, its hands, or fingers, nor should the same attitudes be repeated among the figures in a narrative painting. If the narrative painting be a very large one, such as a fight with slaughter of soldiers —where there are only three ways of fighting, that is, the thrust, the back-hand and the slash—even in this case you must be careful that all those who slash shall be seen from different sides. That is to say, some have their backs turned, while some are seen from the side and others from in front, and all the other views of the same three movements will partake of these three simple motions. Therefore we call all the others participants in one of these three simple motions. But compound motions in battles are matters of great artifice and of great vivacity and movement, and these movements are called compound when, *107* for example, a single figure shows you/the legs from in front and the side of the shoulder in profile. Of these compound motions something will be said in another place.

*122* 385. *Of the motions of figures.* Never make heads straight on the shoulders, but turn them to the right side or to the left, even though they look down, or upward, or straight ahead, because it is necessary for them to look lively and awake and not asleep. And do not depict the front or the rear half of the whole person *122v* /so that too much straightness is displayed, one half above or below the other half; and if you should wish to use stiff figures, do so only in portraying old people. Also, do not repeat the

movements of the arms or legs in the same figure nor in the bystanders and those near at hand, unless the needs of the situation
that is represented require it.

In these precepts of painting an inquiry is made as to the best
way to understand the nature of motions that carry conviction,
as orators do with words, which they say must not be repeated
except in exclamations. But in painting this does not happen, because exclamations occur in different successive moments, but
repetitions of an action are seen all at the same time.

386. *Of a single figure not in narrative painting.* Again, do not *114v*
repeat the same movements in the parts of the body of a figure
which you represent as alone. That is, if the figure appears to
be running alone, do not paint both hands in front, but one forward and the other behind, because otherwise the figure could not
be running, and if the right foot is forward, the right arm should
be in back and the left one forward, because unless the figure
is so disposed, it cannot run well. If/you depict one who is seated, *115*
he should have one leg thrust somewhat forward and show the
other in line with the head, and the arm above should change
in position and go forward. This will be discussed fully in the
book on movements.

[DECORUM AND PROPRIETY]

387. *Of the observation of decorum.* Observe decorum, that is, *125v*
the appropriateness of the action, clothing, and place, and respect
the high or low rank of that which you represent; that is, a king
should have a beard, and a serious expression and attire, and the
place depicted be adorned, the bystanders should be respectful
and admiring, with fine attire suitable to the dignity of a royal
court. Common people should be shown unadorned, disarrayed
and abject; and the bystanders should be similar, with low and
presumptuous gestures, and all of them should correspond to
such a composition. The acts of an old man should not be similar
to those of a young one, nor those of a woman like those of a
man, nor those of a man like those of a child.

388. *Of motions appropriate to men of varying ages.* Motions will *110*
be appropriately of greater or lesser liveliness and dignity, ac-

cording to the age, well-being and importance of him who makes the motion; that is, the motions of an old man or of a child will not be lively as are those of a young man, and the motion of a king or other dignitary ought to be one of greater gravity and

*110v* worthy of more reverence than those of a porter/or any other ordinary man.

*115v* 389. *Variety of attitudes.* The actions of men are to be expressed according to their ages and ranks, and vary according to sex: that is, male and female.

*127* 390. *Of the poses of children.* Infants and old men should not
*127v* make lively motions with/their legs.

*125v-126* 391. *Kinds of men in narrative composition.*/Ordinarily, in usual narrative compositions, introduce few old men, and separate them from the young ones, because old men are few and their habits do not agree with those of the young, and where there is no conformity in habits there is no friendship, and where there is no friendship, separation is created. But where, in narrative compositions, there is gravity and men are taking council, introduce few young men, because young men deliberately avoid councils and other noble things.

*127v* 392. *Of the poses of women and girls.* Women and girls should not have their legs raised nor too far apart, because that shows boldness and general lack of modesty, while straight legs indicate timidity and modesty.

*125v* 393. *Of the age of figures.* Do not mix a number of boys with as many old men, nor young men with infants, nor women with men, unless the situation which you represent requires you to mix them.

*115v* 394. *Of the attention of bystanders at an unusual event.* At any event worthy of notice all the bystanders react with various gestures of amazement while they consider the event, as when justice punishes malefactors. And if the occasion is one of devotion, all the bystanders direct their eyes to the object of devotion with varying expressions of piety, as the elevation of the Host at the sacrifice of the mass and similar manifestations. If the event is one that calls for laughter or tears, it is not necessary that all bystanders turn their eyes to its cause, but a great many of them should be gay or lament at the same time with different/ *116* gestures, and if the occasion inspires fear, the frightened faces of those who flee should make a great display of fear and flight, with various expressions, as will be said in the fourth book on movement.

395. *Each motion of the figure should be painted in such a way* *110* *that it gives a lifelike effect.* The painted movement appropriate to the mental state of the figure, should be shown with great liveliness, and in the figure depict great emotion and fervor. If this is not done, such a figure will be called twice dead, for it is dead because the figure is an imitation, and dead again, when it does not display motion, either of the mind or of the body.

396. *How the hands and arms must, in all their actions, display* *123v* *the intention of the mind that moves them.* The hands and the arms must, whenever possible, display in all their actions the intention of the mind that moves them, because by means of them whoever has feeling and understanding can follow the mind's intent in all movements. Good orators, when they wish to persuade their hearers of something, always accompany their words with gestures of their hands and arms, although some fools do not so ornament their speeches and on the tribunal seem to be statues of wood through whose mouths the voice of a man, concealed in the tribunal, is conducted by a speaking-tube. This practice is a great defect in the living, and is/even more so in painted *124* figures which, if unaided by their creator with lively gestures, appropriate to the intention that you imagine to be in such a figure, will be judged twice dead, that is, dead because not alive, and dead in lack of gesture. But to return to our intent, here below will be represented and discussed many emotions; that is: of anger, of pain, of sudden fright, of weeping, of flight, of desire, of command, of negligence, of solicitude and the like.[8]

[8] Hand 1 has written at the end of this section: Ma'Notta lettore, che ancora che, Mess, leonardo, prometta di trattare de tutti li sopra detti acidenti, che per questo nóne parla, com'io credo, per smenticanza o'per qualch' altro disturbo, come si po uedere, a'l' originale, che dietro a' questo capitulo scriue, l'argumento

*123* 397. *Of the variety of faces.* The expression of faces should be varied according to the emotions of man, in fatigue, in repose, in anger, in weeping, in laughter, in shouting, fear, and the like.

*123v* At the same time the parts of the body and/the whole attitude should respond to the change in the face.

*109v* 398. *Of the gestures of figures.* Portray figures with a gesture which will be sufficient to show what the figure has in mind, otherwise your art will not be praiseworthy.

*115* 399. *Of the attitudes of men.* Let the attitudes of men and the parts of their bodies be disposed in such a way that these display the intent of their minds.

*123v* 400. *How the figure is not praiseworthy if it does not display the passion of the spirit.* That figure is not praiseworthy if it does not, insofar as is possible, express in gestures the passion of its spirit.

*110* 401. *Of motions appropriate to the mind of him who moves.* The motions and attitudes of figures should display the true mental state of the moving figure, in so true a way that they cannot signify anything else.

*110* 402. *Of the movements of the parts of the body when man is represented, and that these should be appropriate.* That figure, whose movement does not conform to the supposed mental attitude of the figure, shows that the limbs are not obedient to the judgment of that figure, and shows the judgment of the painter also to be of little value.

*125* 403. *If the figures do not express the mind, they are twice dead.* If the figures do not perform lifelike actions, and express the concept of their minds with their limbs, those figures are twice dead, because they are dead to begin with, since painting is not

---

d'un altro senza il suo capitulo et e', il seguente, Del figurare l'irato et in quante parti si diuida tal acidente. (But note, reader, that although Master Leonardo promises to treat all the emotions mentioned above, he does not speak of them, I believe, through forgetfulness or some other accident, as can be seen in the original, for after this chapter he writes the heading of another, without writing the chapter, and it is the following: Of representing an angry man and into how many parts that emotion is divided.) This chapter is numbered 369 by Ludwig, but it is omitted by Borzelli from the text, and placed in a note.

in itself alive but expressive of things alive without being alive in itself, and if it does not add the vivacity of action, it becomes twice dead.

Be sure to take pleasure in studious observation of those who talk together with gestures of their hands. If they are people whom you can approach and so hear what causes them to make such gestures, do so. The details of particular individual actions are very well seen in the case of the dumb, who do not know how to draw, although there are few of these who do not aid themselves by drawing figures. Learn, then, from the dumb to make those gestures with the limbs which express the ideas in the minds of/speakers. Consider those who laugh, and those who *125v* weep, consider those who shout with rage, and likewise all the emotions of our minds. Observe decorum and note that it is not suitable, either with regard to the place or to the action, for the master to act as does the servant, nor the infant as does the adolescent, but rather a small child should act like an old man who can hardly sustain himself. The boor should not act as does a noble and well-mannered man, nor the strong like the weak, nor courtesans like good women, nor males like females.

404. *Of the attitudes of figures.* I say that the painter should note *115v* the attitudes and the motions of men which come about because of some immediate emotion. Let them be noted down or memorized, and do not wait until the action of weeping has to be copied from one who poses as if weeping, but without cause for grief; for drawing it then, such an action, since it does not arise from a real situation, will be neither lively nor natural. But it is good to have noted it first in a natural situation, and then to pose somebody in that act, and then to draw it.

[GESTURES APPROPRIATE TO EMOTIONS AND THEIR INTENSITY]

405. *Of movements.* Make the motions of your figures appropri- *122v* ate to the mental conditions of those figures; that is, if you conceive a man that is enraged, let his face not look the contrary, but depict it so that nothing but rage can be discerned in it; and do the same with regard to joy, melancholy, laughter, tears and the like.

*124v* 406. *Of common motions*. The movements of men are as varied as are the emotions which pass through their minds. And each emotion moves men more or less, depending on its greater or lesser force, and also on the age of the man, for in the same situation a young man will act otherwise than an old one.

*122v* 407. *Of the same emotions that occur in men of diverse ages.* The same degree of change ought not to be expressed through *122* the motions of the body, in the ferocious act/of an old man, as in that of a young one; and a violent act ought not to be represented in a young man as it is in an old one.

*124* 408. *Of motions appropriate to the mind of one who moves.* There are some emotions without bodily gestures and some with bodily gestures. Emotions without bodily action allow the arms to fall, and so the hands, and every other part which shows action. But emotions that have corresponding bodily actions cause the body and its parts to move in accordance with the motion of the mind, and of this many things will be said. There is a third motion which partakes of both attributes, and a fourth which is neither one nor the other, and these last are those of the senseless or *124v* rather those who have lost their senses, and this is to be put/in the chapter on madness and on buffoons and their morris-dances.

*124v* 409. *How mental stimuli move a person with the greatest facility and ease.* Mental stimuli or thoughts produce in the body simple and easy action, and not great coming and going, for the object of attention is in the mind which, concentrated upon itself, does not direct the senses to bodily expression.

*124v* 410. *Of the motion occasioned in the mind by some object.* The motion of man caused by an external object is either caused by an immediate object or not. If it occurs immediately he who moves first turns the eye—the most necessary sense of all—toward the object. His feet remain in place, and he only moves his thighs, hips and knees in the direction toward which the eye has turned. There will be long discussions concerning such problems.

411. *Of great and small degrees of emotion.* Furthermore, do not 122v
portray great movements for small or slight emotions, nor small
movements for great emotions.

412. *Of attitudes.*[9] Friendly gestures pointing to things that are 123
near either in time or space should be made with the hand not
too far removed from the person, but if the things are far away,
the hand of the pointer should also be extended and the face
turned toward what he points out.

413. *Of the beauty of faces.* Do not paint muscles with harsh out- 109
lines, but let soft lights fade imperceptibly into pleasant, delightful shadows; from this come about grace and beauty of form.

414. *Quality of expressions of faces.* Depict your faces so that 108
they do not all have the same expression, as one sees done in
most cases, but give them different expressions, according to
ages, complexions, and natures, either bad or good.

415. *Method for remembering the shape of a face.* If you wish to 109
have facility in remembering the expression of a face, first commit to memory many heads, eyes, noses, mouths, chins, and
throats, necks, and shoulders. For example, noses are of ten kinds:
straight, crooked, concave, with a projection higher or lower than
the middle, aquiline, flat, turned up, round, and pointed. These
are good to remember insofar as the profile is concerned.

   In full face, noses are of eleven kinds: even, thick in the middle,
thin in the middle, with thick tips, and thin at the beginning,
thin at the tip and thick at the beginning; nostrils broad and
narrow, high and low, with uncovered openings and with openings covered by the tip.

   You will also find diversity in the other details, things that you
should draw from life and commit to memory, or when you
have to draw a face from memory take with you a little book
wherein are noted down similar features, and when you have
glanced at the face of the person you are to portray, look then at
the parts, which nose, or mouth is like his, and make a little
mark to recognize it, and then at home put it together. Of

---

[9] Hand 3 has added to the heading: De gl'atti demostratiui. (Of demonstrative
gestures.)

monstrous faces I do not speak, since these are remembered without effort.

*108v and* 416. *Of making a man's portrait in profile after having seen him*
*illus.* *only once.* In this case it is necessary to commit to memory the varieties of the four different features in profile, which would be the nose, mouth, chin, and forehead. We shall speak first of noses, which are of three sorts, that is, straight, concave, and convex. Of the straight there are only four kinds, that is, long, short, high at the end, and low. Concave noses are of three sorts, of which some have a concavity on the upper side, others in the middle and still others on the lower side. Convex noses also vary in three ways; some have a projection on the upper part, some in the middle, and others on the lower part. Those which have a projection in the middle of the nose vary in three ways, that is, they are straight, or concave, or really convex.

*108 and* 417. *Of the features and description of the face.* The middle parts
*illus.* of the nose which constitute the bridge can differ in eight ways: that is, first, they are equally straight, or equally concave or equally convex; or if unequally straight, concave, or convex, third, they are straight on the upper and concave on the lower part; fourth, straight above and convex below; fifth, concave above and straight below; sixth, concave above and convex below; seventh, convex above and straight below; eighth, convex above and concave below.

The transition from the nose to the brow is of two sorts: that
*108v* is, it is either concave or it is/straight. The forehead has three variations: it is flat, or concave, or it is round. Flat foreheads are divided into four kinds; that is, convex on the part above, or convex on the part below, or really convex above and below, or really flat above and below.

[EXPRESSIONS OF THE FACE]

*107v* 418. *Of the motions of features.* Various are the expressions of the face due to emotions, of which the first are: laughter, weeping, shouting, singing in high or low tones, admiration, anger, joy, melancholy, fear, the pain of martyrdom, and others, of which mention will be made.

First of laughter and weeping, wherein the mouth, cheeks, and closing of the eyes are very similar, and only the eyebrows and the interval between them differ. All this will be discussed in the proper place, that is, the variety of appearances which the face, as well as the hands and the whole person assumes with each of these emotions, and these you, painter, must of necessity know, and if you do not, your art will truly show bodies that are twice dead.

Again I remind you that movements should not be so extravagant nor so excessively active that a peaceful scene seems to be a battle or a morris-dance of drunken men, and above all, that the bystanders in a situation which the narrative painting represents, should show interest in it, with attitudes that display admiration, respect, pain, suspicion, fear, joy,/or whatever is called 108 for.

And your narrative paintings should not show one figure above the other with different horizons on the same wall, so that the painting seems to portray a shop with merchandise for sale in rectangular drawers.

419. *Of movements in the human face.* Emotions move the face 108 of man in different ways, for one laughs, another weeps, one becomes gay, another sad, one shows anger, another pity, some are amazed, others are afraid, distracted, thoughtful or reflective. In these states the hands and the whole person should follow the expression of the face.

420. *Of laughing and weeping and the difference between them.* 127 Between one who laughs and one who weeps there is no difference in the eyes, or mouth, or cheeks, but only in the rigidity of the eyebrows which are drawn together by him who weeps and are raised by him who laughs. He who weeps also tears his garments and hair with his hands, and scratches his face with his finger nails, and this does not occur with laughter.

421. *Of the same.* Do not depict the face of one who weeps with 127 the same expression as that of one who laughs, just because they often resemble one another; they should in truth be shown differently, as weeping is a different emotion from laughter. In

weeping the eyebrows and the mouth change according to the several causes of tears. One weeps for anger, another for fear, some for tenderness and joy, some for suspicion, some for pain and torment, and some for pity and pain because of lost relatives or friends. Among those who weep one shows himself to be in despair, another is moderate; some are tearful and some are shouting, some raise their faces to heaven and lower their hands, their fingers twisted together; others seem fearful and raise their shoulders to their ears, and so on, according to the reasons mentioned. He who sheds tears raises his eyebrows until they join and draws them together, producing wrinkles in the middle of his forehead, and turns down the corners of his mouth, but he who laughs raises them, and his eyebrows are unfurrowed and apart.

126v 422. *How the figure of an angry man is depicted.* You will show the figure of an angry man holding another down on the ground by the hair of his twisted head, his knees on the other's ribs, and his right arm raising his fist on high. His own hair will stand on end, his eyebrows are lowered and drawn together, his teeth are clenched, the corners of his mouth turn down in a curve, his neck is swollen and in front is full of wrinkles because he is bending over his enemy.

126v 423. *How a man in despair is depicted.* You will show the man in despair stabbing himself with a knife, having torn his garments with his hands. Let one of his hands be shown in the act of tearing open his wound, he himself standing on his feet, but with his legs somewhat bent, and his whole body also bent toward the ground; his hair torn and disarrayed.

126 424. *Of representing one who speaks among a number of persons.* To represent one who speaks among a number of persons, learn to consider the subject with which he is concerned, and arrange gestures for him related to that subject; that is, if the subject be one of persuasion, his gestures should be to this purpose, and if the subject be to explain numerous matters, show him who speaks holding apart two fingers of the right hand with one finger of the left, while the two smaller fingers are turned down,

The face should show excitement, and be turned toward the people, with the mouth a little open, so that the man seems to be speaking, and if he is seated, he should seem to rise a little, with his head forward, and if he be on his feet while speaking, make him bend his chest and head a little toward the people, whom you should represent as quiet and attentive, all looking the orator in the face and gesturing in admiration. The mouth of some old man is to be shown tightly closed in admiration of the words heard, the lower corners of his mouth drawn back, making many creases in his cheeks, and his eyebrows/are raised until *126v* they meet, making many wrinkles on his forehead. Some figures are to be shown seated, the fingers of their hands laced around a tired knee, others with one knee over the other, on which they place a hand, and a bent old man supports his bearded chin in his hand.

425. *Of physiognomy and chiromancy.* False physiognomy and *109* chiromancy I shall not discuss at length, because there is no truth in them and this is clear because/such chimeras have no *109v* scientific foundations. It is true that the face shows some indication of the nature of men, their vices and complexions; in the face the marks which separate the cheeks from the lips, the nostrils from the nose, and sockets from the eyes, show clearly whether these are cheerful men, often laughing; and those who show few such indications are men who engage in thought; and those, the planes of whose features are in great reliefs and hollows are bestial and angry men, of little reason; and those who have very clearly marked lines between the eyebrows are irascible; and those who have horizontal lines strongly marked on their foreheads are men full of concealed or public lamentations; and similar things can be said of many parts of the face.

But what of the hand? You will find many men in great armies killed at the same hour with the knife, and many dying at the same hour in shipwreck and none of these has a sign in the palm similar to that of any other.

[CONDITIONS AND REQUIREMENTS OF PAINTING]

140   426. *Painting, its division and components.*[10] Light, darkness, color, body, form, location, remoteness, nearness, motion, and rest.

Of these ten parts of the function of the eye, painting has seven: light, darkness, color, form, location, remoteness, and nearness. I exclude those which remain, body, motion, and rest. Light and darkness mean shadow and light, or brightness and obscurity, and color. I do not include body, for painting is on a surface, and a surface does not have body as this is defined in geometry.

To put it better, that which is visible is included in the science of painting. Therefore, the ten predicates of the eye mentioned above are, according to reason, the subjects of the ten books into which I divide my discussion of painting. But light and darkness make one single book, which treats of light and shadow and comprise one book only, since shadow is surrounded by or in contact with light, and the same is true of light and shadow, while on the borders light and shadow are always mixed.[11]

160v   427. *Of the ten functions of the eye, all pertaining to painting.* Painting includes all the ten functions of the eye; that is, darkness, light, body, color, form, location, remoteness, nearness, motion, and rest. My little work is woven together of these functions, reminding the painter according to what rules and in what fashion he should reproduce with his art all of these things, the work of nature and the beauties of the world.

153   428. *Of the judgment that you have to make upon a painter's work.* The first thing is for you to consider the forms, whether they have the relief that is required by their location and the light that illuminates them; the shadows should not be the same at the outer edges of a narrative painting as in the center. For it is one thing to be surrounded by shadows and another to have shadows on one side only.

153v   Those forms/are surrounded by shadows which occur toward

10 Hand 1 first wrote "componimenti" in the heading, but then changed it to "componitori."

11 The apparent contradictions in 426, 427 and 428 are typical of how Leonardo, in noting his observations at various times and in varying circumstances, was feeling his way.

the center of the narrative painting, for they are shadowed by the forms placed between them and the light. And those are shadowed on one side only which are placed between the light and the main group in the painting, because where the action occurs there is least light, which causes that portion of the painting depicting the action to be its darkest part, and where there is no action there the splendor of light is seen so that this portion represents the bright part of such a painting.

The second thing is that the distribution or division of the figures should be made according to the episode in the story you have selected.

The third is that the figures should, in lively fashion, be intent on their particular concerns.

429. *How a good painting is to be recognized and what quali-* 132v *ties it must have to be good.* The first thing to consider if you want to be able to recognize a good painting, is that the motion therein should be appropriate to the state of mind of him who moves. Second, that the greater or lesser relief of objects in shadow should be adjusted to the distances. Third, that the proportions of the parts of the body should correspond to the proportions of the whole. Fourth, that the appropriateness of the location should correspond to the decorum of the actions therein. Fifth, that the allocation of the parts of the body should be adjusted to the kind of men portrayed; that is, delicate limbs for the delicate, thick limbs for the thickset, and likewise fat for the fat.

430. *Of the first four parts that are required of the figure.* Atti- 130v tude is the first and most important part of the portrayal of a figure; a good figure painted in a bad attitude is disagreeable, but even the live figure with the highest degree of beauty loses in value when its actions are not suited to the function they have to perform. Certainly and without any doubt, the question of attitude is a matter for greater reflection than is the excellence in itself of the painted figure, for the excellence of a figure can be achieved through imitation of life, but the movement of such a figure must come about through great discrimination of the painter's intelligence. The second important part of the figure

is for it to have relief; the third is good drawing; and the fourth
is good coloring.

*132v*  431. *How the true picture exists on the surface of the flat mirror.*[12]
The mirror with a plane surface contains in itself the true picture
on that surface; and the perfect picture, made on the surface of
some plane material, is similar to the surface of the mirror. You,
painter, find on the surfaces of flat mirrors your master, who
teaches you about brightness and darkness and the foreshortening
of objects; and among your colors there is one which is brighter
*133*  than the illuminated parts of the image/of such an object, and
likewise among those colors there is one which is darker than
any darkness of that object, whence it comes about, that you,
painter, should not make your paintings like those of that mirror,
when it is viewed with a single eye, for two eyes go farther
around an object smaller than the eye.

*132*  432. *How the mirror is master of painters.* When you wish to
see whether your painting altogether conforms with the thing
drawn from nature, take a mirror and reflect the living thing
in it. Compare the thing reflected with your picture and consider
well whether the subject of both representations is in conformity
in both cases.

The mirror, above all, should be taken as your master, the flat
mirror, that is, for in many respects things on its surface have a
similarity to paintings. You see a painting made on a flat surface
display things so that they seem to be in relief, and the mirror
does the same thing on a plane; the painting has only a single
surface, as does the mirror. The painting is intangible insofar as
that which seems round and detached cannot be surrounded with
the hands, and the same is true of the mirror. The mirror and
the painting show in the same fashion things surrounded by
shade and light; both seem to extend a good deal beyond the
*132v*  surface./

And if you know that the mirror, by means of outlines and
shadows and lights makes things seem detached, and you have
among your colors shadows and lights more powerful than those

---

[12] Hand 1 has added to the heading: QVESTO cap¹º seguitarebbe meglio dinanzi
a'quello disopa. (This chapter had better come before that above.)

of the mirror, certainly, if you know how to put them together well, your painting will also seem a thing in nature, seen in a large mirror.

433. *Which painting is the more laudable*. That painting is most  *133* praiseworthy which conforms most to the object portrayed. I put this forward to embarrass those painters who would improve on the works of nature, such as those who represent a child a year old, whose head is a fifth of his height while they make it an eighth; and the breadth of the shoulders is similar to that of his head, and they make it half the breadth of the shoulders; and thus they proceed reducing a small child a year old to the proportions of a man of thirty. They have so often made this error and seen it made that they have adopted it in practice, which has so penetrated and become established in their corrupt judgment that they make themselves believe that nature or whoever imitates nature commits a great error in not doing as they do.

434. *What is the primary objective of the painter*. The primary  *133* purpose of the painter is to make a plane surface display a body in relief, detached from that plane, and he who in that art most surpasses others deserves most praise, and this concern, which is the crown of the science of painting comes about from the use of shadows and lights, or, if you wish, brightness and darkness. Therefore whoever /avoids shadows avoids what is the glory of  *133v* the art for noble minds, but gains glory with the ignorant public, who want nothing in painting but beauty of color, altogether forgetting the beauty and marvel of depicting a relief on what in reality is a plane surface.

435. *Which is of more importance in painting: shadows or out-*  *133v* *lines*. The shadow in a picture is matter for much greater investigation and reflection than its outlines. The proof of this is shown by the fact that the outlines can be traced by means of veils or glass panes placed between the eye and the thing to be traced, but shadows are not attained by any such method because their edges are indistinguishable and usually confused, as will be shown in the book on shadow and light.

140v 436. *Painting and its definition*. Painting is a composition of light and darkness, combined with the different variations of all the simple and compound colors.

[TO JUDGE AND AVOID ERRORS AND DEFECTS]

157 437. *How figures often resemble their masters*. This happens because it is our judgment which guides the hand in the creation of the outlines of figures until they prove satisfactory. Because judgment is one of the powers of our souls, with which it composes the form of the body wherein it resides, according to its will, when it has to remake a human body with the hands, it gladly remakes that body of which it was the first inventor. Thus it comes about that it gladly falls in love with things resembling it and is beloved of them.

107 438. *Of the arrangement of the parts of a man's body*. Measure on yourself the proportion of the parts of your body, and if you find any part in discord with the others, make a note of it and be careful not to use it in the figures composed by you. Remember this because it is a common vice of painters, to delight in making things similar to themselves.

131v 439. *Of the painter's judgment of his own work and that of others*. When one's work is equal to one's judgment, that is a bad sign for one's judgment; and when one's work surpasses one's judgment, that is worse, as happens when a painter is amazed at having done so well; and when judgment looks down on the work, that is a good omen and a young man so endowed will, without doubt be an excellent worker. He will compose few works, but they will be of a kind to make men stop and contemplate their perfection with admiration.

131v 440. *Of the painter's judgment of his own work*. We know for certain that errors are more often recognized in the work of another than in one's own work, so that often while criticizing minor errors in another's work, you will not see your own greater faults. To avoid such ignorant behavior, see that you are first good in perspective, then, that you have complete knowledge of the measurements of man and other animals, and are also a good architect, that is, insofar as concerns the form of buildings and other things that rest on the earth, which are infinite in form; and the more forms you know, the more you will attract praise to your work, and those things in which you are not versed, do not refuse to draw/from nature. *132*

But to return to what was mentioned above, I say that while you are painting you should have a flat mirror and often look at your work in it. When it is seen reversed and seems to be by the hand of another master, you will judge your errors better than you otherwise would. It is also good to get up often and take a little recreation, because when you return your judgment is improved, for staying long at work deceives you greatly. It is good also to move away from your work because it seems smaller and more is grasped in a glance, and the discordant and disproportionate parts and colors of objects are recognized from a distance better than they are close at hand.

441. *Of the practice sought with great anxiety by the painter.* *131*
And you, painter, who desire a great deal of practice, must/un- *131v* derstand that if you do not do work on a good foundation of things studied from nature, you will produce works of little honor and less profit; but if you do them well, your works will be few and good, bringing you great honor and much benefit.

442. *Discourse upon practice.* And you, painter, try to produce *130v* works, which must attract attention to themselves, and make the observers stop with great admiration and delight, and do not first attract them and then drive them away, as does the air to those who at night time leap naked from bed to determine the quality of the air, whether it be cloudy or serene, and immediately, driven away by its coldness, return to the bed from which they arose. But make your works like the air which in warm weather brings men from their beds, and keeps them enjoying the fresh air in summer with delight. Do not try to practice before you are proficient, for avarice/vanquishes glory, the glory de- *131* servedly to be gained from such an art.

Do you not see that among human beauties it is a very beautiful face and not rich ornaments that stops passers-by? And this I say to you who adorn your figures with gold or other rich trimmings, do you not see beautiful young people diminish their excellence with excessive ornamentation? Have you never seen women in the hills wrapped in plain and poor draperies possessing greater beauty than those who are adorned?

Do not paint affected curls or hair-dressings such as are worn by fools fearful that a single, misplaced lock will bring disgrace upon them and that bystanders will be diverted from their own thoughts and talk of nothing else and blame them. Such people have the mirror and comb for their advisors, and the wind that disarranges their carefully dressed hair is their main enemy.

Depict hair which an imaginary wind causes to play about youthful faces, and adorn heads you paint with curling locks of various kinds. Do not do like those who plaster hair with glue, making faces appear as if turned to glass, another increased madness for those for whom it is not enough that mariners coming from eastern parts should bring gum arabic to prevent the wind from changing the order of their ringlets, so that they must still keep seeking a remedy.

### [THE LIGHTING OF FIGURES]

*133v* 443. *How figures should be illuminated.* Light should be employed as it would exist in the natural location where you suppose your figure to be. That is, if you suppose that your figure is in the sunshine, make the shadows dark with great stretches of lights, and imprint the shadows of all the surrounding bodies on the ground. If you represent your figure in bad weather, show little difference between the lights and shadows and make no shadow at the feet. If the figure is indoors, show a sharp distinction between the light, the shade, and the shadow on the ground, and if you represent a shaded window and a white room, show but little difference between lights and shadows. If the figure is illuminated by fire, make the lights reddish and powerful, and *134* the shadows heavy, and the sharply defined shadow/cast on the walls or the ground, and the farther away the shadow is from the body, the broader and larger it becomes, and if that figure is illuminated partly by the fire and partly by the air, make the illumination of the air more powerful and that of the fire almost red, as fire is. Above all let your painted figures be illuminated by a large light from above. The people whom you see on the streets are all illuminated from above, and know that there is not a person so well known to you, that if he were illuminated from below you would not have difficulty in recognizing him.

444. *Precept.* Figures are more attractive when they are placed *156v* under the universal light of the sky than when they are lighted by small individual lights, because large lights that are not powerful bring out the relief of bodies, and works made with such lighting appear attractive from a distance. Those which are/ *157* painted with individual lighting are greatly shadowed, and works made with so many shadows, viewed from distant positions, never look like anything but stains.

445. *Of painting.* The outlines and form of any part of bodies in *154* shadow are hard to recognize, but/the parts of those bodies placed *154v* between the lights and shadows have the greatest degree of clarity.

446. *Precept of painting.* Where shadow borders on light, observe *134v* where there is more brightness and more obscurity, and where the shadow is more or less softened/toward the light. Above all *135* I remind you not to make the shadows on young people as sharply defined as on rocks, because flesh is slightly transparent, as you see on looking at your hand placed between your eye and the sun, where it appears reddish and luminously transparent and is or appears to be more colored. Put a middle value between the lights and the shadows. If you would see what shadow is required for flesh, cast a shadow on it with your finger, and depending on whether you would have it brighter or darker, place your finger near or far from the painting and reproduce that.

447. *Of objects.* That part of the object will be most illuminated *164* which is closest to the luminous body that illuminates it.

448. *Of the side of the opaque body.* That side of the opaque *149v* body will be more shadowed or illuminated which is nearest to the shadowed body that darkens it, or to the luminous body which illuminates it.

The surface of every opaque body takes on the color of its opposite object, but does so with greater or lesser impression, depending on whether that object is near or remote and of greater or lesser power.

Things seen between the light and the shadow will seem to be in greater relief than those which are in the light or in the shadows.

*164* 449. When the object occurs between the eye and the light along the central line which extends between the center of the light and the eye, then the object is completely deprived of light.

*136* 450. *Of the difference of forms in shadows and lights, in diverse situations.* Small lights throw large and sharply defined shadows on shadowed bodies. Large lights throw small shadows with indistinct edges on shadowed bodies. When the small light is included within a large but less powerful light, as is the sun in the air, then the less powerful light takes the place of a shadow on the bodies illuminated by it.

*137* 451. *Of the windows of rooms in which figures are drawn.* The window of the painter's rooms should be made of linen, without cross-bars, and gradually covered toward its edges with increasing
*137v* degrees of darkness, in/such a way that the edge of the light does not coincide with the edge of the window.

*135* 452. *Of places which should be selected in order to give objects*
*135v* *relief and grace.*/In streets that lead to the west, when the sun is at noon, and the walls are so high that the one turned toward the sun does not reflect on bodies which are in shadow, then the sides of the face take on the obscurity of the sides of the walls opposite to them, and so will the sides of the nose, and all of the face turned to the entrance to the street will be illuminated. On this account, the eye of the observer standing in the middle of the entrance to the street will see the front of that face illuminated and those sides which are turned to the sides of the walls will be seen in shadow. To this there will be added the attractiveness of shadows with pleasing dissolution, which are entirely devoid of any sharp outline. This will come about because of the length of the rays of light which pass below the roofs of houses, penetrate between walls, and end on the pavement of the street, where they rebound and are reflected on the shadowed planes

of faces, brightening them somewhat. The length of the above-mentioned light from the sky confined by the edges of roofs and their façades, illuminates almost as far as the beginning of the shadows which are below the projections of the face, gradually changing in brightness, until it terminates over the chin with imperceptible shading on every side.

It is as if the light were A E. The line F E of the light illuminates as far as beneath/the nose, and the line C F only *136 and* illuminates as far as beneath the lip. The line A H extends as *illus.* far as beneath the chin. Here the nose remains very bright because it faces all the rays of light, A B C D E.

453. *Painting in a universal light.* In a multitude composed of *140v* men and animals always make the parts of their figures or bodies darker, the lower they are, and the closer they are to the center of the multitude, even if the figures are in themselves of uniform color. This is necessary because/less light of the sky that illumi- *141 with* nates bodies reaches the lower spaces between those animals than *illus.* in the higher portions of the same spaces.

This is proved by the figure placed in the margin, where A B C D stands for the vault of the sky, the general illuminant of bodies below it. N, M are the bodies that limit the space S T R H between them, in which space the position F is clearly seen. This is illuminated only by the part of the sky at C D which is there illuminated by a smaller part of the sky than is the position E, which faces the part of the sky A B, which is three times larger than the part of the sky D C. Therefore E is three times as much illuminated as F.

[THE BACKGROUNDS OF FIGURES]

454. *What background a painter should use for his works.* Since *134v* experience shows that all bodies are surrounded by shadow and light, I desire that you, painter, should arrange it so that that part which is illuminated borders on a dark object, and that the shadowed side border on a bright object. This rule will give great aid in bringing out relief in your figures.

*141* 455. *Of backgrounds proportioned to the bodies against them, and first of plane surfaces of a uniform color.*[13] Backgrounds of any plane surface of uniform color and light will not seem separated from that surface, since they are of the same color and light. Therefore, conversely, they will seem separated if the converse conclusion follows.

*136* 456. *Of dividing and detaching figures from their backgrounds.* You must place your dark figure against a bright background, and if your figure is bright, put it against a dark background, and if it is both bright and dark, put the dark side against a bright background and the bright side against a dark background.

*142v* 457. *Painting.* Among objects of the same degree of darkness, magnitude, shape, and distance from the eye, that will appear to be smallest which is seen against the background of greatest brilliance or whiteness.

This is shown us when the sun is seen behind trees without leaves, when all their branches, seen against the sun, are so diminished that they remain invisible, and the same thing will happen to the shaft of a spear placed between the eye and the sun.

Whether two parallel bodies placed upright, seen through mist, must look thicker at the top than at the foot, is proved by the ninth book, which states: mist or thick air, penetrated by the solar rays appears whiter, the lower it is.

*143* Things seen from a distance are disproportionate, and this/ comes about because the brightest part sends the eye its visual image with a more vigorous ray, than does the dark part. I saw a lady dressed in black, with white drapery on her head, which looked twice as large as the width of her shoulders, which were clothed in black.

*156v* 458. *Of making objects appear detached from their backgrounds, that is from the walls on which they are depicted.* Objects against a bright and illuminated background display much more relief than against an obscure one.

The reason for this proposition follows: if you wish to give relief to your figure, depict it so that that part of the body which

[13] Hand 1 had begun the heading here as: Pittura di figura (Figure-painting), but then crossed it out at this point.

is farthest from the light partakes least of that light, hence it is left darker, and since it terminates against a dark background, its outlines become indistinct, on account of which, if there is no reflected light, the work remains unattractive. From a distance only the luminous parts can be seen, whence it comes about that dark objects seem to be parts of the background, and things seem cut off and less in relief than they should be the greater the amount of darkness.

459. *Precept.* Among objects that are equally dark and equally *154v* distant, that one will appear to be darkest which is outlined against the whitest background and so conversely.

460. *Of the edges of illuminated objects.* The edge of that il- *153v* luminated object will seem darkest which is seen against the brightest background, and so that will appear brightest which is seen against the darkest background. But if the edge is flush with and seen against a background as bright as itself, then its demarcation will be imperceptible.

461. *Painting. Of form and body.* Regular bodies are of two *141* sorts, one has curved surfaces which are oval or spherical; and the other angular surfaces, which are regular or/irregular. *141v*

Spherical or oval bodies always seem separated from their backgrounds, even when they are the same color as the background, and this also happens with those that have angular outlines. This occurs because they are so constructed that shadows are cast by any of their sides, and this cannot occur with plane surfaces.

462. *Of the outlines of a white object.* Do not make sharp pro- *150v* file lines for the contours of a body that has another body as its background for that body will stand out by itself.

If the outline of a white object is against another white object, and if it is curved, it will create a dark outline naturally, and will be the darkest part of the luminous side; if it has a dark background, that outline will appear the brightest part of that luminous side.[14] That object will appear most detached and

[14] Before the last sentence of this section, an asterisk is inserted in the text, and repeated at this point in the margin.

farthest from another which is seen against a background most different from itself.

137    463. *Of the natures of contours of bodies upon other bodies*. When bodies with a convex surface are seen against other bodies of the same color, the edge of the convex body will seem darker than the body contiguous to it.

The outline of the shaft of a spear standing upright against a wall will seem very dark against a white background, and against a dark background it will appear very much brighter than any other part of it, even though the light which descends onto the shaft is of even brightness.

153    464. *Of painting*. A most important part of painting is the background of painted objects. Backgrounds in which the outlines of natural bodies have a convex curvature are always recognizable as forms, even when the colors of those bodies are the same as the background. This comes about because the convex outlines of bodies are not illuminated in the same way as the background, since such an outline is often brighter or darker than the background. But if the outline is the color of the background, doubtless there can be no clarity in painting the outline of such a form. This composition in painting is to be avoided by painters of intelligence, for it is the purpose of the painter to make his bodies stand out against their backgrounds, and in the case mentioned above the contrary happens, not only in the depicted object but also in actuality with objects that really are in relief.

[COLOR AND RELIEF]

149v    465. *Painting*. The surface of every opaque body takes on the color of its opposite object, and the more so as that surface approaches greater whiteness.

The surface of every opaque body takes on the color of the transparent medium lying between the eye and that surface, the more so when that medium is denser, or when greater space lies between the eye and that surface.

The outlines of opaque bodies are less clear the farther away they are from the eye that sees them.

466. *Precept.* That which is painted in black and white will ap- *154v*
pear in greater relief than will anything else. I remind you,
painter, to clothe your figures in the brightest colors that you
can, because if you make them dark in color, they will have little
relief and will scarcely be visible from a distance, and this will
be so because all shadows are dark. If you make drapery dark,
there will be little contrast between light and dark, but with
bright colors there will be a great contrast.

467. *Of the relief of forms distant from the eye.* That opaque *153v*
body will appear to be in least relief which is most distant from
the eye. This happens because the air lying between the eye and
that opaque body, being brighter than the shadow of such a
body, vitiates the shadow and brightens it, taking away the intensity of its obscurity, and thus the body loses its relief.

468. *Of flesh tones and shapes distant from the eye.* The painter *154*
should show forms and objects remote from the eye only as
stains, and not give them shadows with sharp outlines, but rather
with indistinct edges. If the forms are to be represented in cloudy
weather, or at evening, then avoid sharply defined lights or
shadows most of all, because the paintings afterward seem daubs
when seen from a distance, and they turn out to be heavy, unattractive works. You must remember that shadows are never
of such a kind that you have to lose their color on account of
the darkness in which they occur, if the place where the bodies
are situated is itself not dark. And do not make sharply defined
profiles, do not cause each hair to stand out, nor make white
lights except on white objects, and where those lights occur they
should display the highest degree of beauty in color.

469. *Whether the surface of every opaque body takes on the* *137v*
*color of the opposite object.* You must understand that if a white
object is placed between two walls, one of which is white and
the other black, you will find that the proportion between the
shadowed and the luminous parts of that object is similar to that
of the walls, and if the object is blue in color instead of white,
the same is true.

When you are about to paint it, do the following: take black
to shade the blue object, similar to the black or shadow of the
*138 and* wall which you have to represent/reverberating on your object,
*illus.* for, if you would work according to certain and true science,
you will work in this way. When you paint walls choose whatever color you wish, and take a little spoon, hardly larger than
an ear-spoon, but larger or smaller according to whether the
works which are to be painted are large or small, and this spoon's
outer lips should be even, and with this measure the amounts
of the colors with which you will effect your combinations.

An example would be that on walls where you had made the
first shadow of three degrees of darkness and one degree of
brightness, if you took, as if you were measuring grain, three
even spoonfuls of simple black and one spoonful of white, you
would beyond a doubt have secured a definite result. Now you
have made one wall white and one dark and are placing a blue
object between the two and you wish this object to have the true
shadows and lights that are suitable to such a blue. Then put
aside that blue which you wish to have remain without shadow
and place the black alongside it. Then take three spoonfuls of
black and mix these with one spoonful of luminous blue to make
the darkest shadow.

Having done this, observe whether your object is spherical,
cylindrical, square, or whatever it may be. If it is spherical, draw
lines from the extremes of the dark wall to the center of the
*138v* spherical object, and where the lines/cut the surface of the object, the larger shadows end between equal angles.

Then begin to brighten it, as it would be in the area N O
which has as much darkness as it takes on from the upper wall,
A D; this is a color which you will mix with the first shadow
of A B, making the same gradations.

[MIST AND SMOKE]

*147v* 470. *Of cities or buildings seen at evening or in the morning in
the mist.* Buildings seen from a great distance at evening or in
the morning, in mist or dense air show brightness only in the
parts illuminated by the sun when it is near the horizon, and the

parts of the buildings which do not face the sun remain almost the color of semi-lighted mist.

471. *Of smoke.*/Smoke is more transparent and also darker to-  *149*
ward the edges of its round masses than toward its center.

Smoke moves with greater obliqueness the more powerful the wind that moves it. Smoke is of as many different colors as the varieties of things that create it.

Clouds of smoke do not throw shadows with sharp outlines, and their borders are less definite the more distant they are from their sources, and objects located behind them are less visible, the denser the clouds of smoke. The whiter they are, the nearer they are to the beginning, and they are bluer toward the end. Fire seems darker the greater the amount of smoke lying between the eye and the fire. Where the smoke is farther away things are less concealed by it.

Make a landscape with smoke like thick mist in/which clouds  *149v*
of smoke are seen in different places, with flames illuminating the densest round clouds of smoke at their source. And the higher the mountains, the more clearly the tops can be seen in contrast to their bases, as is also true when they are covered with mist.[15]

472. *Where smoke is brighter.*/Smoke seen between the sun and  *149*
the eye will be brighter and more shining than any other part of the landscape whence it arises. The same thing occurs with dust and mist, which will seem dark to you if you are between them and the sun.

473. *Of the smoke from cities.* Smoke is seen better and more  *161v*
sharply in the east than in the west, when the sun is in the east,/  *162*
and this comes about for two reasons. The first is that the sun with its rays shines through the particles of smoke, making them bright, and rendering them visible. The second is, the roofs of

[15] At the end of this section Hand 1 has written: Era sotto di questo capitulo un rompimento di montagna per dentro delle quali roture scherzaua fiame di fuoco disegnate di penna et ombrate d'acquarella da uedere cosa mirabile et uiua. (Below this chapter there was a cleft in the mountain, an opening within which played a flaming fire, drawn by pen and shaded with watercolor, an admirable and vital thing to see.)

houses from which smoke comes seen toward the east at such a time are shadowed, since their oblique sides cannot be illuminated by the sun; and the same thing happens with dust; both are more luminous the denser they are, and they are denser toward the middle.

162 474. *Of smoke and dust.* When the sun is in the east, the smoke of the city will not be seen in the west, because it is not penetrated by the sun's rays, nor is it seen against a dark background, because the roofs of houses display to the eye the same side that they display to the sun, and against this bright background the smoke from them is hardly seen.

But dust under such circumstances appears darker than does smoke, because it is of denser matter than smoke, which is of humid matter.

[LIGHTS AND SHADOWS WHEN THE SUN IS IN THE WEST]

151v 475. An object illuminated by the sun is also illuminated by the air in such a way that two shadows are created of which that is darker whose center is in direct line with the center of the sun.

143v and 476. *Of the solar rays that penetrate openings in the clouds.* The
illus. solar rays that penetrate through the openings between varying densities and round masses of clouds illuminate all the places that they strike, even those in darkness, or tinge all the shadowed places which are behind them. These places show themselves in
144 the interstices/among those solar rays.

151v 477. The central line of the original light and of the derivative light coincides with the central line of the primary and derivative shadows.

148v and 478. *Why the shadows of bodies on white walls are blue at sun-*
illus. *set.* Shadows created by the redness of the sun when close to the horizon are always blue. This comes about because of the eleventh proposition which states: The surface of every opaque object partakes of the color of its opposite object. Therefore, since the whiteness of the wall is deprived of color, it is tinged with the color of its opposite objects which, in this case, are the sun and the sky, because the sun turns red at evening, and the sky

looks blue. Where there is shadow, there is no view of the sun, according to the eighth proposition of the book on shadows, which states: No luminous body has a view of the shadow cast by it. Where there is no view of the sun on that wall, it is in view of the sky. Therefore, according to the eleventh proposition the derivative shadow strikes the wall with a blue color, and the background/of that shadow, which faces the redness of the sun, *149* takes on the red color.

479. *Of dust*. Where dust arises because of the passing of some *149* animal, it is brighter the higher it rises, and darker the less it rises, when it is between the sun and the eye.

480. *Precept of painting*. Although across long distances percep- *150* tion of the nature of many things is lost, nevertheless, those which are illuminated by the sun are rendered more certain in their appearance, and the others seem enveloped in a vague mist.

Because with every degree of depth the air gains in thickness, things which are lowest look the most indistinct and vice versa.

/When the sun reddens the clouds on the horizon, things *150v* which through distance are clothed with blue take on that redness, which results in a mixture of blue and red, which makes the countryside gay and cheerful, and all the things that are illuminated by that redness, if they are dense, will be very clearly visible and turn red. The air, because it is transparent, will be thoroughly infused with that redness, whence it will tend to have the color of lilies.

The air which is between the sun and the earth, when the sun rises or sets, will always envelop things that are behind it, more than any other kind of air, and this comes about because it is whiter.

481. *Precept*. When the sun is in the west, the clouds which are *151v* between it and you are illuminated below, since they face toward the sun, while the others that are nearer are dark, but of a reddish darkness, and those that are transparent cast few shadows.

482. *Precept*. The sun provides a beautiful spectacle when it is *152 and* in the west, and illuminates the high buildings of cities, and *illus.*

castles, and the tall trees of the countryside, and tinges them with its color. Everything else has little relief, because, illuminated only by the air, the other things differ but slightly in their shadows and lights, and therefore do not stand out very much. The things which rise highest are touched by the solar rays, and, as has been said, are tinged by their color. Wherefore you must take the color with which you make the sun and use it in every bright color with which you illuminate bodies.

*151v*  483. When the sun is in the west, the mist which falls thickens the air, and things which do not face toward the sun remain obscure and indistinct, and those which are illuminated by the sun grow reddish and yellowish according to the way the sun appears on the horizon. The houses, also, which are illuminated by the setting sun become very clearly visible and especially the buildings and houses of cities and villages, because their shadows are dark. Their sharp forms seem to arise from indistinct and uncertain foundations, because there everything is the same color, since it is not in the light of the sun.

[PERSPECTIVE IN SPACE]

*154v*  484. *Discussion of painting.* Perspective, insofar as it relates to painting, is divided into three principal parts; the first is that of diminution, which gives the dimension of bodies at different distances; and the second is that which treats of the diminution of the intensity of colors of such bodies; the third is that which diminishes the perceptibility of those bodies at different distances.

*156 and illus.*  485. *Which seems in higher relief, the relief near the eye or that far from the eye.* The opaque body which is nearest to the eye will appear to be in greatest relief, and it follows that the most distant will show least relief, that is, will appear least detached from its background.

The proof is as follows: Let P be the front of the object P H, which is nearer to the eye A, than is N, the front of the object N M, and the background D F is that which should be seen after the first two objects by the eye A. Now we see that the eye A sees all the background D F beyond the object P H, and sees

only D G of the background, beyond the second object N M.[16]
Therefore, we say that there is the same proportion between the
perceptible degree of relief in the two objects as there is between
the two backgrounds, that is, between the background D G and
the background D F.

486. *Precept.* Objects in relief near at hand when looked at with *156v and*
one eye seem like a perfect painting. If eyes A and B look at *illus.*
point C, C will appear to you at D F, but if you look at it with
one eye, M,[17] it will seem to you to be at G. Painting will never
change to the eye in this way.

487. *Why objects perfectly drawn from nature do not seem to* *155v and*
*be in the same relief as the natural object.* It is impossible for a *illus.*
painting, even though executed with the greatest perfection of
outline, shadow, light, and color, to seem in the same relief as
the natural model, unless that natural model is looked at from
a great distance with one eye.

The proof is as follows: Let the eyes, A B, look at the object
C, with the convergence of the central lines from the eyes, A C
and B C, and those lines converge to the object at the point C,
and along the other lines, on the sides of the central line, the
eyes see the space G D behind the object; the eye A sees the
whole space F D, and the eye B sees the whole space G E. Thus,
the two eyes see the whole/space F E behind the object C. The *156*
object C remains transparent, according to the definition of
transparency, by which nothing is hidden. This cannot happen
to him who looks with one eye at an object larger than his eye,
as it could not happen when the eye looks at objects smaller than
the pupil. This is shown in the second diagram. Because of
what has been said, we can conclude our investigation, because
the painted object covers all the space that is behind it, and it
is in no way possible to see any part of the background behind
it within the outlines of the object.

488. *Precept.* Why does a painted object, which reaches the eye *152v and*
at an angle of the same width as an object in nature that is *illus.*

[16] The diagram appears to be inconclusive.
[17] M and G are interchanged in the MS text.

farther away, not seem as distant? Let us say that on the wall
B C[18] I paint something that must seem to be a mile away, and
153   then place beside it something that/truly is a mile away, and the
two objects are so arranged that the section of the wall A C cuts
the pyramid at an angle of the same size; to two eyes they will not
seem to be at an equal distance.

155   489. *Why, of two objects of equal size, will the painted one seem
larger than the one in relief.* The reason for this is not as easy
to explain as many others, but I shall endeavor to solve the
problem, if not completely, at least as far as I can. As reason
shows us, perspective results in the decrease in the size of objects, the farther they are from the eye. This is confirmed by
experience. Therefore, visual lines which occur between the object and the eye and extend to the surface of the painting, all
terminate at the same surface, but the lines which occur between
the eye and a work of sculpture, have various terminations and
lengths. That line is longest which extends to an object that is
more distant than the others, and so that object seems smaller.
Since many lines are longer than others, and there are many details each more distant than the other, it follows that they look
smaller, and since they appear smaller, they finally make the object, which is their sum, smaller, by means of decreasing the
155v   entire mass./

But this does not happen in painting. Since lines terminate at
the same distance, the result is that they are without decrease in
length, and small details which are not diminished do not diminish the sum of the whole object. For this reason a painting
does not decrease as does sculpture.

[DECREASE OF SIZE IN PERSPECTIVE]

160 and   490. *Precept of painting*/Perspective is the bridle and guide of
illus.   painting.

The size of the painted shape should show from what distance
the object is seen. If you see a shape as large as it is in nature
you know that it appears near the eye.

    18 Note that there are two B Cs in the diagram; the one here referred to is the
vertical line.

491. *Of linear perspective.* Linear perspective includes the func- *146v* tion of visual lines and serves to prove, by means of measurement, how much the second object is smaller than the first, the third than the second and so by degrees to the farthest of the objects seen.

I have found by experiment that, in objects of the same size, the second, if it be distant from the first by as much as the first is distant from your eye,/it is half again smaller than the first. *147* Furthermore, if a third object of the same size as the other two which are in front of it is as distant from the second as the second is from the first, it will be only one third of the size of the first object, and so on, graduating by degrees. Thus at equal distances there will always be a proportionate decrease to that of the second object compared with the first, provided that the interval does not surpass twenty braccia.

At a distance of twenty braccia a figure like yours will lose 2/4 of its size, and in forty 3/4 and 5/6 in sixty braccia and it will decrease gradually. When the background is removed from you by a distance twice your size, an interval of twenty braccia makes a great difference between the first position and the second.

492. *Why the convergence of all the visual images that come to* *163 and* *the eye occurs at a single point.* Objects of equal size located at *illus.* various distances will be seen within a smaller angle in relation to their distance from the eye. B D is equal to C E but C E appears smaller to the eye than B D in the degree that it is distant from the point A as the angle C A E shows with respect to the angle B A D.

493. *Precept.* Among objects of equal height which are higher *151* than the eye, that which is farthest from the eye will seem lowest. And if the object is below the eye, that nearest to the eye will seem lowest. Lateral parallels will come together in a point.

494. *Precept.* Among objects of equal height, that which is *152-152v* farthest/from the eye will be lowest. *and illus.*

Note that the first cloud, even though it is lower than the second, seems to be higher, as the intersecting of the pyramid of the first low cloud at N A, shows you, and that of the second, higher one, at N M, below A N, on the intersection. This comes about when you seem to see a dark cloud higher than a light one illuminated by the rays of the sun in the west or in the east.

*152 and illus.* 495. It also often happens that a cloud seems dark without being in the shadow of another cloud that is separated from it, and this happens according to the location of the eye which sees only the shadowed side of the near cloud and the shadowed and light sides of the other.

*137v and illus.* 496. *Why, when measuring a face and then painting it life size, it will appear larger than nature.* A B is the breadth of the face, which is placed on the paper by the artist who measures it at the distance C F from the eye of the observer. A C is where the cheeks are, but A B must be back of C D by the distance A C and then the temples would be seen in perspective along the lines A F and B F so that there would be the difference of C O and R D. In considering the surface of the paper on which the whole height is drawn, it must be concluded that for the artist who uses perspective, the lines C F and D F are shorter by measurement than A F and B F which constitute the truth, and it is this that brings about the difference of C O and R D as has been stated.

*139v and illus.* 497. *To make a figure on a wall of 12 braccia appear to be 24 braccia in height.* If you would depict a figure or some other object which is to appear to be twenty-four braccia in height, go about it in this manner: in the first place represent one half of the man you would depict on the wall M R; then place the other half on the vault M N. However, first draw the figure on the flat floor of a hall before drawing it on the vault which is above; then, drawing a curve in the form of the vault on which you plan to place your figure, draw your figure in profile in the size that you desire, carrying all the lines to the point F, so that they cut the surface of the wall M N; they represent the figure on the wall which is similar to that drawn on the surface of the flat floor, and you will have all the heights and projections of the figure.

And depict the breadth or thickness which occurs on the

straight wall,/M R, in proper proportion, for as it extends up- 140
ward on the wall, the figure diminishes. Part of the figure on
the vault you will have to diminish as if it were straight, and this
will be the figure which you will take from the surface M R,
with its true breadths; and then you will reduce the portion on
the curved surface which is higher. That will be a good method.[19]

498. *To make a figure which appears to be forty braccia high in* 139 and
*a space of twenty braccia, with corresponding members, the* illus.
*figure to stand straight on its feet.* In this and every other case
the painter ought not to mind how the wall or surface that he
paints upon is placed, especially if the eye of the observer of the
picture is to see it from a window or other opening, since the
eye does not have to regard the evenness or curvature of that
surface, but only the things depicted on that wall representing
various places in the imagined countryside.

But this figure would be executed better on the curved surface
F R G/because there are no angles there. 139v

499. *Of avoiding disproportion in the surroundings.* It is a very 136
great vice in the work of many painters, to depict men's houses
and surroundings in such a way that the gates of the city do
not come up to the knees of its inhabitants, even though they
are nearer to the eye of the observer than is the man who indicates that he wishes to enter. We have seen porticos filled
with men on the roof, with the columns that/supported it in 136v
the fist of a man who leaned against it as on a thin cane. Other
like things are greatly to be avoided.[20]

[LOSS OF DISTINCTNESS WITH DISTANCE]

500. *How high the point of sight ought to be placed.* The point 134
of sight should be placed as high as the height of a man/of 134v

[19] Lettering in diagram is not in accord with text.

[20] At the end of this section, before which Hand 3 has placed the words "al
medesimo," (with the same), we find a heading: Corispondino i corpi si per
grandezza come per uficio alla cosa di cui si tratta. (Bodies should correspond
in size as well as in function to the matter concerned.) Hand 1 immediately adds
the observation: Questa propositione e prima difinita che proposta adonque leg-
gierai di sopra. (This proposition is set forth rather than explained; therefore,
read what precedes it.) This heading is 426a in Ludwig's edition, and it is
numbered 420 by Borzelli.

ordinary size whose eyes are fixed on the far edge of the plain which borders on the sky. This point must be placed at the height of the border of the plain and sky, excepting the mountains which are excluded.

141v 501. *Painting. That part of the body loses its distinctness first which is of least extension.* Of the parts of those bodies which are distant from the eye, that will first lose definiteness which is smallest in shape; and it follows that the part of greatest extension will be the last to lose definiteness. Therefore, painter, do not finish in detail the small portions of those objects that are far removed from the eye, but follow the precept given in the sixth book.

How many are they who in representing cities and other subjects distant from the eye, cause the outlines of the buildings to appear very sharp, as if they were in the closest proximity! This is impossible in actuality because there is no vision so powerful that it can see distant outlines with true clarity as if in close propinquity, because the outlines of those subjects are, in effect, the outlines of their surfaces, and the boundaries of the surfaces are lines, which are not part of any of the breadth of that surface, nor yet of the air, which covers the surfaces.

142 Therefore, that which is not a part of/anything is invisible, as is proved in geometry. If you, painter, would make those outlines sharp and noticeable, as is customary, do not seek to represent the object at a great distance for such a method makes it appear close. Also, the angles of buildings should not be represented in portraying distant cities, because even nearby it is impossible to see them, since those angles are the meeting of two lines in a point, and the point has no parts, and is therefore invisible.

145 502. *Which are those parts of bodies which lose distinctness because of distance.* Those parts of bodies which are smallest will be the first to lose clarity because of distance. This happens because the visual images of smaller objects at equal distances come to the eye with a narrower angle than larger ones do, and the perception of distant things is of that much less clarity, the smaller they are. It therefore follows that when the greater volume reaches the eye from a long distance and through a very

small angle so that it is almost lost to perception, then the smaller quantity entirely loses perceptibility.

*503. Why a man seen at a certain distance is not recognized.* 146
The perspective of decrease in size shows us that the more distant an object is the smaller it becomes. If you observe a man who is a bow-shot's length away from you and if you hold the minute hole of a small needle to your eye, through it you can see many men at that same distance whose visual images are perceptible to the eye and who also all find room within that hole. Therefore, if a man/who is a bow-shot's length away is perceptible to 146v the eye and occupies a small part of a hole within a needle, how within so small a space can you distinguish a nose, a mouth, or any detail of the body? Not seeing him in detail, you cannot recognize the man; the parts of his body do not show by which men are made different from one another.

*504. Why objects, the more they are removed from the eye, are* 145v
*the less perceived.* That thing will be least perceived which is farthest from the eye. This happens because those parts are lost first which are most minute, and then the less minute are lost at a greater distance, and thus successively, ensuing little by little, the while losing the details, perception of the remote object is lost, in such a way that finally all its parts, together with the whole, are lost, and the color also is lost because of the thickness of the air lying between the eye and the object seen.

*505. Of the parts of surfaces which first are lost through distance.* 136v
As you withdraw from shadowed bodies, first to be lost are their outlines; secondly, with greater distance the intervals that divide parts of bodies that touch one another are lost; thirdly, the breadth of the legs at the feet; and thus in succession the more minute parts are lost until, at a great distance there remains only an oval mass of indistinct shape.

*506. Of outlines.* The outlines of objects in the second plane will 153v
never be as clear as/those of objects in the first. 154
    Therefore, painter, do not distinguish as sharply between objects in the fourth and fifth plane, as you do between those in the first and the second, because the outlines of one object im-

pinging upon another follow the course of a mathematical line, which is not really a line, because the termination of one color is the beginning of another color, and is not therefore to be called a line, because nothing intervenes between the outlines of one color which is placed opposite another color, except the outline itself, which is imperceptible even when viewed near at hand. Therefore, painter, do not accentuate it in distant things.

150 507. *Precept of painting.* When you paint objects at great distances and show them clearly and sharply, those objects do not appear to be distant but seem near at hand. Therefore in your portrayal see that those things have the right clarity to indicate the distances, and if the thing that you have as an object has indistinct and uncertain outlines, show this in your reproduction.

Distant things appear to have indistinct and uncertain outlines for various reasons; one of these is that the object comes to the eye through such a small angle and so diminished that the eye functions as it does with very small objects, which, although near to the eye, cannot be distinguished as to shape, particularly in such details as claws on the feet of ants and the like. Another reason is that between the eye and distant objects there lies much air which becomes dense and thick, and through its whiteness it tinges the shadows and veils them, and makes of the obscurities a color between black and white, which is blue.

145 508. *Of objects seen from afar.* The outlines of that object will be less clear which are seen at a greater distance.

146v 509. *Which are the parts which first are lost to notice in bodies which are removed from the eye, and which are preserved the longest.* The part of the body which is far away from the eye, and which least preserves its visibility, is that which has the smallest shape. This occurs with the luster of spherical or cylindrical bodies and the slimmest parts of the body, as, for example, in a deer, which ceases to give the eye the images of its legs and horns before those of its body are lost, since the body being larger preserves its image better. But the first things that are lost through distance are the outlines which bound the surfaces and shapes of bodies.

510. *How, according to reason, small figures should not be fin-* 134v
*ished.* I say that the objects which appear small in size do so
because they are far from the eye. Since that is so, it follows
that there is much air between the eye and the object seen, and
so much air impedes the clarity of form of those objects, and
minute details of those bodies are indiscernible and unrecognizable. In such cases, painter, indicate small figures but do not
finish them in detail for if you do otherwise you will misrepresent
the effects of nature, your teacher. An object remains small because of the great distance that lies between the eye and that
object, and a great distance includes much air, and a great deal
of air is in itself a dense body which impedes vision and removes
minute details from the eye.

511. *Of the boundaries of bodies called outlines or contours.* Out- 136v
lines of bodies are so little conspicuous that at each small interval
lying between the object and the eye, the eye does not grasp the
image of friend or relative, and does not recognize him, unless it
be by his clothing, but gains knowledge of the figure by means
of the whole together with the parts.

512. Among objects of equal density, those which are nearest to 151
the eye will seem most sparse and open, and those which are
farthest away will look most compact.

513. The appearance and substance of objects at every degree of 164
distance lose degrees of power; that is, the more remote from
the eye an object is, the less its appearance will be able to penetrate through the air.

[PERSPECTIVE OF COLOR]

514. *Why faces seem obscure from a distance.* We see clearly 146
that all the images of visible things which we have as objects,
large as well as small, reach the community of senses through
the small opening for light in the eye. Through such a small
entrance pass the images of the greatness of the sky and of the
earth. The face of man being almost nothing amid such great
images because of the distance which diminishes it, occupies so
small a part of that opening for light in the eye, that it is al-

most imperceptible. Having to pass from the surface to the impressionable power through a dark medium, that is an empty nerve which seems dark, those visual images, not being of powerful color, are tinged with the darkness of the way by which they arrive, and when they reach the impressionable power they seem dark.

No other reason can be established in any manner. If that point which is in the eye is black, it is because it is full of a transparent humor as is the air, and it functions as would a hole made in a board, which seems to be black. Things seen in air of mingled brightness and darkness are confused in obscurity.

*163v* 515. *Of the nature of the medium lying between the eye and the object.* The medium occurring between the eye and the object is of two kinds; that is, either it has a surface, as does water, or a crystal and other transparent objects; or it is without a common surface, as is air, which adheres to the surfaces of bodies which are included within it, but that air has no continuous surface, except where it ends, above and below.

*163v and illus.* 516. *Effects of the medium which is enclosed by a common surface.* The medium which is enclosed by a common surface never renders to the eye in its true location the object which is behind it.

The proof is: let the crystal O R have parallel surfaces through which the eye, A, sees N M half of the object N G, behind it, through the part B O of the crystal, and sees the rest of the object, M G, through the air beneath the crystal. By means of the seventh proposition of the fourth book, it is explained that the visual line of the upper part of the object is bent on entering the crystal and makes the line N B A, and the line of the lower part, M G, is seen in its true location, according to the seventh proposition of the fourth book, as is shown by the lines which pass through the air beneath the crystal in M G A. Therefore, half the object N M, increases in the crystal, B O, and the other half diminishes in the air, which is beneath the crystal at O P.

*164* 517. *Of the interposing of transparent bodies between the eye and the object.* The greater the transparent body between the eye and the object, the more the color of the object will be transmuted into the color of the transparent object in between.

518. *Of blue, which distant landscapes appear to be.* Of objects *145* far from the eye, of whatever color you wish, that will appear to be bluest in color, which is the darkest, either naturally or accidentally. That object is naturally dark which is dark in itself and that one is accidentally so which is darkened by shadow cast by other objects.

519. *Of painting.* The blue of the air is a color compounded of *154v* light and darkness; light, I say, is air illuminated by the particles of humidity infused into it; and darkness, I say, is the pure air which is not divided into atoms, that is, into particles of humidity, through which the solar rays have to penetrate.

Of this an example is seen in the air which exists between the eye and mountains, which are shadowy because of the shadows of the great abundance of trees there, or are shadowy in those parts which are not struck by the solar rays, and this air becomes blue. But the air is not blue that lies between the eye and the luminous parts of the mountains, and is still less so in the parts covered by snow.

520. In the distance, first lost are the outlines of bodies that have *150v* similar colors, where the outline of one extends over that of the other, as the outline of an oak over that of another similar/ *151* oak. In the second place, with greater distance the outlines of bodies of medium color that border upon one another are lost, as for example, green trees against plowed land, or walls and mountains and rocks that have crumbled. Last of all to be lost are outlines where brightness borders on darkness, or where darkness does so on brightness.

521. *Precept on perspective in painting.* When you do not rec- *162* ognize differences of brightness or obscurity in the air, then the perspective of shadows is thrown out of your work, and you must rely on the perspective of the diminution of bodies, and on the perspective of the diminution of colors, and on the diminution of the clarity of objects opposite the eye. Perspective makes the same object appear more distant and there is loss in the intelligibility of the shape of any object.

The eye, without moving, will never know, by means of linear perspective,/how much distance there is between the ob- *162v* ject that lies between it and another object, except through the perspective of colors.

136v   522. *Of surface conditions that are lost first in receding from shadowed bodies.* In color the first thing to be lost with distance is the luster, which is the smallest part of color, and is a light within a light. The second is the light area because it is smaller than the shadow. Thirdly, the principal shadows are lost, and at
137   last there remains a medium,/indistinct obscurity.

148 and   523. *Of spots of shadows that appear on distant bodies.* The
illus.   throat or other straight perpendicular, which has some projection above it, will always be darker than the perpendicular face of that projection; this occurs because that body will appear most illuminated which is exposed to the greatest number of rays of the same light.

You see that A is illuminated by no part of the sky F K, and B is illuminated by I K of the sky, and C is illuminated by H K of the sky, and D by G K, and E by the whole sky from F to K. Thus, the breast will be of the same brightness as the forehead, nose, and chin.

But what I should remind you of about faces is that you should consider how, at different distances, different kinds of shadow are lost, and there remain only the essential spots, that is, the pits of the eye and places of similar significance. Finally
148v   the face remains/obscure, because the lights on it which are small in comparison with the medium shadows are consumed, for which reason at a distance the quality and quantity of lights and principal shadows are consumed, and every quality is blended into a medium shadow. This is the reason why trees and all objects at a certain distance appear darker in themselves than if those same objects were near the eye. From this obscurity in the air, which lies between the eye and the object, it comes about that that object becomes brighter again and tends toward blue, but it turns blue in the shadowed part sooner than in the luminous parts, where it shows its own colors more.

159v   524. *Of water clear and transparent down to the bottom below the surface.* When water is so transparent that the bottom can be

632. *Of shadows.* A shadow will never be truly similar to the 185*v*
contour of the body from which it derives, even if it is spherical,
unless the light is of the same shape as the shadowed body.

If the light is long in shape, and its length extends upwards
the shadows of bodies illuminated by it will extend in breadth.

If the length of the light is on a diagonal, the shadow of a
spherical body will become long in its height. Thus, whatever
the length of the light, the shadow will always have length in
the opposite direction, intersecting the length of the light like
a cross.

If the light should be broader and shorter than the shadowed
body, the impact of the derivative shadow will be longer and
narrower than the primary shadow.

/If the light should be narrower and longer than the shadowed 186
body, the impact of the derivative shadow will be broader and
shorter than the primary shadow.

If the length and breadth of the luminous body should be equal
to the length and breadth of the shadowed body, then the contours of the derivative shadow will be of the same shape as the
primary shadow.

633. *Of the outlines of a compound shadow.* The derivative com- 178*v*
pound shadow is of infinite length because it is pyramidal, with
the pyramid originating at its point. And this is proved, because
at whatever point that pyramidal length is cut, its angle is never
destroyed, as happens with the simple derivative shadow.

634. *That the outline of a simple shadow will be less clear than* 177
*the outline of a compound shadow.* The outline of the simple
shadow will be less clear than the outline of the compound
shadow, the nearer the shadowed body is to the luminous body.
This comes about because the pointed angle of the shadow and
the compound light is more obtuse.

The simple derivative shadow, created by a body smaller than
its luminous body always has its base toward the shadowed body.
But the shadow with compound light will have its pointed angle
toward the light.

*187v* 635. *Nature of the derivative shadow.* The derivative shadow increases and decreases in accordance with the increase or decrease of its primary shadow.

*140v* 636. The more a cast shadow/is mixed with light, the farther away it is from the shadowed body.

*187v* 637. *On the extension of the derivative shadow.* The outlines of the derivative shadows around the shadowed body expand the
*188* more the greater the size of the light/that creates them.

*178v* 638. *What shadow does a shadowed body cast which is greater than the luminous body?* If the shadowed body is greater than the luminous body, then the simple derivative shadow will have sides converging to a potential angle of the luminous body, and the angles of the shadow and the compound light will all face the luminous body.

*211* 639. *Between bodies of equal size that which is illuminated by*
*211v and* *the greater light will have a shorter shadow.*/Those bodies which
*illus.* are nearer to their original light or more remote from it will have shorter or longer derivative shadows.

*211v* 640. In this experiment the proposition stated above is confirmed, when the body M N is embraced by a larger part of light than is the body P Q.

    Let us say that U C A B D X is the sky, which produces the
*212* original light, and S T is a/window where the luminous visual images enter, and M N and P Q, are the shadowed bodies placed against that light. M N will have the smaller derivative shadow, because its original shadow is small and the derivative light is large, for however large the original light C D is, P Q will cast more derivative shadow, because its original shadow is larger than that of M N. Its derivative light is smaller than that of the body M N, because that part of the hemisphere A B that illuminates it, is smaller than the hemisphere C D which illuminates the body M N.

*215v and* 641. *Every shadow, with all its differentiations, which, with dis-*
*illus.* *tance, increases in width more than its source, has external lines which converge between the light and the shadowed body.* This

proposition appears clear and is confirmed in experience, so that if A B is a window without any crossbars, the luminous air which is to the right at A is seen from the left at D, and the air which is to the left at B illuminates the point C from the left, and these lines intersect at the point M.

642. *Each shadow cast by bodies in a room is directed along the* 214v *line of its center to a single point created by the intersection of the luminous lines in the center of the breadth and depth of the window.* The principle stated above appears clearly through experiment, for if you represent a place with a window open to the north, at S F, you will see the/horizon at the east produce 215 *and* a line which, touching the corners of the window O F, ends at *illus.* D, and the horizon of the west produces its line touching the two corners of the window R S, and ends at C. This intersection occurs precisely in the center of the breadth and depth of the window. Placing two rods, as in the places G H, will better confirm this principle for you. You will see the line cast by the center of the real shadow directed to the center M of the window, and toward the horizon N F.

643. *Bodies scattered about in a room illuminated by a single* 212 *and* *window will have shorter or longer derivative shadows depend-* *illus.* *ing on whether they are more or less in line with that window.* /The reason why shadowed bodies that are located more nearly 212v in line with the middle of the window will have shorter shadows than those located at the sides, is that they will be exposed to the window in its real shape, while when seen from the sides it is foreshortened. To the body in the middle, the window appears large, and to those at the sides it appears small. The body in the center views a large part of the hemisphere, that is, E F, while those at the sides see a small portion that is, Q R beholds A B, and, also, M N[5] beholds C D. The body in the middle, because it is in more light than those at the sides, is illuminated much farther down than its center, and so the shadow it casts is shorter, and as often as A B enters into E F, so many times the pyramid G 4 enters exactly into L Y.

[5] M N in the diagram should be located analogously to Q R.

212v
illus. on
212 644. *The center line of each derivative shadow lies in a straight line with the center of the original shadow, with the center of the shadowed body with that of the derivative light, with the center of the window and finally with that part of the meridian deriving from the celestial hemisphere.* Y H is the central line of the derivative shadow, L H that of the original shadow. L is the center of the shadowed body, L K of the derivative light. U is the middle of the window, and E is the final center of the original light produced by that part of the hemisphere of the sky which illuminates the shadowed body.

[THE AMOUNT OF LIGHT AND SHADOW VARIES WITH
THE POSITION OF THE EYES]

199 and
illus. 645. *Of the medium shadow contained between the principal lights and shadows.* The medium shadow appears that much greater in extension the more the eye that sees it is in line with the center of its magnitude. That is called a medium shadow which tinges the surfaces of shadowed bodies, beyond the principal shadow, and reflected light is contained therein, and it becomes darker or brighter, the nearer or more remote it is from the principal shadow. Let M N be the darkest shadow. The rest is more and more lighted as far as the point O. The rest of the figure is not connected with this proposition, but it will serve for the next one.

199 646. *Of the position of the eye that sees more or less shadow depending on the movement that it makes around the shadowed* 199v *body.* The proportions of the quantities which/the shadowed and the illuminated sides of shadowed bodies have in relation to one another, vary as much as there are differences in position of the eye that sees them. The proof is:[6] let A M [N] O be the shadowed body. P is the luminous body which embraces it with its rays P R and P S, and illuminates the side M D N, while the remainder, N O M, remains dark. The eye which sees such a body may be Q, which, with its visual rays, embraces that shadowed body and sees all of D M O, a view in which it sees D M, the side illuminated, much smaller than N O, the shadowed

[6] The diagram referred to is that in the paragraph preceding.

side, as is proved in the pyramid D G (Q in diagram) O cut
at K H equally distant from its base, divided at the point I.
Similarly the degree of brightness and obscurity for the eye will
vary in as many ways as the position of the eye varies.

647. *In what position the shadow of spherical bodies is never* 199v and
*seen.* The eye, which is located within the pyramid of reflected *illus.*
light from the illuminated surface of shadowed bodies will never
see any shadowed part of that body. The pyramid of reflected
light of illuminated visual images may be A B C, and the illuminated side of the shadowed body may be the part B C D, and
the eye which is within such a pyramid may be E, where all the
illuminated visual images, B D C, can never converge, unless it
be at the luminous point A, from which a shadow is never seen,
without being quickly destroyed. It follows, therefore, that E,
not seeing/anything except the illuminated side O D P, is less 200
able to see the outlines of the shadow B C, than is A, which is
so much more distant.

648. *Which that light is whose shadow can never be seen even* 216
*when the eye is farther away from the shadowed sphere than is*
*the light and is behind the light.* When the luminous body is
equal to or greater than the shadowed sphere, then the eye which
is in back of the light can never see any part of the shadow of
the shadowed body, because of the difference in their rays.

Let C E D F be the shadowed sphere, A B is/the luminous 216v and
body equal in size to the shadowed one, and the shadow of such *illus.*
a spherical body may be C F D. I say that the eye, L, which is
behind the light A B, at whatever distance you wish, can never
see any part at all of the shadow, according to the seventh proposition of the ninth book which states: parallel lines never converge to a point. Because A C and B D are drawn parallel, they
enclose exactly half of the sphere, and the lines N M, which meet
at the point L, form a point from which the half of the sphere
with its diameter C D can never be seen.

649. *Of the eye which at a great distance will never have its* 216v and
*view of the shadow of the shadowed body blocked when the* *illus.*
*luminous body is smaller than the shadowed body.* But when the

luminous body is smaller than the shadowed body, there will always be found some distance from which the eye can see the shadow of that shadowed body.

Let O P E F be the shadowed body, and the light be A B, less in whatever proportion you wish than the shadowed body. I say that the eye N, which is behind the light, will never be prevented from seeing some part of the shadow of the spherical shadowed body, as the straight directions of the lines show.

*200 and illus.* 650. *That position or rather that distance around the spherical body at which there is never lack of shadow.* But when the eye is more distant from the shadowed sphere than the body which illuminates it, then it is impossible to find a position where the eye is entirely deprived of the shadowy image of such a body. The proof is: let B N C (S) be the shadowed body, A the luminous body, B N C is the shadowed side, and B S C that illuminated. And let the eye be more remote from the shadowed body than is the light A. The eye sees all the shadow B D C E, and if the eye moves in a circle around that body at the same distance, it is impossible that it should entirely lose that shadow, for if, in its movement, it loses one part of that shadow on one side, through its movement it gains some on the other side.

*230v* 651. *Of the shadows and lights of cities.* When the sun is in the east and the eye above the center of a city, the eye will see the southern part of that city with its roofs half in shadow and half in light, and so with the northern part. The eastern part will be all in shadow, and the western all in light.

[SHADOWS IN LANDSCAPE VARY WITH THE POSITION OF THE SUN AND OF THE EYES]

*225v* 652. *Of the sun and the eye placed in the east.* When the sun and the eye are in the east, then all the parts of surfaces which are in view of the sun will appear illuminated to the eye, according to the ninth proposition of this book.

*225* 653. *When the sun is in the east and the eye is toward the north*
*225v* *or south.*/When the sun is in the east, and the eye is toward the north or south, then the eye will see the primary shadows of

bodies to the east and the lights on bodies to the west and is just in the middle between the lights and the shadows of bodies.

654. *Of the sun in the east, and the eye in the west.* When the *225v* eye in the west sees the sun in the east, then the opaque bodies lying between the east and the west will display their shadows to the eye.

It follows that such a landscape is half bright and half dark.

655. *Reminder to the painter.* Therefore, painter, when you rep- *225v and* resent your landscape or countryside with light to the right or *illus.* to the left, remember the above conclusion, setting forth how shadows have to cover bodies to a greater or lesser extent, in the measure that they are nearer or farther away from the source that illuminates them.

656. *Of the distinctness of the shadows in landscapes and of the* *208v* *objects located therein.* If the sun is in the east and you look to the west, you will see that all illuminated objects are entirely de- prived of shadow, because you see what the sun sees; and if you look to the south or toward the north, you will see all the bodies surrounded by shadow and light, because you see both what the sun sees and does not see; and if you look toward the path of the sun, all the bodies will show you their shadowed parts, be- cause that part which you see cannot be seen by the sun.

657. Among shadows of the same quality, that which is nearest *176v* to the eye will seem least dark.

### [MOVEMENT OF SHADOW]

658. *Of the motions of shadows.* The motions of shadows are *181* of five kinds; the first we shall mention is that in which the de- rivative shadow moves with its shadowed body, and the light that causes the shadow remains immobile. We shall call second that in which the shadow and the light move, but the shadowed body is immobile. The third will be that in which the shadowed body and the luminous body move, but the luminous body does so more slowly than the shadowed one. In the fourth motion of shadow, the luminous body moves more rapidly than the shad- owed body. In the fifth, the motions of the shadowed and the

luminous bodies are equal one to the other. This matter will be treated individually in its proper place.

*179v and illus.* 659. *Of the shadow that moves with greater velocity than its shadowing body.* It is possible for the derivative shadow to move many times faster than the original shadow. The proof is: let A be the luminous body, B the shadowed body, which moves from B to C along the line B D, and at the same time the derivative shadow of the body B, moves through the whole space B E, which could contain the space B C thousands of times.

*180 and illus.* 660. *Of the derivative shadow which/is much slower than the primary shadow.* It is also possible that the derivative shadow be much slower than the primary shadow. The proof is: let the shadow-casting body B C move on the plane N E through the whole space C E, and the derivative shadow falls on D E, the wall opposite. I say that the original shadow B C will move through the whole space B D, while the derivative shadow will not leave D E.

*180* 661. *Of the derivative shadow which is equal to the primary shadow.* The motion of the derivative shadow will be equal to the motion of the primary shadow when the luminous body which causes the shadow is equal in speed to that of the shadowed body, or, if you prefer, of the primary shadow. This is not otherwise possible, because whoever walks toward the west from morning to evening will, for the first part of the day, have a shadow moving more slowly in front of him than he goes, while during the latter half of the day the shadow will be much faster in flying backward than the shadow-casting body is in going forward.

*183 and illus.* 662. *Of the motion of a shadow.* The motion of the shadow is always more rapid than the motion of the body which creates the shadow, provided the luminous body is unmoved. The proof is: let the luminous body be A, and the shadowed B, and the shadow D. I say, that in an equal amount of time the shadowed body will move from B to C, while the shadow D moves to E, and the proportion between velocity and velocity during the same time, is that between length and length of movement. Thus, that proportion which the length of the movement made by the shad-owed body has from B to C, to the length of the movement of the shadow from D to E, is the same as the respective velocities of movement.

But if the luminous body is equal in speed to the movement of the shadowed body, then the shadow and the shadowed body are equal in movement one to the other. And if the luminous body is more rapid than the shadowed body, then the movement of the shadow will be slower than the movement of the shadow-ing body. But if the luminous body is slower than the shadowed body, then the shadow will be more rapid than the movement of the shadowed body.

663. *Of the remoteness and nearness when a man leaves and ap-proaches the same light and of the variations in his shadows.* The shadows and lights of the same body alter as much in shape and extent, as do the variations of a man's position in approaching and withdrawing from the light. *210 and illus.*

The proof follows: let the man be B C, who, in the light from A, throws the shadows B C F. Then the man moves from C to E, and the light remains fixed. The shape and the size of the second shadow D E G is different from the first.

664. *Of the changes which a fixed light brings to the shadows which are created on bodies that, without moving their feet, bend over, or down, or arise.* The proof follows: let F be the fixed light, and the man standing fixed in his place be A B, who bends over toward C B. I say that the shadow will change infinitely from A to C, because the movement is made in space, and space is a continuous quantity, and consequently divisible to infinity. Therefore, the shadows are altered to infinity: that is, from the first shadow A O B to the second shadow B C R. Thus our proposition is proved. *210 and illus.*

665. *Of the human body which turns in place and receives the same light on various sides and gives rise to infinite variations.*[7] The shadows which, together with lights, envelop an irregular *238*

[7] The word "humano" in the heading is changed by Ludwig to "allumato," and by Borzelli to "luminoso."

body, will be as various in obscurity and assume as many different shapes as there are variations in position which that body makes in its circumvolution. The same result is brought about when the body turns while the light stays fixed, as when the light moves around an immobile body.

*238v and illus.* The proof is: let EN be the immobile body and the mobile light be B, which/moves from B to A. I say that when the light was at B, the shadow of the globular mass of cloud D extended from D to F, which, while the light moved from B to A, moved from F to E, and so this shadow is changed in quantity and form, because its present place is not of the same form as the place which it left. Such change of form and of quantity is infinitely variable, because if the whole place which was at first occupied by the shadow is in itself completely different and of continuous quantity, and every continuous quantity is divisible to infinity, then it is concluded that the quantity of shadow and its form are variable to infinity.

225 666. *Of the location of lights and shadows of objects seen in the country.* When the eye sees all the sides of bodies in view of the sun, it will see all those bodies without shadow. This is proved by the ninth proposition which states: the surface of every opaque body takes on the color of the opposite object. Thus, since the sun is the opposite object, all those parts of the surface of bodies which are in view of it will take on the brightness of the sun which illuminates them. The eye sees those bodies and it is impossible for it to see any side of those bodies, other than that in view of the sun. Therefore, it will not see the primary shadow nor the derivative shadow of any of those bodies.

[BRIGHTNESS IN ILLUMINATED BODIES]

223 667. *Rule for giving the proper shadows and the proper lights to a form or body with several sides.* The greater or lesser obscurity of shadow, or the greater or lesser brightness of light that falls on the facets of a body with several sides, will correspond to the greater or smaller size of the angle occurring between the central line of the luminous body, which strikes the center of the illuminated side, and the surface of that illuminated side.

Thus, if the illuminated body were an octagonal column,/the  223v and
front of which is here shown in the margin, let the central line  illus.
be R A, which extends from the center of the luminous body R
to the center of the side S C, and also let the central line R D
extend from the center of the luminous body to the center of the
side C F. I say that there will be the same relation between the
quantity of light which the side S C receives from the luminous
body and that which the second side C F receives from the
same light, as between the size of the angle B A C, and the
angle E D F.

668. *On what surfaces is true and equal light to be found.*/That  208v-209
surface will be equally illuminated which is equally distant from  and illus.
the body that illuminates it. For example, if from the light A,
which illuminates the surface B[8] C D, lines were drawn equal to
that surface, then by the definition of the circle that surface will
be equally illuminated in every part; but if the surface is plane
as is shown in the second illustration, E F G H, then, if the
edges of the surface are equally distant from such lines, the
middle H will be the part nearest to that light, and will be the
more illuminated than the edges the nearer it is to its light E.
But if the edges of such a plane surface are unequally distant
from the light, as is shown in the third figure, I K L M, then
the nearest part and the farthest part will be illuminated in proportion to their distances from the body which illuminates them.

669. *Of the brightness of derivative light.* The finest brightness  209
of derivative light is to be seen where all the luminous body, with
half of its/right or of its left field of shadow in view.  209v and
  The proof follows: let B C be the luminous body, and its right  illus.
and left fields of shadow be D C and A B, and the shadowed
body, smaller than the luminous, may be N M, and the wall
P S is where the visual images of shadow and light are impressed.
I say, therefore, that the finest brightness of light of all the points
on that pavement will be on the wall P S at the point R. This is
manifest because R is in view of all the luminous body B C, with

---

[8] The MS reads A C D; this seems to be a reference error by Hand 1, since
on the diagram this must be B C D.

half the dark field A D, that is C D, as is shown us by the converging straight lines of the pyramid of shadow C D R, and the luminous pyramid B C R. Therefore, R is in view of as great a quantity of the dark field C D as it is of the luminous B C, but the point S is in view of the shadowy A B, and also of the shadowy C D, and these two dark spaces are twice the size of the luminous B C. But the farther you move from S toward R, the more you lose of the obscurity A B. Also, the farther you move from R to O, the less you will see of the luminous body, and thus the pavement R O will grow more obscure the nearer it is to O.

*210*     Through such analysis we have proved that R is the/brightest part of the base line O S.

*190 and*   670. *What part of the illuminated surface will be of the greatest*
*illus.*   *brightness.* That part of the illuminated body will be most luminous which is nearest the object which illuminates it. The proof is: let the side of the illuminated object be U C X, and the object which illuminates it be A B. I say that the point C is more illuminated than any other on the side of that body, because the luminous angle A C B which strikes it is larger than any other angle which can be created on that surface.

*198 and*   671. *Of the particular light of the sun or other luminous body.*
*illus.*   That side of an illuminated body will be of most intense brightness which is struck by the luminous ray between the most similar angles, and the least illuminated will be that which occurs between the most dissimilar angles of those luminous rays.

The angle N of the side which is toward the sun, being struck by the sun at equal angles, will be more intensely illuminated than any other part of that illuminated body, and the point C will be illuminated less than any other part because that point is struck by the solar body at angles more dissimilar than those at any other part of the plane to which the rays of the sun extend. Of the two angles let the greater be D C E and the lesser E C F, and A N O and B N R, which I should represent first, are equal angles, and for this reason N will be illuminated more than any other part.

672. *How one should know what part of the body ought to be* 218v 219 *more or less luminous than the rest.*/If A is the light, and the head is the body illuminated by it, that part of the head which receives on it the ray between the most nearly equal angles will be most illuminated; and that part which receives the rays between angles less equal will be less luminous.

This light acts like a blow;/the blow which falls between equal 219v and illus. on 219 angles has the greatest degree of power, and when the blow falls between unequal angles, it will be as much less powerful than the first as the angles are more unequal. For example: if you throw a ball against a wall of which the extremities are equally distant from you, the blow will fall between equal angles, but if you throw the ball against that wall, standing at one of its extremities, the ball will fall between unequal angles, and the blow will not be effective.

673. Where the angles made by the direct lines are more nearly 219v and illus. on 219 equal, there will be more light, and where they are more unequal, there will be more darkness.

After it has been proved that every light emanates from a single point, or seems to do so, the side illuminated by it will make that part more luminous on which the radial line between two equal angles falls, as is shown above along the lines A G, and also along A H, and similarly along L A, and that part of the illuminated side will be less luminous upon which the incidental line strikes between two more dissimilar angles, as appears in B C D. In this way also you can realize which parts are without light, as is shown at M and K.

674. *Light which falls on shadowed bodies between equal angles* 213v *has the greatest degree of brightness, and that body is in greater darkness which receives light between less equal angles; both light and shadow function through pyramids.* The angle C has the greatest degree of brightness because it/faces all the window 214 and illus. A B and all the horizon of the sky M X. The angle D has little difference from C, because the angles that place it in the center are not so dissimilar in proportion compared with those that are lower and it lacks only that part of the horizon which is between Y and X. Although it acquires as much from the opposite side,

nevertheless its line is of little strength because its angle is smaller
than that/alongside. The angles E D, have less light, because
there they do not face as much of the sky as does C, and the
light M S and the light U X are lacking there, and the angles
between which they fall are very unlike; the angle K and the
angle F are each placed between angles very dissimilar one from
another and therefore give little light, because K is in view only
of the light P T, and F is in view only of T Q; O G is the least
degree of light, because it does not face any part of the light of
the horizon, and those are the lines which compose a pyramid
similar to the pyramid C, and this pyramid L is of the greatest
degree of shadow because it also falls between equal angles.

And those angles of the pyramids are directed and turned toward one another by a straight line which passes from the center
of the shadowed body and connects the luminous visual images
with the center of the light, images multiplied within the boundaries of the window marked by the points A B. As they expand,
they produce a brightness which surrounds the derivative shadow
created by the shadowed body at the points 4 and 6. The forms
of shadow are multiplied in O G and finish at 7 and 8.

675. *Of that part of a body which will be most illuminated by a
light of even quality*. That side of a body will be brightest which
receives the impact of light at the largest luminous angle.

The proof is: let the hemisphere of the sky be R M C, which
illuminates the house K D O F. I say that the part of the house
will be most illuminated which receives the impact of light at
the widest angle.

Therefore, at F, where N F C strikes, there will be more intense brightness of light, than where the angle E D C strikes,
where the proportion of the lights is the same as that of the angles,
and the proportion of the angles/will be the same as is that of
their bases N C and E C, where the larger exceeds the smaller
by the whole part N E. Thus at A, under the eaves of the roof
of the house, there will be less light than at D, and this diminution will be in proportion as the base B C of this angle B A C is
smaller than the base E C, and thus it always follows proportionately, provided the light is of even quality.

214v

201 and
illus.

201v and
illus.

And the same that is said above is confirmed in every body illuminated by our hemisphere, and is here shown in the part of the spherical object beneath the hemisphere K and F which at the point B is illuminated by all the part A to C, and at the part D by the hemisphere E F, and at O by G[9] F, and at N by M F, and at H by S F, and thus you have learned where the greatest degree of light and the greatest degree of shadow are in any body whatsoever.

676. That part of a shadowed body will be most luminous which is illuminated by the largest amount of light. *201v and illus.*

Therefore, taking A B C as the shadowed body, and D F N as the luminous body, that is the illuminated hemisphere, the point C has double the light of the side B, and three-quarters more than A, because C is illuminated by the sky D G F E, and B by the sky D F, which is one half smaller than D E, and the side A is illuminated by only the fourth part of D E, that is, by G D.

677. The surface of every opaque body takes on the/color of the object opposite it. *201v-202 and illus.*

Let D be the opaque body, A N the luminous body, A C a body of dark color, C D the plane illuminated by the hemisphere A F M N. By reason of what has been said, R will be more illuminated than O, O than S, S than T, and the same will occur on the sides that are turned to A C, a dark body, and the same on those that are turned to the illuminated place C D. From this the light and shadow and reflected light derive.

678. The shadow made by the sun, and lying beneath the projections of the coverings of buildings, gains in darkness with every degree of height. *202 and illus.*

679. *Which part of the sphere is more illuminated.* That side of *220v* spheres which is illuminated will be of most intense brightness, which is accompanied by the least number of images of shadow.

The proof is: let F N O be the shadowed spherical body, and A B C the luminous hemisphere, and the/plane A C the density *221 and illus.*

---

[9] G, referred to in the text and missing from the diagram, should be marked at the intersection between M and E.

of the earth. I say, then, that the part of the sphere F N, will be of the most intense brightness, for it is not in view of any part of the earth A C, and in itself it is of equal brightness because it is illuminated by equal arcs of the hemisphere A B C; that is, the arc A R E is equal to the arc R B S, and to the arc B S C, and according to the precept that when two things are equal to a third they are equal to one another, therefore, P F N are equal in brightness.

*196v* 680. *Of the nature of the light that illuminates shadowed bodies.* The universal light of the sky surrounds the part of the shadowed body which faces it, and illuminates and varies the illumina-
*197* tion of that part with greater or lesser brightness,/depending on whether the parts of such an illuminated body are exposed to a greater or lesser quantity of that universal light.

*191* 681. *Precept of painting.* Under the universal light from the sky,
*191v and* shadows occupy little space/on the surfaces of bodies. This comes
*illus.* about because the great amount of light from our hemisphere of the sky surrounds shadowed bodies down to the least parts, when the horizon does not interfere, and especially if the body is raised above the earth.

Let F be the shadowing body, E the earth, A B C D our hemisphere of the sky. A D is the horizon of this hemisphere, and the density of the earth U X obscures as much of the shadowed body as it has in view, but the horizon also views the same parts, illuminates the same places, and makes indistinct the visual images of the earth, which would be disposed to make dark shadows underneath the object, if it were not impeded.

*198* 682. *Of the universal light of the air where the sun does not*
*198v and* *strike.*/That object will appear most illuminated which is ex-
*illus.* posed to the largest quantity of the luminous body. According to what has been said, E will be more illuminated than A, since E faces a larger amount of sky, with a view of R S, which A does not see, since it beholds only the sky B C D.

[POSITION AND DEGREE OF SHADOWS]

*193v* 683. *Of the qualities of lights and shadows on shadowed bodies.* I say that shadows have little strength on the sides of bodies which are turned to the cause of the light, and so also the shadows among shadows turned to the cause of those shadows. Those shadows and lights are shown to be of great strength which occur between the cause of the shadows and the cause of the light.

684. *Of the universal light mixed with the particular light of the* 198v and *sun or other light.* Without doubt, that part of the shadowed illus. body which is exposed to the least quantity of the universal or specific luminous bodies will be least illuminated.

The proof is: let A be the body of the sun placed in the sky N A M. I say that the point O of the shadowed body will be more illuminated by the universal light than the point R, because O sees and is seen by all of the parts of the universal light N A M, and the point R is not seen except by a part of the sky, M T. Furthermore, O is seen by the whole quantity of the sun, which is turned toward it, and R does not see any part of that sun.

685. *Of the imperceptible outlines of shadows.* That part of the 193v shadow will be most dark which is suffused with the least amount of light.

686. *What part of an opaque sphere is least illuminated.* That 221 and part of an opaque sphere will be most deeply in shadow which illus. is exposed to the smallest number of luminous rays. Although this is very similar to the first proposition above, I shall not neglect to prove it, because the proof is somewhat different.

[10]Let the shadowed body be F N O, and the hemisphere A B C, and the density of the earth be the line A C. To begin with, I say that the upper part of the sphere, F P N, will be equally illuminated by all the hemisphere A B C, and this I have shown, for the three parts which are given as equal, that is, A R E, which illuminates the point F, and R B S which illuminates P, and G[11] S C which illuminates N; therefore, according to the seventh proposition of the ninth book, F P N, the upper part of the sphere is of equal brightness, and the seventh of the ninth states that all those parts of bodies which are illuminated at an equal

---

[10] The diagram for this proof is that for the chapter immediately preceding in the MS.

[11] G should be interpolated in diagram at the intersection of C N P with the arc.

*221v and illus.* distance by equal and similar lights will always/necessarily be of equal brightness, a condition which occurs at F P N.

There follows the second demonstration. Let A B C be the shadowed spherical body, D F E the illuminating hemisphere; D E is the earth, which in this instance causes the shadow. I say that, according to the preceding, all the part of the sphere A N B is without shadow, because it is not in sight of the density of the earth, and all the remainder of the surface of that sphere is shadowed with more or less obscurity, depending on whether a greater or smaller amount of the density of the earth is accompanied by a smaller or larger quantity of light from the hemisphere. Therefore the point C, which is in view of a smaller amount of the hemisphere and a larger amount of the earth, will be darker than any other part of the shadow, that is, it is in view of only R D and S E of the hemisphere, and in view of all the earth D E. The brightest is A B, because it has in view only the extremities of the earth, D E.

That part of any sphere which is illuminated will be as much smaller as the part of the luminous body that it views is smaller.

*221v and illus.* The proof is: let A H be the shadowed body, C I E may be our hemisphere. It follows that A, a part of the shadowed body, will be less illuminated because it is in view of a smaller part of the luminous body, that is, of a smaller part of the daylight of *222 and illus.* our hemisphere, as/the two parts B C and D E show.

Therefore, that part of the spherical body which is illuminated by a greater amount of the luminous body will be of larger shape. This is proved by the converse of the preceding.

If the smallest light B C, D E, of our hemisphere illuminates a very small part of the sphere A H, the same light of that hemisphere will illuminate the largest part of the spherical body; that is, if B C and D F of the following figure illuminate only the part N M R, the remainder of the hemisphere, including the parts B C and D F, will illuminate the rest of that sphere. This is so, because, although B C and D F illuminate N M R, they also illuminate the part K N of the sphere, and the other L R, on the opposite side.

Here the opposition says that it does not want so much science, that it is enough to practice drawing from nature. The reply is that there is nothing more deceptive than to rely on our own opinion, without any other proof, as experience always proves to be the enemy of alchemists, necromancers, and other ingenuous simpletons.

687. *Of the shadow of the opaque sphere placed in the air.* The *216v* part of an opaque sphere will be most shadowed which is exposed to the greatest amount of darkness.

Let the dark object be the plane D C, and the luminous hemisphere be/D N C, and the spherical body placed between the *217 and* light of the hemisphere and the darkness of the earth be B C P O. *illus.* I say that the part of O Q P will be darker than any other part of the sphere, because it alone is exposed to all three sides of the darkness D C, of the earth opposite, and it sees less of every other side.

The proof is one of the elements of geometry which states: the line drawn from the center of a circle to the angle of the tangent is perpendicular and falls between two right angles. It follows that the line which comes from the center X of the sphere terminates in right angles on S C at the point O, in view of the density of the earth D C, and therefore O is in view of the earth. P, which is opposite does the same, for the same reasons, as does Q, and every part that lies in the space between O and P. But Q is of the most intense obscurity, because it is in the center above the earth, which O and P are not, for they are nearer the ends of the density of the earth, and begin to be in view of the horizon of the hemisphere, and they are mingled with its light.

688. *Of the shadow of the opaque sphere which is placed on the* *217 and* *earth.* But the opaque sphere in contact with the earth will have *illus.* a shadow of greater obscurity than the preceding one, which only has the earth in view as the object opposite it.

The proof is: let the opaque sphere N M S rest on the earth A C at the/point S, and the arc A B C may be our hemisphere. *217v* I say that the shadow which the sphere makes on the earth where it rests is darker than the preceding, according to the eighth proposition which states: every thing participates in its cause, whence it follows that the earth, cause of such a shadow, will produce a darker shadow, which will be inherently darker. Therefore, the shadowed object is darker than that illuminated— this is the conclusion.

191 and illus. 689. *Of the quality of obscurity in shadows.* The degrees of darkness of derivative shadows vary infinitely, with greater or lesser power in relation to the greater or lesser distances at which the impacts of the derivative shadows occur.

The proof is: let the sun be A, which creates the shadow N P H I, into which enters the light of the air, which surrounds the sun's rays, that is, E B R S above, and F C R S below, and lights up that shadow, which is very dark in the space N P O, where there is no view of the sun, nor air, except in the extremities at B C.

270v and illus. 690. *Which part of the sphere is least illuminated.* That part of the shadowed body will be least illuminated which is exposed to the smallest part of the luminous body.

The proof is: let A S Q R be the shadowed body and the luminous body may be its hemisphere N C E F. I say, that the part A and the part O, because they face the equal arcs B[12] C E D and C E D F, are in view of equal quantities of light, and are for this reason equally illuminated by them.

But R faces the smaller arc E D F and receives less light, and P faces only D F, which is smaller than E D F, for this reason remains less luminous, and Q remains still less luminous, for it faces only the extremity of the horizon F.[13]

## [DARKNESS OF DIFFERENT SHADOWS]

199 691. *Whether a large light of little strength is as strong as a small light of great strength.* The shadow created by a small and powerful light is darker than the shadow created by a larger light of less strength.

---

[12] The text reads ACED, which is an obvious error. The intersection of the diagonal A with the arc between N and C is here arbitrarily designated as B for clarity.

[13] This passage is confused, so that Ludwig proposed two different reconstructions of it. Cf. *Quellenschriften*, XVII, 321n.

692. *Of the light that is changed into shadow*. The place il- 188
luminated by the air will become shadowed if it is surrounded
by the impact of the sun's rays. This comes about because the
greater light makes the illumination of a smaller light seem
obscure.

693. *Of the shadow that is changed into light*. A place shadowed 188
by the sun will remain illuminated by the air after the setting of
the sun, since the lesser light is always a shadow of the greater
light.

694. *Of simple shadow of the first degree of obscurity*. The 181v and
simple shadow is that which can be seen by no reflected light, *illus.*
but will be augmented only by an opposite shadow.

Let the sphere G be placed in a concavity B C E F, and the
specific light be A, which falls on B, and is reflected on D, and
rebounds with a second reflection on the sphere G, which has its
simple shadow on one side in the angle E, which faces neither/ 182
the direct nor the reflected light with any degree of reflection.
Thus the shadow of the sphere receives the reflection of the
simple shadow E, and for this reason, it is called a simple
shadow.

695. *What light makes the shadows of bodies most different* 200 and
*from their lights*. That body will make shadows of greatest dark- *illus.*
ness which is illuminated by light of greatest brilliance.

The point A is illuminated by the air which is illuminated by
the sun. There is the same proportion between the illuminated/A 200v
and the illuminated B that there is between the light of the sun
and that of the air.

696. *What body is it which, with the same color and distance* 208
*from the eye, has lights that least differ from its shadows?* That
body will display the least difference between its shadows and
its lights which is in air of the greatest/darkness, and conversely 208v
so, when it is in air of the greatest brightness. This is manifest
when a body is placed in darkness, and cannot be perceived;
but when objects are placed in the brilliance of the sun, the
shadows seem to be darkness itself compared to the parts struck
by the sun's rays.

[COMPARISON OF SHADOWS]

*177v*  697. *How primary and derivative shadows are connected.* The derivative shadow is always combined with the primary shadow. This conclusion is proved by itself, because the primary shadow is the basis of the derivative one, but they differ only so far as the primary shadow tinges the body to which it is attached and the derivative is diffused through all the air penetrated by it.

The proof is:[14] let the luminous body be F and the shadowed body be A O B C, and the primary shadow which is attached to the shadowed body, the part A B C. The derivative shadow, A B C D, originates together with the primary. Such a shadow is called simple, for it is one in which no part of the luminous body can be seen.

*181v*  698. *Of the death of the derivative shadow.* The derivative shadow will be completely destroyed on bodies illuminated by the universal light.

*185v*  699. *Where the derivative shadow is most obscure.* That derivative shadow will be darkest which is nearest to its cause, and those which are remote will be lighter.

That shadow is sharpest and clearest which is nearest to its origin, and the least sharp is the most remote.

A shadow looks denser toward its edges than toward its center.

*181v*  700. *Of the maximum power of the derivative shadow.* With specific lights the derivative shadow is made greater in power, the smaller the extent of the light and the more powerful it is in brightness.

*239v*  701. *Which shadow is darkest.* That part of the shadow will be darkest which is nearest to its origin.

*186*  702. *Of the various degrees of obscurity of the shadows surrounding the same shadowed body.* Of the shadows surrounding the same shadowed body, that will be darkest which is created by the most powerful luminous body.

[14] A pencilled comment in the margin reads: Notta errore nella figura. (Note an error in the diagram.) The diagram is not appropriate. Cf. note: Ludwig, *Quellenschriften*, XVII, 310.

703. *Of the shadow made by one body between two equal lights.* 186v
That body which is located between two equal lights will send
out two shadows, which will be directed along straight lines to
the two lights, and if the body mentioned is moved and placed
nearer to one light than the other, the shadow, which it directs
toward the nearer light, will be less dark than that which is directed toward the farther light.

704. *Where the derivative shadow is darkest.* That part of the 188
derivative shadow will be darkest which is nearest to its cause.
And the contrary follows: that part of the derivative shadow is
least dark which is farthest from its cause.

705. The darkness of the derivative shadow diminishes by as 176
much as it is farther away from the primary shadow.

706. *Of a derivative shadow created on another derivative shadow.* 187v and
The derivative shadow created by the sun can be cast on a deriva- *illus.*
tive shadow created by the air.
    The proof is: let the shadow of the object M, which is created
by the air E F in the space D C B, and let the object N, by
means of the sun, G, make the shadow A B C and the remainder
of the shadow D M, which in this place does not face the air
E F nor the sun either; therefore, it is a double shadow, because
it is created by the two objects, that is, N and M.

707. *Of the compound derivative shadow.* The more the com- 177 and
pound derivative shadow is removed from the simple derivative *illus.*
shadow, the more darkness it loses. This is proved by the ninth
proposition which states: that shadow becomes less dark which is
exposed to a greater quantity of a luminous body. Then let A B
be the luminous body, and $L^{15}$ O the shadowed one, and let
A B F be the luminous pyramid, and $L^{15}$ O K the pyramid of
the simple derivative shadow. I say that G will be one quarter
less illuminated than F, because F faces all the light A B, and
G lacks one quarter of the light A B; for only C $B^{15a}$ which is
three quarters of the luminous body, illuminates G./And H 177v

[15] For the sake of clarity, because of the duplication of the letter B, read "L"
for "B" in the shadowed body.
[15a] The manuscript here reads C F in error.

faces D B, half of the luminous body A B, so H has half the light of F. And I faces one quarter of the light A B, that is, E B, so I is three quarters less luminous than F. And K faces no part of that light, so in that place there is absence of light and the beginning of the simple derivative shadow. Thus we have explained the compound derivative shadow.

177v  708. *How the simple shadow is connected with the compound shadow.*[16] The simple shadow is always connected with the compound shadow. This is proved by the previous passage in which it is said: the primary shadow becomes the basis for the derivative shadow. Because the simple shadow and the compound one

178  are derived from the same/body, and are connected with one another, it is necessary that the effect participate in the cause. And since the compound shadow is in itself not other than the diminution of light, and begins where the luminous body begins and ends where the luminous body ends, it follows that such a shadow is created between the simple shadow and the simple light.

The proof is: let the luminous body be A B C, the shadowed one D E, and the simple derivative shadow be D E F, and the compound derivative shadow be F and K. The simple derivative shadow does not face any part of the luminous body, while the compound derivative shadow always faces the luminous body, in greater or lesser part, depending on the greater or lesser degree of remoteness of its parts from the simple derivative shadow. The proof is: let such a shadow be E F K, which, with half its size F K, that is, I K, faces the half of the luminous body A B, which is A C. This is the brightest part of that compound shadow, and the other darker half of the same compound shadow, that is, F I, faces C B, the second half of the luminous body. Thus we have explained the two parts of the compound derivative shadow, and how one is brighter or less dark than the other.

178  709. *Of the simple and compound primary shadow.* The simple and the compound shadow have the same proportion to one an-

[16] The scribe has added at the beginning: et la sua figura è la 2ª disopā (and its figure is the second above). A comment in the margin reads: Notta errore nella figura. (Note an error in the diagram.) The diagram referred to (McM. 707, Urb. 177) and its lettering do not agree with the text of this section.

other in primary shadows attached to shadowed bodies that they have in derivative shadows separated from those same shadowed bodies. This is proved because the simple and compound primary and derivative shadows are connected with one another, without interruption, as though the primary shadow were the origin and cause of the derivative shadows.

710. *Whether the primary shadow is stronger than the derivative shadow.* The primary shadow, being simple, will be equal in darkness to the simple derivative shadow. The proof: let the simple primary shadow be D E, and the simple derivative shadow be F G. I say this because of the fourth proposition of this book, wherein it is stated: darkness is absence of light. Therefore the simple shadow is that which receives no illuminated reflection, and thus remains dark, as is D E which is not exposed to the light A, nor does the simple derivative shadow F G face it, and therefore these shadows are of equal density, for both are without light and luminous reflection. *180v and illus.*

711. *Which shadow is darker, the primary or the derivative.* The primary shadow is always darker than the derivative shadow, provided it is not affected by a reflected light striking it, which makes it the background for the impact of the derivative shadow. Let B C D E be the shadowed body, and A be the light which causes the primary shadow B E C and throws the derivative B E C H I. I say that if the illuminated reflexes F H and I G do not spoil the primary shadow B E with F H, and C E with I G, the primary shadow will remain darker than the impact of the derivative one, provided that both shadows are thrown on a surface of equal darkness or of equal brightness of color. *176 and illus.*

712. *How the derivative shadow, when it is surrounded wholly or in part by an illuminated background, is darker than the primary shadow.* On a plane surface, the derivative shadow which is, wholly or in part, surrounded by a luminous background, is always darker than the primary shadow. Let the light be A, and the object which has the primary shadow be B C, and the wall be D E, which receives the derivative shadow on the part N M, and what remains, D N and M E, is illuminated by A. *184v and illus.*

The light D N reflects on the primary shadow B C, and the light
M E does the same. Therefore, the derivative N M, not facing
the light A, remains dark, and the primary shadow is illuminated
by the illuminated background, which surrounds the derivative
shadow. And so the derivative shadow is darker than the primary.

*184v* 713. *How the primary shadow which is not attached to a plane
surface is not of even darkness.* The proof is: let the primary
shadow attached to the object be B C D, toward which the derivative shadow F G faces, and furthermore, the illuminated
*185 and* backgrounds E F and G H face toward it. I say that such a body/
*illus.* will be more illuminated at the edge B than in the middle D,
because B faces A, the original light, and the derivative light
E F is seen by means of reflected rays, and the derivative shadow
F G is not attached to it, because F B D is the angle of the
tangent made by the straight line F B and the curve B D. The
derivative shadow F G faces all the rest of such a body depending, more or less, on whether the line F G can be made the base
of a triangle with a larger or a smaller angle at its point.

### [REFLECTED LIGHTS IN SHADOWS]

*180v* 714. *Nature or condition of shadow.* No shadow is without a
reflection which augments or weakens it, and that reflection augments it which is created by something darker than the shadow,
while another reflection weakens it when created by something
brighter than the shadow.

*180v and* 715. *What an augmented shadow is.* The augmented shadow is
*illus.* one in which only its own derivative shadow is reflected. Let A
be the luminous body, B C the primary shadow or the basic one,
and D G will be the shadow cast.

*185* 716. *Conditions governing objects darkened by each shadow.*
Among shadowed objects of equal darkness, shape, and size, that
one will darken most from a shadow opposite which is nearest to it.

*222* 717. *Of the proportion of illuminated parts of bodies to their
222v and* *reflected lights.* There is the same proportion between the side
*illus.* illuminated by the incident/light and that which is illuminated

by the reflected light, as there is between the incident and the reflected lights.

The proof is: let A B be the incident direct light which illuminates the spherical body C D on C N D, and passes on with its rays to the object E F, reflecting from it on C M D. I say that if the light A B has two degrees of strength, and E F has only one, which is half of two, the reflected light C M D will be half the light C N D.

718. *Of the medium shadow which falls between the illuminated* 198v *and the shadowed parts of bodies.* Between the illuminated and the shadowed parts of bodies there falls the medium shadow whose outlines vary greatly, for where it meets the shadow it is converted into shadow and where it meets an illuminated part/ 199 it partakes of the illuminated part. If the original light is from a specific source, then, provided the body has a polished surface, there will be lustrous areas which will have edges whose medium shadow will be as sharp as that shadowed side permits.

719. *Of the darkest side of shadow on spherical or columnar* 222v *bodies.* The darkest part of the shadow of spherical or columnar bodies will occur between the incident light and the reflected light.

720. *Where the reflection of light must be dimmest.* If the light 228v and S illuminates the body R H P, it makes the primary shadow illus. brighter above, toward the light, than below where this body rests on a plane, according to the fourth proposition of this book, which states: the surface of every body takes on the color of the object opposite it. Then the derivative shadow, which is thrown on the pavement in the place M P, rebounds to the part of the shadowed body O P, and the derivative light which surrounds this shadow, that is, M N, rebounds on O R. This is the reason why such shadowed bodies never have luminous reflected light on the borders that rest on the pavement.

721. *Of shadow interposed between incident light and reflected* 228 *light.*[17]/The shadow that comes between the incident and the re- 228v

---

[17] The heading: DE REFLESSI (Of reflected lights), precedes this group of sections. Hand 1 had first written as the heading of this section: Delli reflessi de

flected light is of great density and appears darker than it is, by comparison with the incident light on which it borders.

228v  722. *Why reflected light is seen little or not at all under universal light.* The reflected lights on shadowed bodies are seen little or not at all under universal light from the sky, and this happens because the universal light surrounds and embraces each one of those bodies whose surface, as has been proved, takes on the color of objects opposite. It is as if the body A were illuminated by the hemisphere G C D, and shadowed by the earth,

229 *and* G F D. Here the surface of the body/is illuminated and shad-
*illus.* owed by the air and the earth, which stands as its object, and it is the more illuminated or shadowed, depending on whether it is exposed to a greater or lesser amount of the luminous body or of the dark one. As is seen, all the part of the hemisphere H C I faces the point K, which does not face any part of the darkness of the earth. Then it follows that K is illuminated more than A, which faces only the part of the hemisphere C D, and this illumination is spoiled by the darkness of the earth R D, all of which is exposed and is seen at the point A, as is proved by perspective.

If we wish to speak of the point B, we find that it is less illuminated than the point A, for B faces half as much of the hemisphere as A does, which faces all of C D, but B faces only E D, which is half of C D, and it faces all of the darkness of the earth, which A faced, that is, the earth R D, to which is added the part R F, which is darker, because it lacks the light of the hemisphere E C, which is not lacking on the earth R D.

For this reason, then, this body cannot have reflected light, because reflected light comes after the principal shadow of bodies, and here the principal shadow is at the point where this body is in contact with the plane of the earth, because there it is entirely deprived of light.

229  723. *In what way reflected light is created under universal light.*
229v *and* /Reflected light is created on bodies illuminated by universal light
*illus.*

---

lumi che risaltano all'ombre (Of the reflected lights that penetrate into the shadows), but then crossed it out in favor of the first heading given above.

when one part of the illuminated body reflects its greatest light in that place where a smaller part of that same light is seen; as for example, when the sky E F faces the place D, and the greater part of the same sky faces H, then the derivative light H is reflected at D. But a special treatise on this will be composed in the proper place.

724. *Of the different degrees of shadow portrayed in painting.* The surface of every opaque body takes on the color of the object opposite, and does so more or less, as the object is nearer or farther away. *204 and illus. on 204v*

The proof of the first part: let A B C be the surface of the opaque body, which we shall suppose to be white, while the object R S is black, and the object N M is also white. According to the ninth proposition of this book, it is proved that every body fills the surrounding air with the visual images of its color and with the resemblance of the colored body. Therefore, R S, the black object, fills the air in front of it with dark color, which terminates at G A B, a side of the opaque body A B C, which is tinged with the color of the object R S, and the white color of the other object N M will whiten all that part of the opaque body at A B C. Therefore, on the opaque body will be found all A G simply taking on the black of R S, and B C the simple white, while on A B, which faces a white and a black object, there will be a color composed of black and white; that is, a surface of mixed color.

Regarding the second part of this proposition, it may be said that it will be much darker at A than at B, because A is nearer to the black body R S than is B, and this is made manifest by the definition of the circle in geometry as in the figure. Beside this, at the angle B, although it is the smallest angle there is, as is proved in geometry, from the angle of the tangent B nothing can be seen but the extremity of the body R S at the point R. Furthermore, there is added at B the brightness of the white object N M, which, even/if it were black, because it is farther from B than A is from R S, would never be as dark as A. *205*

725. When a specific light illuminates its object, an object which has something of bright color illuminated by the same light op- *202v*

posite gives rise to a counter light, that is, a reflection, or rather a reverberation.

That part of the reflected light which in part envelops the surface of bodies will be that much less bright than the illuminated part of the air, as it is less bright than the air.

197 726. *How bodies surrounded by universal light create specific lights on many of their own sides.* Individual lights are created on the surfaces of shadowed bodies, even when as a whole they are surrounded from above by the universal light of the sky without the sun, as when a dark cloud covers it. This comes about because of the inequalities of the surfaces of those bodies, by reason of the parts joined to them, which, coming between that light and the shadowed body, deprive that body of a great quantity of the universal light; whence the light that penetrates between the limbs and the body becomes individual light; that is, a part of the whole light which embraces the external parts of each limb.

[DISTINCTNESS IN THE EDGES OF SHADOWS]

184 727. *Which derivative shadow will show the sharpest outlines.* That derivative shadow will show the sharpest outlines, whose shadowed body is most distant from the luminous body.

195 728. *Of shadow and light.* That object will have shadows and lights with the most indistinct outlines which lies between the largest dark and bright objects.

The proof is: let the object be O, which lies between the shadowy N M and the luminous R S. I say that the shadowy object/
195v and includes almost all the object with its pyramid N A M, and the
illus. pyramid from the luminous R C S does the same on the opposite side.

And that which is proposed is proved by the eighth proposition of the fifth book, for it states that that side of a sphere will be darkest which most completely faces the darkness placed opposite to it. It follows that C is darker than any other part of that sphere.

The second figure also proves this: B A C faces all the darkness E G F, and that darkness is not distributed on B A C with equal intensity, because it is not distributed in uniform quantity, for A, which faces all the obscurity E F, is much darker than B, which faces only the half E G, and the same thing happens at C, where part of the shadow G F is seen.

729. *Why a shadow which is larger than its cause has indistinct* *186v* *outlines*. The air which surrounds the light is almost of the same nature as that light with regard to brightness and color, but the farther away it is, the more it loses its likeness. The object/which *187* makes a large shadow is near to the light and is illuminated by the light and the luminous air, wherefore this air leaves the out-lines of the shadow indistinct.

730. *Whether a derivative shadow is darker in one place than in* *183v* *another*. The derivative shadow will be the darker the nearer it is to the shadowed body, or rather, to the primary shadow, and thus it comes about that its/outlines are sharper at its origin *184* than in the parts distant from that origin.

731. *Of the derivative shadow distant from the primary shadow.* *180 and* The edges of the derivative shadow will be the more indistinct *illus.* the more distant they are from the primary shadow. The proof: let A B be the luminous body, C D the primary shadow and E D is the simple derivative shadow, while C G E is the in-distinct end of the derivative shadow.

732. *Of the outlines of the derivative shadow*. The outlines of *187v* the derivative shadow are less distinct under universal light from the sky than under a specific light.

733. Absolute darkness is absolute absence of light, and, because *238v* their quantity is continuous, there is infinite variation between light and darkness; that is, between darkness and light there is a pyramidal light potential/which, since it is always divided in *239* half toward its point, leaves the remainder always more luminous than the part taken away.

[SHADOWS AFFECTED BY THE DENSITY AND COLOR OF BODIES]

734. *Quality of shadows*. Where equal absences of light occur *183* there will be the same proportion between the darkness of the

shadows created, as there is between the degrees of darkness of the colors to which such shadows are attached.

*217v* 735. *Of the shadows of somewhat transparent bodies.* No transparent body throws a dark shadow unless it is shadowed by many other similar bodies, such as the leaves of trees which make shadows on one another.

*190v* 736. *What body takes on the deepest shadow.* That body will take on shadow of the greatest darkness which is the densest, *191* although the bodies themselves be of the/same color. I say that the shadow of a green drapery will be darker than that of a leafy tree, even if the green of the drapery and of the leaves of the tree be of the same quality, and this is caused by the fact that the drapery is not transparent, as is a leaf, and does not have illuminated air between its sides, as does the foliage of trees, which makes the shadowed parts indistinct.

*191* 737. *Of the shadow of the verdure of meadows.* The verdure of meadows has very little, almost imperceptible shadow, especially where the plants are very small, with thin blades of grass, and for this reason shadows cannot be created there, since the great hemisphere of the sky surrounds the small blades in a ring, and except where there is grass with broad blades the shadows of plants are scarcely perceptible.

*197v* 738. *Of shadows and in what bodies they cannot be very dark and so also of lights.* Where shadows of great density cannot be created, neither can lights of great brightness be created.

This happens with trees that have thin, narrow leaves, such as willows, beeches, junipers, and others, and also with transparent fabrics such as taffeta, veiling and the like, as well as in the case of curly, thin hair. And this happens because the whole body of each one of the species mentioned shows no lights in its details, except imperceptibly, and their images do not move from the place in which they are created. The shadowed parts of such details do likewise, and the whole does not create a dark shadow, because of the penetration and illumination of the air in those parts near the center as well as those beyond. If there are variations, these are almost imperceptible, and thus the illuminated parts of the whole cannot be much different from the parts in shadow, because, as has been said, since the luminous air penetrates all the details, the illuminated parts are so near the shadowed details that the visual images/sent to the eye make an *198* indistinct mixture of very small bright and dark particles, composed in such a way that nothing can be discerned but a blurred mass, like a mist. The same thing happens with veilings, spun fabrics and the like.

739. *Which colors vary most from light to shadow.* Among col- *205* ors, there will be the greatest difference between the lights and the shadows in those which are most like white, because white has a brighter illumination and a darker shadow than has any other color, although neither white nor black is included in the number of colors.

740. *What surface shows the greatest difference between bright- 208 ness and darkness.*[18] A black surface and such also as most take on a reflected black, shows less difference between its shadowed and its illuminated parts than any other, because the illuminated part shows itself to be black, and the shadowed part cannot be other than black, but with a little variation it gains somewhat greater darkness than the illuminated black part.

741. But simple color is never seen, and this is proved by the *140v* ninth proposition which says: the surface of every body takes on the color of the object opposite it, even when it is the surface of a transparent body, such as air, water, and the like. For the air takes its light from the sun, and its darkness from the loss of that sun, so that it is tinted with as many different colors as occur between it and the eye. The air in itself has no color, nor has water, but humidity, which is mixed with it in the middle region is that which thickens it, and when it thickens, the solar rays which strike it illuminate it, and the air which exists from the middle region upward is dark, and as light and dark compose the color blue, the air is tinged with this blue in greater or lesser degree, as the air is mixed with more or less humidity.

[18] In the heading, "maggior" was an error, contradicted by the text.

[DARKNESS OF SHADOW RELATED TO BACKGROUND AND CONTEXT]

*185 and illus.* 742. *What background makes shadows darker.* Among shadows of equal darkness that one will appear darkest which is thrown against the brightest background. It follows that the shadow which is cast on the darkest background will appear least dark. This is proved in the case of a single shadow which, at its farthest point, borders on a white field where it appears darkest while, on the other side, where it borders on itself, it looks dark *185v* in lesser degree./Let the shadow of the object B D fall along D C, which is blacker at N C, because it borders on the white ground C E, than it is at N D, which borders on the dark N C.

*196* 743. *Of lights between the shadows.* When you represent a body, remember, while you compare the strength of the lights of its illuminated sides, that the eye is often deceived, since that seems brighter which is really less bright. The cause of this arises through comparison for if there are two sides of unequal brightness and the less bright borders on a dark side, and the brighter borders on a bright area, such as the sky or a similar source of brightness, then that which is less bright or lucid will seem more lucid, and the brighter side will seem darker.

*176* 744. That shadow looks darkest which is surrounded by the most brilliant whiteness, and, on the contrary, it appears least visible where it is thrown against the darkest background.

*176-176v* 745. *Of shadow.* A shadow will seem darker, the nearer it is to the light. All the shadows being of the same color, that which is found with the most luminous background will seem to be darkest.

*190* 746. *Of shadows depicted on the shadowed side of opaque bodies.* Shadows depicted upon shadows of opaque bodies need not be as clear as those which are depicted on the luminous sides of the same bodies, nor do they have to be created by original light, but they may be caused by derivative light.

*193v* 747. *Of the appearance of lights and of shadows.* That shadow *194* will appear darkest which is/nearest the luminous part of the body, and thus, conversely, that will look least dark, which is nearest the darkest parts of bodies.

748. *Of lights.* The light will look brightest which is nearest to 194 darkness, and the light will look least bright which is nearest the most luminous parts of bodies.

749. *Of outlines of bodies through the medium of background.*[19] 240 The outlines of bodies always seem intensified to greater darkness or brightness than other parts in contrast to their backgrounds. That which is said happens according to the seventh proposition of this book, which proves that the outlines of white objects seem brighter, in the degree that they border on dark background, and the outlines of shadowed objects seem darker, to the degree that these border on white. The principal example of this is shown when a white object is partially exposed to the sun, and the illuminated part seems very pure in comparison with the shadow, and the shadow darkest in comparison with the bright part. This is well seen on the sides of walls and on other plane surfaces.

750. *How bodies accompanied by shadow and light always dif-* 219v *ferentiate their contours from the color and light of that which borders their surface outlines.* If you see a body whose illuminated part/falls and terminates on a dark field, the part of this light 220 and which will seem brightest is that which borders on the dark field *illus.* at D; and if the illuminated part borders on a bright field, the contour of the illuminated body will seem less bright than at first, and its utmost brightness will appear between the contour of the side F and the shadow. The same thing happens with the shadow, for the contour of that part of the shadowed body which lies in a bright place at L, will seem much darker than the rest. If this shadow ends on a dark field, the contour of the shadow will seem brighter than at first, and its utmost density will be between that contour and the light, at point O.

751. *Why the borders of shadowed bodies sometimes look bright-* 226 *er or darker than they are.* The borders of shadowed bodies look brighter or darker than they are, in the degree that the background on which they border is darker or brighter than the color of the mass that surrounds them.

[19] An unidentified hand has added to the heading: mediante li cāpi (by means of the background).

224 752. *Why the illuminated area around a derivative shadow seems brighter inside a house than in the open country.* The bright area which surrounds the derivative shadow is brighter near that shadow than in parts farther away. This happens when the area receives the light from a window and it does not happen in the open country. It happens because etc. [*sic*]. This will be explained in its proper place in the book on shadow and light.

188v 753. *That shadows should always participate in the color of the shadowing body.* Nothing appears in its natural whiteness, because the locations in which objects are seen render them proportionately clearer or less clear to the eye, as the location is darker or less dark. This is illustrated by the moon in the sky, which by day appears to possess little brightness, but at night appears with so much splendor that it makes itself the image of the sun in the day, as it drives away darkness. This comes about for two reasons. The first is the striving of nature to display objects as more perfect in the images of their colors, the more these are unlike one another. The second is that the pupil of the eye is larger at night than in the day, as has been proved, and a larger
189 *and* pupil sees a luminous body with a more splendid/brilliance than
*illus.* the smaller pupil, as is proved when anybody looks at the stars through a small hole made in a sheet of paper.

[LIGHTS AND SHADOWS: ORIGINAL AND DERIVATIVE]

189 754. *Of shadows on a body and which primary shadows are darkest.* Those primary shadows are darkest which are created on the surface of the densest body; and on the contrary, those are brightest which are created on the surfaces of the least compact bodies. This is obvious since the visual images of those objects, which
189v tinge bodies placed opposite them with their colors/impress themselves with greatest vigor on bodies with the densest or most polished surfaces. The proof is: let R S be the dense body placed between the luminous object N M and the shadowed object O P. According to the seventh proposition of the ninth book, which states: the surface of every body takes on the color of its opposite object, we shall say, then, that the side A R B of that body is illuminated, because the object N M is luminous. Likewise we

shall say that the opposite side C S D is shadowed because its object is dark, and thus our proposition is proved.[20]

755. *Which side of the surface of a body is most impregnated with the color of its object.* The surface of a dense body which is least exposed to other objects of other colors takes on most intensely the color of the object opposite. Therefore, we can use the same figure for our proposition. Let us suppose that the body surface A R B is not exposed to the obscurity O P. It will be entirely deprived of shadow, and likewise, if the surface C S D is not exposed to the luminous N M, it will be entirely deprived of light.

*189v*

756. *Every shadow produced by a shadowed body smaller than the original light will cast a derivative shadow tinted with the color of its origin.*/Let the origin of the shadow E F be N, and be tinted with its color. The origin of H E is O, and likewise is tinted with its color, and so also the color of V H is tinted with the color of P, because it is created by it, and the shadow of the triangle Z K Y is tinted with the color of Q, because it derives from Q.

*212v*

*213 and illus.*

F is the first degree of light, because all the window A D illuminates it there, and so the shadowed body M is of similar brightness.[20a]

Z K Y is a triangle/which contains the first degree of shadow, because the light A D does not reach into that triangle. X H is the second degree of shadow, because it is illuminated by only a third of the window, C D. H E is the third degree of shadow, because it faces two thirds of the window, B D. E F is the last degree of shadow because the ultimate degree of the light from the window illuminates the place F.

*213v*

757. *That part of a shadowed body is least luminous which is in view of the least quantity of light.* The part of the body M is of the first degree of light, because it faces all the window A D along the line A F, and the second degree of N, because it faces the light B D G along the line B E. O is of the third degree be-

*213v and illus. on 213*

---

[20] Text of this section is incomplete, and references to diagram are erroneous.

[20a] Textual reference to diagram is incorrect.

cause it faces the light C D along the line C H. P is the next to
last because it faces C D along the line D V, and the last degree
is Q because it faces no part of the window.

As many times as C D is contained in A D, by so much N R S
is darker than M, and this is so of all the rest of the shadowless
field.

186  758. *Of the outlines which surround derivative shadows at their
impact.* Where the outlines of simple derivative shadows fall,
they are always surrounded by the color of illuminated objects,
which give forth their rays from the same side of the luminous
body which illuminates the shadowed body, creating the shadow.

179-179v  759. *What variations does the derivative shadow possess?*/There
are two variations of derivative shadow; one is that which is mixed
with the air opposite the primary shadow; the other is that which
strikes an object that cuts across the derivative shadow.

202  760. An object seen inside a room illuminated by a specific light
202v  from a high window,/will show great differences between its
lights and shadows, especially if the room is large or dark.

208  761. *Of small lights.* Lights made by small windows also cause
a great difference between the lights and the shadows, especially
if the room illuminated by them is large. This is not a good
setting to use.

[THE STRENGTH OF LIGHTS AND SHADOWS]

226  762. *In what part of shadowed bodies the colors will appear to
be of greatest beauty.* The greatest beauty of any color that does
not contain luster, is always in the greatest brightness of the most
illuminated side of the shadowed bodies.

192v  763. *Of the quality of shadows and lights.* The difference be-
193  tween lights and their shadows is/much greater on bodies in
strong lights, than on those in dark places.

207v  764. *Of the quality of the air in shadows and lights.* That body
will cause the greatest contrast between the shadows and lights
which is exposed to the greatest light, such as the light of the sun,
or the light of a fire at night. But this device is to be employed

seldom in painting, because such works are crude and without attractiveness.

That body which is in a medium light causes little contrast between the lights and the shadows, and this happens at twilight or when it is cloudy. Such works are soft, and give grace to every kind of face. As in everything, extremes are faulty; too much light makes for crudeness, while too much darkness does not allow anything to be seen; the median is good.

765. *Of the color of shadows and how dark they become.* As all colors in obscurity are tinged by the darkness of night, so the shadow of any color ends in that darkness. Therefore, painter, do not make it a practice that in your ultimate obscurities colors that border on one another have to be identified, for nature does not allow this, and as you profess to imitate nature so far as your art permits, do not cause it to be thought that you seek to improve on its errors. For there is no error in nature, and you must know that the error is in you and, given the principle, it is necessary that you follow a method to achieve an end harmonious with that principle. *206v*

766. *Of the false color of the shadows of opaque bodies.* When an opaque body casts its shadow on the surface of another opaque body which is illuminated by two different lights, then the shadow will not seem to be that of the same opaque body but of another object. *205v*

The proof is as follows: let N D E be the opaque body and let it be white, and be illuminated by the air A B and by the flame C Q, and let there be placed between the flame and the opaque body the object O P, the shadow of which is cut by the surface at D N. Now at D N the redness of the fire does not illuminate it,/but rather the blue of the air, whence D N takes on blue and N F is exposed to the flame. Therefore, below, the blue shadow borders on the redness from the flame on that opaque body, and above it borders on a violet color; that is, D E is illuminated by a mixture of the blue of the air, A B, and of the redness of the fire, $Q^{21}C$, and is almost the color of violet. Thus *206 and illus.*

---

[21] The original text reads DC, an obvious error for QC.

we have proved that shadow to be false; that is, it is neither the shadow of white, nor that of redness, which surrounds it.

190   767. *Which part is of medium shadow on the surface of a shadowed body*. That part of the surface of a shadowed body will be of medium brightness and of medium shadow which is equally exposed to the brightness and darkness. Therefore on the line K H[22] there will be a shadow as much less dark than its simple primary shadow C S D, as it is less bright than the simple original light A R B.

239v   768. *Precept*. Bodies illuminated by lights of diverse colors do not have illuminated parts of the surfaces which are consistent with the colors of the shadowed parts.

Very rare are the times when the colors of the surfaces of opaque bodies correspond properly to the colors of their illuminated parts.

That which is propounded occurs because the objects which cast shadows on these bodies are not the natural color of those bodies, nor are they of the same natural color as that which illuminates those bodies.

[LUSTER]

195   769. *Of illumination and luster*. Illumination is participation in light and luster is the mirroring of that light.

197   770. *Of shadowed bodies which are polished and lustrous*. On shadowed bodies which have a polished and lustrous surface, those which are illuminated by a specific light vary in their shadows and lusters in various locations, depending on the mutations of the light or of the eye that sees them. In this case the specific light may be immobile and the eye moving, and conversely, which amounts to the same thing with respect to the mutations of lusters and of the shadows on the surfaces of those bodies.

197   771. *Of universal lights on polished bodies*. Universal lights surrounding polished bodies give a general brightness to the surfaces of such bodies.

[22] The diagram is that of McM. 754, Urb. 189v.

772. *Of those bodies which have light without luster.* Opaque 227v
bodies which have a dense and rough surface never create a
luster on any portion of the illuminated side.

773. *What difference there is between the illuminated part of* 226
*the surface of shadowed bodies and the lustrous part.*/The side 226v
of a shadowed body which is illuminated will seem less illuminated the nearer it comes to its lustrous part, and this is caused
by the great difference between them along their edges, because
the less luminous part appears dark at the edge, and the luminous
part of the luster appears bright. But the surfaces that receive
these impressions are like blurred mirrors, which catch indistinct
images of the sun and the sky, which are their field, and do
likewise with the light from a window in relation to the darkness
of the wall in which the window is made.

774. *What difference there is between luster and light.* The dif- 227
ference between luster and light is that luster is always more
powerful than light, and light is of greater extent than luster.
Luster moves with the eye, or with its cause, or with both, but
light is fixed in a definite place, if the cause that creates it does
not move.

775. *How luster generated upon a white field is of little power.* 227
Among lusters of equal power, that will appear to be of least
brilliance which is created on the whitest surface.

776. *Of the size of lusters on polished bodies.* Among the lusters 227
created on spheres equally distant from the eye, that will have
the smallest shape which is created on the sphere of least size.
    See how, on little grains of quicksilver, which are almost im-
perceptible in quantity, the lusters are equal in size to the grains,
and this occurs because the visual power of the pupil of the eye
is larger than the little grain, and as has been stated surrounds
it for that reason.

777. *Of the lusters of shadowed bodies.*[23] Among lusters of equal- 226v
ly polished bodies, that will contrast most with its background
which is created on the blackest surface, and this occurs because

[23] The heading DE LVSTRO (Of luster) precedes this and the following sections.

lusters are created on polished surfaces which are like mirrors, and because all mirrors return to the eye what they receive from objects. Every mirror that has the sun as its object renders that sun with the same color, and the sun is more powerful against a dark background than against a bright one.

226v 778. *How luster is more powerful against a black background than against any other.* Among lusters of equal power that will appear of the greatest brightness, which is seen against the darkest background. This is somewhat similar to the foregoing yet it 227 is changed, because/the foregoing tells of the difference that the luster has from its background, and this section tells about the difference that a luster in a black area has from that created against other backgrounds.

220 and 779. *Of the highest points of light which turn and change as the*
illus. *eye that sees the body changes.* Let us suppose that the body is this round one figured here in the center, and that the light is the point A, and that the illuminated side of the body is B C, and the eye is at the point D. I say that when the eye is at the point D, the luster, because it is entirely on that side, will appear at the point C, and to the degree that the eye changes from D to A, the luster will change from C to N.

227 780. *Of light and luster.* The lights which are created on the polished surfaces of opaque bodies will be immobile on immobile 227v bodies, even/though the eye of the observer moves. But the lusters will be seen on these bodies in as many places on the surface, as there are places to which the eye moves.

227v 781. *Which bodies those are that will possess luster but not an illuminated part.* Opaque, dense bodies with a polished surface are those which have all the luster in as many places on the illuminated side as there are locations which can receive the angle of incidence of the light and of the eye.

227v 782. *Of luster.* Luster on a polished surface will take on much more of the color of the light that illuminates the lustrous body, than of the color of that body.

The luster of many shadowed bodies is entirely of the color of the illuminated body, as is the case with objects of polished gold, silver, or other metals, and similar objects.

The luster of leaves, grass, and jewels takes on little of the color of the object where it is created, but much of the color of the body that illuminates it.

The luster produced inside dense transparent substances/pos- *228* sesses the finest degree of the beauty of that color, as is seen in ruby-blends, colored glass, and such substances. This occurs since all the natural color of the transparent body comes between the eye and that luster.

The reflected lights of dense and lustrous bodies are of much greater beauty than the natural color of those bodies, as is seen in folds of gold cloth that are open, and in other similar objects, since one surface reverberates on that opposite and the other reverberates on it, and they do this successively to infinity.

No lustrous and transparent body can show a shadow on itself which is received from any object, as it is seen in the case of the shadows of bridges over rivers, which are never seen, unless on muddy waters; on clear waters they do not appear.

Luster is to be seen on objects in as many different locations as the places from which it is seen are different.

When the eye and the object are without movement, the luster will move on the object with the light which causes it; when the light and the object are without movement, the luster on the object will move with the movement of the eye which sees it.

Luster occurs on the polished surface of any body which will hold more light, the more that body is dense and polished.

### [REFLECTED COLOR IN SHADOWS]

783. *Where and in what color shadows lose most of the natural* *200v* *color of the shadowed object.* White that is not exposed to direct light or any kind of reflected light, is that which first loses its own natural color in its shadow; if white can be called a color.

But the color of black increases in the shadows and decreases in the illuminated parts, and it decreases more when the illuminated part is exposed to a light of greater strength.

Green and blue augment their color in medium/shadows, but *201* red and yellow gain in color in the illuminated parts, as does white. Mixed colors partake of the nature of the colors that compose the mixture; that is, black mixed with white produces gray, which is not beautiful in the ultimate shadows, as is pure black, nor is it beautiful in the light, as is pure white, but its greatest beauty is between light and darkness.

201 784. *Which color of body will make a shadow more different from light; that is, which will be darker.* The illuminated parts of that body which is of a color nearest to white will have shadowed parts farthest from brightness.

206 785. *Which object most tinges with its likeness the white surfaces of opaque bodies.* That object which is of a kind most re-
206v moved from white will tinge/the surfaces of opaque white bodies most with its likeness. That which appears to be farthest from white is black, and it is this which will tinge the surface of an opaque white more than any other color.

229v 786. *How white bodies should be represented.* If you would represent a white body surrounded by a great deal of air, pay attention to the colors of the objects opposite, for white has no color in itself, but is tinged and transformed in part by the color which is in these objects. If you see a woman dressed in white in the country, that part of her which is exposed to the sun will be bright in color, in such a way that in part it will hurt the eyes
230 as the sun does. That part/of the woman which is exposed to the luminous air, through the weaving and penetrating of the sun's rays on it, will tend toward blue since the air is blue. If, on the surface of the earth near by there be a meadow, and the woman finds herself between the illuminated meadow and the sun, you will see the parts of those folds which face the meadow tinged with the color of the meadow by reflected rays. Thus the body continues to transform itself through the colors of the luminous and nonluminous objects near by.

If you, poet, know how to speak and write the description of forms, the painter will describe them so that they seem alive, with shadows and lights, composing the expressions of faces, and you cannot achieve with the pen what is achieved with the brush.

787. *Which principal shadow on the surfaces of bodies will have* 190
*less and which more difference from the luminous sides?* The
shadow of black bodies, provided it is the principal one, will
have less difference from its principal lights than the/surface of 190
any other color.

788. *How every shadowed body creates as many shadows as* 186
*there are luminous parts that surround it.* Shadowed bodies
create shadows of as many sorts and as many colors around their
bases as there are illuminated colors opposite which surround
them; but each is as much more powerful than the other, as the
luminous body opposite is of greater brightness. This is shown
when several lights are placed around a single shadowed body.

789. *Of the colors of lights that illuminate shadowed bodies.* A 206v
shadowed body placed between adjacent walls in a dark place,
which is illuminated on one side by a very small candle light,
and on the opposite side by air through a very small vent, if/it 207 *and*
be white, will appear yellow on one side and blue on the other, *illus.*
provided the eye is in a place illuminated by the air.

790. *Of the colors of the visual images of objects which tinge the* 205v *and*
*surfaces of opaque bodies.* Many are the times that the surfaces *illus.*
of opaque bodies, while becoming tinged with the colors of the
opposite objects, take on colors which are not those of the objects.

The proof is: let the opaque body be C D, and A B be the
object opposite, which we may suppose to be yellow, and the
opaque body blue. I say that all the part of the surface D N C of
the opaque body which is blue, will appear to be green, and the
same would happen if the opaque body were yellow and the
object opposite blue. This comes about because when different
colors are mixed, they are transformed into a third which partakes of both, and therefore yellow mixed with blue makes
green, which is a compound of its components. This is understood to be obvious by the painter who reflects on the matter.

791. *Of shadow and light.* Every part of the surface which sur- 195v
rounds bodies is partly transmuted into the color of the thing
which is placed before it as an object.

## *Example*

If you put a spherical body in the middle of various objects, that is, so that on one side it is illuminated by the sun, while on the other side there is a wall which is green or some other color and is also illuminated by the sun, the plane on which it rests 196 may be red,/and the two transverse sides should be dark. You will see the natural color of that body take on the colors of these objects. The strongest will be that of the luminous body, the second will be that of the illuminated wall, and the third, that of the shadow. There still remains a certain quantity of the surface which takes on some of the color of the edges of the coloring bodies.

[THE COLORS OF SHADOWS IN RELATION TO
COMPOSITION AND REPRESENTATION]

206v 792. *Of conditions of the surfaces of bodies.* The surface of every opaque body takes on the color of the object opposite, and the color on the surface will be more perceptible, the whiter the surface of such a body and the nearer such a color is.

193 793. *Of lights and shadows and their colors.* No body ever shows itself entirely in its natural color.

That which is set forth can happen because of two different conditions, the first of which occurs through interposition of an object between the body and the eye. The second condition comes about when the things that illuminate that body retain in themselves the quality of some color.

The part of the body illuminated by the luminous body without color would display its own natural color, and under such illumination it would not be exposed to any object other than that light. This can never be seen, except in the color blue placed on a plane facing the sky, on top of a very high mountain, so that it cannot be exposed to any other object, and provided the setting sun is covered with low clouds, and the cloth is of the color of the air.

But in this case I remind myself that pink also increases in 193v beauty/when the sun, which illuminates it, turns red in the west, as do the clouds which lie between, although in this case it might also be accepted as true, because rosy red illuminated by reddish light, displays beauty more than elsewhere and this is an indication that the lights of colors other than red take away its natural beauty.

794. *Of shadows and lights on objects.* The surface of every 193v shadowed body takes on the color of the object opposite.

The painter should pay great attention to placing his subjects among objects of various strengths of light and illuminated by various colors, for no subject so surrounded ever shows itself entirely in its true color.

795. *Of the consistency of shadows with their lights.* You should 225v have great regard for the objects surrounding those bodies which you wish to represent,/according to the first proposition of the 226 fourth book, which proves that the surface of every shadowed body takes on the color of the object opposite. But you should arrange deliberately to have green subjects such as meadows and other suitable things opposite the shadows of green bodies, so that shadows that take on the color of such an object may not degenerate and seem the shadow of a body other than green. This comes about because, if you put illuminated red facing a shadow which is green, this reddish shadow will cause the shadow to become a color that will be most ugly and will be very different from the true shadow of green. What is said of this color is meant for all others.

796. *Which part of the surface of a shadowed body it is on which* 189v *the colors of the objects are mingled.* Throughout all that part of the surface of a shadowed body/which is exposed to the colors of 190 several objects, there will be mingled the visual images of those colors. Therefore, the part of the shadowed body A B C D[24] is covered with mingled lights and shadows, since in that place it faces the light N M, and the dark O P.

797. *Of the light on shadowed bodies which are almost never of* 192 *the true color of the illuminated body.* Almost never can we say that the surface of illuminated bodies is of the true color of those bodies.

[24] The diagram is that for McM. 754, Urb. 189v.

The seventh proposition of the fourth book states the reason for that which is set forth, and it is again shown to us, when a face in a dark place is illuminated on one side by a ray of illuminated air, and on the other side by the beam of a lighted candle, in which case without doubt it will seem to be of two colors. But before the air and its light fell on the face, the light of the candle seemed its proper color, as did the light of the air when it alone was present.

If you take a white ribbon and put it in a dark place and through three small openings you cause it to catch the light from the sun, from fire, and from the air, the ribbon will be of three different colors.

*191v* 798. *Of shadows which are not consistent with the illuminated side*. Shadows on opaque bodies which are true shadows of their illuminated sides are very rare.

This is proved by the seventh proposition of the fourth book, which states that the surface of every shadowed body takes on the color of the object opposite. Thus the illuminated color of faces having a black color as an object, takes on black shadows, and so it will do with yellow, green, blue and every other color placed opposite it. This happens because each body sends its likeness through all the surrounding air, as is proved in perspec-
*192* tive, and is seen in the case of the sun,/for all the objects placed in front of it participate in its light and reflect it on the other objects. This is seen also in the case of the moon and the other stars, which reflect to us the light given them by the sun.

Darknesses do likewise, for they envelop with their obscurity whatever is included in them.

*239v* 799. *Precept*. The true color of the shadow and of the light on
*240* each body/is seen where the walls of the room in which that body is found are of the color of the body that is enclosed within them, and the color of the shade of the window which illuminates that room is also of the color of the body included there. Thus, with its shadowed parts the room creates shadows upon the enclosed body, which will be of a color corresponding to that of the body in shadow; and the parts illuminated by the color of the window

will be consistent with the color of that illuminated body and with the color of its shadow.

800. *Which are the objects related to the flesh which cause them* 207 *to show shadows in harmony with the lights.* Light from flesh-colored glass, and the room of a man tinted with the same flesh-tone, and the/garments also, will make his face appear with the 207v true lights and shades of flesh. This is a most useful way to make the flesh appear beautiful, but such advice is contrary to the advice with regard to figures posed in the open country surrounded by many colors, because if the figure is afterwards posed in such a landscape, the result obtained would be contrary to the third proposition of the ninth book of this work.

801. *How shadows with lights appear when they are in contrast* 207 *to one another.* Black clothes make the flesh of men appear in greater relief than white garments, and this comes about according to the third proposition of the ninth book, which states: the surface of every opaque body takes on the color of the object opposite. It follows, therefore, that the parts of the face that are exposed to black objects take on black, and for this reason the shadows are dark, and in great contrast to the illuminated parts of that face.

But white garments cause the shadows of the face to take on their whiteness, and for that reason the parts of the face will display little relief to you because the bright and the dark will have little contrast. It follows that in this case the shadow of the face will not be the true shadow of the flesh.

802. *Of the shadows of faces when seen along streets that are* 207v *wet, and which do not seem to be consistent with the flesh-tones.* This problem arises with regard to something that often happens when the face is high in color or white, and its shadows tend toward yellow. This occurs because wet streets tend toward yellow more than do dry ones, and the parts of the face which are turned toward these streets are tinted by the yellowness and darkness of the streets, which are opposite them.

803. *What is really the true shadow of the colors of bodies?* The 206 shadow of a body ought not to take on any other color than that of

the body to which it is attached. Therefore, since black is not counted in the number of colors, the shadows of all the colors of bodies are made darker or less dark with black used as needed in a given place, provided that the color of the body is never entirely lost, except in the complete darkness contained within the boundaries of the opaque body.

Therefore, painter, if you would imitate nature, tinge somewhat the walls of your studio with white mixed with black, because white and black are not colors.

[GENERAL OBSERVATIONS ON PERSPECTIVE]

241 and
illus.
804. *Of perspective*. When with both eyes you see two equal objects which are each in themselves smaller than the space between your eyes, then the second object will seem larger than the first. The pyramid A C embraces the first object, and the pyra-
241v mid B D embraces the second object. Now/the object M will seem as much larger than N, as the breadth of the pyramid B D is larger than A C.

218
218v and
illus.
805. *How the contours of shadowed bodies seen by the pupil of one eye/are not in the same place on that body*. The contours of opaque bodies, seen by the pupil of one eye are not in the same place on that body.

The proof is: let the pupil of the eye A B see the upper part of the opaque body N. I say that the lower part, B, of such a pupil, will see the contour of that body at the point D, terminating on the wall O R at the point E. The upper part A, of the pupil, will see the contour of the opaque body C terminating at F on that wall. Therefore, since C and D are not at the same place on the opaque body, we have proved our point.

218 and
illus.
806. *Of the outlines of opaque bodies*. The true outlines of opaque bodies are never seen with sharp precision. This happens because visual power does not occur in a point, as is proved in the third proposition of the fifth book on perspective, where it is stated: visual power is diffused throughout the pupil of the eye.

Thus, the pupil of the eye A B C sees the edge of the body N at the extremity M, occupying all the space D E F on the wall G H, because A, the upper part of the pupil, sees the edge of the body M at the point D, and the center of the pupil, B, sees another edge lower down at the point E, which is higher than D, and the lower part of the pupil, C, sees another edge of the body lower down, which is carried high up on the wall. In this manner the cause of the indistinctness of outlines of shadowed bodies is proved.

807. *Of the contours of bodies which lose clarity first.* The contours of opaque bodies/lose their distinctness at a very short distance. The outlines which show the shapes of the surfaces of dense bodies are called contours and are here referred to as losing distinctness. These contours do not have substance, and therefore do not appear sharp and distinct, the less so the more distant they are from the observer.

217v
218

808. *How that opaque body will have the most indistinct outlines which is nearest the eye that sees it.* The contours of opaque bodies will be more confused the nearer they are to the eye that sees them.

218v and illus.

That which is propounded is proved by showing A B, the pupil of the eye, seeing the contours of the body E at C D, very distant from one another, so that they remain indistinct. The eye sees the contours N and O of the body F, which is more distant, as nearer to one another, and consequently it comes to see them as being more definite than those of the body E.

809. *Of the error of the painter regarding the size of trees and other objects in the country.* Consider well, painter or miniaturist, how far from the eye your painting should be looked at, and pretend that at that distance you see an air hole, or opening, if you wish, or a window, through which objects can penetrate to your eye, and truly you will/judge that things seen thus are so very small that not only the parts but the whole seems almost impossible to represent.

233v

234v and illus.

For example, if the eye were O, and the opening of a quarter braccio, equal to your painted panel, may be A B, distant half a braccio from your eye, then through this space you will see all the things that could be seen the length of a horizon one hundred miles long, and these will be seen so indistinctly and in such diminution that not only can you not represent any part in detail, but you can hardly put so fine a point on a brush that it will not be larger than any great building placed ten miles away.

*231*  810. *Common perspective.*[25] Among things equal in movement that will seem slowest which is most distant from the eye.

Let us suppose that in the same length of time equal lengths of movement are made at different distances from the eye, such as from A to F, from G to K, and also from L to M. I say that there will be the same relation between velocities and between *231v and* lengths of movement, that there is between distances of the/ *illus.* thing seen which moves, and the eye that sees it.

Let L M be in triple proportion of distance from the eye, O, compared with the distance A F from O. I say that with regard to velocity and length the movement L M will appear to be a third of the movement from A to F,[26] performed in the same length of time and of movement. The proof is that within the distance A F from the eye at O, L M appears to have moved only the space C D, while A has moved to F, and the space C D will be found to enter three times into the space A F. Therefore, the space A F is three times as great as the space C D, and because both movements are made within the same space of time, the movement A F seems three times as fast as the movement C D. This is what was to be proved.

[THE PERSPECTIVE OF COLOR, AIR, AND SHADOW]

*189*  811. *Of white objects distant from the eye.* When a white object is distant from the eye, the farther it is removed the more it loses its whiteness, and all the more so as the sun illuminates it, because it takes on the color of the sun mingled with the color of the air lying between the eye and the white object. If the sun be in the east, the air appears dullish red because of the vapors that arise, but if the eye turns to the east, it will see only the shadows of white taking on blue color.

---

[25] Hand I wrote, as a title for the following group of sections: DELLE OMBROSITA ET CHIAREZZE DE MONTI (of the shadowed and bright parts of mountains). He then wrote and later crossed out the heading which he used for the chapter translated in McM. 826.

[26] The original text here reads in error A to B.

812. That color will best be seen from the most distant place *205* which is most removed from black.

813. At equal distances that will appear to have the sharpest out- *205* lines which is seen against a background most unlike it in brightness or darkness.

814. *Of the shadows of distant objects and their colors.* The shad- *189* ows of distant objects will take on more of the color blue, the darker and more distant they are. This happens because of the brightness of the air which comes between the darkness of shadowed bodies that lie between the sun and the eye which sees it. But if the eye turns in the direction opposite to the sun, it will not see a similar blue.

815. *All colors in distant shadows are unknown and indistin-* *205* *guishable.* All the colors in shadow are unknown at a distance, because an object that is not touched by the principal light is not powerful enough to send its visual image to the eye through the more luminous air, since the lesser light is overcome by the greater.

An example: when we are inside the house, all the colors which are on the sides of the walls are seen clearly and sharply if the windows of the room are open. But if we go out of the house and, from a little distance, look through the windows again to see the paintings made on those walls, instead/of those *205v* paintings we shall see a continuous obscurity.

816. *How shadows appear at great distance.* Shadows are lost at *192* great distance, because the quantity of luminous air lying between the eye and the object seen tinges the shadow of that object with its color.

817. *Of various objects near to one another seen at a great dis-* *200v* *tance.* When objects, very small and near to one another, are seen at a great distance in such a way that their shapes lose distinctness, there is then caused a mixture of their visual images, which takes on primarily that color which envelops the greatest portion of those objects.

230   818. *Of the eye that is in a bright light and looks toward a dark place.* In shadows no color in the second plane is of the same brightness as that in the first plane, even though they are similar in themselves.

This is proved by the fourth proposition of this book, where it is stated: the surface of that body will be tinged the more by the transparent medium lying between the eye and that body, the greater the thickness of the medium.

Thus it is concluded that the second color, placed in the center of a transparent dark medium, will produce more darkness between it and the eye than will the first color, which is nearer to that eye. There will be the same relation between the darkness of one and that of the other that there is between the quantities 230v   of the dark medium with which they are/tinged.

230v   819. *Of the eye that sees objects in a bright place.* In illuminated air no color in the second plane will be as dark as the same color which is nearer in the first plane.

This is proved by the preceding statement, because greater thickness of the bright air lies between the eye and the second color, than between the eye and the first color, and consequently the difference of these colors will be proportionate to the quantities of air occurring between the eye and these colors.

200v   820. *Of the position where the object appears darkest.* At an equal distance from the eye, that object will appear darkest which is seen in the highest location, and this happens because the air becomes thinner the higher it is, and covers the objects less than where the air is thicker. Thence it comes about that the tops of hillocks on the flanks of mountains appear to be darker at their summits than at their bases.

208   821. *Is the greatest difference between shadows and lights in near or in distant objects?* That shadowed body will show least difference between its lights and shadows which is farthest from the eye. The opposite is true when the body is near the eye, because of the brightness of the luminous air which lies in greater thickness between the eye and the shadowed body when it is distant than when it is near.

[BRIGHTNESS AND SHADOW ON MOUNTAINS]

822. Painter, remember not to diminish the perspective of colors *238v*
more than that of the shapes where such colors are created.

And do not diminish the linear perspective more than that of
colors, but follow the diminution of both according to the rules
of the eighth and seventh propositions.

It is true, however, that in nature the perspective of colors
never breaks its laws, but the perspective of sizes is free, because
near the eye you find a little hill, and at a distance a very large
mountain, and so too of trees and buildings.

823. *Of the summits of mountains that are revealed to the eye,* *233 and*
*one above the other, and how their proportions with regard to* *illus.*
*distance are not in accord with their proportions with regard to*
*color.* When the eye sees the summits of mountains at an equal
distance from one another and equal in height, below it, it will
not see the colors of the summits of those mountains diminish in
color in the same proportion as the distances do, because they
reach the eye through different thicknesses of air.

The proof is: let O, P, Q be the summits of three mountains,
which are of the same color and at the same distance from one
another, and let A be the eye, which is higher than those summits.

I say that the proportions of the distances of the summits of
the mountains from one another, will not be the same as the
proportion of diminution of color of those summits and this
comes about because, since A O is two, A P four, and A Q six,
the air from N to O is not half the air between M and P, but
two-thirds, and the space from the eye, A O, is half the space
A P, and the space N O is about two-quarters of the/space S Q, *233v*
which, according to the space between the mountains should be
a third.

824. *Of the peaks of mountains as seen from above.* The peaks *231v and*
of mountains, seen one beyond the other from above, do not *illus.*
grow bright in proportion to the distances of those mountain
peaks from one another, but do so much less, according to the
seventh proposition of the fourth book, in which it is stated: the
distances of landscapes seen from above grow darker toward the

horizon, and those which are seen at the same distance as the
232 first but from below always/grow lighter.

This comes about according to the third proposition of the
ninth book in which it is stated: the thickness of the air seen from
below is much brighter and more resplendent than that seen from
above, and this happens, because the air seen from above is somewhat penetrated by the dark visual images of the earth, which is
below them, and so it appears to the eye to be darker than that
which is seen from below, for that air is penetrated by rays of the
sun that reach the eye with great brilliance.

Thus the same thing happens with mountains and the landscapes in front of them, the visual images of which, passing
through the air, appear dark or bright, depending on the darkness or brightness of the air.

*232 and*  825. *Of air which makes the bases of mountains appear brighter*
*illus.* *than their peaks.* The peaks of mountains always appear darker
than their bases. This occurs because these peaks penetrate thinner air than their bases do, according to the second proposition
of the first book in which it is stated: that region of the air is
much more transparent and thin, the farther it is from the water
and the earth. It follows, therefore, that the peaks of mountains
which reach the thin air display more of their natural darkness
than those which lie in the air below, which, as has been proved,
is much denser.

*232v and*  826. *Why distant mountains appear/darker at the summit than*
*illus.* *at the base.* With regard to that which has already been said on
the preceding page, I continue by saying that although the spaces
between the mountains, A O, O P, and P Q, are equal in proportion, the summits of these mountains, O, P, Q, do not observe
the same proportion in respect to their brightness, as they would
if they were of the same height, because, if they were of the
same height, their extremities would be in air of equal density,
and then the proportions of distances and of colors would be the
same. But such an arrangement cannot be shown to the eye because, if the eye is as high as the summit of the mountain, it is
necessary that the summits of all the mountains that are beyond
the first one should be at the height of the eye and of the first

mountain, and from this it follows that the second mountain and the third, and also the others that follow, would not exceed nor be exceeded in height by the first mountain, nor by the eye. Therefore, as the surface of the summit of the first mountain is even with the summits of all the mountains that are behind the first, these cannot be seen, except for the summit of the first one. Thus this demonstration is vain, for example: let A be the eye, B the summit of the first mountain, C, D, the other summits; and you see how the summit B/meets (the height of) the other two summits, C and D, and the eye A sees the three summits B, C, D, within the outlines of the mountain B. And the distances and colors of these are similar in proportion, but neither the distance nor the color is seen.  *233*

827. *Why mountains seen at a great distance appear darker at* *234* *the summit than at the base.* The air, which acquires degrees of density in relation to every degree of nearness to the earth and also of distance, is the reason why the higher the summits of mountains rise, the more their natural darkness becomes apparent, because they are less impeded by the density of the air at the summit than at the base, and so, also, when they are near at hand than when they are far away.

The proof is: O P, D S, C R, A K are degrees of air which get thinner the more they rise. A F, F H, H K are the other, horizontal degrees, where the air acquires/greater thinness, the *234v and* nearer it is. It follows that the mountain E is darker at the sum- *illus. on* mit than at the base, because, as has been said, the air is more *234* dense below than higher up; also, the mountain E is darker than the mountain G, because there is less density of air between D E than between D G. And the summit G, since it is higher than its base, is similar to mountain E, becoming darker the higher it is, and at an equal distance, say Y G, it would seem darker than the summit E, because it rises in air, which impedes it less because it is thinner.

Thence it does not follow that the darkness of mountains is in proportion to their nearness, which would follow if the summits of mountains were of equal height, but G, because it rises higher, does not observe it, because it penetrates into thinner air.

*234v and* 828. *Why mountains appear to have summits that are darker*
*illus.* *than their bases when seen at a great distance.* The density of the
air has as many differences in thinness, as its differences in height
above the earth and water, and it is thinner and colder the
farther it is away from this earth. As a result of the first cause
the mountain P looks lighter than the mountain O, since there
is more air between the eye A and the mountain P than there is
between A and the mountain O, and thus also the mountain Q
will be brighter than the mountain P, but this brightness in relation to the brightness of P, will not be in proportion to the dis-
*235* tances between them, because/Q is in thinner air than P, wherefore it looks darker than the proportion of distance requires.

*237v and* 829. *Of mountains.* At various distances one discerns the sum-
*illus.* mits of hills and mountains much better than anything on them.
This happens because with every degree of distance from the eye
toward the east, there results a degree of loss in the brightness or
whiteness of the air. It is twice as bright from F to B as from
F to A.

*235v and* 830. *Of mountains and their treatment in painting.* I say that the
*illus.* air lying between the eye and mountains seems brighter at P
than at A, and this happens for different reasons, of which the
first is that the air lying between the eye and P is greater in
quantity than that which lies between the eye and A, and is consequently brighter. The second is that the air is denser in the
valley P than at A, a mountain top.

*235v* 831. *Of the air that is seen between mountains.* The air looks
more luminous and bright toward the side of the sun than on
the opposite side.

*235* 832. *How mountains shadowed by clouds take on a blue color.*
Mountains shadowed by clouds take on the color blue when the
atmosphere about the clouds is bright. This is caused by the fact
that air illuminated by the sun is very bright, and the image of
*235v* the darkness of the mountain shadowed by clouds, passing/to
the eye through the brightness of the air, becomes blue in color,
as has been proved in the fifth proposition of the second book.

833. *Of the summits of mountains that do not diminish in color* 233v and illus.
*according to the distances between these summits.* When the
summits of mountains are equally distant from one another, and
have equal differences in height between them, they will also
have equal differences in height and in thinness of air, but not
equal diminution of color, because the highest will be darker
than it ought to be according to the distance.

This is proved, because the summit O is all in dense air and is
greatly whitened by this air; P is seen by the eye, A, in less dense
air than O, as shown by R A in comparison with P R, which is
all thinner air, so that it (P) is almost as white as O; Q is seen
through all the dense air, I A, and within the thinner K I, and
also within the still thinner L K. It is thus lighter than O, but
not in the degree that the distance calls for.

834. *How one should not represent mountains as though they* 235
*looked as blue in winter as in summer.* Landscapes representing
winter ought not to portray mountains as blue as one sees mountains to be in summer, and this is proved by the fourth proposition of this book in which it is stated: among mountains seen
at a great distance that will seem bluer in color which is darker
in itself.

Therefore, when the trees have lost their leaves, they look gray,
but when they have their leaves, the trees are green. Since green
is darker than gray, by that degree the green will look bluer
than the gray, according to the fifth proposition of this book.
The shadows of trees covered with leaves are as much darker
than the shadows of trees that have lost their leaves, as the trees
covered with leaves are less thin than those that do not have
leaves. Thus we have proved what we proposed.

The definition of the blue color of the air furnishes the reason
why landscapes are bluer in summer than in winter.

835. *Of mountains.* The summits of mountains and of hills will 237v and illus.
seem darker because a great number of trees grow close together,
and the flat ground between them is not seen. Such intervals are
brighter, as can be seen in the valleys, and for the same reason,
the country seems darker in the midst/of its heights. 238

[THE SHAPE AND COLOR OF MOUNTAINS]

194 836. *Of lights and shadows which tinge the surfaces of the countryside.* The shadows and lights of the countryside take on the
194v color/of their causes, because the compound obscurities of the
· densities of clouds added to the absence of solar rays tinge whatever they touch with their colors. But the surrounding air, excepting the clouds and shadows, illuminates that place and causes
it to take on the color blue.

The air penetrated by solar rays coming between the darkness
of the earth and the eye which sees it, again tinges that place
with the color blue, as is proved by the fact that the blue of the
air is created by light and darkness. But the part of the countryside illuminated by the sun takes on the color of the air and of
the sun. It takes on the color of the air in greater degree, because
the air, greater in extent, is near, and provides an area for innumerable suns, as far as the eye is concerned. These landscapes
take on blue the farther they are from the eye, and this blue becomes brighter as it rises toward the horizon; and this is due to
humid vapors. Objects are less distinct in shadow than in light,
and the universal light of the sky includes within it the shadowed
bodies and leaves them with little relief, when the eye comes
between the shadowing body and the light, and there shadow
is invisible to the eye. But in such circumstances bodies at the
sides will show a greater or smaller quantity of their lights, depending on whether these bodies are nearer or farther from the
straight line that extends from one to the other horizon, passing
through the two eyes that view such a landscape.

235v 837. *Painting which shows the necessary shaping of the Alpine
mountains and hills.* The shapes of those mountains that are
called the chain of the world are created by the courses of rivers,
originating from the rain, snow, and hail dissolved by the rays
of the summer sun, a dissolution which brings waters together
from many small rivulets, flowing from various directions into
236 greater rivers. They increase in magnitude as they increase/in
motion, until they come together in the great waters of the ocean,
always taking away from one of the banks and giving to the
other, until they achieve the whole breadth of their valleys. And

they are not content with this, but consume the roots of the mountains at the sides, which, falling into those rivers, close the valleys, and as if these wished to be avenged, prevent the course of that river and convert it into a lake, where the water in slow motion seems pacified, until the dam created by the fallen mountain is again consumed by the course of that water.

Therefore, we shall say that water which is confined in the narrowest and shortest course, consumes least the place through which it passes. Conversely, where it is very broad and deep it consumes most. It follows from this that mountains have more durability at their highest peaks than at their bases. This is true because there are no rivers on the peaks of mountains and since they are clothed in snow most of the time and receive little rain, the few drops of moisture remaining after absorption by the dry peak can generate only small trickles, which are not even muddied by the particles of earth they flow over because these are held in place by the old roots of small plants.

Toward the base, the furious course of the assembled waters, not content with the earth they have carried away, continually removes hills covered with trees, together with very large rocks, rolling them over for a great/distance, until it has reduced them *236v* to very small pebbles, and finally to fine sand.

838. *Painting, and how mountains grow.* Because of that which *236v* has been concluded just before this, it is necessary to concede that the bases of mountains and hills are continually being cut back, and, since this is so, it cannot be denied that valleys increase in breadth. Because the breadth of the river cannot afterward occupy the breadth of its enlarged valley, it is always changing its location, and leaving its course in that place where it has taken away most material; it rolls over and takes away the pebbled clay until, after it has carried away the material previously left, it regains its former bed, which it does not leave again until a similar occurrence removes it from that place. Thus from rain to rain, the river goes on carrying away substance from each valley.

839. *Painting and portraying the characteristics and component* *236v* *parts of mountainous landscapes.* The grass and trees will be paler in color, in the degree that the soil that nourishes them is

meager and lacking in humidity. The soil is drier and more
meager on rocks, of which mountains are composed. The trees
will be smaller and thinner the nearer they are to the summits
of mountains, and the soil will be more meager the nearer it
237 approaches those summits; and more abundant and rich the/
nearer it is to the concavity of the valleys.

Therefore, painter, you will show the summits of mountains
composed of rocks, in large part not covered by soil, and the
grass that grows there in large part turned pale and dry through
lack of moisture, and the sandy and meager soil appearing among
the pale grass. And show small bushes, dwarfed and aged and
diminutive in size, with short, thick branches and few leaves,
revealing in large part their decayed, dry roots interwoven with
the cracks and broken places of the decomposed rocks, created
by chips broken off by men and by winds. In many places rocks
are seen hanging over the hills of high mountains, clothed with
thin and pale corrosion, and in some places showing their true
colors because of the percussion of bolts of lightning from the
sky, bolts which have been stopped by those rocks and not without revenge in the way of damage.

And as you descend farther toward the bases of the mountains,
the trees are more vigorous and thick with branches and leaves,
and their verdure is of as many kinds as there are species of
plants that compose the forest. This spread of branches is manifested in various ways and in varying densities of branches and
leaves, and also in varying shapes and heights; some trees having
thick branches and leaves, such as the cypress and the like, and
others with sparse and expansive branches such as the oak, the
chestnut and others; some with minute leaves, and others with
slender ones, such as the juniper, the plane tree and the like;
some masses of trees having become separated by spaces of dif-
237v ferent sizes,/and others united, without division by meadows or
other spaces.

## [LIGHT, SHADOW, AND RELIEF]

196 840. *Of bright and dark*. Light and shadow together with foreshortening, constitute the ultimate excellence in the science of
painting.

841. *Of the four fundamentals which must be considered pri-* *196v*
*marily in painting shadows and lights.* There are four fundamentals which must be considered in painting; these are quality,
quantity, location, and figure. By quality is meant what shadow
and what part of the shadow is darker or less dark. Quantity is:
how large the size of a certain shadow is in comparison with
others near by. Location is: in what way it should be placed and
on what side of the part to which it is to be attached. Shape is:
what the shape of that shadow is, that is to say, whether it is
triangular, or somewhat round, or rectangular, et cetera.

The aspect of the shadow is also to be included as qualifying
it, that is, if the shadow is long in shape, what is the aspect of
the sum of that length; for example, whether the shadow of a
brow is directed toward the ear; whether the lower shadow of
the eye socket is directed toward the nostril, and so on, placing
these shadows as they come together in their various aspects.
Aspect, then, should come before location.

842. *Of brightness and darkness.* Brightness and darkness, that *196*
is, light and shadow, have an/intermediary which can neither *196v*
be called bright nor dark, but participates equally in the bright
and the dark; it is sometimes equally removed from both the
bright and the dark, and is sometimes nearer one than the other.

843. *Of the principal shadow which falls between direct and re-* *217v*
*flected light.* Note the true shape of the principal shadow, which
lies between the reflected and the direct light. Such a shadow is
not cut off, nor has it an end, except as the part to which it is
attached has an end, and its sides are at varying distances from
its center, with varying outlines which border on the direct and
the reflected light. Sometimes the shadow appears to have sharp
and sometimes imperceptible outlines, sometimes it bends and
sometimes it preserves its straightness, and sometimes the outlines are unequally distant from the center of the principal
shadow. On this subject a book will be composed.

844. *Why the true shape of a body that is enveloped in light and* *208v*
*shadow and with outlined surfaces is recognizable.* Light and
shadows are a most certain manner of making known the shape

of any body, because one color of equal brightness or darkness cannot display its relief, but acts as a plane surface, which, with all its parts at an equal distance, is equally distant from the brilliance that illuminates it.

224v 845. *Of giving aid by means of artificial lights and shadows to the simulation of relief in painting.* To increase relief in painting, interpose a beam of bright light, which separates the shape from the obscured object between the shape represented and that visual object which receives shadow. On that same object make two bright parts, which come together in the center of the shadow cast on the wall by the shape before it. Often portray limbs which you wish to show as somewhat separated from the bodies, as when the arms cross the chest, so that, between the fall of the shadow on the chest and the shadow of the arm itself some light which seems to pass through the space which is between the chest and the arm remains. The more you desire the arm to appear to be distant from the chest, so much larger make the light. Use your ingenuity to set the bodies against backgrounds, so that the part of those bodies which is dark ends on a bright ground, and the illuminated part of the body terminates on a dark ground.

224v 846. *Of surrounding bodies with varying lines of shadows.* See that the shadows produced on the surfaces of bodies by different objects always advance like waves with diverse twistings, as a
225 result of the differences of surface in the parts that produce the/ shadows and in the object that receives them.

195v 847. *Of lights and shadows.* I remind you to see that you give its share of the possession of shadow and light to every part of the body and also to every least part which shows an indication of relief.

196 848. *Of shadows and lights.* You who represent the works of nature, observe the quantities and qualities and shapes of the lights and shadows on each muscle, and note from the lengths of their forms with what muscle they and their straight central lines are connected.

229v 849. *What lights make the shape of muscles appear clearest and sharpest.* Of those lights, which should give a true perception

seen, that ground will be seen the more clearly the slower the motion of the water. This occurs because the waters which are slow in motion have a surface without waves. Because of the even surface the true shapes of the pebbles and sand at the bottom of that water are seen./But this cannot happen with water *160 and* in rapid motion, because of the waves that are created on the *illus.* surface, and the visual images of the various shapes of the pebbles, having to pass through the water, cannot be carried to the eye on account of the different degrees of obliqueness of the sides and fronts of the waves. Their curvature on the crests and in the troughs carries the visual images outside of the straight lines of vision, twisting the straight lines in many directions and showing us their shapes in confused fashion. This is demonstrated in curved mirrors, that is, mirrors with mingled flat, convex, and concave surfaces.[21]

525. *Of the foam of water.* The foam of water appears least white *160* when it is farthest from the surface of the water. This is proved by the fourth proposition of this book, wherein it is stated: That submerged object will be the most transmuted from its natural color into the green color of the water that has the greatest amount of water above it.

526. Distant objects which are near rivers are less clearly visible *151* than those which are remote from streams or swamps.

[CONFLICTS BETWEEN PERSPECTIVES]

527. *Of the diminution of colors and bodies.* Observe the diminu- *164* tion of the qualities of colors with the diminution of the bodies to which they belong.

528. When the air that lies between the eye and an object becomes *151* thickened,/it makes that object appear uncertain and indistinct *151v* in outline to you, and makes it seem larger in shape than it is.

[21] Hand 1 has added, at the end: tolto in margine (taken from the margin [?]), apparently referring to the drawing, after which he continues: Questa figura sara messa nella 42ᵃ della prospettiua sanza la quale la dimostratione dell'acqua trasparente nulla uale. (This figure should be put with the 42nd section of the book on perspective; without it the explanation of transparent water is of no value.)

This comes about because linear perspective does not diminish the angle that carries its visual images to the eye, while the perspective of color removes it to a greater distance than it is in actuality, so that one factor removes it from the eye and the other preserves its size.

142 529. *Why the same countryside sometimes looks larger or smaller than it is.* Sometimes open countryside looks larger or smaller than it is, because of the intrusion of air thicker or thinner than ordinary, which lies between the horizon and the eye. Among horizons at equal distances from the eye, that looks more remote which is seen through thicker air, and that looks nearer which is seen through thinner air.

The same thing seen at equal distances seems larger or smaller as the air between the eye and that thing is thicker or thinner.

If the object seen is at a distance of a hundred miles, a hundred miles of uniform and thin air, and if the same thing is seen at a 142v distance of that hundred miles, a hundred miles of/uniform but thick air, with a density four times that of the air mentioned before, without doubt the same objects, seen first in the thin air and then in the thick, will seem four times larger in thick air than in thin air.

Unequal objects seen at equal distances will seem equal, if the thickness of the air between the eye and those things is unequal, that is, when thick air comes between the eye and the smaller object. This is proved through the perspective of colors, which shows that a great mountain, seeming small in measurement, seems greater than a small thing near to the eye, as it is often seen that a finger near to and in front of the eye covers a great mountain distant from the eye.

162v and 530. *The eye placed at a high level which sees objects high and* illus. *low.* When the eye, placed in a high position, sees the high summits of mountains, together with their bases, then the colors of the bases of the mountains will seem more distant than the colors of their summits. This is proved by the fourth proposition of this book, which states: Among colors of the same kind, the most remote will be most tinged with the color of the medium lying between it and the eye which sees it.

It follows that since the bases of mountains are seen through thicker air than their summits, these bases seem more remote from the eye than the summits do, seen by the same eye through thinner air. Let the eye be located at the height A, from which it sees the summit of the mountain B after the air A B comes between, and it sees the base D of the same mountain after the air A D, a shorter space than A B, comes between. Because the air A D is thicker than the air A B, the base of the mountain, as already stated, will seem more distant than its summit.

531. *The eye placed at a low level which sees objects low and high.* But when the eye is located at a low level, it will see the bases of the mountains and their summits, and then the colors of that mountain will seem much less clear than in the preceding case. This happens because the summit and base of the mountain are seen through air/that is thicker than before, in the degree that the eye which sees it is at a lower level.

*162v*

*163 and illus.*

Then let the eye be N, and the summit and the base of the mountain be O P. Therefore, the visual line P N in this figure being lower than the visual line of the aforementioned figure D A, it is necessary that the color of the base in the second demonstration should differ more from its natural color than the base of the first demonstration, and the same is to be understood with regard to the summits of mountains.

[DISTORTIONS OF PERSPECTIVE]

532. *Of objects that the eye sees below it, combined with mist or thick air.* The closer the air is to water or land, the thicker it is. This is proved by the nineteenth proposition of the second book which states: that object rises least which has greatest inherent weight, and it follows that the lightest object rises more than does the heavy one. Thus our claim is proved.

*144*

533. *Of cities and other things seen through thick air.* Buildings of cities seen below the eye in misty weather or in air thickened with smoke of fires, or other vapors, will always be less clear the lower they are, and conversely they will be sharper and clearer the higher they are. This is proved by the fourth proposition of this book which declares: air is thicker the lower it is, and thinner

*143 and illus.*

the higher it is. This is shown by the figure for that fourth proposition in the margin. Let us say that the tower A E is seen by the eye at N in the thickness A E of the air, which I divide into four degrees which are thicker the lower they are.

The less the quantity of air that intervenes between the eye and the object, the less the color of that object takes on the color of the air; and it follows that the greater the quantity of air intervening between the eye and the object, the more the object takes on the color of the intervening air.

*143 and illus.* To/demonstrate this: let N be the eye, to which converge the visual images of the five parts of the tower A E, that is, A B C D E. I say that if the air were of uniform thickness, there would be the same proportion between participation in the color of the air that is acquired at the foot of the tower E, and the participation of the color of the air which is acquired at the part of the tower B, as there is in the proportion between the length of the line E M and the line B S, but because of previous statements which prove that the air is not uniform in its thickness, but thicker, the lower it is, it is necessary that the proportion of the colors with which the air is tinged by the parts of the tower E and B should be greater than the proportion mentioned above, so that the line M E, beside being longer than the line S B, which it passes in the air, has a thickness progressively unequal.[22]

*147* **534. *Of bodies seen in the mist*.** Things seen in the mist appear to be much larger than their true size, and this comes about because the perspective of the medium lying between the eye and the object does not agree in color with the size of that object. Because the mist is similar to the indistinct air lying between the eye and the horizon in clear weather, a human body near the eye, seen behind mist near at hand, appears to be at the distance of the horizon, whereas a very large tower would look smaller than that man close by.

*144v* **535. *Of the view of a city in thick air*.** The eye which sees below it a city in thick air will see the tops of the buildings as darker

[22] The text and the figures show that this section is defective, the necessary letters M S appearing only in the second diagram, fol. 143v; Cf. notes: Ludwig, *Quellenschriften*, XVII, 275.

and clearer than their bases, and it sees those tops against a bright background, because it sees them in low and thick air. This comes about because of the preceding precept.

536. *Of buildings seen in thick air.* That part of a building will 144 *and* be least clear which is seen in air of the greatest thickness, and *illus.* so conversely it will be clearest when it is seen in the thinnest air. Therefore, the eye, N, seeing the tower A D, will see, at each degree lower, a less clear and brighter part, and at each degree higher a part that is clearer and less bright will be seen.

537. *Of the lower contours of distant objects.*[23] The lower out- 144v lines of distant objects will be less perceptible than their upper outlines. This happens especially with mountains and hills, the summits of which have as their background the sides of other mountains behind them. Their upper outlines are seen more sharply than their lower ones, because the outline above is darker, since it is less covered by thick air, which occurs in locations that are depressed. It is this which makes the outlines at the base of hills indistinct. The same thing happens with trees and buildings and other objects which rise up into the air. Thence it comes about often that high towers, seen at a long distance, seem thick at the top and thin at the bottom, because the part at the top shows the angles of the sides which join the front, and the thin air does not conceal them, as does the thick air at the base. This happens as established in the seventh proposition of the first book which states: where the air is thick between the eye and the sun, it is more luminous below than up high. And where the air is whiter, it conceals dark things from the eye, more than if this air were blue. This is seen in the case of distant battlements of fortresses, where the spaces/between the battlements are actually 145 equal to their breadth, though the space seems much greater than the battlement. At an even greater distance the space conceals and covers the whole battlement, and such a fortress usually looks like a straight wall, without battlements.

538. *Why objects placed higher in the distance are more obscure* 147v *than those that are lower, even when the mist is uniform in*

---

[23] Above this heading, Hand 1 had first written and then crossed out: Delle Remotioni delle campagne. (Of distant things in the country.)

*thickness.* In mist or other air, thick because of vapor, smoke, or by reason of distance, that object will be clearest which is highest, and of objects of equal height that will seem darkest *148 and* which is against/the deepest mist.
*illus.*
This happens to the eye, E,[24] which, seeing A, B, C, which are towers equal in height, sees C, summit of the first tower, and at R, where the tower is lower down in the mist by two degrees of depth, and the eye sees the summit of the tower B in the middle, in a single degree of mist. Therefore the summit C, will appear darker than the summit of the tower B.

*144* 539. *Which object is apparent from afar.* A dark object will look brighter, when it is farther from the eye; it follows conversely that a dark object will look darker when it is closer to the eye.

Therefore, the lower parts of anything that is placed in thick air will look more distant at the bottom than at the top, and for that reason the base of a mountain near at hand will look farther away than the crest of that same mountain which is actually more distant.

*145v* 540. *Why parallel towers appear in the mist to be narrower at the foot than at the top.* At a long distance parallel towers in the mist look thinner at the base than at the top, because the mist which makes a background for them is thicker and whiter below than above. The third proposition of this book states: a dark object against a white background diminishes in size to the eye; and the converse states: a white object placed against a dark background looks larger than against a bright background. Hence, it follows that the lower parts of the dark tower having as background the whiteness of the low, thick mist which increases over the lower outlines of the tower, are decreased with regard to perceptibility, but this is something which the mist cannot do with the upper outlines of the tower, where the mist is thinner.

*147* 541. *Of the heights of buildings seen in the mist.* That part of a building near at hand looks most indistinct which is farthest *147v* from the ground, and this comes about because/there is more

[24] The diagram labels the eye H.

mist between the eye and the summit of the edifice, than between the eye and its base.

In the mist, the distant tower with parallel sides looks thinner
toward the base. This comes about from the preceding, which
states: the mist appears whiter and thicker the nearer it is to the
earth, and from the second proposition of this book, which states:
a dark object will appear to be smaller in shape, in the degree
that it is seen against a background of powerful whiteness. Therefore, since the mist is whiter at the bottom than at the top, it is
necessary that the darkness of the tower should appear narrower
at the bottom than at the top.

### [REFLECTIONS IN WATER]

542. *Of objects reflected in the water.* Reflections in the clearest 163
water will be most true in color to the object reflected.

543. *Of objects reflected in muddy water.* Reflections in muddy 163
water always partake of the color of that which makes the water
muddy.

544. *Of objects reflected in running water.* Of reflections in run- 163
ning water, that image will seem longest and least distinct in
outline,/which is impressed on the water that flows fastest.    163v

545. *Of the shadows cast by bridges upon water.* The shadows 158v and
of bridges are never seen immediately above the water, unless *illus.*
the water has first lost its function of reflection because of turbu-
lence. This is proved by the fact that clear water has a lustrous
and polished surface, and reflects the bridge in all places at equal
angles between the eye and the bridge, and reflects air underneath the bridge where the shadow of the bridge is. But turbid
water cannot do this, because it does not reflect, but receives the
shadow as would, indeed, a dusty road.

546. *Of the likenesses, bright or dark, that are imprinted upon* 158v
*places shadowed and illuminated found between the surface*
*and the bottom of clear waters.* When the visual images of dark
or of luminous objects are impressed on the dark and illuminated parts of bodies occurring between the depths of the
water and its surface, then the shadowed parts of those bodies

which are covered with the shadowed images become darker,
and their luminous parts do the same. But if luminous images
are impressed upon the shadowed and luminous parts, then the

*159 and illus.* illuminated parts of those bodies become much brighter,/and
their shadows lose their great density, and these bodies appear
to be less in relief than the bodies struck by dark images. This
happens, because, as has been said, shadowed images augment the
shadows of shadowed bodies, which, even though they are exposed to the sun, penetrate the surface of the water. With their
shadows they become distinct from the lights of those bodies, and
the shadow is added to the obscurity of the dark image, which is
reflected on the surface of the water, and thus the shadow of
those bodies is augmented, becoming darker.

And even if the dark image itself tinges the illuminated parts
of such submerged bodies, it does not lack the brightness given by
the sun's rays, which, though it be somewhat altered by that dark
image, affects the relief but little, because it draws so much
strength of form from all the shadowed parts that the submerged bodies show more relief than those which are altered
by a luminous image. This image, although it brightens their
illuminated as well as their shadowed parts, causes the variations
of those shadowed parts to be of such brightness that submerged
bodies under such conditions appear to have little relief.

As an example, let the pond N M T V have a shingle, or plants,
or other shadow-casting bodies at the bottom of its clear water
which takes its light from the rays coming from the sun at D.

*159v* And let one/side of the shingle have on it the obscure image
which is reflected on the surface of the water, and the other side
of the shingle have on it the image of the air D C S M. I say
that the side of the shingle covered by the dark image will be
more easily visible than the side of the shingle that is covered
with the brightness of the bright image. The reason is that the
side struck by the dark image is more easily visible than that
struck by the bright image, as visual power is overcome and impaired by water illuminated by the air, which is reflected in it,
and consequently visual power is augmented on the side darkened
by the water. In this case the pupil of the eye is not of uniform

strength. On one side it is hurt by too much light and on the other strengthened by darkness.

Therefore, what is said above does not come about except through causes which do not relate to water and the images of visible things. It comes about only because of the eye, which is hurt by the brilliance of the reflections of the air, and is strengthened on the other side by a dark reflection.[25]

[NATURAL PHENOMENA]

547. *Precept.* The eye which has the largest pupil will see objects with the largest shapes. *151*

This is shown on looking at a celestial body through a small hole made with a needle in a piece of paper, where, because no more than a small part of its light can function, that body seems to diminish as much in size as the part of the light that is seen is less than the whole.

548. *Of portraying the four seasons of the year or things connected with them.* In the autumn you will portray things according to the progress of the season. That is, at the beginning the leaves of the trees on the oldest branches commence to grow more or less pale, depending on whether the tree is represented as growing on sterile or fertile soil. Even more pale and reddish are leaves of those trees which were first to produce fruit. Do not, as many/do, paint all kinds of trees, even when equally distant, *157v* in the same green. For, speaking of fields, as well as plants and other kinds of ground, and of stones and roots of trees, they are always varied. Because nature is infinitely variable, not only as regards species but different colors are found in the same trees, that is, on some twigs the leaves are more beautiful and larger than on other branches. Nature is so delightful and abundant in its variations that among trees of the same kind there would not be found one which nearly resembles another, and this is so not only of the tree as a whole, but among the branches, the leaves, and the fruit, for not one will be found which is precisely like another. Therefore, observe this and vary them as much as you can.

[25] Hand 1 has added, at the end: tolto in margine. (Taken from the margin [?].) Text reads B for D in diagram.

*157* 549. *Of portraying the parts of the world.* You must also be careful that, in maritime places which face the south or near them, you should not represent winter by means of trees and fields, as you would in places remote from the sea and toward the north, except for trees that shed their leaves every year.

*135* 550. *Of representing a wooded place.* Trees and plants that have many small branches should have less somber shadows. The trees or plants with more leaves occasion greater shadow.

*157v* 551. *Of painted wind.* In the representation of the wind, beside the bending of branches and the twisting of leaves in a direction contrary to that from which the wind comes, there should be represented the whirling of fine dust, mixed with the murky air.

*157v* 552. *Of the beginning of a shower.* The rain falls through the air, obscuring it with a yellowish-black tinge, taking the light of the sun on one side and the shadows on the opposite side, as is seen in mist. The earth grows dark, for the splendor of the sun is taken away by the rain. Things seen beyond the rain have indistinct and unintelligible outlines, and the objects which are nearest to the eye are clearest, and those things which are seen in shadowed rain are clearer than those in illuminated rain. This
*158* happens because objects seen in shadowed rain/lose only their principal lights, but those seen in illuminated rain lose both light and shade, for the luminous parts mingle with the luminosity of the illuminated air, and the shadowed parts are brightened by the same brightness of the illuminated air.[26]

*158* 553. *Of the arrangement of a storm of winds and of rain.* The air is seen tinged with nebulous darkness at the approach of a tempest or storm at sea. This is a mixture of rain and wind, with serpentine twistings in the tortuous course of threatening lightning bolts. The trees bend to earth, with the leaves turned inside out on the bent branches, which seem as though they would

[26] At the end of this section, Hand 1 has added: Era a meggio questo capitulo una citade in iscorto sopra della quale cadeua una pioggia rischiarata a locho a locho dal sole tocca d'aquarella cosa bellissima da uedere pur di man propria dell'-autore. (In the middle of this chapter there was a foreshortened view of a city, on which rain fell, illuminated here and there by the sun; touched with water-color, a very beautiful thing to see, also by the author's own hand.)

fly away, as if frightened by the blasts of the horrible and terrifying wind, amid which is diffused the vertiginous course of the turbulent dust and sand from the seashore. The obscure horizon of the sky makes a background of smoky clouds, which, struck by the sun's rays, penetrating through openings in the clouds opposite, descend to the earth, lighting it up with their beams. The winds that drive the dust raise it into the air in globular masses, and these masses have an ash color mingled with reddish rays of the sun that penetrate them. The animals, without a guide to lead them to safety, are terrified and run about in circles./ *158v* Claps of thunder, created by the globular clouds, throw off infuriated bolts of lightning, and their light illuminates the shadowed countryside in various places.

554. *How one ought to make an imaginary animal seem natural.* *135* You know that no animal can be portrayed each one of whose members does not have some similarity with those of another animal. If, therefore, you would have an imaginary animal appear natural, and assuming, let us say, that it is a dragon, for the head take that of a mastiff or hound, and give him the eyes of a cat, the ears of a porcupine, the nose of a greyhound, the brow of a lion, the temples of an old cock, and the neck of a sea turtle.

[TECHNICAL ADVICE]

555. *Where he who looks at a painting ought to stand.* Let us *134 and* suppose that A B is the picture seen, and D is the light. I say *illus.* that between C and E you will comprehend the painting badly, and most of all, if it is painted in oil or varnished, because then it will be lustrous and have almost the nature of a mirror, and for this reason, the more you approach the point C the less you will see, because there the rays of light rebound from the window on the painting, but if you can stand between E and D, your view will be good especially so the nearer you approach D, because that place is less subject to the reflected rays.

556. *Of sculpture.* If you want to make a figure of marble, make *160v* it first of clay, and when it is finished and dried, place it in a box which is large enough, after you have removed the figure

from that place, to receive the marble block within which you would reveal a figure like the one of clay.

*161*    Then, when the clay figure has been placed in the box,/take white rods that can enter through corresponding holes, and push each rod inside each hole as much as is required for each rod to touch the figure in a different place; stain with black the parts of the rods that remain outside the box. And make a mark on each rod and its hole in such a manner that they will correspond. Next, take the clay figure out of the box and put in your block of marble; remove enough marble so that all your rods will be hidden in the several holes up to the black marks, and to do this better, arrange that the bulk of the box can be raised while the bottom of the box remains under the marble. In this way you can very easily raise it with iron bars.

*161*  557. *To make a painting with an everlasting varnish*. Paint your well-designed picture on paper smoothly stretched on a frame, then give it a good, thick priming of pitch and brick-dust that has been well pulverized, and afterward a priming of white lead and yellow, then color and varnish it with old oil, clear and thick, and apply to it a very smooth glass.

But it would be better to make your picture on a clay surface that is well glazed and very smooth, and then over this glazed surface put the priming of white lead and yellow. Next color and varnish, and afterward apply the glass with very clear varnish on this glaze. But first let the coloring dry well in an oven that is warm but not hot, and then varnish it with oil of walnut and amber, or walnut oil thickened in sunlight.

*161v*    /If you would make thin, smooth glass, blow the pipe between two panels of bronze or well-polished marble, and blow so hard that they spread apart with your breath. The glass will be so smooth and thin that you can bend it. You can then apply it with varnish to the painting, and because this glass is so thin it will not break. You can also pull a plate of this glass out to any length and breadth after placing it in a small hot furnace.

*161v*  558. *How to use color on linen*. Place your linen on a stretcher and give it a coat of thin glue, and let it dry. Draw and paint the flesh tones with bristle brushes, and thus, while the paint is fresh, you can make the shadows as smoky as you wish. The flesh tones will be of white lead, lake and yellow. The shadow will be black and red with a bit of lake, or, if you wish, hard red chalk.

When you have painted the gradations of shadow, let them dry. Then retouch when dry with lake and gum that has stood some time together with the gummy liquid, which is better, because it does its work as a binder without shining. Again, to make the shadows darker, take the above-mentioned gummy lake and ink, and with this you can shadow many colors because it is transparent, then make the shadow with blue and lake; do this against the shadows, I say, because against the lights you will shade with simple gummed lake over lake without binder, because without binder you glaze over vermilion that has binder and has dried.

# PART FOUR

## OF DRAPERIES

### [FOLDS OF DRAPERIES]

*167* 559. *Of draperies that clothe figures.* Draperies that clothe figures should show that they cover living figures. Show the attitude and motion of such a figure with simple, enveloping folds
and avoid the confusion of many folds, especially over protruding parts of the body, so that these may be apparent.

*169v and* 560. *Of folds of draperies in foreshortening.* Where the figure
*illus.* is foreshortened, portray a larger number of folds than where
it is not foreshortened, and the limbs should be surrounded by
numerous folds swirling around them. Let A be the position of
the eye; M N puts the middle of each circle of drapery farther
*170* away from the eye/than its ends; N O shows them straight
because they are in front of the eye; P Q puts them on the
opposite side. Be sure to make this difference in the folds that
surround the arms, legs, or other parts of the body.

*167* 561. *Of draperies that clothe figures in much-folded or stiff manner.* The draperies that clothe figures should have folds that are
solid or broken according to the kind of fabric, be it thin or
thick, that you would represent. You can use both sorts in the
composition of narrative paintings, to satisfy various opinions.

*168* 562. *Of draperies.* Garments should be diversified with different
kinds of folds which vary according to the kind of garment. If
the fabric is thick and loosely woven, make long, thin folds, like
macaroni, and if it is of medium thickness and tightly woven,
make the folds smooth, with small angles. Above all, with every
kind of fabric remember to make the folds, between one break
in the surface of the cloth and the next, thick in the middle and
thin on the sides. The smallest thickness of the fold should be
in the middle of the rounded angle of the fold.

*168v* 563. *Of the nature of the folds in draperies.* That part of the fold
*169 and* which is farthest from its/contracted ends will revert most to its
*illus.* original nature. Everything naturally seeks to maintain its being

as it is, and fabric, because it is of equal density and thickness, both on the reverse and on the right side, tends to lie flat. When it is, by some crease or fold, compelled to abandon that flatness, it follows the nature of that force in the part of itself where it is most contracted, and you will find that part which is farthest from those contractions reverting most to its first nature, that is, to be extended and ample.

Example: let A B C be the fold of drapery mentioned above, A and C the places where the fabric is folded and contracted. I indicated to you that that part of the fabric which is farthest from the contracted ends would revert most to its first nature. B is more distant from A C, and the fold A B C is broader at B than in any other place.

*167* 564. *Of the draperies that clothe figures, and their folds.* Fabrics that clothe figures should have folds suited to gird the limbs clothed by them in such a way that folds with dark shadows are not placed on the illuminated sides and folds with too much brightness are not made on the shadowed sides. The outlines of folds should surround the limbs covered by them, but should not do so with outlines that cut the limbs nor with shadows that *167v* sink in farther than the surface/of the clothed body. Indeed, the drapery should be arranged in such a way that it does not seem uninhabited; that is it should not seem simply a piling up of drapery as is so often done by many who are so much enamored of groupings of various folds that they cover the whole figure with them forgetting the purpose for which the fabric is made which is, where possible, to clothe and surround grace-fully slim limbs and not to cover illuminated projections of limbs with puffed up forms so that they resemble bladders. I do not deny that some handsome folds should be made, but let them be placed upon some part of the figure where they can be as-sembled and fall appropriately between the limbs and the body.

Above all, diversify the draperies in narrative paintings; in some make the folds with smooth breaks, and do this with thick fabrics, and some should have soft folds with sides that are not angular but curved. This happens in the case of silk and satin and other thin fabrics, such as linen, veiling and the like. Also, make draperies with few but large folds in thick fabrics, such as are seen in felt, when used in capes and bed coverings.

These reminders I give, not to masters, but to those who do not wish to teach, who are certainly not masters, because whoever does not teach is afraid that he will be deprived of gain, and whoever esteems gain most abandons the study which is contained in the works of nature, teacher of painters; and what these have learned, they cast into oblivion, and what they have not learned by now they will not learn later.

565. *Of the eye which sees the folds of drapery that surround a* 170v *man.* The shadows lying between the folds of cloth surrounding human bodies will be the darker the more directly they are in front of the eye and opposite the concavities where such shadows are created. This applies to instances when the eye is situated in the center, between the shadowed and the luminous sides of the aforementioned figure.

[FABRICS AND FOLDS]

566. *Opinion regarding draperies and their folds, which are of* 168v and *three sorts.*[1] There are many who love breaks in folds of drapery *illus.* with angles that are acute, harsh, and sharp; others prefer them with almost imperceptible angles, others without any angles, but with curves instead. Within these three categories, some desire thick draperies with few folds, others thin ones with a great number of folds, while others take a middle ground. You will follow all three of these opinions, putting some of each in your narrative painting, adding to them some old mended draperies, and some new, abundant draperies, and some that are wretched, according to the position in life of him whom you clothe, and apply colors in the same way.

567. *Of draperies in motion or static.* The draperies with which 168 figures are clothed are of three sorts; that is, thin, thick, and medium. Thin ones are lightest and liveliest in motion. Therefore when a figure is running, consider the motions of that figure, because it bends now to the right, now to the left. When it

---

[1] "Openioni" of the heading in Urb. 168v is altered in modern Italian editions, such as that of Borzelli, to read "operazioni."

rests on the right foot, the drapery on that side rises from the foot, reflecting by its undulation the impact of the foot on the ground. At the same time, the leg behind relates in the same way to the drapery that rests upon it, while the part of the drapery in front presses, with diverse folds, upon the chest, body, 168v thighs, and legs, and/all the drapery flies back from the body, except from the leg that is back. Medium draperies show less motion and thick ones almost none, unless a wind contrary to the motion of the figure aids them to move.

The upper or lower ends of draperies follow the bending of the figure; toward the feet they are disposed according to whether the leg is straight, bending, twisting, or striking against them. They must approach or withdraw from the joints, in accordance with whether the figure is walking, running or jumping, or move without other motion of the figure when the wind itself strikes them. And the folds should be modified in accordance with the kinds of draperies, and whether these are transparent or opaque.

[FIGURES AND THEIR DRAPERY]

167 568. *Of clothing figures gracefully.* Practice the rule in painting your draperies of making the parts that cling to the figure show its manner of movement and attitude, and show those parts of the drapery which are not attached to the figure in a light, graceful manner, which will be described.

169v 569. *Of making few folds in draperies.*[2] Figures that are dressed in a mantle should not display the nude so much that the mantle seems to be directly over the flesh, unless, indeed, you would wish to show that the mantle does rest directly on the flesh, but you must think of the fact that between the mantle and the flesh there are other garments which prevent the display of the shape of the body above the surface of the mantle. That form which you do portray, depict in so large a way that underneath the mantle there appear to be other garments. Portray almost the true size of the parts of the body only in a nymph or an angel, who are shown dressed in very thin garments, driven or pressed by the blowing of winds. In these and others like them you can very well display the forms of their bodies.

[2] The heading of this section is not connected with the content.

570. *Of the folds of draperies.* Folds of cloth in any action of the 170v
figure ought always to outline its action so as not to cause am-
biguity or confusion about the true attitude of the figure to anyone who sees it./No fold, with the shadow in its depths, should 171
cut off any limb, that is, it should not seem that the depth of
the fold is deeper than the surface of the clothed limb. If you
represent figures clothed in several garments, it should not appear
that the topmost garment encloses within itself the stark bones
of the figure, but covers the flesh as well, and the fabrics clothe
the flesh with as much thickness as is required by the multiplica-
tion of layers.

Folds of cloth that surround the body must decrease their
thickness toward the extremities of the limb surrounded.

571. *Of folds.* The length of folds that lie closest to the limbs 171
should wrinkle on the side which is shortened by the bending
limb, and stretch out on the side opposite to the bend.

572. *How folds should be made in draperies.* Many folds should 169
not encumber a drapery, but make them only where they are
held by the hands or arms, and the rest should be allowed to fall
simply and naturally. And the figure should not be crossed by
too many outlines or creases of folds.

Draperies should be drawn from the actual object; that is, if
you wish to represent a woolen drapery, make the folds ac-
cordingly; and if it is silk or fine cloth, or coarse material such
as peasants wear, or linen, or veiling, diversify the folds of each
kind of material, and do not/make a habit, as many do, of 169v
working from clay models covered with paper or thin leather,
because you will greatly deceive yourself by so doing.

[DECORUM AND GRACE IN DRAPERIES]

573. *Of the way to clothe figures.* Observe decorum in clothing 168v
your figures according to their station/and their age. And above 168
all, see that draperies do not conceal movement; and that the
limbs are not cut off by folds nor by the shadows of folds. As
much as you can imitate the Greeks and the Latins in the manner
of revealing limbs when the wind presses draperies against them,
and make few folds; make many folds only for old men in positions of authority who are heavily clothed.

170 574. *Of ways of clothing figures and of diverse garments.* The garments of figures should be in keeping with age and decorum; that is an old man should wear a long robe, and a young man should be adorned with a garment which does not extend above the shoulders, except for those who have professed religion. As far as possible avoid the costumes of your own day, unless they belong to the religious group just mentioned. Costumes of our own period should not be depicted unless it be on tombstones in churches, so that we may be spared being laughed at by our successors for the mad fashions of men and leave behind only things that may be admired for their dignity and beauty.

I remember, in my childhood, having seen with my own eyes, men both great and small, with all the edges of their garments scalloped at all points, head, foot, and side, and it even seemed such a fine idea at that time that they pinked the scallops. They wore hoods of the same fashion, as well as shoes, and scalloped cock's combs of various colors, which came out of the main seams of their garments. Furthermore, I saw the shoes, caps, purses, weapons, the collars of their garments, the edges of jackets reaching to the feet,[3] the trains of their cloaks, and indeed everybody 170v who would look well was covered/up to the mouth with points of long, sharp scallops.

At another time the sleeves began to grow in size and they became so large that each one by itself was larger than the gown alone. Later, gowns began to rise above the neck, so much that they finally covered the whole head. Then, they began to take them away so that the clothes could not be held up by the shoulders because they did not hang from them. Afterward, garments began to lengthen, so that men always had their arms full of their own clothes, in order not to tread on them with their feet. Later they reached such an extreme that men were clothed only as far as the flanks and the elbows, and were so tight that they suffered great torture, and many burst inside. The shoes were so tight that the toes were pushed over one another, and became covered with corns.

[3] The words "li stremi de giuponi da piedi" are translated by Ludwig as "die untern Ränder der Panzerhemden!" Cf. note: Ludwig, *Quellenschriften*, XVII, 288.

# PART FIVE

## OF SHADOW AND LIGHT

[DEFINITION AND DIVISIONS OF SHADOW AND LIGHT]

575. *What is shadow?* Shadow, in the proper sense of the word, *175* is to be considered a subtraction from light falling on the surfaces of bodies; its beginning is in the ending of light, and its end is in darkness.

576. *Of the essence of shadow in itself.* Shadow is in the nature *175* of universal things, all of which are more powerful at the beginning, and become weak at the end. I refer to the beginning of every form and quality, visible and invisible, and not to things brought from a small beginning to a great growth by time; as, for example, a great oak, which has a weak beginning in a small acorn; so that I shall say the oak is most powerful where it begins to grow in the earth, that is, at the point of its greatest thickness.

Darkness is, then, the first degree of shadow, and light is the last. So, painter, make the shadow darkest near its source, and end it so that it is converted into light,/and seems to be without end. *175v*

577. *What are shadow and light?*[1] Shadow is absence of light *175v* and only results when dense bodies are opposed to luminous rays. Shadow is of the nature of darkness; illumination is of the nature of light. One conceals, the other reveals. They are always together, and associated with bodies. Shadow is of greater power than light, for it prohibits light of which it entirely deprives bodies, and light cannot dispel all shadow from dense bodies.

578. *Of shadow and light.* Darkness is absence of light, and *195* light is absence of darkness. Shadow is the mingling of darkness with light, and it will be of greater or lesser density as the light with which it is mingled is of lesser or greater strength.

[1] One of the original editors of Urb. 1270 has added to the heading: et quale è di maggior Potēza (and which is of greater power).

*175* 579. *From what does shadow derive?* Shadow derives from two dissimilar sources of which one is corporeal and the other spiritual; the body that is shadowed is corporeal and the light is spiritual. Light and body are the cause of shadow.

*175v* 580. *What are shadow and darkness?* Shadow is diminution of light; darkness is absence of light.

*175* 581. *What difference there is between shadow and darkness.* The difference between shadow and darkness is this: shadow is a subtraction of light, but darkness is complete absence of light.

*176v* 582. *What differentiation is there from shadow to darkness?* That is called shadow where some part of the luminous body or that which is illuminated can be seen. Darkness is that state in which no part of the luminous or illuminated body can be seen, through incidence or reflection.

*175v* 583. *Into how many parts is shadow divided?* Shadow is divided into two[2] parts, of which the first is called primary shadow; the second, derivative shadow.

*175v* 584. *Of shadow and its division.* Shadows on bodies are created by dark objects placed in front of those bodies, and are divided into two parts, of which the first is called primary, and the other derivative.

*179 and illus.* 585. *How many kinds of shadow are there?* The kinds of shadows are of two sorts, of which one is called primary, and the other derivative. The primary shadow is that which is attached to the shadowed body, and the derivative one is that which derives from the primary.

*195* 586. *Of derivative light.* Derivative light results from two things; that is, original light and the shadowed body.

*179* 587. *How many are the sorts of primary shadow.* The primary shadow is unique and single, never varying. Its edges face the edge of the luminous body, and the edges of the illuminated side of the body to which it is attached.

2 One of the original editors has altered "quante" to "due."

**588.** *In how many ways does primary shadow vary?* The primary shadow varies in two ways, of which the first is simple and the second is compound. The simple shadow is that which goes toward a dark place, and for this reason, such a shadow is dark. The compound one is that which goes toward an illuminated place with various colors, and then such a shadow will be mixed with the kind of colors of the objects placed opposite it. *179 and illus.*

**589.** *What difference is there between simple shadow and compound shadow?* Simple shadow is that which exists where no part of the luminous body can be seen; and compound shadow exists where some derivative light is mingled with the simple shadow. *176v*

**590.** *Of two kinds of shadows and into how many parts they are divided.* The kinds of shadow are divided into two parts, one of which is called simple, and the other compound. That is simple which is caused by one light and one body only; that is compound which is created by several lights on a single body or by several lights on several bodies. *175v*

**591.** The simple shadow is divided into two parts; that is,/primary and derivative. That which is attached to the surface of the shadowed body is primary; the derivative shadow is that which starts out from the body just mentioned and extends through the air, and meeting resistance, stops at the place where it strikes with the shape of its own base. *175v-176*

**592.** The same is to be said of compound shadows. *176*

**593.** *What is the difference between compound light and compound shadow?* Compound shadow is that which participates more in the shadowed body than in the luminous. Compound light is that which participates more in the luminous body than in the shadowed. We shall say then that compound shadow and compound light take their names from that in which they participate most; that is, if an illuminated body is exposed to more shadow than light, it may be said that it is covered with compound shadow, and if it is covered more by the luminous than by the shadowed, then, as has been said, it may be called compound light. *176v*

176v 594. *How compound light and compound shadow always border*
177 *on one another.*/Compound lights and compound shadows always border on one another; but the outer edge of the compound shadow is simple shadow, and the edge of the compound light is always the simple light.

187 595. *What difference is there between a shadow attached to a body and one which is separated from it?* An attached shadow is one that never leaves the illuminated body; for example, a ball placed in the light always has one side covered by a shadow, which is not separated from it when the ball changes its place. A separate shadow may or may not be created by the body. Let us suppose that the ball is a braccio distant from a wall, and that the light is on the opposite side; the light will throw on the wall precisely as much expansion of shadow, as is found on the side of the ball which is turned to the wall. Part of the separated shadow does not appear, when the light is below the ball,
187v and the/shadow is thrown toward the sky and, finding no resistance in its way, becomes lost.

183v 596. *Whether shadow can be seen through the air.* Shadow can be seen through misty or dusty air, and this becomes apparent, when the sun penetrates through small openings into dark places, for then the shadow is seen between the two or more rays of the sun which pass through those small openings.

179 597. *How many sorts of shadow there are.* There are three sorts of shadow, of which one derives from a specific light, such as the sun, moon, or a flame; the second is that which derives from a door, window, or other opening, through which a large part of the sky is seen; the third is that which derives from the universal light, such as the light of our hemisphere of sky, when it is without the sun.

195 598. *Of lights.* The lights that illuminate opaque bodies are of four kinds: that is, general, such as that of the air which is within our horizon; specific, as that of the sun, or of a window, or door, or other limited, open space; the third is reflected light; while the fourth is that which passes through translucent matter such as linen, or paper, or similar things, but not transparent

matter, like glass, or crystal, or objects which produce an effect as if nothing were lying between the shadowed body and the light which illuminates it. Of these things we shall speak separately in our discourse.

## [ATTACHED SHADOWS]

599. *Of shadows and lights and colors.* That side of the shadowed 193 body will appear most luminous which is illuminated by the strongest light.

In shadowed bodies, the quantity of shadow will exceed the quantity of illumination by as much as the quantity of darkness to which it is exposed exceeds that of the brightness which illuminates it.

600. *Of the variations of shadows when the sizes of the lights 188 that create them vary.* The shadow of a body increases by as much as the light which creates it diminishes without change of location.

601. *Which body takes on the greatest quantity of shadow.* That 190v and body will be covered with the greatest quantity of shadow which *illus.* is illuminated by the smallest luminous body. Let A B C D be the shadowed body; G is the small luminous body, which illuminates on that shadowed body only the part A B C, so that the side A D C remains much greater than the luminous A B C.

602. *Which body, exposed to light, increases its shadowed side.* 210v and When the luminous body is smaller than the body illuminated *illus.* by it, the shadow of the illuminated body increases by as much as it approaches the luminous body. Let A be the luminous body, smaller than the shadowed R S G L, and illuminate all the side R S G, included within its luminous rays A N and A M, wherefore the shadowed part, by the necessity of such rays, leaves all R L G in shadow. After that I bring toward the luminous rays this same shadowed body, D P E O, which will be enclosed within the straight luminous rays A B and A C, and it will be touched by those rays at the point D and the point E, and the line D E divides the shadowed side from the luminous or, D P E from D O E, a shadowed side which is necessarily

larger than the shadowed side of the more remote body R L G. All this comes from the luminous rays which, because they are straight, are more separated from the middle of such a shadowed body, the nearer it is to the luminous body.

603. *Which body takes on the greatest quantity of light.* That body takes on the greatest quantity of light which is illuminated by the greatest light. Let A B C D be the body illuminated, E F is the body which illuminates it. I say that because the luminous body is so much greater than the illuminated body, the illuminated side B C D will be much larger than the shadowed side B A D. This is proved by the straightness of the luminous rays E G, F G.

604. *Of lights and shadows.* Shadow is the diminution or absence of light. That shadow will be largest on the shadowing body, which is illuminated by the smallest light. It follows that the greater the quantity of light by which the body is illuminated, the less is the quantity of shadow which remains on that body. A is the luminous body,[3] B C is the shadowed body, B is the side of the body which is illuminated, C is that which remains without light, and the shadowed body is greater than the luminous. E is the luminous body greater than the shadowed body opposite it, F G is the shadowed body, F is the side illuminated, and G is the shadowed side.

605. *What luminous body is it from which only half of a shadowed sphere is seen?* When the shadowed spherical body is illuminated by a spherical luminous body of equal size then the shadowed and the luminous sides of the shadowed body will be equal to one another. Let A B C D be the shadowed spherical body equal to the luminous sphere E F. I say that the shadowed side A B C of the shadowed spherical body/is equal to the luminous side A B D, and it is proved thus: the parallels E F S T are tangent to the fronts of the diameter A B; that is, the diameter of the shadowed sphere passes through the center of that sphere, which, as it is divided by the said diameter, is divided equally, and one side will be all shadow, and the other will be all luminous.

[3] The diagram is omitted.

606. *Whether it is possible that at any distance a luminous body* 204 and
*can illuminate only half of a shadowed body smaller than itself.* illus.
It is impossible that, at any distance, a luminous body, larger
than a shadowed one, should be able to illuminate exactly half
of the shadowed body.

That which has been said is proved by parallel lines which are
created equally distant from one another. Between equidistant
lines are included nothing but spherical bodies of equal diam-
eters: therefore, the outlines of two unequal spheres cannot be
contained within two parallel lines.

607. *Equality of shadows on unequal shadowed and illuminated* 203v and
*bodies at various distances.* It is possible for one shadowed body illus.
to take equal shadow from luminous bodies of different sizes.

F O G R is a shadowed body of which the shadow is FGO,
created by the lack of a view of the luminous D E at a near
distance, and of the illuminating body B C at a remote distance.
This comes about because both luminous bodies are cut off from
the view of the shadow F O G, because of the straight lines
A B, R C.

We shall say the same of two luminous bodies at different
distances from a larger shadowed body; that is, the luminous
large R S and the small luminous A C, differently remote from
the shadowed body, N M O P.

608. *Of variations in the shadow without diminution of the light* 188
*that causes it.* The shadow of a body increases and decreases by
as much as the space between the light and the shadowed object
increases or decreases when the object itself is smaller than the
luminous body.

609. *Which body, the closer it approaches the light, diminishes* 210v
*the more on its shadowed side.* When the luminous body is
greater than the body/illuminated by it, the shadow of the 211 and
lighted body will diminish the closer it approaches the luminous illus.
body. Let A B be the luminous body larger than the shadowed
body X Y R H, which, approaching nearer the luminous body
at C E O D diminishes its shadow because it is more greatly
encompassed beyond its center by the luminous rays, when it is
near the body that illuminates it, than when it is more remote.

*211 and* 610. *Which body it is that does not increase or diminish its shad-*
*illus.* *owed or its luminous side whatever the closeness of the body that*
*illuminates it.* When the shadowed and the luminous bodies are
equal to one another in size, then no distance or lack of distance
between them will have the power to diminish or to increase their
shadowed or illuminated parts. Let N M[4] be the shadowed body
which, taken from the position C D, nearer to the luminous A B,
has not increased or diminished the quantity of its shadow. This
happens because the luminous rays which embrace it are in
themselves parallel.

[CAST SHADOWS AND THEIR SHAPES]

*183v* 611. *Of compound derivative shadow.* The compound derivative
shadow is of two sorts: that is, columnar and spreading.

*178v* 612. *Of the termination of the simple shadow.* The simple derivative shadow requires brief analysis compared with the compound derivative one because the compound shadow, as already
said, originates at the angle of the simple shadow, but the simple
shadow has its origin at its base. And it is evident that wherever
the pyramid is cut by a shadowed body, such a division never
destroys its base.

*176* 613. The primary shadow is always the base of the derivative
shadow. The outlines of derivative shadows are straight lines
from that base.

*178v* 614. *What shadow does the light make which is equal to the*
*shadowed body in the form of its shadows?* If the shadowed body
is equal to the luminous body, then the simple shadow has parallel sides and is infinite in length. But the compound shadow and
light will be pyramidal in shape with the angle turned toward
the luminous body.

*179v and* 615. *How many shapes does the derivative shadow have?* The
*illus.* shapes of the derivative shadow are three in number; the first
is pyramidal, derived from a shadowed body smaller than the
luminous body; the second with parallel sides, is derived from
the shadowed body equal in size to the luminous body; the third

4 N M should read E F.

is one which expands to infinity, and that which is columnar in shape is infinite also as is that which is pyramidal, for after the first pyramid it comes to an intersection and there creates an infinite pyramid with its point against that of the finite pyramid, provided that it finds infinite space in which to expand.

**616. *Of derivative shadow and where it is greatest.*/**That derivative shadow will be greatest in extent which is created by the largest light and this is so conversely. This is proved as follows: A B, a small light, makes the derivative shadows C G E and D F H, which are small. Take the next figure: N M, the light of the sky, which is universal, makes the large derivative shadow R T X and also the space O S U, because the part of the sky P N makes that shadow R T X, and the space L M, a part of the sky, makes the opposite shadow O S U.   *181-181v and illus.*

**617. *That derivative shadows are of three kinds.*** Derivative shadows are of three kinds, of which one is spreading, the other columnar, and the third converging to the place where there is an intersection of its sides. These, after this intersection, are of infinite length, or infinitely prolonged/straightness. If you should say that the shadow ends at the angle of the conjunction of its sides, and does not pass beyond, this is denied, because in the first proposition of the book on shadows it is proved that that thing is entirely ended of which no part exceeds its limits. The contrary of this is seen in such a shadow, for while such a derivative shadow is created, obviously there are created the shapes of two pyramids of shadow, the angles of which are joined.   *182*   *182v*

Thus, if according to those of opposite view, the first pyramid of shadow is ended by the point of the derivative shadow, where then does the second pyramid of shadow originate? The opposition says that it is caused by the point and not by the shadowed body. This is denied with the aid of the second proposition of this book, where it is stated: shadow is a condition created by the shadowed bodies lying between the location of this shadow and the luminous body, and therefore it is clear that the shadow is created, not by the point of the derivative shadow, but only by the shadowed body, itself.

*183v* 618. *Of the simple derivative shadow.* The simple derivative shadow is of three sorts, one of which is finite in length, and two are infinite. The finite shadow is pyramidal, and one of the infinite shadows is columnar and the other is spreading. All three have rectilinear sides. But the converging shadow, that is, the pyramidal one, is created by a shadowing body smaller than the luminous one. The columnar shadow is created by a shadowed body equal in size to the luminous body, and the spreading shadow by a shadowed body larger than the luminous body.

*182 and*　619. *Of the three varying forms of derivative shadows.* There are
*illus.*　three varieties of derivative shadows, of which one is broad in its origin, and the farther it is removed from its source, the narrower it becomes. The second possesses infinite length, with the same breadth as its source. The third is that which at every degree of distance from the breadth of its source acquires degrees of greater breadth.

*182*　620. *Variations in each of the three derivative shadows mentioned.* The derivative shadow derived from a shadowed body smaller than the body which illuminates it will be pyramidal in shape, and will be the shorter the nearer it is to the luminous body. The parallel shadow, however, does not vary in such a case, while the spreading shadow becomes broader, the nearer it is to its luminous source.

*183-183v*　621. *Of the pyramidal shadow.*/The pyramidal compound shad-
*and illus.*　ow produced by a body with parallel sides will be narrower than the shadowed body, the farther away from that shadowed body the simple derivative shadow is intersected.

*215v*　622. *Each shadowed body lies between two pyramids, one dark and the other illuminated, the one seen and the other not, and this happens only when the light enters through a window.* Take
*216 and*　it that A B is the window, and R is the shadowed/body; the
*illus.*　light at the right, 3, passes the body on the left side of the shadowed body at G and goes on to P. The light at the left, K, passes to that body on the right side, at I, and goes on to M. These two lines intersect at C and create pyramids. Then A B touches the shadowed body at I G and creates its pyramid, F I G. F is dark

because it never sees the light A B I G. C is always luminous
because it is in view of the light.

623. *In how many ways is the impact of the derivative shadow*   184 and
*transformed?* The impact of the derivative shadow has two varia-   illus.
tions, that is, the straight and the oblique. The straight is always
shorter than the oblique, which can extend to infinity.

624. *In how many ways does the extent of the impact of the*   184 and
*shadow vary from the original shadow?* The shadow, or rather,   illus.
the impact of the shadow, varies in three ways, in those spoken
of above; that is, converging, diverging, and constant. The diverging shadow has a greater impact than the primary shadow.
The constant always has an impact equal to the primary shadow.
The converging makes two sorts of impact, that is, one on converging and the other on diverging, but/the converging shadow   184v
always has a smaller impact than the primary shadow, and its
diverging part does the opposite.

625. *That derivative shadows are of three sorts.* Derivative shadow   182v
is of three kinds; that is, that which when thrown on the wall
will be larger than its base, or smaller than that base, or equal to
it. If it is larger, it is a sign that the light which illuminates the
shadowed body is smaller than that body, and if it is smaller, the
light is larger than the body. If it is equal, the light is equal to
that body in size.

626. *Impact of the derivative shadow and its conditions.* The im-   181
pact of the derivative shadow will not be similar to that of the
primary shadow, except under the following conditions: first,
that the shadowed body does not have angles, is not pierced or
jagged; second, that the shape of the luminous body be similar
to the shape of the shadowed body; third, that the size of the
luminous body be equal to that of the shadowed body; fourth,
that the surface of the rays of shadow be of equal length on each
side; fifth, that the impact of the derivative shadow be created
between equal angles; sixth, that this impact be on a flat and
continuous wall.

*187v* **627. Of the shapes of shadows.** The derivative shadow will never be entirely similar to the shadowed body which creates it, if the light which bounds the outlines of that body with its rays is not of the same shape as that body.

*187 and illus.* **628. How the separate shadow is never similar in size to its cause.** If the luminous rays are, as experience confirms, caused by a single point, and diverge and spread through the air in a circular course around this point, they grow wider as they diverge; the object placed between the light and the wall must always cast a larger shadow on the wall, since the rays which strike it are wider when they reach the wall.

*186v* **629. Why the shadow larger than its cause is disproportionate.** The distortion of the proportions of that shadow which is larger than its cause comes about because the light, being smaller than the object, cannot be equidistant from the extremities of that object, and that part of the shadow which is more distant increases more than do those which are nearer.

*188 188v and illus.* **630. Of the derivative shadow created by a light of long shape which strikes on an object similar to itself.**/When the light passes through a small opening, long and narrow in shape, and strikes a shadowed object with a shape and position similar to its own, then the shadow will have the shape of the shadowed object. This is proved as follows: let the opening through which the light penetrates into a dark place be A B, and the columnar object, with a shape equal and similar to the shape of the opening, be C D, and E F be the impact of the rays of shadow from the object C D. I say that such a shadow cannot be greater nor smaller than that opening at any distance, provided the light is conditioned in the aforesaid way. This is proved by the fourth proposition of this book, which states: all the rays of shadow and light are rectilinear.

*186v* **631. That the body which is nearer the light makes the larger shadow and why.** If an object placed in front of a particular light is very close to it, you will see it cast a very large shadow on the opposite wall, and the farther you remove that object from the light, the more the shape of that shadow will diminish.

of the shape of the muscles, the universal ones are not good, but specific lights are perfect, and the more so the smaller in shape these lights are. A demonstration of this should be made by placing the light on several sides, for if the light were fixed it would illuminate only a small part of the muscular body, and the rest would remain dark, and consequently would not be recognized.

850. *Of the shadow and light of shadowed bodies.* All the sides 239 of bodies which the eye sees between the light and the shadow have to be sharply terminated by shadow and light, and the sides turned to the light will be indistinct so that there will be little difference between the lights. If there is no reflected light the shadowed sides, like those illuminated, show little difference between the darker and the less dark.

851. *Of the breadth of shadows and of primary lights.* The ex- 192 pansion and contraction of shadows, or, rather, the greater and smaller breadth of shadows and lights on opaque bodies, will be found on the greater and smaller curvature of the/sides of the 192v bodies where they are created.

852. *Of the greater or lesser density of shadows.* Greater density 192v of shadows is created on the side where the parts of the body are most curved, and the least density will be found on the flattest sides.

### [SPECIFIC LIGHTS]

853. *Where shadows deceive the judgment which determines* 192v *their greater or lesser density.* Among shadows of equal density, that will appear least dark which is surrounded by lights of least power, as are the shadows which are created by reflected lights. Therefore, painter, see that you do not deceive yourself by changing such a shadow.

854. *Where lights deceive the judgment of the painter.* Among 192v lights of equal brightness, that will appear most powerful which is smallest and is surrounded by the darkest background.

855. *Of specific light.* Specific light is the cause of giving better 231 relief to shadowed bodies than is universal light. This is shown by the comparison of one part of the countryside illuminated by

the sun with one shadowed by a cloud and illuminated only by the universal light of the air.

222v 856. *How the shadows cast by specific lights are to be avoided because their ends are like their beginnings.* Shadows cast by the sun or by another specific light are without grace for the body to which they adhere for the parts of such a body remain indistinct, with conspicuous boundaries between the shadow and light, and the shadows are as strong at the end as at the beginning.

[BRIEF RULES REGARDING LIGHTS]

239v 857. *Of light.* That light will be greatest in quantity which is created on a body with a slight curvature, provided the light is produced by one cause.

Those bodies which are illuminated by the air without sun create shadows without perceptible contours.

Those bodies which are illuminated by the air with the sun cast shadows with contours of extreme sharpness.

241 and 858. *Of reflected light.* An illuminated object is less luminous
illus. than that which illuminates it, by as much as its reflected side is less luminous than the illuminated side.

That object will be most illuminated which is nearest to the light.

As many times as B C enters into B A, so much more will A D be illuminated than D C.

That wall which is most illuminated seems to have shadows of the greatest density.

238 and 859. *Precept.* Lights and shadows are as varied as the locations in
illus. which they are found.

When the shadowed part of bodies is intensified by a dark object opposite, that shadow becomes as much darker than it was at first as this intensification is less bright than the air.

The form cast by the derivative shadow will never be the shape of its original source, if the original light is not of a shape similar to that of the body which casts the shadow.

[THE LIGHTS IN NARRATIVE PAINTINGS]

202v 860. And you, painter, who undertake narrative painting, portray your figures with as much variety of light and of shadow, as the objects which cause them are various, and do not paint them in a generalized manner.

The side of the surface of every body will take on as much variety of color as there is on those objects which are opposite it.

The landscape illuminated by the sun will cause the shadows of any object to appear to be very dark, and to him who sees it on the side opposite that of the sun, it will seem darkest and distant objects will seem near.

But when you see things along the line of their exposure to the sun, these things will appear to you to be without shadow, and objects near by will seem far away and indistinct in shape.

The object which is illuminated by the air without sun will be darker where it is exposed to less air, and also in relation to the extent of the dark place that it faces.

/Things viewed in the open country show little difference be- *203* tween their shadows and their lights, and their shadows are almost imperceptible and without any outlines, so that they lose themselves as they extend toward the luminous parts, like smoke, and become darker only where the object is deprived of air.

An object seen in places that have little light, or at twilight, also shows little difference between its lights and shadows, and if the time be complete night, for the human eye the difference between light and shadows is imperceptible, to such a point that the object entirely loses shape, and is then apparent only to the keen eye of nocturnal animals.

Objects that seem vague to you because of their distance should be portrayed with indistinctness, otherwise they will not appear to be at the distance that they are. Do not edge their contours with a definite outline, because the contours are lines or angles, and because they are the last of least things, they are invisible, not only from a distance, but also close at hand.

If the line and also the mathematical point are invisible, the outlines of things, also being lines, are invisible, even when they are near at hand. Therefore, painter, do not give contours to objects far from the eye, at a distance where not only those outlines but even the parts of bodies are imperceptible.

Everything that is illuminated takes on the color of that which illuminates it.

Shadowed objects retain the color of the object that shadows them.

203v    /The greater the light on the illuminated object, the darker the shadowed body that has it as a background seems to be.

239  861. *Of bodies illuminated by the air without the sun.* You will paint the shadows of figures or other bodies seen in the air without sun, according to the fifth proposition of the fourth book which teaches us that that part of any illuminated body will be most illuminated which faces the greatest part of the body which illuminates it. Therefore, consider, and draw the imaginary lines from the body which illuminates to the illuminated body, and see to it that the more of the luminous body there is in view, the more the body is illuminated, and here reflected lights appear little. This is common to all objects that are in illuminated air, when some cloud covers the light of the sun, or when the sun has just gone down and the sky gives forth a dead light, in which the contours of shadows with their lights on shadowed bodies appear imperceptible.

239  862. Those outlines of shadows will be least perceptible which derive from the greatest quantity of light.[27]

The reflected lights, or the shadows, which are contained be-
239v  tween the incident and the reflected light, will be of/greater density in any one place when they are greater in quantity.

This happens because when these are greater in quantity, then, according to the seventh proposition of the ninth book, the reflected and the incident lights are more distant; so that the shadow is not greatly affected.

192v  863. *Of the shadow on bodies.* When you represent dark shadows on shadowed bodies, always represent the cause of this darkness, and do the same with reflected lights, because dark shadows are derived from dark objects, and reflected lights from objects of little brightness, that is, from diminished lights. There is the same relation between the illuminated parts of bodies and the

27 Borzelli uses the first sentence of this section as a heading.

part of bodies lighted by reflection, that there is between the cause of the light on these bodies and the cause of this reflection.

864. *Of the shadows and lights by means of which natural ob-* 197v
*jects are imitated.* There are some who wish to see dark shadows in all their works, and so they condemn whoever does not do as they do. These men will be partly satisfied by producing dark shadows and lighter shadows; the dark ones in dark places, and the lighter ones outdoors under a general light.

865. *Of the illumination of the lowest parts of bodies crowded* 230v
*together, as in picturing men in battle.* When men and horses labor in battle, the parts of their bodies will appear darker as they are nearer to the earth which supports them. This is proved by the walls of wells, which become/darker, the deeper they go, 231 *and* and this occurs because the deepest part of the well faces and is *illus.* exposed to less of the luminous air than any other part of it. The ground, which is of the same color, and supports the legs of the men and horses is always more illuminated between equal angles than are the legs above it as already indicated.

866. *Of giving the proper lights to illuminated objects according* 222v
*to their locations.* One should pay great attention to the lights adjusted to objects illuminated by them, for in the same narrative painting there may be parts that are in the open country under the universal light of the air, and others that are/under porticoes, 223 where individual and universal lights are mingled, and others under specific lights, that is, rooms that receive light from a single window.

Of these three kinds of light, it is necessary for the first to encompass large areas, according to the fourth proposition of the first book, which states: there is the same proportion between the sizes of illuminated bodies that there is between the sizes of the objects that illuminate them. And also in these it is required that there be reflections from one body to the other, where the light enters through narrow places among the bodies illuminated by the general light, because the lights that penetrate among bodies near to one another are affected in the same way as the lights that penetrate through the windows and doors of houses, which we

call specific lights. And so we shall make appropriate mention
of this in the proper place.

[ADVICE ON THE REPRESENTATION OF
LIGHTS AND SHADOWS]

220  867. *The manner in which shadows made by objects should ter-*
220v and  *minate.*/If the object is the mountain figured here, and the light
illus.  is the point A, I say that from B to D, and likewise from C to F
there will be no light except that of reflected rays, and this comes
about because the luminous rays do not proceed except by straight
lines, and so do the secondary rays, which are reflected.

224  868. *Of placing lights.* First put a general shadow on all the side
which is not exposed to the light, then put in the medium shad-
224v  ows and the principal ones, in contrast to/one another. And so,
create the general light with a medium light pigment, then, for
contrast, add the medium and principal lights similarly.

223v  869. *Rule for placing the true brightness of lights on the sides of
the aforesaid body.* Take a color similar to that of the body which
you would copy, and take the color of the principal light with
which you would illuminate that body.

Then, if you find that the above-mentioned angle[28] is double
the smaller angle, take away one part of the natural color of the
body which you would copy and give it two parts of the color of
light which you wish it to receive, and you will have made this
light double the lesser light. Afterward to make the half light,
224  take away/one part of the natural color of the above-mentioned
body, and add only one part of the color of light, and thus with
the same color you will have made a light which is double in one
case as compared with the other, because to one quantity of color
there is given a similar quantity of light, and to the other quantity there are given two quantities of light.

If you wish to measure these quantities of color exactly, use a
small spoon, with which you can take equal quantities of pigment, as is shown here and when you have taken the color with
it, level it with a small straight-edge, as they do with measures
of grain, when they sell it.

[28] Cf. McM. 667.

870. *Way of making the shadow on bodies consistent with the* 225
*light and the body.* When you paint a form and you wish to see
if the shadow is consistent with the light, so that it be not redder
or yellower than the real color that you wish to shadow, do this:
make a shadow on the illuminated part with your finger, and if
the accidental shadow made by you is similar to the natural
shadow made by your finger on your work, it is well. Then, with
your finger nearer or farther away, make darker or lighter shadows, which you should always compare with those you have
painted.

871. *Precept for depicting shadows.* Shadows and lights of dis- 240
tant bodies should be made under the same light, for if you made
your mixture of colors in the sun, to portray objects in view of
the sun, and then you made the mixture of colors of the shadows
of bodies in shadow to portray objects that are not exposed to the
sun, and/you then placed both mixtures in shadow, a true likeness 240v
would not result, because you have to consider that the same quality of colors, placed in shadow, will be the true shadow of that
which is placed in the sun, and if you put sun on the shadowed
body as well as on that illuminated, you would see that the
painted shadow and the light are the same color.

872. *Of the representation of colors at any distance.* When you 240v and
would copy a color, take care that when you stand in a shadowed *illus.*
place, you do not seek to depict a luminous place, since you
would deceive yourself with such an imitation. What you have
to do in such a case, if you would practice with the certainty that
belongs to mathematical demonstration, is to compose all the
colors that you have to simulate, comparing the simulated ones
with the real colors in the same light, so that the color you make
may coincide with the natural color.

Let us say that you wish to depict the side of mountains exposed to the sun: place your colors in the sun and there make
your color mixtures and in the sunlight compare these with the
real color. Suppose that the sun is at noon, and I represent a
mountain in the west, which is half shadowed and half luminous,
but I wish to depict only the luminous part. I take a little piece of
paper covered with that color which seems to me similar to that

241 of the mountain,/and I put it alongside the real color in such a way that there is no space between the true and the simulated, exposing it to the sun's rays, and adding different colors until each seems true, and I will continue thus with respect to every kind of shadowed and luminous colors.

# PART SIX

## OF TREES AND VERDURE

### [THE STRUCTURE OF PLANTS]

873. Therefore, painter, if you do not have such rules as these, to 248v avoid the condemnation of those who know these matters, be prepared to represent everything from nature and do not dispense with study, as do those who work for the sake of money only.

874. *Of the branches of plants.* First: every branch of any tree 243 that is not pulled down by its own weight, curves and raises its extremity toward the sky.

Second: the twigs on the branches of trees that grow below, are larger than those that grow above.

Third: all the twigs growing toward the center of the tree wither away in a short time because of excessive shade.

Fourth: those branches are most vigorous and favored which are nearest the upper parts of trees. The causes of this are the air and the sun to which they are exposed.

Fifth: the angles at which the branches extend are usually equal to one another.

Sixth: but these angles become more obtuse as the branches become old.

/Seventh: the side of that angle becomes more oblique which is 243v and made by a thinner branch. illus.

Eighth: every bifurcation of branches, when joined together, recomposes the thickness of the branch from which it grows. For example: A B joined together make E; C D joined together make F; E F joined together make the thickness of the principal branch or trunk O P, and this thickness O P is equal to the total of the thicknesses of A B C D. This comes about because the sap of the thickest branch divides itself among the branches.

Ninth: the contortions of the main branches are as numerous as the growths of those of their ramifications, which are not directly opposite one another.

Tenth: that twisting of branches is greatest where its branches are alike in thickness. See the branch A C and also B C; because they are equal to one another, the branch A C D is bent more than the one above, N O A, whose branches are more dissimilar.

Eleventh: the attachment of the leaf always leaves a trace of itself below its branch, and this grows together with the branch until the bark cracks open due to the age of the tree.

*247*
*247v and*
*illus.*
875. *Of the branches of plants and their foliage.* The branches of some trees, such as the elm, are/wide and thin, like an open hand seen foreshortened. These display the arrangement of their leafy masses as follows: those below show their upper sides, and those which are highest show the under side, and some of those in the center show the under and some the upper side. The upper side is turned toward the tip of the ramification. The part in the center is foreshortened more than any other part of those which are turned with their points toward you, and those branches at the middle height of the tree seem longer which are toward the outer sides of the trees. These ramifications appear like the leaves of the fern which grows in the clay of streams.

Other branches have a round form such as the trees whose twigs and leaves are so arranged that the sixth branch is above the first; while others are thin and transparent, such as the willow and the like.

The extremities of plants, unless pulled down by the weight of fruit, turn toward the sky as much as possible. The right sides of leaves are turned toward the sky in order to receive the nourishment of the dew which falls at night.

The sun gives spirit and life to plants and the earth nourishes them with moisture. I tested this by leaving only the smallest root of a gourd-bearing plant in the ground, and this I kept nourished with water, and the plant brought to perfection all the fruit that it could, which was about sixty large gourds of the broad variety.

*248*
/I applied my mind to this form of life with diligence and learned that the dew at night was what penetrated the stems of large leaves with humidity, to give nourishment to the plant and its offspring.

The rule for leaves grown from the last branch of the year is for the two brother-leaves to move in opposite directions; that is, turning around the stems of the leaves on their branches in such a way that the sixth leaf above comes out above the sixth below. The motion of their turning is this: if one turns toward its companion on the right, the other turns to the left. The leaf is the nipple or rather the breast for the branch or fruit which grows the following year.

876. *Of the branches of plants.* Trees which expand a great deal, *246v* have angles of division which separate their branches, and these are more obtuse the lower down their point of origin is, that is, the closer it/is to the thickest and oldest part of the tree. Thus on *247* the youngest part of the tree, the angles of its branches are most acute.

877. Branches of trees are arranged in two ways, that is, they are *245 and* either opposite one another, or not so. If they are not opposite one *illus.* another the branch in the middle will bend now toward one branch, then toward another. If they are opposite one another, the middle branch of the tree will be straight.

878. *Of the branches of trees.* Branches of trees, when loaded *245* with fruit and leaves, change position from that which they assume during the winter.

879. The branch always grows over the point at which the leaf *245v* is attached and fruit does so also.

880. The thickness of branches, as they bifurcate, varies almost *245* imperceptibly, and if anyone were to assemble the twigs which are produced by the principal branches, these would add up to an equal thickness.

881. When the trunk of the tree divides into three or more prin- *245v and* cipal branches at the same height, then the outer surfaces of these *illus.* branches are higher opposite each other than toward the center of the tree, opposite which there are great concavities. This happens when the angles between branches are smaller than those between branches and the trunk of the tree.

For example: A and B are branches separated by smaller angles, as also are B and C, than are A and C, and therefore these branches which have thickened more rapidly and more massively draw nearer at B C, and their junction is raised higher than the junction at A C, which accounts for the fact that the junction in the middle is lower.

This is the result of a factual premise: let the three circles be N M O which touch one another at points along the lines N M and M O and O N, and do not touch in the center./Being unable to grow together except where they touch, these circles are attached where they are in contact and not in the centers. When they grow thick the point at which they are attached is raised, as is shown above in Y C, and in cases where this point of junction is raised, the centers where they do not touch remain low and concave.

*246v*

*252 and illus.* 882. *Of the center of the thickness of trees.* In the division of the plant, its center will never be in the center of the thickness of its branches. This comes about because these branches are never round, and it also happens because there is more sap in the inner portion of the tree than toward the outer side. That is to say C, which is the point of junction of the branches A C and C E is as much farther away from the center of the branches B and D as the outer sides A E fork away from the centers B D.

[THE GROWTH OF LEAVES, STEMS, BRANCHES,
AND TRUNKS OF TREES]

*249v* 883. *Of the proportion of branches to their nourishment.* The *250* proportion of the thickness of all the branches of one/year of growth is the same in relation to the thickness of their trunk as that of the nourishment of the trunk to the nourishment of the branches; that is, the nourished organism exists in proportion to its nourishment.

For, if a branch of a tree is cut off, and there be grafted or inserted one of its own twigs, in time this twig will grow much larger than the branch which nourishes it, because the nourishment or vital saps rush to the defense of the injured place; which, in this instance is the place of the graft. When many buds of plants are grafted in a circle about a cut stump, that very year they will compose a greater mass than the surface of the cut trunk.

884. *Of the form that trees have where they approach their roots.* 255
The lower trunks of trees do not keep their round breadth when
they approach the origin of their branches or their roots. This
comes about because both the higher and lower branches are the
sources by which plants are nourished, for in the summer they
are nourished from above by means of their leaves, with the dew
and rain which they receive, and during the winter they are
nourished from below by means of the contact which the earth
has with their roots.

885. *Of the growth of trees and in which direction they grow* 250
*most.* Larger branches do not grow toward the center of the
tree. This comes about because every branch naturally seeks the
air and avoids shadow, and shadows are more powerful on the
lower parts of branches, which face the earth, than on those parts
which turn to the sky. It therefore follows that the course of the
water and dew which descends and which the night multiplies,
keeps the lower part more humid than the upper and for this
reason, the branches have more abundant nourishment in that
part, and therefore grow more.

886. *Which branches of trees are those which grow most in one* 250
*year.* The largest branches/are always those which are produced 250v
by that part of the bough which faces the earth, and the smaller
ones grow from it above the largest branch. The lower branch
grows to this size because the sap of the branch, when it is not
struck by the heat of the sun, always falls to the lower part of
the branch, and nourishes more there where it is in greater abundance. For this reason the bark grows thicker here than it does
above, and this is a fundamental reason why the twigs of the
branches are much larger below than above, and for this reason
also trees put forth many branches in the lower portion. This is
why a branch does not put forth large twigs which strike against
the branch which is above it, and so plants do not grow with
confusion, nor take away the air from one another through the
nearness of so many branches and so much foliage for they give
way to one another. And if a branch, as has been said, grows
downward somewhat, that branch which grows toward it, grows
but little upward.

247 and
illus.

**887. *Of growth of leaves upon their stems*.** Never does the thickness of a branch diminish with respect to the space that there is from leaf to leaf beyond the thickness of the bud which is above that leaf, a thickness which is lacking in the branch which extends as far as the following leaf.

Nature has arranged the leaves of the last branches of many trees so that the sixth leaf is always above the first, and this follows successively unless the rule is impeded. This has two advantages for the tree. The first is that if a branch or fruit is produced the following year from the twin vein of the bud, which is above and in contact with the attachment of the leaf, the water which bathes the branch can extend to nourish the twin by stopping in the concavity of the origin of that leaf. The second advantage is that when the branches grow the next year, one will not cover the other, because when there are five branches turned in five directions, the sixth grows far enough away above the first to avoid this.

249   **888. *Of the branches of trees*.** All the branches of trees have the origin of their sixth leaf above that of the sixth leaf below, except, etc.[1]

These have hollow stems, such as the blackberry and the like, except the white jasmine, which always has a pair of stems placed at right angles placed over the preceding.

All trees that have the sun behind them are dark toward the center.

248   **889. *Of the growth of branches on plants*.** [2]The growth of the branches of trees on their principal trunk is like that of the growth of their leaves, which develop in four ways, one above the other. The first and most general is that the sixth leaf above always grows above the sixth below; the second manner is for the third pair of leaves to be above the third pair below; the third manner is for the third leaf to be above the third below.

[1] "Etc." should read "in the instances stated before."
[2] In this chapter, space was left vacant to be filled with a diagram. This drawing was never inserted. A later hand has written "O" in the center of this space, and an unidentified hand has written in the margin, in pencil: "niente" (nothing).

890. *Of the diversity that branchings of trees show.* There are *251 and*
three ways in which trees branch. One of these is that they put *illus.*
forth branches in opposite directions, one on the side toward the
east and the other toward the west so that they do not face one
another directly, but in the middle of the space opposite. Another
is to put them in pairs at the same time and facing one another,
but if two are on the east and west sides, the next two will face
south and north. The third manner of branching always results
in the sixth branch being directly above the first and this is true
successively.

891. *Of plants that send forth their branches opposite to one an-* *251 and*
*other.* All plants that send out equally thick branches by degrees, *illus.*
like steps, one opposite to the other, are always straight, as is the
silver fir, A B. This straightness comes about because the oppos-
ing parts, being equal in thickness, draw an equal amount of/sap *251v*
or nourishment, and cause the branches to be of equal weight,
whence it follows that since equal causes produce equal effects,
this equality maintains the straightness of the tree.

892. *Of chance which bends the aforesaid plants.*/But when the *251v*
aforesaid trees put forth branches that are unequal in thickness,
then that tree does not preserve its straightness, but bends on the
side opposite to the thicker branch, and this happens because
necessity compels the tree to be in the center of equal weights,
for if it were not, it would soon collapse in even a small wind,
when that wind blew from the direction in which the thickest
branch grows.

[THE BARK OF TREES]

893. *Of the bark of trees.* The growth in thickness of plants is *250v*
brought about by the sap which, in the month of April, is created
between the inner bark and the wood of the tree. At that time
the inner bark is converted into bark, and the outer bark acquires
new cracks in the depth of the existing cracks.

894. The bark of trees always cracks along the length of the *245v*
tree, except the bark of the cherry tree, which opens in a circle
around it.

245   895. The bark of a young tree does not crack.[3]

243   896. *Of the branching of trees.* The swelling of bark from which
the leaf of the twig springs, grows in the same proportion that
the branch does and is always manifest until old age cracks the
bark.

244 *and*   /Let P B C be the thickness of the branch and B C D be the
*illus.*   leaf that is attached to the branch throughout the space B O C,
which is one third of the thickness of the branch. O is the bud
which the twig grows above the leaf. I say, then, that since a
third part of the thickness of the branch surrounds the attachment of the leaf, when the branch P B C grows to the size
H G S, the attachment of the leaf will still be surrounded by a
third part of the thickness of the branch, as it is shown in G S.

That branch of the tree will be most curved which grows lowest in the mass of its branchings.

244   897. *Of the branching of trees.* The swelling of bark, produced
by the conjunction of branches, is very marked at the fork when
the branches become attached together as they thicken in their
early years. In late years this remains concave.

[THE AGE OF TREES]

249   898. *Of the branching which, during the same year, is sent forth
again on the end of branches that have been cut.* The quantity
of shoots that grows on a cut branch compared with the quantity
of shoots which that branch should ordinarily produce that same
year, is that of the quantity of the inner bark which lies between
the bark and the wood, and corresponds to the circumferential
line made on the cut end of the branch, in comparison with the
249v   length of the diameter of/this shoot. This comes about because
the nourishment which passes through the diameter, and cus-
tomarily rises to nourish the branches of that year, not finding
them, stops and nourishes that branch which grows at the end
of the bark and the inner-bark.

But this rule seems to suffer exceptions because, if all the

[3] The single sentence in this section of Ludwig's edition is used as the heading
in that of Borzelli.

branches, due to all the nourishment, were to sprout that year, they would reproduce such a quantity of branches that if they were united, they would reconstruct a thickness equal to that of the branch which has been cut off. Thus, if the top edges of the bark and inner-bark of the cut plant recomposed one continuous branch on the tips where the branch has been cut and if this embraced the entire circumference of the wood, it would again that same year create a volume of wood equal to the thickness of the branch which it embraces. This seems impossible, however much the air, rain, and dew should aid it, for the circumference of all the branches together, which this tree, without having been cut, should produce that year is much greater than is the circumference of the inner-bark on the whole edge of the cut bark, and consequently it would derive more nourishment than those that remain do, because in the bark and inner-bark is the life of the plant.

But this will not be discussed in full here, because it is reserved for elsewhere, and it does not relate to painting.

899. *Of the proportion that the branchings of plants have to one another*. There is the same proportion between the branching of each tree produced in the same year and the trunk as there is between the antecedent and subsequent/growth of all other years both past and future. That is, every year the branches which each plant has acquired, when their thicknesses are calculated together and united after they have finished growing, are equal to the branch which it produced the previous year and which produced them. Thus they continue and so they will be found in the future. For example: the branches A D and B D, the last ones on the tree, will be equal to the branch D C, which has produced them. *244v*

*245 and illus.*

900. *Of the branching of trees*. That part of the tree will appear and will, in actuality, be of greatest age which is closest to its point of origin, as the wrinkling of the bark shows. This is seen in walnut trees which often have a great part of their bark stretched and polished over the old and wrinkled bark, and are as different in youth and age as their main branches indicate. *246 and illus.*

The age of trees which have not been injured by men can be counted in years by their branchings from the trunk. For example, A, B, C, D, E, F are circles, with each growth of a principal branch putting forth that branch which is nearest to the center of the tree.

Trees have as many differences in age as they have principal branches.

The youngest part of the tree will have bark which is more polished and smoother than any other part.

The southern sides of trees show greater youth and vigor than the northern sides.

*246v*  /The oldest part of the bark of a tree is always that which cracks first.

That part of the tree will have the roughest and thickest bark which is oldest.

The circles of the branches of trees which have been cut off show the number of its years, and also show which years were wetter or drier, according to the greater or lesser thickness of these branches.

The branches also show the direction toward which they were turned, because they are thicker on the north side than on the south, and for this reason the center of the tree is nearer to the bark on the south than on the north. Although these things do not serve painting, yet I will note them, so as to leave out as little about trees as is possible.

Those tops of trees will grow most which are nearest to the main trunk of their tree.

The leaves which grow first and fall last are those which are produced on the main heights of trees.

The tree which grows oldest has the smallest branches.

The branch which extends in most continuous thickness and is straightest is that which creates the smallest twigs around it.

### [ANALYSIS OF THE ELM AND WALNUT]

*264v and*  901. *Description of the elm.* The ramification of the elm has its
*illus.*  longest shoot on top and the smallest shoots are the first and the last but one, when the main branch is straight. The distance from the attachment of one leaf to the next is very nearly half

the length of the largest leaf, because the leaves have an interval between them which is about a third of the breadth of this leaf.

The leaves of the elm are thicker at the end of its branch than at the beginning, and their breadths vary little when looked at from one place.

In the composition of leafy trees care should be taken not to repeat too often the color of a plant which has as its background the same color in another tree, but rather to vary the color with brighter, darker, or greener verdure.

The leaf always has its right side to the sky so that it may better *265* receive on all its surface the dew which descends from the air with slow movement. These leaves are distributed in the trees in such a way that one covers the other as little as possible, by interlacing one over the other as ivy is seen to do when it covers the walls. This interlacing serves two purposes which are to leave intervals between the leaves which the air and the sun can penetrate and second, so that the drops that fall on the first leaf can also fall on the fourth and sixth leaves and so on.

902. *Of the leaves of the walnut.* The leaves of the walnut are *265* distributed throughout all the shoots of that year and are more distant from one another and greater in number in relation to the youth of the branch from which they are put forth. The younger the tree is, the closer they are to their points of growth and they are fewer in number in relation to the origin of the branch on which they grow to an older branch. Fruits originate at the end of the twig whose larger shoots are on the lower side of the stem on which they grow. This happens because the weight of the sap causes it to be more apt to descend than to rise and for this reason the branches which grow uppermost and reach toward the sky are small and thin, with leaves spread out with equal distribution of their tips and if the small stem faces the horizon the leaves lie flat. This comes about because leaves universally turn their reverse sides toward the earth.

[THE STRUCTURE OF TREES AND THE EFFECTS
OF LIGHT, WIND, AND POSITION]

903. *Precept.* Some of the branches and twigs of trees are pointed *267* and others are round.

The thickest tips of branches of trees send out the largest leaves, or leaves in larger quantity than does any other end of a branch.

The tips of branches and twigs always become full of leaves first.

*267v*    The thickest ends of branches are always on the main branches of the tree, and conversely the thinnest ends of branches are the farthest from the main trunk.

*244*    904. *Of the smaller branchings of trees.* The leaves which constitute the final foliage of trees are more visible in the upper than in the lower part of the tree and this occurs more in walnut trees than in others because the foliage of walnut trees is composed in groups of seven leaves as you see in the margin in A. These *244v and* leaves bend downward because of their weight/and often rest *illus.* upon one another and form a very bright spot which is apparent at a great distance. When you are near to such a cluster you see the high lights on each leaf and on the underside of the branches the leaves hang obliquely from their stems, casting shadows upon others below. For the reason stated it is concluded that such foliage has more distinguishable leaves above than below, since above it is not covered by other leaves while, on the lower part, being covered by leaves higher up, individual leaves are not entirely distinguished by the eye. At the top, because the leaves hang from their stems and are not far from the branch, and below they grow much farther away, the upper leaves of these stems are less distant from the mass of all the leaves than the last leaves below. This all happens under a particular light because under the universal light the leaves have light but not high lights. All the trees which have foliage composed of groups of leaves appear as described above, even when they have broad leaves, such as the plane tree, the lime tree, the fig tree and the like.

*267v*    905. *Precept on trees.* Some branches and the trees from which they stem are entirely governed by nature and others are hindered by natural defect, and these dry up, either entirely or in part, and others do not achieve their natural size because they have been cut off by men, and some are stunted because they have been deformed by lightning or winds or other storms.

The trees which grow near the seacoast, where they are exposed to winds are all bent by the wind, and they grow bent and remain so.

906. *What tree is most deformed in regard to its thickness and of* 252v
*least height and most durability.* That tree will be most deformed in regard to its thickness which grows on the highest site, in the thinnest forest, and farthest from the center of such a forest.

907. *Which tree in forests grows with the most consistent thick-* 252v
*ness and to the greatest height.* That tree will grow with the most consistent thickness and to the greatest height which grows in the lowest and narrowest valley and in the thickest forest and farthest from the borders of that forest.

908. *Of the bark of trees.*/The bark of trees always has greater 250v-251
cracks toward the south than toward the north side.

909. *Of the north side of the trunks of trees.* The north side of 250v
old trees always has the bark on the lower side of its trunk which is covered with greenish moss.

[VISUAL CONDITIONS OF TREES]

910. *Of the states of the foliage of trees.* Four states of the foliage 251v
of trees are: luster, light, transparency, and shadow. If the eye looks down on this foliage, the illuminated part will seem to be greater in quantity than the shadowed part, and this occurs because the illuminated side is larger than the shadowed side and is subject to light, high light and transparency. For the moment I shall leave transparency aside and describe the appearance of the illuminated part, which is considered the fourth of the qualities of colors which vary on the surfaces of bodies. This is a medium quality, which means that it is not the principal light but a secondary one, which is accompanied by a secondary rather than a principal shadow. This medium, illuminated part comes between the high light and the shadowy quality which, in turn, comes between the medium illuminated part/and the principal 252
shadows.

The third state, which is transparency, occurs only in transparent objects, and not in relation to opaque bodies. But I am speaking, at present, of the leaves of trees and it is necessary to describe the second state of foliage which is important in depicting plants. This has not been employed by anyone before me insofar as I am aware. It is, as has been stated, the portion of the foliage situated in the lower part of the tree.

*253v and illus.* 911. *Of the ends of branches of leafy trees.* The primary shadows which the first leaves cast upon the second leafy branches are less dark than those which these shadowed leaves cast upon the third leaves and also less dark than those cast by the third shadowed leaves upon the fourth. This brings forth the fact that the illuminated leaves which have the third and fourth leaves which are in shadow, as their backgrounds, appear in greater relief than those which have the first shadowed leaves as their background.

For example, if the sun were E, and the eye N, and the first leaf illuminated by the sun were A, which has as its background the second leaf B, I say that this leaf would stand out less, since it has as its background that second leaf, than if it projected farther out and had as its background the leaf C, which is darker because more leaves lie between it and the sun. The leaf A would *254* stand out still more if it/had as its background the fourth leaf, that is, D.

*251v* 912. *Of the sparse tops of trees.* The sparse tops of thin trees with thin foliage do not cast perceptible shadows, because their branches are thin and few, with few and thin leaves, and the parts which are not transparent remain illuminated.

*261* 913. *Of trees that send forth straight branches.* The willow and other similar trees from which branches are cut every three or four years, send out very straight branches, and their shadows fall toward the center from which those branches spring, and toward the edges they cast little shadow because of their very small leaves and sparse, thin branches. Thus the branches which rise toward the sky will produce little shadow and little relief, and those branches which grow down from the horizon originate in the dark part of the shadow and little by little become brighter toward their ends. These branches display deep relief, because they are in different degrees of brightness against a shadowed background.

That tree will be least shadowed, which has most sparse branches and foliage.

914. *Of the universal light that illuminates trees.* That part of the *255v* tree will appear to be enveloped in least dense shadow which is farthest from the earth.

It is proved thus: let A P⁴ be the tree, and N B C be the illuminated hemisphere. The lower part of the tree faces the earth P C, that is, the part O, and it is exposed to a little of the hemisphere in C D, but the higher part in the concavity A is exposed/ *256 and* to the greatest amount of the hemisphere, that is, B C, and on *illus.* this account, because it does not face the density of the earth, it remains more illuminated.

But if the tree is thick with foliage, as are the laurel, the fir, or the box-tree, then the situation is different, for, although A does not face the earth, its foliage is divided into many shadows, which reverberate on the reverse of the leaves above them. The shadows of these trees are darker the nearer they are to the center of the tree.

915. *Which part of the branch of the tree will be more shadowed.* *262v* That part of the branch of the tree will be darkest which is farthest from its extremities, if the tree has a uniform distribution of branches and foliage.

916. *Of the sizes of shadows and lights on leaves.* The branches *255* and foliage of trees are seen from below, above, or from the center. If they are seen from below, then the light will be universal and the shadowy part will be greater than the illuminated part; if they are seen from above, the illuminated part will be larger than the shadowed part, and if they are seen from the center, the illuminated part will be as large as that in shadow.

[THE ILLUMINATION AND SHADOW OF TREES]

917. *Of the illumination of trees.* When the eye is situated so that *255* it sees that side of the trees illuminated which is exposed to the luminous body,/one tree is never seen illuminated as is another. *255v and* The proof is: let the eye be C, which sees the two trees B, D, *illus.*

⁴ Read A P for A B in original text.

which are illuminated by the sun A. I say that that eye C will not see the lights on one tree to be as they are on the other, for the tree which is nearer to the sun will appear as much more shadowed than that which is farther away, as one tree is nearer than the other to the convergence of the rays of the sun which come to the eye.

Notice that nothing but shadow of the tree D is seen by the eye C, yet by the same eye C, the tree B is seen half in light and half in shadow.

257   918. *Of trees below the level of the eye.* Trees below the level of
257v  the eye, although they are, in actuality, of equal/height, color, and density of foliage, will not be prevented from increasing in density with every degree of distance they have from the eye. The tree which is nearest to you and of which you see the illuminated side, which is that part which displays itself to the light of the sky, appears with a brighter effect because you are above it. That one which is farther away you see as though it were farther beneath, and its shadowed parts are displayed to you so that it seems to you to be darker. If there were not a greater amount of air lying between the eye and the second tree than there is between the eye and the first tree which lightens this darkness, the perspective of colors would diminish in the opposite manner.

254v   919. *Of the difference of shadows of trees in the same light in a landscape under a specific light.* When the sun is in the east the trees east of you cast large shadows, and those to the south are half in shadow while those to the west are entirely illuminated. These three differentiations are not enough, however, for it is better to say that the entire tree toward the east is in shadow and that which grows toward the southeast is three-quarters in shadow, while the shadow of the tree directly south covers half the tree. One quarter of the tree toward the southwest is in shadow and the tree directly west has no shadow at all.

262   920. *Of plants in the south.* When the sun is in the east, trees in the south and north have almost as much light as shadow. The amount of light is greater the farther west they are, and the amount of shadow is greater the farther east they are.

921. *Of the shadows of trees*. When the sun is in the east, the 261 trees to the west of the eye appear to have very little, almost imperceptible, relief if the air which lies between the eye and the trees is very dusty. According to the seventh proposition of this book,/these trees are without shadow, and although there is 261v shadow in each division of the foliage, it happens that because the visual images of the shadow and the light which reach the eye are confused and intermingled, and because of the smallness of their size and form they cannot be envisaged.

The principal lights are in the middle of the trees, and the shadows toward the edges, and the spaces between are marked by the shadows in these intervals when the forests are thick, but when they are sparse the outlines are but little to be seen.

922. *Of the shadows of trees*. Shadows of trees in landscapes do 259 not appear to be the same in trees at the right as in those at the left, particularly when the sun is at the right or at the left. This is proved by the fourth proposition which states: opaque bodies lying between the light and the eye appear to be entirely in shadow, and also by the fifth proposition which states: the eye placed between the opaque body and the light sees the opaque body all illuminated; and furthermore by the sixth proposition which states: if the eye and the opaque body are between the darkness and the light, the opaque body will be seen half in shadow and half in light.

923. *Of trees in the east*. When the sun is in the east, trees seen 261v by one looking toward the east will have light surrounding their shadows, except toward the earth, and unless the tree was pruned in the past year. Trees toward the south and the north will be half shadowed and half light, to a degree which depends on whether they are more or less to the east or to the west.

The eye at a high or low level sees changes in the shadows and the lights of trees, for at a high level the eye sees trees with little shadow and at a low level the eye sees them with much shadow.

The foliage of trees is as varied as their species are different.

924. *Of trees in the east*. When the sun is in the east, trees in the 261v east are dark toward the middle, and their outer areas are bright.

*261v* 925. *Of the shadows of trees in the east.* The shadows of trees in the east cover a large part of the trees and are darker the more *262* thickly the trees/are covered with leaves.

[THE TRANSPARENCY OF LEAVES AND THE
COLOR OF THEIR SHADOWS]

*260v* 926. *Of the color of leaves.*[5] If the light comes from M, and the eye is at N, the eye will see the color of the leaves A and B, all taking on the color of M, that is, of the air; B and C, will be transparent and will be seen from the reverse, appearing a most beautiful green tending toward yellow.

*261*   If M is the luminous body which illuminates the leaf S, all eyes that see the reverse of that leaf will see it as a most beautiful bright green, because it is transparent.

Many are the times that groups of leaves are without shadow and are transparent and the right side has a high light.

*260v and* 927. *Of dark leaves in front of transparent ones.* When leaves are *illus.* placed between the light and the eye, then the leaf nearest the eye will be the darkest and the most distant will be the brightest, provided that it does not have the air as its background. This happens in the case of leaves which are beyond the center of the tree, that is, toward the light.

*252* 928. *Of the transparency of leaves.* When the light is in the east, and the eye looking toward west, sees the plant from below, it perceives the eastern side of the tree to be transparent in great part, except those parts which are covered by shadows of other leaves. The western side of the tree will be dark because it receives the shadow of half of the foliage, that is, of the part turned toward the east.

*257* 929. *Of trees.* When trees are looked at by one facing the sun, they appear to be a more beautiful green than they were at first because of the transparency of the leaves, while toward the center of the tree the leaves seem very dark. The leaves which are not transparent show their right sides, whose high lights are much in evidence.

[5] The illustrations are missing.

But if you look at trees with dense foliage from the side opposite the sun, you will see them with few shadows and much gleam on the leaves.

930. *Of the green of leaves.* The most beautiful greens that the *257* leaves of trees display are seen when they are placed with their mass between the eye and the air.

931. *Of the aspects of landscapes.* When the sun is in the east, all *265v* the illuminated parts of trees display most beautiful greens, and this happens because the leaves illuminated by the sun within half of the horizon, that is, the eastern half, are transparent.

Within the western semicircle the greens are of poor hue in the humid air, muddy with the color of dark ashes, because these leaves are not transparent like those in the east, whose air is bright and increasingly so the more humid it is.

932. *Of trees seen from below.* When trees are seen from below *264 and* and against the light, side by side and close together, the far side *illus.* of the first will be transparent and bright in great part, and will have as its background the dark part of the second tree, and this will be so successively with all of the trees which are situated according to the aforesaid conditions.

⁶Let S be the light, R the eye, C D N the first tree, A B C the second. I say that the eye at R will see the part C F in large part transparent and bright because of the light at S, which/is in view *264v* on the opposite side, and it will be in view against the dark background B C, because this obscurity is the shadow of the tree A B C.

But if the eye is situated at F, it will see O P dark against the bright background N Q.

The nearest to you of the transparent shadowy part of trees is darkest.

933. *Of trees that are between the eye and the light.* The front *258v* of trees which are between the eye and the light is bright, and this brightness comes from the mass of transparent leaves which is seen from behind, with lustrous leaves seen from the right side.

⁶ Read diagrams as illustrating different views of two trees.

And their background below and behind is of dark foliage, because it is shadowed by the front part of the tree.

This happens with trees that are higher than the eye.

266 934. The eye that follows the course of the wind will never see the leaf of any tree, other than the reverse side except those on the branches that face the wind, or the leaves of laurel and other similar trees, which have very strong stems.

256 935. *Of lights on dark leaves.* The lights on leaves will partake more of the color of the air which is reflected on them, if the leaves are dark in color. This is caused by the fact that the brightness of the part illuminated which comes from the blue of the air mixed with the darkness, composes the color blue. It is mirrored on the polished surface of leaves and increases the blue which the brightness of the air usually creates on dark objects.

256v 936. *Of the high lights on the foliage of trees.* The leaves of trees commonly have a polished surface, because of which they mirror in part the color of the air, and because the air takes on white since it is mixed with thin and transparent clouds, the surfaces of these leaves, when they are naturally dark, like those of the elm, and when they are not covered with dust, have high lights which appear to be blue. This happens according to the seventh proposition of the fourth book which shows that brightness compounded with darkness produces the color blue.

These leaves will have high lights that are bluer as the air which is mirrored in them is more pure and blue, but if these leaves are young, like those at the tips of branches in the month 257 of May, then/they will be green tending toward yellow,[7] and if their high lights are produced by the blue air which is mirrored in them, then these will be green according to the third proposition of the fourth book which states: the color yellow mixed with blue always produces the color green.

The high lights of all the leaves of a dense surface will take on the color of the air, and the darker the leaves are, the more they will function like mirrors, and as a consequence these high lights will become blue.

[7] On Urb. 256 the words "traenti al giallo" (tending toward yellow), have been added a second time, beside the first line of the heading.

937. *Of trees which are illuminated by the sun and by the air.* 256v
Trees illuminated by the sun and the air, with leaves which are
dark in color, will be illuminated on one side by the air alone,
and therefore the illumination will partake of blue. And on the
other side, they will be illuminated by the air and the sun, and
that side which the eye sees illuminated by the sun will be
lustrous.

938. *Of the light on foliage of verdure tending toward yellow.* 256-256v
The leaves of foliage tending toward yellow do not have to mirror the air to have blue luster, for as everything that appears in
a mirror partakes of the color of that mirror, so that the blue of
the air mirrored in the yellow of foliage appears green, because
blue and yellow mixed together compose a most beautiful green,
the color of the lusters of bright foliage tending toward the color
yellow will be yellow-green.

939. *Of the shadow of the leaf.* Sometimes a leaf has three inci- 260 and
dental conditions; that is, shadow, high light, and transparency; *illus.*
for example, if the light were from N on the leaf S, and the eye
at M, it would see the part A illuminated, B shadowed, and C
transparent.

The leaf with a concave surface, seen in reverse from below,
sometimes appears half shadowed/and half transparent. For ex- 260v and
ample, let P O be the leaf, and the light M, and the eye N, which *illus.*
sees O shadowed because the light does not strike it at equal
angles on the right side nor on the reverse, and let P be the right
side, illuminated with a light which shines through to the reverse side.

940. *Of the darkness of a tree.* That side of the tree which has a 257
background of air is much darker than that which stands against
the background of a forest, mountain, or hill.

[SHRUBS AND GRASS]

941. *Discussion of kinds of blossoms in the flowering branches* 243
*of shrubs.* Some of the flowers that grow on the branches of
shrubs bloom first at the very top of those branches, and others
open the first flower at the very lowest part of the stem.

268 942. Those leaves of shrubs will be most indented which are closest to its seeds, and the least indented ones will be the nearest to its root.

262 943. *Of meadows.* When the sun is in the east, the greens of meadows are of a most beautiful color because they are transparent to the sun, something which does not happen with meadows to the west, while the green colors of southern and northern grasses are of medium beauty.

267v 944. *Of grass.* Some grass is in shadow and some in light, and if the eye looks toward the shadows, it will see the shadowy grass have as a background the brightness of the illuminated grass. But if the eye is toward the light, it will see the illuminated grass have as a background the darkness of the shadowy grass.

262 945. *Of the grass of meadows.* Where grass takes shadow from the trees that grow among it, that portion which is on this side of the shadow has blades illuminated against a shadowy background, but the grass which is in the shadows of the trees has dark blades against a bright background, that is, against a background which is beyond the shadow.

266 946. *Precepts concerning plants and verdure.* Trees and meadows appear much brighter seen along the course of the wind, than heading into it. This comes about because each leaf is paler on the reverse than on the right side, and whoever looks at it along the course of the wind, sees its reverse side, and whoever looks at it against the wind sees it shadowed, because its ends bend, and cast shadows toward its center, and furthermore the leaves are seen on the reverse side.

The whole of that tree is bent most by the pressure of wind which has the thinnest and longest branches, such as willows and the like.

266v If the eye is between the advance and the flight of the/wind, the trees will seem to have thicker branches toward the advance of the wind, than toward its flight, and this happens because the wind that strikes the tops of the trees turned toward it, presses them against the stronger branches, causing them to be compact there and to have little transparency. But the branches opposite that are struck by the wind, which penetrates through the per-forations of the mass of the tree, are blown away from the center of the tree and appear more sparse.

Among trees of equal thickness and height, that one will be most bent by the wind, the ends of whose lateral branches are but little distant from the center of the tree. This is caused by the fact that the position of its branches is close to the center and gives no protection for the middle of the tree against the advance or pressure of the wind.

Those trees are most bent by the course of the wind which are the highest.

Trees that are most dense with leaves are most bent by the striking of the wind.

In great forests, and in fields of grain and in meadows, the waves made by the wind look like those seen on the sea or on beaches.

947. That tree will produce the darkest shadow which has the *266v* most abundant and thickest leaves, such as the laurel and the like.

Straight limbs which are not weighed down by their leaves or their fruit, are all directed to the central point of their branching.

All the thick branches which each tree sends out year by year, when each year's growth is put/together, will be equal to the *267* first trunk.

The lower trunks of old trees growing in humid and shadowed places are always covered with green moss.

The youngest tree has a bark more polished than the older one.

The upper branches of trees are more heavily covered with leaves than the lower ones.

The outer parts of forests have trees more heavily covered with leaves than those in the interior.

The ground of those forests will be least covered with grass where the forests are thickest.

[THE COLOR AND BRIGHTNESS OF TREES AS
AFFECTED BY DISTANCE]

948. *Of the illuminated side of verdure and mountains*. At a *256* great distance that side of verdure which is illuminated by the most powerful light will appear most natural in color.

258v  949. *Of the incidental color of trees.* The incidental conditions of color in the foliage of trees are four: shadow, light, high light, and transparency.

253  950. *Branches and twigs of trees at diverse distances.* The trees in the first plane show their true shapes to the eye, and each cluster of leaves growing on the last twigs of the trees shows sharply its lights, high lights, shadows and transparent parts; in the second plane within the distance from the horizon to the eye, all the clusters of leaves appear like points on the twigs; at the third distance all of the twigs seem to be points sown among the larger branches; at the fourth distance the larger branches are so diminished that they remain only as indistinct shapes in the tree; then follows the horizon, which is the fifth and last distance, where the tree is completely diminished in such a way that it is like a point in shape. Thus I have divided the distance from the eye to the true horizon, which ends on a plane, into five equal parts.

258  951. *Of the luminous parts of the verdure of plants.* Luminous parts of the verdure of trees in the vicinity of the eye appear to be brighter than those of more distant trees, and their shadowed parts appear darker than those of the more distant trees.

258v    The bright parts of distant trees are darker/than those of adjacent trees, and their shadowy parts seem brighter than the shadowy parts of those adjacent trees. This comes about because the concurrence of the visual images becomes confused and mixed on account of their great distance from the eye that sees them.

254  952. *Why the same trees seem brighter near at hand than at a distance.* There are three reasons why trees of the same kind seem brighter near at hand than at a distance. The first is because shadows look darker near at hand and because of this darkness the illuminated branches which border on them appear brighter than they are. The second is that when the shadow is farther from the eye, the air which lies between that shadow and the eye with greater thickness than it used to, lightens the shadow and makes its color take on blue, for which reason the luminous branches do not at first look as dark as they are, though later they seem darker. The third reason is that the visual images of

brightness and obscurity which these branches send to the eye are mingled at their edges and become confused. Also the shadowy parts are always greater in quantity than the luminous parts, and the shadowed parts gain greater clarity at a distance than do the few bright parts. For these three reasons the trees look darker from a distance than near at hand. Also, the luminous parts appear larger as they become more powerfully illuminated, and they appear more powerful the less thickness of air lies between the eye and them.

953. *Why trees at a certain distance are brighter the farther away* 254 *they are.* After a certain distance, the greater the distance from the eye, the brighter trees look, so that at last/they are as bright 254v as the air at the horizon. This comes about because of the air which lies between those trees and the eye. Since this is of a white quality, the greater the amount that lies between the trees and the eye, the greater the whiteness with which it covers the trees, and while the trees in themselves take on a dark color, the whiteness of the air lying in between makes the dark parts more blue than the illuminated parts.

954. *Of the light of branches and foliage.* For the reasons given 254v above the details of the branches and foliage of illuminated trees such as the separation of each leaf from other leaves by shadowed parts, are lost to view because they are very small and also because they are occupied and overcome by the illuminated part which does not diminish as much as the shadowed part at a distance. Thus the leaves of a branch, seen at a distance, and being of one color—despite the fact that, with a good view,/something 255 of the shadows in the intervals between the leaves is distinguishable—do not give an accurate impression of darkness. This results from two causes, the first of which is the thickness of the air which lies between the eye and the shadowed object. The second cause is the very small visual images become somewhat confused at their edges and in clarity when seen at such a distance, and since the illuminated part is clearer than the shadowed part, the shadows appear to be of little density.

[DISTANCE AND CLARITY IN THE CONTOURS OF TREES]

248v 955. *Of trees.* If the branch of the tree comes to your view fore-shortened, its leaves will appear in full view or nearly so. If the
249 branch/appears in its true form, its leaves will appear to you distorted, that is, foreshortened.

When, at a distance, a tree does not present its true shape to the eye, or is deceptive with regard to its leaves, there yet remains the shape of the clusters of branches which have a certain quantity and quality. When, because of distance, the shape of the clusters of branches is lacking, there remains for the eye only the amount of its brightness and darkness, and if you would judge it at a still greater distance, you will have only the color which distinguishes it from other, different objects, and if these are not different they will not be distinguished.

258v 956. *What outlines distant trees display against the air which forms their background.* The outlines which the branches and foliage of trees display against the illuminated air, have a shape tending toward the spherical the farther distant they are, and the nearer they are, the less they show of this spherical shape. For
259 and example, A, the first tree, because it is near/to the eye displays
illus. the true shape of its branching, which almost disappears in B,
on 258v and is entirely lost in C, where, not only are the branches of the tree not seen, but the whole tree is recognized only with great effort.

Every shadowed body, of whatever shape one wishes, seems spherical at a great distance. This happens because, if it is a rectangular body, at a short distance its angles are lost, and a little farther away the smaller sides are lost. Thus, before the whole is lost, the parts are lost, since they are smaller than the whole. Just as a human figure, under the same conditions, first loses legs, arms, and head, before the torso; and then loses the extremities of length before those of breadth. If these extremities became equal, they would form a square, providing the angles were left, but when no angles remain a round form results.

253 957. *Of the part of trees at a great distance which remains clear.*
253v /When trees are at great distances from the eye that sees them,

only the whole masses of their principal shadows and lights are apparent, but those shadows which are not principal ones are lost through diminution, so that if a small illuminated part lies in a large shadowed space, it is lost and does not affect that shadow in any way, and the same thing happens with a small shadowy part against a large illuminated background.

958. *Of the withdrawal of the country into the distance.* Make 257v the extremities of trees in places somewhat distant almost imperceptible and little differentiated from their background.

[HOW TREES ACQUIRE BLUENESS WITH DISTANCE]

959. *Of distances more remote than those aforementioned.* But 253v when trees are at a greater distance, then the shadowy and the luminous masses are confused by the air lying in between, as well as by their diminution, so that they will seem to be all of one color, that is, blue.

960. *Of the azure color which distant trees acquire.*/The blue 257v-258 which trees in distant places acquire is created more in the dark than in the luminous parts. This comes about because of the light of the air lying between the eye and the shadow, which is tinged with the color of the sky, and the luminous parts of trees are the last to lose their greenness.

961. *Of landscapes.* The shadowy parts of distant landscapes take 263v on the color blue more than do the illuminated parts. This is proved by the intensification of blue, with which air without color is tinged, for if this did not have darkness above it, it would remain white, because the blue of the air in itself is composed of light and of darkness.

962. *Why the shadow of leafy branches does not appear* 262v *powerful at their luminous parts as in the parts opposite.* The illuminated part of branches of trees at a great distance causes the shadowed parts which are among the illuminated details to become indistinct. This happens because the illuminated parts increase the size of their forms at a distance, and those of the shadowed parts diminish to such an extent that they are not perceptible to the eye, and the visual images which come to the eye

are those of indistinct objects, because such shadowed and illuminated visual images blend, and as the luminous parts maintain their forms better, the combination appears to be of that kind
which is seen in the larger part of the branch.

*265v* 963. *Of the openings through trees.* The openings through the
bodies of trees made by air, and the openings for air through
masses of trees, are not visible to the eye at a long distance, because where the whole is comprehended with effort, the parts
are known with difficulty, but a confused mixture results which
takes on the appearance of that which is greater in quantity. The
openings in the tree are particles of illuminated air, which are
much smaller than the tree, and so they are lost to perception before the tree itself, but this does not mean that for this reason
they are not there. By necessity there is a mixture of the air and
of the darkness of the shadowed tree, all of which come together
as a mass to the eye which sees them.

*265v* 964. *Of trees which cover the perforations of one another.* That
part of the tree will show fewest openings to the air, in back of
which there is the greatest amount of another tree which comes
between the tree and the air.

For example, in the tree A the openings are not covered, nor
*266 and* in B, because there is no tree behind it. But only half of C shows
*illus.* /openings to the air, that is, C O is covered by the tree D, which
is covered by the tree E, and a little farther beyond all the openings are lost.

*258v* 965. *Of the appearance of chance conditions.* At a distance there
is produced a mixture of the chance conditions affecting the
foliage of trees. That foliage participates more in such chance
conditions which is largest in mass.

[DESCRIPTION OF MISTY LANDSCAPES]

*263* 966. *Painting of the mist which covers the landscape.* The mists
which are mingled with the air become thicker the lower they
fall, so that the rays of the sun are more resplendent therein provided the mist lies between the sun and the eye. But if the eye
lies between the sun and the mist, that mist appears dense, and

this density is more powerful, the lower it is, as has been proved. Both kinds of mist remain dense like a cloud, when the cloud/ 263v comes between the sun and the mist, but the mist lying between the sun and the eye through an extent of space somewhat distant from the eye, takes on a great deal of the splendor of the sun, and all the more so as it comes nearer to the solar body. In such instances the buildings of cities appear darker the more they are situated in luminous mist, because then they are closer to the sun, and because it has been said that mist is of unequal thickness; that is, it is thicker the nearer it is to earth, and it takes more splendor from the sun, the lower it is. For this reason parallel buildings, such as towers and bell towers, which are in it appear less heavy the nearer they are to their bases. This is true because that dark body appears smaller which is located in luminous air. The reason is set down in the thirty-second proposition of my book on perspective.

967. *Of landscapes in the mist at the rising or at the setting of* 263v *the sun.* Of landscapes to the east of your eye, I say that at the rising of the sun, or indeed with mists, or other thick vapors lying between the sun and the eye, these will be much brighter/toward 264 and the sun and less splendid on the opposite side, that is, the western *illus.* side. But if they are without mists or vapors, the eastern side, or rather that side which lies between the sun and the eye, will be darker in relation to its proximity to the eye. This accidental condition will occur on that side which is nearest the sun, that is, which seems to be more directly under the sun; and on the opposite side in clear weather it will do the contrary. In misty weather it will do the contrary of what it does in fine weather.

[ADVICE ON THE REPRESENTATION OF LIGHT
AND SHADE IN LANDSCAPE]

968. *Of landscapes in painting.* Trees and mountains represented 262 in painting should show shadows from that side of the picture from which the light comes and their illuminated parts should be shown from that side from which/the shadows come, so that 262v and the light and shadow is shown in those parts where the eye sees *illus.* both light and shadow. This is proved by the figure in the margin.

255v 969. *Reminder to the painter about trees.* Remember, painter, that the densities of shadows in one kind of tree are as varied as the thinness or density of their branchings are varied.

248v 970. *Of trees.* Toward the depths of valleys and the land near valleys, trees are always larger and thicker than toward the tops of hills. The tops of mountains are more wooded than their flanks, for there is no concourse of waters there to wash against them as there is on the flanks.

262v 971. *Of the view of trees.* Between trees which grow along cause-
263 ways, you will make/the shadows cast by the sun interrupted, so that they appear like the clusters of branches from which they derive.[8]

In the foreground the landscape which you see between the tops of trees in meadows and other spaces and in intervals between trees is bright; but when, because of distance, you begin to lose those intervals, you see only the contours of the trees, which, even though they are of the same color as the meadows, are more shadowed toward the center of the tree because of their thickness and diminution than are the meadows. This brings about a quality of darkness which with distance can be lightened and blended into the color of the horizon.

[THE DIFFICULTY OF DEPICTING TRANSPARENT LEAVES]

267v 972. *Of foliage.* Some leaves have brightness because of their transparency, since they are placed between the eye and the light, and some of them have this through the simple illumination of the air, and some because of their high lights.

The transparent leaf displays a more beautiful color than its natural one, the leaf illuminated by the air shows its natural color more; the high-lighted leaf takes on more of the color of
268 the air,/which is mirrored in the density of the surface of the leaf than of its natural color.

That leaf which has a hairy surface does not have sheen.

[8] On Urb. 263 space was left for a diagram, but this drawing was never supplied, and a later hand has written, in pencil, at the margin of the empty space: "niente" (nothing).

. That bush is least shadowed which is sparsest and has the thinnest branches.

973. *Of the shadows of transparent leaves.* The shadows on trans- *259v* parent leaves seen from the reverse side, are the same shadows which are on the right side of the leaf, and which show through on the reverse together with the luminous part, except for the luster which never shows through.

When one green is behind another green, the high lights and transparencies of the leaves appear to be of greater power than those which border on the brightness of the air.

And if the sun illuminates the leaves which lie between it and the eye, and this eye does not see the sun, then the high lights of the leaves and their transparencies are excessive.

It is very useful to make some branches low. These should be *260* dark and have illuminated verdure as their background, which should be somewhat distant from it.

That part of dark verdure seen from beneath is densest which is nearest to the eye, that is, most distant from the luminous air.

974. *Of the shadows and transparencies of leaves.*/Because the *259-259v* leaves of trees are transparent they do not cast great darkness on the leaves shadowed by them, but cast shadows of little density, which achieve the beauty of greenness; the leaves placed third below the first become doubly dark from the darkness of the second leaf, because there are two leaves that shadow it, and the third does likewise and the fourth continues to multiply this darkness and so they could go on to infinity.

And so, painter, when you make clusters of large leafy branches, make them more illuminated on the outside than toward the center of the tree, and make the clusters of branches nearer to the light even more illuminated and the clusters of those clusters more also, and the last leaves still more illuminated, and most of all the tips of the leaves turned to the light.

All the leaves and foliage of a tree between the eye and the sun are transparent and are seen aided by the light of the sun, and this transparency displays the highest degree of beauty in green; this is so rather by virtue of the rays of the sun which illuminate the tree from the opposite side, than because of its natural color.

258 975. *Of the sun which illuminates the forest.* When the sun illuminates the forest, the trees in the woods appear to have sharply determined shadows and lights, and for this reason they seem to approach you, and are of a more recognizable shape; and that part of them which is not exposed to the sun, seems uniformly dark, except for the thin parts which lie between the sun and you, which become bright because of their transparency. The quantity of lights on the trees illuminated by the sun is less than that illuminated by the sky, because the sky is larger than the sun, and in this instance the larger cause produces the larger effect.

When their shadows are smaller, trees seem to be more sparse, especially when they are of one color, and when by nature they are sparse in limb and thin of leaf, such as peach and plum trees and the like, because their shadow retreats to the middle of the tree, they seem diminished and the branches, all of which remain outside the shadow, seem to form a background of one color.

260v 976. *Of young trees and their leaves.* Young trees have more transparent leaves and more polished bark than old ones, and this is especially true of walnut trees, which are brighter in May than in September.

The shadows of trees are never black, because wherever the air penetrates there can never be complete darkness.

260 977. *Of never portraying foliage transparent to the sun.* Never represent leaves which are transparent to the sun. These are indistinct, because on the transparency of one leaf there will be impressed the shadow of another leaf which is above it, and this shadow is sharply bounded and of a determinate density and sometimes it takes up a half or a third of the leaf that it shadows, and thus that cluster is confused and its portrayal is to be avoided.

The upper shoots of the lateral branches of a tree are nearer to the main branch than are those below.

That leaf is least transparent which receives light between most unequal angles.

The lowest branches of trees that produce large leaves and heavy fruit, such as walnut trees, figs, and the like, always direct themselves toward the earth.

[ADVICE ON PAINTING LANDSCAPES]

978. *Of trees and their lights.* The true practical method to repre- *256* sent the countryside, or if you wish to say, landscapes with trees, is to select a site with the sun covered so that the country receives universal light and not the particular light of the sun, which creates shadows that are sharply marked and quite different from the lights.

979. *Of composing the color of the underpainting of trees for* *267* *painting.* The way to compose the colors of the underpainting of trees which have the air as a background, is to make your colors as they would be on a night of little light when you would see all the trees to be of a dark color, broken through by the light in the air, and this will enable you to see the simple shape sharply, without the hindrance of different colors of light or dark green.

980. *Of the shadow of verdure.* The shadow of verdure always *262* takes on blue, and so does every shadow of all other objects, and it becomes more blue the farther from the eye it is, and less blue the nearer it is.

981. *Precept, for imitating the color of leaves.* Those who do not *268* wish to rely entirely on their own judgment in duplicating the true colors of leaves, should take a leaf from that tree which they desire to represent, and mix their color based on this, and when there is no difference between their color and the color of the leaf, then you can be certain that your color is an exact duplication of that leaf, and you can do the same with other objects that you wish to represent.

[THE SELECTION AND TREATMENT OF PLANKS]

982. *Why planks are many times not straight in their grain.* When *248 and* the branches of a second year which follow those of the past year *illus.* are not of a similar thickness compared with the previous branches, but grow out laterally then the vigor of the branch

below is twisted to nourish the higher one, although it may grow only a little to the side. But if such branches are uniform in their growth, the veins on the trunk will be straight and equidistant in relation to every degree of height in the tree.

252v 983. *Of the planks which keep straight best.* The panel made from that part of the tree which turns most toward the north will be that which bends less than others, and it will best maintain its natural straightness.

And this is because on that side it is little exposed to the sun and moves the sap of the tree but little. This does not occur on the south side, because it is exposed to the sun all day and this
253 moves the sap on that side of the tree from/the east side to the west side with the course of the sun.

252v 984. *Of trees and sawn planks which never bend of themselves.* When you wish the cut tree not to bend, saw it in the center along its length, and turn the divided parts, one against the other; that is, the part of the plank which was at the bottom, put against the top of the other plank, turn the top against the bottom, and then join the planks together. Such a construction will never bend.

253 985. *Of the cracking of planks when they dry.* That tree which grows farthest from the edges of the forest will produce straightest cracking in its boards as they dry and that tree will have boards which produce most crooked cracks which grows nearest to the southern edge of the forest.

253 986. *Of planks that do not open up when they dry.* When you desire that the wood should not produce any cracks while drying, boil it a long time in ordinary water, or keep it for a long time at the bottom of a river, until its natural vigor is consumed.

# PART SEVEN

## OF CLOUDS

### [THE ORIGIN AND WEIGHT OF CLOUDS]

987. *Of the creation of clouds.* Clouds are created from the hu- midity infused through the air, which gathers because of cold, which is carried through the air by the winds. These clouds generate winds when they are created, as well as when they are destroyed. They are created when the sparse and vaporized humidity, hastening toward the creation of clouds, leaves the place empty/from which it escapes.

Because there is no vacuum in nature, it is necessary for the parts of the air surrounding the flight of the humidity to refill the vacuum which is beginning and this motion is called wind; but when, because of the heat of the sun, these clouds dissolve into air, there is generated a contrary wind, created by the destruction and evaporation of the cloud. As has been said, both of these conditions are causes of wind.

These winds are generated in every part of the air which is changed by heat or cold, and their motion is straight and not curved, as those who believe the opposite claim. If it were curved, it would not be necessary to raise or lower the sails of vessels to hunt for high or low wind. That sail which has been struck by a wind would be continually accompanied by the wind as long as it lasted, but the contrary is shown us by the experience of seeing the surface of the water with brief, diverging movements in different parts of the sea. This is manifest proof that the winds descend from on high from different places and with varying degrees of obliqueness in their motion, and that, from their beginnings, they disperse in different directions. Because the sea has a spherical surface, the waves often continue after the wind abandons them, and the sea continues to move as a result of the initial impetus.

988. *Of the clouds and their heaviness and lightness.* A cloud is lighter than the air which lies beneath it and heavier than the air which is above it.

275 989. *Of clouds.* Clouds are mists raised on high by the heat of the sun and their elevation is arrested where the weight acquired by them becomes equal in power to that which moves them. The weight which they acquire comes from their condensation, and their condensation derives from the heat infused into them, which takes refuge from the edges which are penetrated by the cold of the middle region of the air. Dampness follows the heat which caused it to rise to wherever that heat escapes, and since it escapes toward the middle of every round mass of cloud, those round masses are condensed with definite surfaces, in the manner of dense mountains, and acquire shadows by means of the rays of the sun which strike them.

The clouds sometimes appear to receive the rays of the sun and become illuminated in the manner of dense mountains, and sometimes they remain very dark, without variation in any part of their obscurity. This comes about through the shadows which those clouds make, that take away the rays of the sun as they fall between the sun and the obscured clouds.

276 990. *Why clouds are made of mist.* Mist struck by various currents of wind is condensed and becomes a cloud with diverse globular masses.

[THE REDNESS OF CLOUDS]

275 991. *Of the redness of clouds.* That redness with which the clouds are more or less tinged originates when the sun is at the horizon in the evening or the morning, because any body which has some transparency is to some extent penetrated by the rays of the sun when the sun appears in the evening or in the morning. And be-
275v cause the parts of clouds which are toward the ends/of their globular masses are thinner than those in the middle, the rays of the sun penetrate them with a more splendid redness than those dense portions which remain dark, being impenetrable by the rays of the sun. And the clouds are always thinner at the points of contact of their globular masses with the air than in the center, as is proved above. For this reason the redness of the clouds is of various kinds.

I say that the eye placed between the globular masses of clouds and the body of the sun will see that the centers of those globular masses are of greater splendor than any other part. But if the eye is on one side, so placed that the lines which come from the globular mass to the eye and from the sun to that eye converge at an angle less than a right angle, then the greatest light of such a round mass of cloud is at the edges of that mass.

We are here speaking of the redness of clouds when the sun is behind the clouds. But if the sun is in front of those clouds, then their globular masses will be of greater splendor than in the intervals between them in the center of the globular masses and concavities, but not so at the sides, which are exposed to the darkness of the sky and of the earth.

992. The clouds are redder, the nearer they are to the horizon; *276v* and they are less red the farther they are from the horizon.

993. *Of clouds.* Make the clouds cast their shadows upon the *277* earth, and make clouds the redder, the nearer they are to the horizon.

994. *Of the shadows of clouds.* The shadows of clouds upon the *276v* earth are to be made with intervals struck by rays of the sun, with greater or lesser brilliance, depending on the greater or lesser transparency of the clouds.

[THE SHADOWS OF CLOUDS]

995. *Of air all cloudy.* Air which is all cloudy renders the coun- *276v* tryside beneath brighter or darker, according to the greater or lesser volume of clouds which lie between the sun and the countryside.

When the heavy air which comes between the sun and the earth is of uniform density, you will see little difference between the illuminated and the shadowed parts of any body.

996. *Of clouds.* When the clouds come between the sun and the *276v* countryside, the green woods appear to have shadows of slight density; the shadows and the lights differ little in darkness or brightness; and because the woods are illuminated by the great amount of light from the hemisphere of sky, the shadows are pur-

sued and take refuge toward the center of the trees and toward
that part of them which is exposed to the earth.

276v 997. *Of clouds beneath the moon.* A cloud beneath the moon is
darker than any of the others, and the more distant ones are
brighter. The part of the cloud, however, which is transparent
within and between the edges of the cloud, is brighter than any
other similar part in the transparencies of the more distant clouds,

277 because with every degree of distance the/centers of clouds become brighter, and their bright parts become more opaque with
pink from the dying red. The edges of their darkness impinging
on their transparent brightness, have smoky and confused outlines, and the bright edges, which border on the air, do the same.
Clouds of little volume are all transparent, and more so toward
the middle than toward the edges. They are of a dead, reddish
color, muddy and confused. And the farther the clouds are separated from the moon, the paler is their light as it approaches the
moon. Thin clouds have no blackness and little twilight, because
the darkness of the night, which is manifest in the air permeates
them.

# *PART EIGHT*

## *OF THE HORIZON*

### [THE POSITION OF THE HORIZON]

998. *What is the true location of the horizon.* Horizons are at
varying distances from the eye, so that what is called the horizon,
where the brightness of the air meets the edge of the earth, is to
be seen in as many places from the same perpendicular to the
center of the earth, as are the heights from which the eye sees
them. If the eye is placed at the level of the surface of the sea, it
sees the horizon near, at a distance of about a mile, but if a man
rises to his full height, then he sees the horizon seven miles away
from him. With every degree of increase in height, the horizon
appears farther away. So it happens that those who are at the top
of high mountains near the sea, view the circle of the horizon
as very far from them, but those who are inland do not have a
horizon at an equal distance, because the surface of the earth is
not equally distant from the center of the world, so that it is not
a perfect sphere, as is the surface of the water of the sea, and
this is the reason why there are such divergent distances from the
eye to the horizon.

But the horizon of the sphere of water will never be higher
than the bottom of the feet of him who sees it, when he stands
in contact with the place where the edges of earth and water meet.

The horizon of the sky is sometimes very near, especially for
him who stands on the flanks of mountain tops, and sees the
horizon begin at that mountain top, but when he turns about
toward the horizon of the sea, he will see it as very far away.

/Very distant is the horizon seen along the sea of Egypt; looking upstream along the course of the Nile, toward Ethiopia, with
its plains on either side. Here the horizon appears indistinct and
unrecognizable, because there are three thousand miles of plain,
which always rise with the height of the river, placing such
thickness of air between the eye and the Ethiopian horizon that
everything becomes white, causing the horizon to be lost to
perception.

These horizons make a very fine sight in painting. It is true that there should be some mountains, behind one another, at the sides, with color diminishing by degrees, as is required by the rule for the diminution of colors seen at great distances.

But to demonstrate how the pyramid of perspective includes infinite space, we shall imagine A B, the eye, which cuts the degrees of distance, D N M O P, and cuts off visual lines on the wall, C D. These visual lines, with every degree of distance from the beginning gain height on the wall, C D, but never reach the height of the eye. Because C D, the wall, is a continuous quantity, it is divisible to infinity, and will never be filled with visual lines, even if the length of the last line were infinite. It would never reach a line parallel to B S, even if the space B S were infinite.

Figures which diminish little are also little removed from the eye. Hence necessarily the edge of the natural horizon is on a level with the eye of the person represented./For example, the figure A T sees the figure R U near it at the farther angle of the pyramid A T B, so the R U is smaller than A T. But this pyramid is not the one that optical perspective requires; therefore, it is not found in practice, because it has infinite space from its base to its point, and the one above has seven miles to the base from that point.

*284 and illus.*

999. *Of the horizon.* The horizon of the sky and that of the earth end on the same line. This is proved as follows: let the sphere of the earth be D N M, and the sphere of the air be A R P, and the eye of the observer of the horizon of the earth is B, and F is the horizon of the earth, where the view of the air ends, and it appears that A of the air joins F of the earth.

*284 and illus.*

1000. *Of the true horizon.* The true horizon must be the termination of the sphere of water, which is immobile, because this immobility constitutes a surface equidistant from the center of the world, as is proved in its place.

*284*

If the sky and the earth were plane surfaces with equidistant space between, without doubt/the horizon of perspective would be at the height of the eye that sees it. But it would be necessary that these parallel spaces be infinite in extension, if they had to

*284v and illus.*

seem to the eye to converge in a line, that is, to be in contact, and this contact would be at the height of the eye of the observer. Because the earth would have a smaller quantity of plane surface than would the sky, it would happen that, when the plane of the sky would have lowered its last edge to the level of the eye, the horizon of the earth would be raised to the height of the navel of the same observer, and for this reason they would not converge to the same eye. But because the sky and earth are not divided by space into parallels, or equidistant planes, but by a space that is convex on the side of the sky and concave on the side of the earth, it happens that every part of the surface of the earth can be a horizon, which could not happen if both the sky and the earth were flat. This is shown with the sky A B, and the earth F E, the eye being at G, and the wall C D, where the horizon A F of the planes of the sky and earth are cut at the points N M.[1]

### [THE HORIZON AND THE HEIGHT OF THE OBSERVER]

1001. *Of the horizon.* If the earth is spherical, the horizon will never reach the height of the eye when it is higher than the surface of the earth. *285 and illus.*

Let us say that the height of the eye is N M, and that the line of judgment, or wall, is B R, and A is the horizon, and that the line G R H is the curvature of the earth. I say, then, that the horizon, according to the straight line A F K, is lower than the feet of the man by all of M F, and lower than the eye, according to the turning of the earth, by all of B O.

1002. If A and B are two men, the horizon N will seem level with their heights. *285 and illus.*

1003. *The eye that sees the horizon of the sea when a man stands with his feet at the level of the sea, sees the horizon lower than itself.* The horizon of the sea will appear lower than the eye of him who has his feet at the edge of the waters of that sea, by the distance from the height of the eye of the observer/of that horizon to his feet. *285 285v and illus.*

This is proved as follows: let N be the bank of the sea, A N

[1] The second diagram is incomplete, Cf. note: Ludwig, *Quellenschriften*, XVII, 351-352.

the height of the man who sees the horizon of the sea at O, where the central line of the world M O falls perpendicularly on the visual line A R, which terminates at O on the surface of the sea, according to the definition of the circle. The central line A M exceeds the central O M with all the excess A N, which is the distance from the feet of a man to his eyes.

*284v* 1004. That thing is highest which is most distant from the center of the earth.

*285* Therefore a straight line is not at an equal height throughout its length, and consequently is not level, so that if you speak of a line of equal height you can mean only a curve.

*284v* 1005. *Of the horizon*. The horizon will never be the same as the height of the eye which sees it.

That figure whose position is fixed and which is nearest to the horizon will have that horizon nearest to its feet.

### [THE HORIZON AND ITS REFLECTION ON WATER]

*285v and illus.* 1006. *Of the horizon mirrored in running water*. Water that runs between the eye and the horizon will not reflect that horizon to the eye, because the eye does not see the side of the wave which faces the horizon, nor does the horizon face the side of the wave which is in view of the eye. Therefore, according to the sixth proposition of this book, our claim is concluded, for this proposition states: it is impossible that the eye see a reflected image which is not in view of the actual object and the eye at the same time.

Let the wave be C B, and the eye A, and the horizon D. I say that the eye A, because it does not see the side of the wave B G, will also not see the image of D, which is mirrored on that side.

*285v-286 and illus.* 1007. *Where the horizon is mirrored on the wave.*/According to the sixth proposition of this book, the horizon would be mirrored on the side of the wave in view of the horizon and the eye. For example, the horizon is shown at F, in view of the side of the wave B C, and this side is also seen by the eye.

Therefore, painter, when you have to represent the inundation of the waters, remember that you will see the color of the water as bright or dark, depending on the brightness or darkness of the site where you are, mixed together with the color of other objects that are behind you.

[REDNESS NEAR THE HORIZON]

1008. *Why the dense air near the horizon becomes red.* The air ²⁸⁶ becomes red on the eastern horizon as well as on the western, provided it is dense; and this redness appears between the eye and the sun. But the redness of the rainbow develops when the eye is between the rain and the sun. The cause of the first lies in the sun and the humidity of the air, but the redness of the rainbow is caused by the sun, the rain, and the eye that sees it. That redness, together with the other colors, is of much greater intensity, the more the rain is composed of large drops, and the more minute the drops, the paler are the colors. If the rain is of the nature of mist, then the rainbow will be white and so completely without hue. But the eye must be between the mist and the sun.

# TABLE OF HEADINGS

In this list bracketed numbers refer to the chapters in the translation. The bracketing of two or more numbers indicates that the chapter in the original has been subdivided in translation.

Record and Signatures of all the portions of the Books in the hand of Leonardo that together comprise the present book of the Treatise on Painting. And first the entire book

signed . . .

[For the symbols referred to, see facsimile pages 330v and 331 (erroneously numbered 231 in the manuscript), and the discussion on page xii and note 6 of the Introduction.]

# A SELECTIVE BIBLIOGRAPHY

COMPILED FROM THE NOTES OF A. PHILIP MCMAHON

AND SUPPLEMENTED BY

## KATE TRAUMAN STEINITZ

LIBRARIAN OF THE ELMER BELT LIBRARY OF VINCIANA

## A SELECTIVE BIBLIOGRAPHY

# A. The Treatise on Painting

## I. MANUSCRIPT COPIES

THE ABBREVIATED MANUSCRIPT COPIES OF LEONARDO'S TREATISE ON PAINTING containing parts of Books II, III, and IV of Codex Vaticanus (Urbinas) 1270 (cf. p. xvii).

CODEX BARBERINUS LAT. 4304. Formerly Barberinus 832. Vatican Library, Rome. 16th Century.

BELT MS. 35. Replica of Codex Barberinus 4304. Elmer Belt Library of Vinciana, Los Angeles. 16/17th Century.

CODEX CASANATENSE 968. Biblioteca Casanatense, Rome. 17th Century.

CODEX CASANATENSE 5018 (Codice del Ministro). Biblioteca Casanatense, Rome. 17th Century.

CODEX LAURENZIANUS, ASHBURNHAM 1299. Biblioteca Medicea Laurenziana, Florence. 16th Century. Incomplete.

CODEX PINELLIANUS (D 467). Ambrosiana, Milan. Written before 1601.

CODEX RICCARDIANUS 2275. Biblioteca Riccardiana, Florence. *Ca.* 1630-1635. Copied by Stefano della Bella from Cod. Pinellianus (D 467). This manuscript was used for the edition of 1792 with the delicate etchings by Stefano della Bella.

CODEX CORSINI 402. Biblioteca dell'Academia dei Lincei, Palazzo Corsini, Rome. 17th Century.

CODEX OTTOBONIANUS 2984. Vatican Library, Rome. 17th Century.

MS. B 271. Biblioteca Comunale dell'Archiginnasio, Bologna. 17th century.

CASSIANO del Pozzo's Manuscripts H 227 and H 229. Ambrosiana, Milan. 1634-1639. (Cf. Carusi, Lettere di Galeazzo Arconati, and A3 below.)

MANUSCRIPT H 227 inf. compiled from several 17th Century manuscripts, one of them on Hydraulics. Fol. 119-124. *Alcune Memorie di D. Ambrosio Mazzenta.*

MANUSCRIPT H 229 inf. consists of 3 parts with chapters of various subjects copied from Ms. A which at that time was in Milan.

CASSIANO del Pozzo's Manuscript H 228 inf. and other manuscripts illustrated by Nicolas Poussin and his workshop.

MANUSCRIPT H 228 inf. Ambrosiana, Milan. Written *ca.* 1740 by Cassiano del Pozzo, with diagrams carefully drawn by his own hand. Figure drawings, possibly Poussin's originals, tipped in. Used by Gault de St. Germain for his edition of 1803.

MANUSCRIPT GANAY. Coll. Marquis Hubert de Ganay, formerly Renouard, Firmin Didot, Comtesse de Béhague, Paris. 17th Century. Said to be handwritten and illustrated by Nicolas Poussin and Gaspar Dughet in preparation for the first printed edition of 1651.

BELT MS 36. Elmer Belt Library of Vinciana, Los Angeles. Formerly Marquise Soragna-Melzi. 17th century copy from Poussin's workshop, the text possibly copied from the Ganay Manuscript.

MANUSCRIPT 84 No. 17. Hermitage, Leningrad. Dated by a note in M. de Chantelou's hand. "Ce livre m'a été donné à Rome au mois d'aoust [*sic*] 1640 par Mr. le Cavalier del Pozzo au voyage que j'y fait pour amener en France Mr. Poussin, Chantelou." The elaborate figure drawings, pasted in as in the Ambrosiana Manuscript H 228 inf. also have the characteristics of Poussin's hand.

MANUSCRIPTS EDWARDS-ESDAILE and NOAILLES. 17th century. Copies from Poussin's workshop cannot be located at present.

COPIES OF THE LATE 17TH CENTURY, some of them made from the printed edition.

MS. DA VINCI, NUOVO METODO. Biblioteca Leonardiana, Vinci. 18th century.

MS. $\frac{C\,3}{43}$ RACCOLTA VINCIANA, Milan. 17th century.

KING's 283. King's collection. British Museum, London. Formerly Consul Smith and P. Antonio Pellegrini. Made from the printed edition of 1651, with awkward drawings.

FRENCH 9145. Bibliothèque Nationale, Paris. Late 17th century. Made from the printed editions.

BELT MS 34. Formerly PHILLIPS MS 21154. Elmer Belt Library of Vinciana. 17th century copy, apparently used as textbook in architects' studios, and perhaps an auxiliary copy for the printer.

SEVEN MANUSCRIPT COPIES IN THE BIBLIOTECA NAZIONALE, FLORENCE. Cf. List A3, Uzielli.

PALAT. 783-(451,-21,2). End of 17th century. Pencil sketches of the Urbinate type.

SEZIONE MAGLIABECCHIANA, CL. XVII, CODICES 18 and 28. Both 17th century. Illustrations of the Urbinate type.

II, III, CODEX 278. 17th century. Illustrations of the Urbinate type.

MS. f 2896 c9. 17th century fragment.

PALAT. 962.-(868.-21,2). 18th century copy from Riccardianus. VAL-
LOMBROSA 1182 Conv. F6 made from the printed edition of 1651.
18th century.

Others of the numerous manuscript copies of the *Treatise* in the
libraries in Venice, Modena, Cortona, Naples, Montpellier and
Athens are not listed here. These are of greater or lesser importance. Some have only recently been discovered and are still
the subject of research. Cf. List F, forthcoming Bibliography by
Kate T. Steinitz. Late seventeenth century copies are numerous.
They appear in private collections and are often offered for sale.
Their number is evidence of the great demand for the *Treatise*
in the late seventeenth and eighteenth centuries.


## 2.  PRINTED EDITIONS

### 1651

*Trattato della Pittura di Leonardo da Vinci*, novamente dato in luce
con la vita dell'istesso autore, scritta da Raffaelle du Fresne. Si
sono giunti i tre libri della pittura, et il trattato della statua di
Leon Battista Alberti, con la vita del medesimo. Paris, Langlois,
1651. Reprinted Bologna, Istituto delle Scienze, 1786.

*Traité de la peinture de Léonard de Vinci* . . . traduit d'italien en
françois par R.F.D.C. [Roland Fréart Sieur de Chambray]. Paris,
Langlois, 1651.

### 1671

Scaramuccia, Luigi. *Le finezze de penelli italiani ammirate e studiate
da Girupeno sotto la scorta . . . di Raffaello d'Urbino*. Pavia,
Magri, 1671. (Contains 24 chapters of *The Treatise*)

### 1716

*Traité de la Peinture par Léonard de Vinci* . . . Nouvelle édition augmentée de la vie de l'autheur. Paris, Pierre François Giffart, 1716.
Reprinted Paris, Deterville, 1796 and 1803.

### 1721

*A Treatise of Painting by Leonardo da Vinci*, translated from the
original Italian . . . London, Printed for J. Senex, 1721. Reprinted
1796.

### 1723

*Trattato della Pittura di Leonardo da Vinci*. . . . Naples, Ricciardo,
1723. (Based on Paris 1651 but without the treatise of Alberti)
Single copy in the Biblioteca Marciana, Venice.

### 1724

*Des vortrefflichen Florentinischen Mahlers Lionardo da Vinci hoechst nuetzlicher Tractat von der Mahlerei,* aus dem Italiaenischen und Frantzoesischen in das Teutsche uebersetzt . . . von Johann Georg Boehm. Nuremberg, J. C. Weigel, 1724. Reprinted 1747 and 1786 with slight variants.

### 1733

*Trattato della Pittura di Lionardo da Vinci,* nuovamente dato in luce . . . da R. du Fresne . . . Naples, Ricciardo, 1733. Based on the first edition, Paris 1651. This edition only includes *Osservazioni di Nicolo Pussino sopra la Pittura,* following Alberti's *Della Statua.*

### 1784

*El Tratado de la Pintura por Leonardo da Vinci* y los tres libros que sobre el mismo arte escribió Leon Bautista Alberti. Traducidos . . . por Don Diego Antonio Rejon de Silva. Madrid, Imprenta real, 1784. Reprinted 1827.

### 1792

*Trattato della Pittura di Lionardo da Vinci* . . . sopra una copia a penna di mano di Stefano della Bella, con le figure disegnate dal medesimo . . . Florence, G. Pagani, 1792. (Edited by Francesco Fontani from Cod. Pinellianus)

### 1802

*A Treatise on Painting by Leonardo da Vinci.* Faithfully translated from the original Italian, and now first digested under proper heads, by John Francis Rigaud. . . To which is prefixed a new life of the author . . . by John Sidney Hawkins. . . . London, Y. Taylor, 1802.

### 1803

*Traité de la Peinture de Léonard de Vinci* . . . avec des notes et observations par P. M. Gault de St. Germain. Paris, Perlet, 1803. Reprinted Geneva, Sestie fils, 1820. (Gault de St. Germain used Ms. H. 228 inf.)

### 1804

*Trattato della Pittura di Leonardo da Vinci.* Società tipografica de'classici italiani. Milan, 1804. (With Memorie by C. Amoretti)

### 1805

*Trattato della Pittura di Leonardo da Vinci* . . . per opera di Baldassare Orsini, direttore dell'Accademia del disegno nell' augusta città di Perugia . . . Perugia, C. Baduel, 1805. 2 vols.

## 1817

*Trattato della Pittura di Lionardo da Vinci tratto da un Codice della
Biblioteca Vaticana* . . . Rome, de Romanis, 1817. A text and an
atlas volume: Disegni che illustrano l'opera del Trattato della pittura . . . tratti fedelmente dagli originali del Codice Vaticano
Roma, 1817. Text edited by Guglielmo Manzi . . . , the first
edition of the Trattato drawn from the full text of Codex Vaticanus (Urb.) 1270.

## 1827

*Verhandeling over de Schilderkunst van Leonardo da Vinci* . . . naar
de Fransche Uitgave van den Jare 1716 door Joannes Vos. Am-
sterdam, S. de Grebber, 1827. (Based on the French Giffart Edition 1716)

## 1835

*Leonardo da Vinci. A Treatise on Painting.* Faithfully translated . . .
by John Francis Rigaud . . . To which is prefixed a *Life* of the
author with a critical account of his works by John William
Brown. London, J. B. Nichols, 1835.

## 1839

*Ammaestramenti per la Pittura,* tratti da varii scrittori. Venice, Tipi
del Gondoliere, 1839. (Extracts from the *Treatise,* pp. 109-139)
"Biblioteca classica di scienze ed arti."

## 1859

*Trattato della Pittura di Leonardo da Vinci* con aggiunte tratte del
Codice Vaticano pubblicato da Guido Manzi. Milan, Società
Tipografica de'Classici Italiani, 1859. (Based on the edition of
1802 with additions from the "Manzi edition" 1817)

## 1877

*A Treatise on Painting by Leonardo da Vinci.* Translated by John
Francis Rigaud with a *Life* . . . by John William Brown. London,
G. Bell, 1877. (Based on the edition of 1835. With new appen-
dices) Reprinted 1892 and 1906.

## 1882

*Lionardo da Vinci. Das Buch von der Malerei,* nach dem Codex
Vaticanus (Urbinas) 1270 herausgegeben, uebersetzt und er-
laeutert von Heinrich Ludwig. Vienna, Braumueller, 1882. 4
vols. (Volumes xv-xviii of *Quellenschriften fuer Kunstgeschichte*)

## 1885

*Leonardo da Vinci. Das Buch von der Malerei.* Neues Material aus
den Originalmanuscripten gesichtet und dem Cod. Vatic. 1270
eingeordnet von Heinrich Ludwig. Stuttgart, Kohlhammer, 1885.

### 1888

*Lionardo da Vinci, Das Buch von der Malerei, Deutsche Ausgabe,* Neue Ausgabe . . . Vienna, Braumueller, 1888. (Same as IV of the edition of 1882)

### 1890

*Leonardo da Vinci, Trattato della Pittura,* condotto sul Codice Vaticano Urbinate 1270 con prefazione di Marco Tabarrini . . . Preceduto dalla vita . . . da Giorgio Vasari con nuove note e commentario di Gaetano Milanesi. Rome, Unione cooperativa editrice, 1890.

### 1901

*Leonardo da Vinci, Treatise on Painting* . . . by J. F. Rigaud. London, Bohn's Artists Library, 1901.

### 1909

*Leonardo da Vinci, Traktat von der Malerei,* nach der Uebersetzung von Heinrich Ludwig, neu herausgegeben und eingeleitet von Marie Herzfeld. Jena, Diederichs, 1909. Reprinted 1925.

### 1910

*Léonard de Vinci Traité de la Peinture,* traduit intégralment pour la première fois en Français sur le Codex Vaticanus (Urbinas) 1270, complété par des nouveaux fragments tirés des manuscrits du Maître, ordonné méthodiquement et accompagné de commentaires par Péladan. Paris, Delagrave, 1910. Reissued eleven times to date.

*Léonard de Vinci, Traité du Paysage,* traduit pour la première fois en français in extenso sur le Codex Vaticanus . . . par Péladan. Paris, Delagrave, 1910. Reprinted 1921.

### 1911

*Léonardo da Vincis Malarbok,* Utdrag i Svensk Ofversattning in Osvald Siren, *Leonardo da Vinci.* Stockholm, Ljus, 1911. (Excerpts, pp. 365-465)

### 1914

*Trattato della Pittura di Leonardo da Vinci.* Introduzione di Angelo Borzelli. Lanciano, Carabba, 1914. (Scrittori italiani e stranieri) 2 vols. Reprinted 1924.

### 1921

*Das Malerbuch von Leonardo,* Ausgewaehlt nach der Uebersetzung von Heinrich Ludwig von Dr. Emmy Voigtlaender. Leipzig, R. Voigtlaender's Verlag, 1921.

### 1934

In Russian: *Book about Painting by Master Leonardo da Vinci* . . . for the first time translated into Russian by A. A. Guber and V.

K. Shileiko. Introductory chapter by B. N. Lazarev. Moscow, Ogiz-Tzogiz, 1934.

## 1939

*Leonardo da Vinci, Trattato della Pittura*. Milan, Vittoria, 1939.

"*The Paragone or first book of the Book on Painting by Leonardo da Vinci*, according to the Codex Vaticanus (Urbinas) 1270." In J. P. Richter, *The Literary Works of Leonardo da Vinci*. London, New York, Oxford University Press, 1939. pp. 13-101.

## 1942

*Leonardo da Vinci el Tratado de la Pintura*. Version española de la ediciòn de 1828 (Rejon de Silva). Buenos Aires, More-Mere, 1942.

## 1943

*Leonardo da Vinci, Tratado de la Pintura*, Version Castellana de Maria Pittaluga. Precedido de la vida . . . per Giorgio Vasari y el ensayo sobre Leonardo y los filosofos de Paul Valéry. Buenos Aires, Losada, 1943.

## 1944

*Leonardo da Vinci, Tratado de la Pintura y del Paysaje, Sombra y Luz*. Texto integro del "Codex Vaticanus" completado con fragmentos de los Manoscritos de Leonardo. Traducción y classificación metódica, de Péladan, Apendice . . . por Joaquín Gil. Buenos Aires, Gil, 1944.

*Leonardo da Vinci Tratado de la Pintura*, Traducción y prefacio de Manuel Abril. Colleccion Crisol, No. 68. Madrid, Aguilar, 1944.

## 1948

*Lionardo da Vinci, Der Paragone*. Der Wettstreit der Kuenste. Düsseldorf, L. Schwann, 1948. (Dramatized by Peter Menniken from Heinrich Ludwig's 1882 edition for performance at the first postwar meeting of Art Historians in Schloss Rheidt, Germany, September 22, 1946)

## 1949

*Paragone, a Comparison of the Arts by Leonardo da Vinci*, with an introduction and English translation by Irma A. Richter. London, New York, G. Cumberlege, Oxford University Press, 1949.

## 1953

Leonardo da Vinci. *Paragone*. Warsaw, Panstwowy Institut Sztuki, 1953.

GHOSTS in Treatise Bibliography

This list of printed editions attempts to be exhaustive and includes 58 entries to present date against 41 listed in Ettore Verga's *Bibliografia Vinciana* to 1930.

(Cf. List G19). The present list omits three Verga entries which the compiler has been able, in ten years of collecting a complete run of editions, to identify as nonexistent. These are:

*Trattato della Pittura di Leonardo da Vinci* . . . Naples, Ricciardi, 1773. Erroneously listed by Ettore Verga, No. 9, as a single copy in the Biblioteca Nazionale in Naples. Research of the Librarians Dott. Guerriera Guerrieri and Kate T. Steinitz, in Naples, July 1951, verifies that due to a clerical error, Verga listed a bibliographical "Ghost," a nonexistent edition.

*Treatise on Painting.* New York, Scribner's Sons, 1877 and Boston, Little Brown, 1887. Listed by Verga, Nos. 30 and 33, without locating a copy. No copy was located since. The publishing houses have checked their archives on request and stated that no record of these editions can be found. It may be presumed that these editions are "Ghosts." (Cf. Maureen Cobb Mabbott. List *19*)

## 3. STUDIES ON THE TREATISE

Alberti, Leon Battista. Cf. Clark, Kenneth and Janitschek, Hubert, below.

Amoretti, Carlo. Cf. below List E4.

Baldacci, Antonio. *Gli alberi e le verdure nel Trattato della Pittura*, 1931. Cf. below List B3. Geology and Physical Geography.

Beltrami, Luca. *Il "Trattato della pittura" di Leonardo da Vinci nelle sue varie edizioni e traduzioni.* Per nozze Guy-Della Torre, Milan, 1919.

Brun, Carl. "Leonardo's Ansichten ueber das Verhaeltnis der Kuenste." *Repertorium fuer Kunstwissenschaft*, xv, 267-281. Stuttgart, 1892.

————. "Leonardo's Anbetung der Magier im Lichte seines 'Trattato della Pittura.'" *Raccolta Vinciana*, x, 45-60. Milan, 1919.

Calvi, Gerolamo. *I manoscritti di Leonardo da Vinci.* Pubblicazzioni dell' Istituto Vinciano in Roma, vi. Bologna, Zanichelli, 1925.

Carusi, Enrico. "Per il 'Trattato della Pittura' di Leonardo da Vinci (contributi di ricerche sui manoscritti e sulla loro redazione)— Capitoli del Trattato della Pittura negli autografi vinciani." *Per il iv centenario.* . . . Bergamo, 1919. pp. 419-439.

————. "Nel quarto centenario dalla morte di Leonardo da Vinci." *Vita e pensiero.* Milan, 1919. pp. 249-258, 533-539.

————. "Lettere di Galeazzo Arconato e Cassiano del Pozzo per lavori sui manoscritti di Leonardo da Vinci." *Accademie e biblioteche d'Italia*, iii, 6, 1929-1930.

————. "Sulla redazione abbreviata del Trattato della Pittura di Leonardo da Vinci." *Accademie e biblioteche d'Italia*, 1928.

Cellini, Benvenuto. *I trattati dell'oreficeria e della scultura per cura di Carlo Milanesi.* Florence, Le Monnier, 1857. pp. 225-256.

Chennevières-Pointel, Philip de. *Recherches sur la vie et les ouvrages de quelques peintres provinciaux de l'ancienne France.* Paris, Dumoulin, 1847-1862.

Cicognara, Conte L. *Catalogo ragionato dei libri d'arte e d'antichità,* I, 58-59. Pisa, Capurro, 1821.

Clark, Kenneth. *A Catalogue of the Drawings of Leonardo da Vinci in the Collection of His Majesty the King at Windsor Castle.* New York, Macmillan; Cambridge University Press, 1935.

————. "Leon Battista Alberti on painting." *Proceedings of the British Academy,* xxx, Oxford University Press, 1946. Cf. below Lists B1, B2 Landscape, E4.

Dalma, Juan. "Leonardo, anticipador de conceptos psicodinamicos modernos." *Revista 'Psicosomatica,'* III, 1-2. Buenos Aires, January-June 1952.

Du Fresne, Raphael Trichet. *Catalogus librorum Bibliotecae Raphaelis Tricheti du Fresne Paris, apud vidam & haeredes,* 1662.

Eitelberger, von R. "Zur Publikation des Libro della pittura des Lionardo da Vinci." *Repertorium fuer Kunstwissenschaft,* IV, 280-292. Stuttgart, 1881.

————. *An idea of the perfection of painting.* Translated into English by J. E. (John Evelyn). In the Savoy, 1668.

Felibien, André, Sieurs des Avaux. *Entretiens sur les vies et les ouvrages des plus excellens peintres anciens et modernes.* Paris, Mariette, 1696.

————. *L'idée du peintre parfait.* London, Mortier, 1707.

Firmin-Didot, Ambroise. *Catalogue des livres précieux, manuscrits et imprimés.* . . . Paris, Firmin-Didot, 1882. pp. 69-73.

Fontanini, Giusto. *Biblioteca dell'elloquenza italiana con le annotazioni del signor Apostolo Zeno.* Venice, Pasquali, 1753.

Franchi, Antonio. *La teorica della pittura.* Lucca, Marescandoli, 1739.

Fréart, Roland, Sieur de Chambray. *Idée de la perfection de la peinture.* Paris, Ysembart, 1662.

Hautecoeur, Louis. "Illioustratsii Poussena k traktatou Leonardo." Starye Gody, marzo 1913.

————. The same in French. *Bulletin de la Société de l'histoire de l'art français.* Paris, Champion, 1913; reprinted in Grautoff, Otto. Nicolas Poussin. Munich. G. Mueller, 1914.

Heydenreich, H. L. "Considerazioni a recenti ricerche su Leonardo da Vinci." *Rinascita* v (1942), pp. 161ff.

————. "Quellenstudien zu Leonardos Malereitraktat." *Kunstchronik.* Munich, 1921. pp. 255ff. Cf. below B3. Other Sciences, E4.

—————. *I disegni di Leonardo da Vinci e della sua scuola conservati nella Galleria dell'Accademia di Venezia.* Florence, Lange, Domsch and Company, 1949.

Janitschek, H. *Leone Battista Alberti's kleinere kunsttheoretische Schriften.* Vienna, Braumueller, 1877. (Quellenschriften zur Kunstgeschichte, XI)

Jordan, Max. "Das Malerbuch des Lionardo da Vinci. Untersuchung der Ausgaben und Handschriften." *Jahrbuecher fur Kunstwissenschaft herausgegeben von D. A. von Zahn.* Leipzig, XV, 1873. Reprinted, Leipzig, Seemann, 1873.

Klaiber, Hans. *Leonardostudien.* Strassburg, Heitz, 1907.

Ludwig, Heinrich. "Leonardo's Malerbuch," *Repertorium fuer Kunstwissenschaft,* V, 204-215. Berlin, 1882. Cf. List II.

Morelli, Jacopo. *I codici manoscritti volgari della libreria Naniana.* Venice, Zatta, 1776.

Murr, Christophe Th. *Bibliothèque de peinture, de sculture, et de gravure.* Frankfort et Leipzig, Krauss, 1770.

Péladan, Sar. "Les artistes français et le Traité de peinture." *Revue hebdomadaire,* V, 381-409. Paris, 1910.

Pierantoni, Amalia Clelia. *Studi sul libro della pittura di Leonardo da Vinci.* Rome, Scotti, 1921.

Poussin, Nicolas. *Correspondance* . . . publiée par Ch. Jouanny. Paris, Schemit, 1911. pp. 420-421. See also Hautecoeur and Steinitz.

Reinach, Salomon. "L'enlèvement de Proserpine par Léonard de Vinci." *Revue archéologique,* I, 377-389. Paris, 1910.

Renouard, Augustin. *Catalogue de la Bibliothèque d'un Amateur,* I, 320-323. Paris, Renouard, 1819.

Richter, Jean Paul. "Leonardo da Vinci's Lehrbuch von der Malerei." *Zeitschrift fuer Bildende Kunst,* XVII, 11-20. Leipzig, 1882.

—————. "Bibliographie der Handschriften Lionardo's." *Zeitschrift fuer Bildende Kunst,* XVII-XVIII, 315-318; 383-388; 88-91; 127-132; 154-157; 190-193. Leipzig, 1882-1883.

—————. "Prolegomena and General Introduction to the Book on Painting," in Richter, *The Literary Works of Leonardo da Vinci.* London, 1883. I, 1-24.

—————. "The History of the 'Trattato della Pittura.' Paragone. Prolegomena . . ." in Richter, 1939. I, 5-111. Cf. above List A2.

Rosenthal, Georg. "Lessing und Leonardo da Vinci," *Neue Jahrbuecher fuer Paedagogik,* XXIX, 418-425. Berlin, 1916.

Rubens, Peter Paul, *Théorie de la figure humaine.* Cf. List 7.

Sandrart, Joachim. *Academia nobilissimae artis pictoriae.* . . Nuremberg, Froberg, 1683. pp. 111-113. German edition, Frankfurt, M. Merian, 1675.

Sarchiani, Giuseppe. *Elogio del dott. Giovanni Lessi*. Florence, Piatti, 1819.

Schlosser, Julius von. *Materialien zur Quellenkunde der Kunstgeschichte*. 3. Heft: Leonardo's Vermaechtnis. Vienna, Hoelder, 1916 and Kunstliteratur, 1924. pp. 140ff. List G.

Seibt, Wilhelm. *Helldunkel, von den Griechen bis zu Correggio*. Frankfurt am Main, Keller, 1885. pp. 36-53.

Seidlitz, Woldemar von. *Leonardo da Vinci. Malerbuch*. Vollstaendige Zusammenstellung seines Inhalts. Berlin, Bard, 1910 and 1919.

————. "Fuer eine neue Ausgabe von Leonardos Traktat." *Mitteilungen des Kunsthistorischen Instituts in Florenz*. Berlin, Cassirer, 1908.

Siren, Osvald. *Leonardo da Vinci . . . och Malerbok*. Stockholm, Ljus, 1911.

————. *Leonardo da Vinci, the Artist and the Man*. New Haven, Yale University Press, 1916.

————. *Léonard de Vinci, L'artiste et l'homme*. Tr. Jean Buhot. Paris-Brussels, van Oest, 1928.

Smith, Joseph. *Bibliotheca Smithiana, catalogus, librorum . . .* Venice, Pasquali, 1755.

Springer, Anton. Bilder aus der neuen Kunstgeschichte. Bonn, Marcus, 1886. 1, 297-326.

Steinitz, Kate Trauman. "Poussin, Illustrator of Leonardo da Vinci and the Problem of Replicas in Poussin's Studio." *The Art Quarterly*, XVI, 1, 40-55.

————. "Poussin, illustrateur de Léonard de Vinci . . ." Communications du Congrès International du Val de Loire (7-12 juillet 1952). Paris Alger, *Etudes d'Art*, Nos. 8-10, 1953-1954. pp. 339-360. (Referred to hereafter as *Etudes d'Art*, Nos. 8-10, 1953-1954)

Uzielli, Gustavo. *Ricerche intorno a Leonardo da Vinci*. Rome, Salviucci, 1884. pp. 283-347: "Elenco dei codici autografi . . . e degli apografi. . . ."

Valéry, Paul. "Introduction à la méthode de Léonard de Vinci." Paris, *Nouvelle Revue* du 15 aout 1895. Reprinted *Nouvelle Revue Française* 1919. (With "Note et digression")

————. *Introduction to the Method of Leonardo da Vinci*. Translated by Thomas McGreevy. London, Rodker, 1929.

————. *Les divers essais sur Léonard de Vinci*. Editions de la N.R.F. [*Nouvelle Revue Française*], 1938.

Vangenstein, Ove C. L. "Per una completa conoscenza dell'opera scientifica e letteraria di Leonardo da Vinci." *Per il IV Centenario.* . . . Bergamo, 1919.

Venturi, Lionello. *La Critica e l'arte di Leonardo da Vinci.* Istituto Vinciano in Rome. Bologna, Zanichelli, 1919.

————. *History of art criticism.* Tr. Ch. Marriott. New York, Dutton, 1936.

————. *Storia della critica d'arte.* Rome, Edizione U, 1945.

Winterberg, Constantin. "Leonardo da Vinci's Malerbuch und seine wissenschaftliche und praktische Bedeutung." *Jahrbuch der preussischen Kunstsammlungen*, VII, 172-202.

Wolff, James. *Lionardo da Vinci als Aesthetiker. Versuch einer Darstellung und Beurteilung der Kunsttheorie Lionardos auf Grund seines "Trattato della pittura."* Strassburg, Heitz, 1901.

# B. Subject Matter of *The Treatise*

## I. PHILOSOPHY AND AESTHETICS

Boas, George. "The Mona Lisa in the History of Taste." *Journal of the History of Ideas*, I, 207-224. Also in *The Wingless Pegasus.* Baltimore, Johns Hopkins Press, 1950.

Bovi, Arturo. *Leonardo, filosofo, artista, uomo.* Milan, Hoepli, 1952.

Cassirer, Ernst. *Individuum und Kosmos in der Philosophie der Renaissance. Studien der Bibliothek Warburg*, x. Leipzig-Berlin, Teubner, 1927.

————. *Individuo e cosmo* . . . Tr. F. Federici. Florence, La nuova Italia, 1935.

Castelfranco, Giorgio. *Il pensiero estetico di Leonardo da Vinci.* Mostra della Scienza e Tecnica di Leonardo 12. Museo Nazionale della scienza e della technica. Milan, 1954.

Clark, Kenneth. "The Demonic Genius of Leonardo da Vinci." *The Listener*, London, April 24, 1952, pp. 664-666.

————. "Leonardo da Vinci. A note on his relation between his science and his art." *History Today*, II, 5: 301-313. London, 1952.

————. "A note on Leonardo da Vinci." *Life and Letters*, II, 9, 122-132. London, 1929. Cf. K. Clark, above List A3, and below B2 Landscape, E4.

Croce, Benedetto. *Conferenze Fiorentine.* Milan, Treves, 1910. pp. 227-256.

Ferrero, Leo. *Léonard de Vinci ou l'œuvre d'art; precédé d'une étude, Léonard et les philosophes, de Paul Valéry.* Paris, Kra, 1929.

Fumagalli, Giuseppina. *Eros di Leonardo*, Milan, Garzanti, 1952. (Received the *Premio Leonardo da Vinci* as the most original and important work of an Italian author published in the Quincentennial year.)

Gantner, Joseph. *Leonardo da Vinci.* Gedenkrede. Basel. Basler Universitaetsreden 30. Heft, 1952.

————. *Rodin und Michelangelo.* Vienna, A. Schroll, 1953. "Rueckblick auf Leonardo." pp. 63-70.

Gentile, Giovanni. "Leonardo filosofo" *Nuova Antologia*, I, 232-250.

————. *Il pensiero di Leonardo da Vinci, Edizione curata dalla Mostra . . . in Milano.* Novara, Istituto Geografico de Agostini, 1940. pp. 163-174. Referred to hereafter as *Mostra Milano*, Novara, 1940.

Gundolf, Friedrich (Gundelfinger, Fr.). "Michelangelo und Leonardo . . . Die Truemmer Leonardo's." *Preussische Jahrbuecher*, CXXIX, 34-45. Berlin, 1907.

————. "Die Truemmer Leonardo's." *Neue Literarische Welt.* Darmstadt, 15 April, 1952.

Huxley, Aldous. "Leonardo then and now," *Leonardo da Vinci 500th Anniversary Exhibition*, Oct. 27-Nov. 16, 1952. The Municipal Art Commission, Los Angeles, Cal. pp. 7-9.

Jaspers, Karl. *Leonardo als Philosoph.* Bern, Francke, 1953. Schriften der "Concinnitas."

McCurdy, Edward. *The mind of Leonardo da Vinci.* New York, Dodd Mead and Co., 1928, and many reprints in New York and London, the most recent 1952.

Marone, Gherardo. "El mundo de Leonardo." *Ars*, XIII, 59. Buenos Aires, 1952.

————. "La sonrisa de 'la Gioconda' y el claroscuro." *Lyra.* Buenos Aires, Numero Anniversario 1952.

Oberdorfer, Aldo. "Leonardo romantico." In *Per il IV Centenario.* Bergamo, 1919.

Pater, Walter. *The Renaissance.* London, Macmillan, 1893. Numerous reprints especially of the passage on la Gioconda.

Peladan, Sar. "Un idéalisme experimental. La philosophie de Léonard de Vinci d'après ses manuscripts." *Mercure de France*, pp. 193-214; 440-461. Paris, 1908.

————. *La philosophie de Leonard de Vinci . . .* Paris, Alcan, 1910.

————. "Les idées philosophiques de Léonard de Vinci. Experimentalisme. . . ." *La nouvelle revue.* N.S. 13, pp. 397-410. Paris, 1910.

Prantl, K. von. "Leonardo in philosophischer Beziehung." *Sitzungs-berichte der Koenigl.* Bayerischen Academie der Wissenschaften. Philos.-Philol. Klasse. 3 Januar 1885.

Ruskin, John. *Lectures on art, delivered before the University of Oxford in Hilary term.* London, G. Allan, 1870.

Séalles, Gabriel. "L'esthétique et l'art de Léonard de Vinci." *Revue des deux mondes,* cxi, 302-330. Paris, 1892.

—————. "L'esthétique de Léonard de Vinci." *Per il IV Centenario.* Bergamo, 1919. Cf. List E4.

Spengler, Oswald. *Der Untergang des Abendlandes.* I. Band. *Gestalt und Wirklichkeit.* Vienna and Leipzig, Braumueller, 1918.

—————. *The decline of the West,* I. New York, A. Knopf, 1926.

Valéry, Paul. Cf. above List A3.

Venturi, Lionello. Cf. above List A3.

## 2. ART

### PROPORTION

Bilancioni, Guglielmo. *L'orecchio e il naso nel sistema antropometrico di Leonardo da Vinci.* Rome, Nardecchia, 1920. Studie di storia della scienza, I.

Bossi, Giuseppe. *Del "Cenacolo" di Leonardo da Vinci.* Libri quattre. Milan, Stamperia Reale, 1810. "Opinioni di Leonardo intorni alle proporzioni del corpo umano," pp. 202-234.

—————. *Delle opinioni di Leonardo da Vinci intorno all'simmetria de'corpi umani.* Milan, Stamperia Reale, 1811. (Separate edition of the proportion chapter of 1810)

Caride, Vicente P. "Leonardo da Vinci y el canon de proporciones en el cuerpo humano." *Ars,* xiii, 59. Buenos Aires, 1952.

Cook, Theodore Andrea. *Spirals in nature and art. A study based on the Manuscripts of Leonardo da Vinci.* New York, Dutton, 1903.

—————. *The Curves of Life. An account of spiral formations . . . with special reference to the Manuscripts of Leonardo da Vinci.* London, Constable; New York, Holt, 1914.

De Toni, G. B. "Leonardo da Vinci e Luca Paciolo." In *Atti del Reale Istituto veneto di scienze, lettere, ed arti,* lxv, 2: 1145-1148. Venice, 1906.

—————. "Frammenti vinciani. V. Intorno al Codice sforzesco 'De divina proportione' di Luca Paciolo e ai disegni anatomici di quest' opera attribuiti a Leonardo da Vinci." In *Atti della Società dei naturalisti e matematici di Modena*, XIII, 52-80. Modena, 1911.

Favaro, Giuseppe. "Il canone di Leonardo da Vinci sulle proporzioni del corpo umano." *Memorie dell'Istituto anatomico della R. Università di Padova*. Venice, Ferrari, 1917. pp. 167-227.

──────. "Misure e proporzioni del corpo umano secondo Leonardo." In *Atti del R. Istituto veneto di scienze, lettere ed arti*, LXXXVIII, 109-190. Venice, 1918.

──────. "Le proporzioni del corpo umano in un codice anonimo del Quattrocento postillato da Leonardo." *Memorie della classe di scienze fisiche. . .* , V, 577-596. Rome, Reale Accademia d'Italia, 1934.

Funck-Hellet, Ch. *Composition et nombre d'or dans les œuvres peintes de la Renaissance. Proportion-symétrie-symbolisme.* Paris, Vincent, Freal, 1950.

Ghyka, Matyla C. *Esthétique des Proportions dans la nature et dans les arts.* Paris, Gallimard, 1927.

──────. *Le Nombre d'or*, Paris, Gallimard, 1931. 2 vols.

──────. *Essai sur le rhythme.* Paris, Gallimard, 1938.

──────. *The Geometry of Art and Life.* New York, Sheed and Ward, 1946.

──────. *Geometrical composition and design.* London, A. Tiranti, 1952.

Giesen, Josef. *Dürers Proportionsstudien im Rahmen der allgemeinen Proportionsentwicklung.* Bonn, 1930.

Hagemeier, Otto. *Der goldne Schnitt.* Ulm, Tapper, 1949.

Holden, Harold M. *Noses.* Cleveland and New York, 1950.

Lomazzo, Jean Pol. *Traicté de la Proportion naturelle et artificielle.* Tr. Hilaire Pader. Toulouse, Colomiez, 1649. Cf. List A3.

Marzoli, Carla. *Studi sulle proporzioni.* Mostra bibliografica. Nona Triennale di Milan, 1951. pp. 114-134.

Mortet, Victor. "La mesure de la figure humaine et le canon des proportions d'après les dessins de Villard de Honnecourt, d'Albert Dürer et de Léonard de Vinci." *Mélange Chatelain.* Paris, Champion, 1910.

Pacioli, Luca. *Divina Proportione.* Venice, Paganius Paganinus, 1509.

──────. *Euclidis Megarensis. . .* Venice, Paganius Paganinus, 1509.

──────. *Divina Proportione, die Lehre vom goldnen Schnitt. . .* neu herausgegeben von Constantin Winterberg. Vienna, C. Graeser, 1889. Quellenschriften fuer Kunstgeschichte. Neue Folge Bd. II.

──────. *La divina proporción.* Buenos Aires, Losada, 1946.

Panofsky, Erwin. *Dürers Kunsttheorie vornehmlich in ihrem Verhaeltnis zur Kunsttheorie der Italiener.* Berlin, Reimer, 1915.

————. "Die Entwicklung der Proportionslehre als Abbild der Stilentwicklung." *Monatshefte fuer Kunstwissenschaft,* xiv (1921), 188-219.

————. *The Codex Huygens and Leonardo da Vinci's Art Theory.* The Pierpont Morgan Library Codex M.A.1139. The Studies of the Warburg Institute. Vol. 13. London, 1940.

Richter, Irma. *Rhythmic Form in Art.* . . London, Lane, 1932.

Rubens, Pierre Paul. *Théorie de la figure humaine.* Paris, Jombert, 1773. With texts and figure engravings by Aveline after Poussin.

————. " 'Théorie de la figure humaine' par G. Pawlowski," *L'Art,* xxxvi, 214-220. Paris, 1884.

Speziali, Pierre. *Léonard de Vinci et la Divina Proportions de Luca Pacioli.* Geneva, Droz, 1953.

Steinitz, Kate Trauman. "A Pageant of Proportion. . ." *Centaurus,* i, 309-333. Copenhagen, Munksgaard, 1951.

Tory, Geoffroy. *Champfleury, auquel est contenu l'art et science de la deue et vraie proportion des lettres attique.* Paris, 1529. Second edition 1549 and facsimile editions, Paris, Bosse, 1931 and New York, Grolier Club, 1927.

Zeising, A. *Neue Lehre von den Proportionen des menschlichen Koerpers.* Leipzig, R. Weigel, 1854.

### PERSPECTIVE

Bosse, Abraham. *Traité des pratiques géométrales et perspectives enseignées dans l'Académie Royale de la peinture et sculpture.* Paris, chez l'Auteur, 1665. The Leonardo passage refers to the first Trattato edition and to the Poussin illustrations.

Francastel, Pierre. "La Perspective de Léonard de Vinci et l'expérience scientifique au XVI siècle." Colloques internatinaux du Centre National de la recherche scientifique, Paris 4-7 juillet 1952, Paris, Presses universitaires, 1953. pp. 61-88. (Referred to hereafter as *Colloques Internationaux,* Paris, 1952-1953)

[Francesca, Piero Della] Petrus Pictor. *De prospectiva pingendi . . . nebst deutscher Uebersetzung von Dr. C. Winterberg.* Strassburg, Heitz, 1899. 2 vols.

————. *De Prospectiva pingendi.* A cura di Nicco Fasola. Florence, Sansoni, 1942. 2 vols.

Gauricus, Pomponius. *De Sculptura ubi agitur de symetriis, de lineamentis, de physiognomia, de perspectiva.* . . . Florence, Junta, 1504.

Guardasoni, Alessandro. *Della pittura, della stereoscopia, e di alcuni precetti di Leonardo da Vinci. Pensieri.* Bologna, Azzoguidi, 1880.

Ivins, Jr., William M. "On the Rationalization of Sight." *The Metropolitan Museum of Art Papers*, No. 8. New York, 1938.

Lambert, Johann Heinrich. *Schriften zur Perspective*, herausgegeben und eingeleitet von Max Steck. Berlin, Luettke, 1943.

Little, A. M. G. "Perspective and Scene Painting." *Art Bulletin*, XIX (1936), 437 ff.

Mesnil, Jacques. "La perspective linéaire chez Léonard de Vinci." *Revue archéologique*, XVI, 54-76. Paris, 1922.

Nielsen, Chr. V. *Leonardo da Vinci og hans forhold til Perspektiven et afsnit af Perspektivens historie.* Copenhagen, Trydes, 1897.

Panofsky, Erwin. *Die Perspektive als "symbolische Form."* Vortraege der Bibliothek Warburg. Leipzig, Teubner, 1927. pp. 258-330. Cf. List 7 above, Proportion.

Schuritz, Hans. *Die Perspective in der Kunst Albrecht Dürers.* Frankfurt, Keller, 1919.

Serlio, Sebastiano. *Il secondo libro di perspectiva.* Venice, Nicolino de Sabbio ad instantia di Marchio Sessa, 1551.

――――. *The second Book of Architecture, entreating of Perspective, made by Sebastino Serly.* London, Robert Peake, 1611.

White, John. "Developments in Renaissance Perspective." *Journal of the Warburg and Courtauld Institutes*, XII, 58-79; 1949, XIV, 42-69. University of London, 1951.

### LANDSCAPE

Bloch, Ernst. "Dargestellte Wunschlandschaft in Malerei, Oper, Dichtung." *Sinn und Form*, I, 5:18-64, Potsdam, 1949.

Buscaroli, Rezio. *La pittura di paesaggio in Italia.* Bologna, Mareggiani, 1935.

Clark, Sir Kenneth M. *Landscape into Art.* London, Murray n.d. (1950?)

De Mattia, Angelo. "Le paysage de Léonard." *Cahiers du Sud*, XXXXV, 313:370-378. Marseilles, 1952.

Gerstenberg, Kurt. *Die ideale Lanschaftsmalerei.* Halle, Niemeyer, 1923.

――――. "Die italienische Landschaftskunst der Renaissance." *Das Kunstwerk*, III, 1:39-47. Baden-Baden, 1949.

Goldscheider, Ludwig. *Leonardo da Vinci, Landscapes and Plants.* New York, Phaidon, 1952.

Guthmann, Johannes. *Die Landschaftsmalerei der toskanischen und umbrischen Kunst von Giotto bis Rafael.* Leipzig, Hiersemann, 1902.

Kallab, Wolfgang. "Die toskanische Landschaftsmalerei im xiv und xv Jahrhundert." *Jahrbuch . . . des allerhoechsten Kaiserhauses,* xxi. Vienna, 1900.

Kiel, Hanna e Neri, Dario. *Paesaggi inattesi del Rinascimento.* Prefazione di B. Berenson. Milan, Electa editrice, 1952.

Salter, Emma Gurney. *Nature in Italian Art. A study of landscape background from Giotto to Tintoretto.* London, Black, 1912.

SCULPTURE

Bode, Wilhelm von. *Italienische Bildhauer der Renaissance. . .* Berlin, Speman, 1887.

——. "Leonardo als Bildhauer." *Jahrbuch der Koeniglich preussischen Kunstsammlungen,* xxv, 125-141. Berlin, 1904.

——. *Florentine Sculptors of the Renaissance.* London, Metheun, 1908.

——. *Florentimer Bildhauer der Renaissance.* Berlin, Cassirer, 1910. (Reproduces article of 1904)

——. *Studien ueber Leonardo da Vinci.* Berlin, G. Grote, 1921.

Cook, Sir Theodore Andrea. *Leonardo da Vinci, Sculptor . . . the Albizzi Madonna.* London, Humphreys, 1923.

Courajod, Louis. *Léonard de Vinci et la statue de Francesco Sforza.* Paris, Champion, 1879.

McCurdy, Edward. "Leonardo da Vinci as Sculptor." *The Nineteenth Century and After,* pp. 1041-1050. London, 1909.

Malaguzzi-Valeri, Francesco. *Leonardo da Vinci e la scultura.* Bologna, Zanichelli, 1922.

Meller, Simon. "Die Reiterdarstellungen Leonardo's und die Budapester Bronzestatuette." *Jahrbuch der Koeniglich Preussischen Kunstsammlungen,* xxxvii, 213-250. Berlin, 1916.

Mueller, Theodor. *Il cavallo von Leonardo da Vinci.* Berlin, Gebr. Mann, 1948.

Schlosser, Julius von. "Aus der Bildnerwerkstatt der Renaissance. Fragment der Geschichte der Renaissance Plastik." *Jahrbuch . . . des Allerhoechsten Kaiserhauses,* xxxi, 2:119-121. Vienna, 1913.

Seidlitz, Woldemar von. "Leonardo da Vinci als Bildhauer." *Der Kunstwart,* xxiii, 429-435. Munich, 1909.

Stites, Raymond S. "Leonardo da Vinci, Sculptor, i, ii, iii." *Art Studies, Mediaeval, Renaissance and Modern.* Harvard University Press, 1926, 1928, 1930-1931. (Subtitle of 1928: "Leonardo's Terracotta Group in the Bargello")

————. "The Bronzes of Leonardo da Vinci." *The Art Bulletin* (1930), XII, 3.

Suida, W. "A Bronze Horse Attributed to Leonardo." *International Studio*, June, 1931.

Valentiner, W. R. "Leonardo as Verrocchio's Co-Worker." *Art Bulletin* (1930), XII, 1, 43-89.

————. "On Leonardo's Relation to Verrocchio." *The Art Quarterly* (1941), IV, 1, 3-31.

————. "Two Terracotta Reliefs by Leonardo." *The Art Quarterly* (1944), VII, 1, 3-21.

————. *Studies of Italian Renaissance Sculpture*. New York, Phaidon, Oxford University Press, 1950.

### ARCHITECTURE

Annoni, Ambrogio. *Dell'edificio "Bramantesco" S. Maria Fontana in Milano*. Milan, Alfieri & Lacroix, 1914.

Baroni, Costantino. "Leonardo architetto." *Mostra Milano*, Novara, 1940.

[Beltrami, Luca.] "Leonardo architetto." Polifilo, *Leonardo e i disfattisti suoi*. Milan, Treves, 1919.

Calvi, Ignazio. *L'architettura militare di Leonardo da Vinci*. Milan, Libreria Lombarda, 1943.

Chierici, Gino. "L'architettura a cupola." *Mostra Milano*, Novara, 1940.

Geymueller, H. von. "Leonardo da Vinci als Architekt." *Die Architectur der Renaissance in Toscana*. Munich, Bruckmann, 1906.

Heydenreich, L. H. *Die Sacralbauten Leonardo da Vincis*. Leipzig, Vogel, 1920.

Sartoris, Alberto. *Léonard architecte*. Paris, Tallone, 1952.

Spinazzola, Vittorio. "Considerazioni su Leonardo da Vinci architetto." *Conferenze Fiorentine*. Milan, Treves, 1910. pp. 107 ff.

Uccelli, Arturo. "La scienza delle costruzioni." *Mostra Milano*, Novara, 1940.

## 3. SCIENCE

### ANATOMY, BIOLOGY, PHYSIOLOGY

From the mass of material we have selected: (1) Leonardo's own anatomical manuscripts; (2) the earliest records of his anatomical studies; (3) the greatest modern publications on Leonardo's anatomy; (4) articles with special reference to the anatomical chapters of the *Treatise*.

Leonardo da Vinci. *Dell'Anatomia, Fogli A*. Pubblicati da T. Sabach-nikoff e G. Piumati. Paris, Rouveyre, 1898.

————. *Dell'Anatomia, Fogli B*. Pubblicati da T. Sabachnikoff e G. Piumati. Turin, Roux e Viareggio, 1901.

————. *Quaderni d'Anatomia*. Comunicazioni dello Istituto Ana-tomico dell'Università di Christiania. Christiania, J. Dybwad, 1911-1916. 6 vols.

Belt, Elmer. "Leonardo da Vinci's studies of the aging process." *Geriatrics*, 7, 3:205-210.

————. "Les dissections anatomiques de Léonard de Vinci." *Col-loques Internationaux*. Paris, 1952-1953. pp. 189-224.

Biaggi, Carlo Felice. *L'anatomia artistica. Mostra Milano*. Novara, 1940. pp. 437-447.

Biasoli, Umberto. *Le conoscenze anatomiche di Leonardo da Vinci*. Milan, Bracciforti, 1913.

Bilancioni, Guglielmo. "La gerarchia degli organi dei sensi nel pen-siero di Leonardo da Vinci." *Giornale di medicina militare*, LXVII, 1244-1271. Rome, 1919.

Blumenbach, Friedrich. *Introductio in historiam medicinae literariam*. Goettingen, Dietrich, 1786.

————. "Von den anatomischen Zeichnungen des Lionardo da Vinci in S. R. Maj. des Koenigs grossen Sammlungen von Hand-zeichnungen." *Medizinische Bibliothek*. Goettingen, Dietrich, 1788.

Bottazzi, Filippo. "Saggi su Leonardo da Vinci." *Archivio di ana-tomia e di embriologia*, VI, 499-547. Florence, 1907.

————. "Leonardo biologo e anatomico." *Conferenze Fiorentine*. Milan, Treves, 1910. pp. 183-223.

Burrows, Jackson H. "Leonardo da Vinci and Nicolas Andry on Posture." *Journal of Bone and Joint Surgery*. British Number, London, November 1952. pp. 541-544.

Castaldi, Luigi. *La figura umana in Leonardo da Vinci*. Siena, Stab. Arti grafiche S. Bernardino, 1927.

Choulant, Ludwig. *Geschichte und Bibliographie der anatomischen Abbildung. . .* Leipzig, R. Weigel, 1852.

————. *History and Bibliography of Anatomic Illustration*. Trans-lated and annotated by Mortimer Frank. University of Chicago Press, 1920, and New York, Schuman, 1945.

De Toni, G. B. "La biologia in Leonardo da Vinci. Discorso letto . . . il 24 maggio 1903." *Atti del R. Istituto veneto. . .* XXIII, 171-196. Venice, 1903.

Disselhorst, Rudolf. "Das biologische Lebenswerk des Lionardo da Vinci." *Leopoldiana*, Berichte der Kaiserlich Leopoldinischen Deutschen Akademie der Naturforscher in Halle. Leipzig, Quelle & Meyer, 1929.

Duval, Mathias and Edouard Cuyer. *Histoire de l'anatomie plastique*. Paris, Soc. Française d'Editions d'art, 1898; and Picard, 1908.

Esche, Sigrid. *Die Anatomiezeichnungen Leonardos*. Dissertation. Berlin, 1943; Basel, Holbeinverlag, 1954.

Favaro, Giuseppe. *Leonardo da Vinci, i medici e la medicina*. Rome, Maglione & Strini, 1923.

————. "L'equilibrio del corpo umano negli studi di Leonardo." *Atti del R. Istituto veneto di scienze, lettere ed arti*, LXXXVI (1926-1927), 227-254.

————. "L'anatomia e le scienze biologiche." *Mostra Milan*, Novara, 1940. pp. 363-372.

————. "Il peso del corpo umano negli studi di Leonardo." *Atti del III Congresso nazionale della Società italiana di storia delle scienze mediche e naturali*. Venice, 1925; Siena, tip. S. Bernardino, 1926.

Herrlinger, Robert. "Die didaktische Originalitaet der anatomischen Zeichnungen Leonardos." *Anatomischer Anzeiger*, 99, 20/22: 367-395. Jena, 1953.

Hunter, William. *Two introductory lectures to his last course of anatomical lectures. . .* London, J. Johnston, 1784.

Keele, K. D. *Leonardo da Vinci on movement of the heart and blood with a foreword by Charles Singer*. London, Harvey and Blythe, 1952.

Knox, R. *Great Artists and great Anatomists*. London, Van Voorst, 1852.

McMurrich, J. Playfair. *Leonardo da Vinci, the Anatomist (1452-1519)*. Baltimore, the Williams and Wilkins Co. for the Carnegie Institution of Washington, 1930.

Marx, Karl F. H. "Ueber Marc'Antonio della Torre und Leonardo da Vinci, die Begruender der bildlichen Anatomie." *Abhandlungen der Kgl. Gesellschaft der Wissenschaften zu Goettingen*, 1849.

O'Malley, Charles D. and De C. M. Saunders, J. B. *Leonardo da Vinci on the Human Body*. New York, Henry Schuman, 1952.

Verdier, Henry. *Léonard physiologiste*. Paris, Rousset, 1913.

## BOTANY

Baldacci, Antonio. Memorie letto alla R. Accademia delle scienze dell' Istituto di Bologna, 1913-1931. Series VII, Vols. I, II, III, X: *Leonardo da Vinci, Botanico e fondatore del metodo sperimentale.* 1914.
*La botanica . . . dai Mss. della Biblioteca del Istituto di Francia.* 1914-1915.
*La botanica del Codice Atlantico.* . . 1915-1916.
*Le piante . . . nel Codice della Biblioteca reale del Castello Windsor,* 1922-1923.
————. *Gli alberi e le verdure nel Trattato della Pittura.* . . Bologna, Azzoguidi, 1931.
————. "La botanica vinciana." *Mostra Milano,* Novara, 1940.
————. "L'adolescenza di Leonardo e il mondo verde." *Raccolta Vinciana,* XIII, 114-129. Milan, 1930.

Bazardi, Alessandro. *La botanica nel pensiero di Leonardo.* Pref. di Elio Baldacci, Milan, Museo Nazionale della Scienza e della Technica, No. 5, 1953.

Cermentati, Mario. *Intorno al 'mapello' di Leonardo da Vinci, Contributi . . . alla storia della botanica.* Rome, Voghera, 1907.

Cortesi, Fabrizio. "Leonardo botanico." *Sapere,* XVII, 387. Milan, 1938.
————. Same in Spanish. *Ars,* XIII, 59. Buenos Aires, 1952.

De Toni, G. B. "Frammenti vinciani VI: Di alcuni appunti e disegni botanici nelle carte leonardesche." *Atti della Societa dei naturalisti e matematici di Modena,* XIV (1912), 138-148.
————. *Le pianti e gli animali in Leonardo da Vinci.* Publicazioni del Istituto Vinciano in Roma IV. Bologna, Zanichelli, 1922.

Goldscheider, Ludwig. ed. *Leonardo da Vinci, Landscapes and Plants.* New York, Phaidon, 1952.

Grey, Sandra Zalaschi. "Flora Vinciana." *Sapere,* XVII, 388-399. Milan, 1938.
————. Same in Spanish. *Ars,* XIII, 59. Buenos Aires, 1952.

Haberlandt, O. "Leonardo da Vinci als Botaniker." *Neue Freie Presse.* January 1, 1884.

Uzielli, Gustavo. "Sopra alcune osservazioni botaniche di Leonardo da Vinci." *Nuovo Giornale botanico italiano,* I, 481ff. Florence, 1869.

## GEOLOGY AND PHYSICAL GEOGRAPHY

Baratta, Mario. *Leonardo da Vinci e i problemi della terra.* Turin, Bocca, 1903.

————. "Importanza per la geologia e la geografia fisica della pub-
licazione dei manoscritti di Leonardo da Vinci." *Bolletino della
Società geologica italiana*, xxx, 1007-1014. Rome, 1911.

Beringer, Carl Chr. *Geschichte des geologischen Weltbildes*. Stuttgart,
F. Enke, 1954.

De Lorenzo, Giuseppe. *Leonardo da Vinci e la geologia*. Publicazioni
dell'Istituto Vinciano a Roma III. Bologna, Zanichelli, 1920.

————. "Leonardo geologo." *Sapere*, xvii, 401-403. Milan, 1938.

Gianotti, Agostino. *Geografia e geologia negli scritti di Leonardo da
Vinci, con prefazione del Prof. A. Desio*. Museo Nazionale della
scienze e della technica, No. 6. Milan, 1953.

Kuiper, Gerard. ed. *The Atmosphere of the Earth and Planets*. Chicago, University of Chicago Press, 1952. p. 72.

La Mer, K. and Milton Kerker. "Light Scattered by Particles."
*Scientific American*, 188, 2, 69-76.

Lyell, Charles. *Principles of Geology or the Modern Changes of the
Earth and its Inhabitants.* . . London, Murrey, 1840. 3 vols.

Oberhummer, Eugen. "Leonardo da Vinci und die Kunst der Renaissance in ihren Beziehungen zur Erdkunde." 9e Congrès International de Geographie, Geneva, 1908.

————. Same in English. *The Geographic Journal*, xxxiii, 540-569.
London, 1909.

Reale Commissione Vinciana. *I manoscritti e i disegni di Leonardo
da Vinci*. I disegni geografici. Fascicolo unico. Rome, La Libreria
dello Stato, 1941. With preface by Mario Baratta, and contribu-
tions by Renzo Cianchi, Roberto Marcolongo, and Enrico Carusi.

Sacco, Federigo. "Geologia e geografia vinciana." *Mostra Milano*, Novara, 1940. pp. 455-466.

Salomon, Wilhelm. "Geologische Beobachtungen des Leonardo da
Vinci." *Sitzungsberichte der Heidelberger Akademie der Wissenschaften*. Math. naturwissenschaftliche Klasse 1928. 8. Abhand-
lung. Berlin, Gruyter, 1928.

Schimank, H. Cf. below, Other Sciences.

Uzielli, Gustavo. "Leonardo da Vinci e le Alpi." *Bolletino del Club
alpino italiano*, xxiii, 81-156. Turin, 1890.

#### MATHEMATICS

Babini, Jose. "Leonardo, matematico visual." *Ars*, xiii, 59. Buenos
Aires, 1952.

Cantor, Moritz. "Ueber einige Konstruktionen von Leonardo da Vinci."
*Festschrift . . . der Mathematischen Gesellschaft in Hamburg,
1890.* Zweiter Teil. Leipzig, Teubner, 1890. pp. 8-15.

————. *Vorlesungen ueber Geschichte der Mathematik.* 2d ed. II, 294-302.

Duhem, Pierre. "Léonard de Vinci et la composition des forces courantes." *Biblioteca mathematica,* III, 338-343. Leipzig, 1902.

Emanueli, Pio. "La matematica vinciana." *Mostra Milano,* Novara, 1940. pp. 201-208.

Libri, Guillaume. *Histoire des sciences mathématiques en Italie depuis la Renaissance des lettres, jusqu'à la fin du dix-septième siècle.* 4 vols. Paris, Renouard, 1838-1841.

Marcolongo, Roberto. "Le ricerche geometrico-meccaniche di Leonardo da Vinci." *Atti della Società italiana delle scienze detta dei,* XL, 259-261. Rome, Bardi, 1929.

————. "I centri di gravità dei corpi negli scritti di Leonardo da Vinci." *Raccolta Vinciana,* XIII, 99-113. Milan, 1930.

Sergescu, Pierre. "Léonard de Vinci et les mathématiques." *Colloques Internationaux,* Paris, 1952-1953.

Valéry, Paul. "Divers essais sur Léonard de Vinci." Paris, *NRF,* 1938.

Venturi, J. B. *Essai sur les ouvrages Physico-Mathématiques de Léonard de Vinci avec des fragments tirés de ses manuscrits. . .* Paris, Duprat, 1797.

————. Same in Italian. Società Geologica Italiana XXX Anniversario dalla Fondazione. Milan, Nugoli, 1911.

Whewell, William. *History of inductive Science from the earliest to the present time.* London, Parker, 1837.

Wind, Edgar. "Mathematics and sensibility." *The Listener.* London, May 1, 1952.

OPTICS

Angelucci, Arnaldo. "La 'maniera' in pittura e le leggi ottiche di luci e colori scoperte da Leonardo da Vinci." *Giornale de Medicina militare,* LXVII, 1191-1217. Rome, 1919.

Argentieri, Domenico. "L'ottica di Leonardo." *Mostra Milano.* Novara, 1940. pp. 405-436.

Bruecke, Ernst Wilhelm von. *Principes scientifiques des beaux-arts . . . suivis de l'optique et la peinture par H. Helmholtz.* Paris, Baillière, 1878.

Elsaesser, Wilhelm. "Die Funktion des Auges bei Leonardo." *Zeitschrift fuer Mathematik und Physik,* XLV, 1900, pp. 1-6.

Perrod, G. "La diottrica oculare di Leonardo da Vinci." *Archivio di ottalmologia,* XIV, 1907, pp. 463-497.

Ronchi, Vasco. "La luce camina veramente in linea recta?" *Sapere,* March 15, 1939.

————. "L'optique de Léonard de Vinci." *Colloques Internationaux*. Paris, 1952-1953. pp. 115-120.

For light and shadow, chiaroscuro, cf. also above Lists A3, B1.

OTHER SCIENCES

Anile, Antonio. "La scienza di Leonardo da Vinci." *Rivista d'Italia*, XXII, 36-44. Milan, 1939.

Calvi, Gerolamo. "Osservazione, invenzione, esperienza in Leonardo da Vinci." *Per il IV Centenario*. Bergamo, 1919. pp. 323-352.

Castelfranco, Giorgio. "Il concetto di forze in Leonardo da Vinci." *Proporzioni*, No. 3. Florence, 1950.

Dannemann, Friedrich. *Die Naturwissenschaften in ihrer Entwicklung und in ihrem Zusammenhange*. 1. Band. Leipzig, Engelmann, 1920.

Dugas, René. *Histoire de la mécanique*. Paris, Dunod, 1950.

————. "Léonard dans l'histoire de la mécanique." *Colloques Internationaux*, Paris, 1952-1953.

Duhem, M. P. "Sur quelques découvertes scientifiques de Léonard de Vinci." *Comptes rendus hebdomadaire des séances de l'Académie des sciences*, Vol. 143, pp. 946-949.

Ellis, Havelock. "Leonardo da Vinci." *The Nation*, xxv, 316-318. London, 1919.

Elsaesser, Wilhelm. "Die Bedeutung Leonardos fuer die exakten Naturwissenschaften." *Preussische Jahrbuecher*, XCVII, 272-294.

Faggi, Adolfo. "Leonardo e il concetto di scienza." *Per il IV Centenario*. Bologna, 1919. pp. 381-383.

Favaro, Antonio. "La place de Léonard de Vinci dans l'histoire des sciences." *Scientia*, xxvi, 137-149. Bologna, 1919.

————. "Leonardo nella storia delle scienze esperimentali." *Conferenze Fiorentine*. Milan, Treves, 1910.

Feldhaus, Franz M. *Leonardo, der Techniker und Erfinder*. Jena, Eugen Diederichs, 1913, and 4 reprints to 1922.

Ferri, Luigi. "Leonardo da Vinci scienziato e filosofo." *Nuova antologia*, XII, 294-334. Rome, 1873.

Grothe, Herman. *Leonardo da Vinci als Ingenieur und Philosoph, ein Beitrag zur Geschichte der inductiven Wissenschaften*. Berlin, Nicolai, 1874.

Hart, Ivor B. *The mechanical investigations of Leonardo da Vinci*. London, Chapman & Hall, 1925. (With translation of "On the Flight of the Birds")

Heller, August. *Geschichte der Physik von Aristoteles bis auf die neuste Zeit*. Stuttgart, Enke, 1882.

Heydenreich, Ludwig Heinrich. *Arte e scienza in Leonardo*. Conferenze milanesi a cura dell'istituto germanico. Milan, Bestetti, 1945.

————. "Le dessin scientifique de Léonard." *Les Arts Plastiques* (Carnets du Séminaire des Arts. 6 serie 1953). Cf. above Lists A3, below E4.

Humboldt, Alexander von. *Kosmos*. Stuttgart und Tuebingen, Cotta, 1845-1862.

Lippmann, Edmund O. von. "Lionardo da Vinci als Gelehrter und Techniker." *Zeitschrift fuer Naturwissenschaften*, LXXII, 291-316. Stuttgart, 1899. Reprinted in *Abhandlungen und Vortraege zur Geschichte der Naturwissenschaften*. Leipzig, Veit, 1906.

Marcolongo, Roberto. *Leonardo da Vinci, Artista scienziato*. Milan. Hoepli, 1939.

————. *La meccanica di Leonardo da Vinci*. Naples, S.I.E.M., 1932. Cf. above, Optics.

Marinoni, Augusto. *Gli appunti grammaticali e lessicali di Leonardo da Vinci*. Milan, Castello Sforzesco, Vol. I, 1944. Vol. II, 1952.

Olschki, Leonardo. *Geschichte der neusprachlichen wissenschaftlichen Literatur*, Vol. I. Heidelberg, Winter, 1919.

Reti, Ladislao. "Le arti chimiche di Leonardo da Vinci." *La chimica e l'industria*, XXXIV, Milan, December, 1952.

Sarton, George. "The message of Leonardo da Vinci. His relation to the birth of Modern Science." *Scribner's Magazine*, LXV, 531-540. New York, 1919.

————. "Léonard de Vinci, Ingénieur et Savant." *Colloques Internationaux*. Paris, 1952.

————. *The Life of Science*. New York, Schuman, 1948. Parts 2, 5. "Leonardo and the birth of Modern Science."

————. "Leonardo da Vinci." *The Metropolitan Museum of Art Miniatures*. New York, 1952.

Schimank, Hans. *Epochen der Naturforschung. Leonardo, Kepler, Faraday*. Berlin, Volksverband der Buecherfreunde, 1930.

Schuster, Fritz. *Zur Mechanik Leonardo da Vincis*. Erlangen, Junge, 1915.

Singer, Charles. *Studies in the History and Method of Science*, Vol. II. Oxford University Press, 1921.

Solmi, Edmondo. *Nuovi studi sulla filosofia naturale di Leonardo da Vinci. Il metodo sperimentale. L'astronomia. La teoria della visione*. Mantua, G. Mondovi, 1905.

Timpanaro, Sebastiano. "La fisica vinciana." *Mostra Milano*, Novara, 1940. pp. 209-213.

Werner, Otto. *Zur Physik Leonardo da Vincis*. Berlin, Internationale Verlagsanstalt. . . 1913.

Zammattia, Carlo. *La Visione scientifica di Leonardo da Vinci*. Mostra della scienza e technica di Leonardo 3. Museo Nazionale della scienza e della technica, Milan, 1954.

# C. Related Works

## 1. THE TREATISE ON MOTION AND
## MEASURE OF WATER

*(Related to Mss. 227 and 229 inf.)*

*Raccolta di Autori Italiani che trattano del moto dell'acque*. Bologna, Marsigli, 1821-1826. Fr. Cardinali. Vol. x, 270-450. Del moto e misura dell'acqua di Leonardo da Vinci.

*Leonardo da Vinci, del Moto e Misura Dell'Acqua*. Libri nove ordinati da Luigi Maria Arconati. Editi sul codice archetipo barbariniano da E. Carusi ed A. Favaro. Istituto vinciano in Roma, Testi Vinciani. Bologna, Zanichelli, 1923.

"Del Moto e misura dell'acqua L'idraulica in Leonardo da Vinci." Edited by Nando de Toni in *Frammenti vinciani* II-x. Brescia and Milan, 1934-1935. Frammenti xi and xii (Multigraphed), 1950.

## 2. EDITIONS OF LEONARDO'S WRITINGS
## ON MECHANICS AND FLIGHT

R. Giacomelli, *Gli scritti di Leonardo da Vinci sul Volo*. Rome, Bardi, 1936.

*I Libri di Meccanica* nella Riconstruzione ordinata di Arturo Uccelli. Milan, Hoepli, 1940.

# D. Facsimile Editions, Anthologies, Selections from Leonardo's Manuscripts

## 1. FACSIMILE EDITIONS

*Il Codice Atlantico*. Saggio . . . Milan. C. Ricordi, 1872.

————. *nella Biblioteca Ambrosiana*. Milan. Ulrico Hoepli, 1894-

1904. Galbiati, Giovanni. *Dizionario Leonardesco . . . delle voci e cose . . . nel Codice Atlantico* and Semanza, Guido e Marcolongo, Roberto. *Indici . . . del Codice Atlantico*. Milan, Ulrico Hoepli, 1939.

*Les Manuscrits de Léonard de Vinci*. A-M. et Ashburnham 2038 and 2037 de la Bibliothèque de l'Institut de France . . . par Ch. Ravaisson Mollien. Paris, Quantin, 1881-1891. 6 vols.

*Il Codice . . . nella Biblioteca del Principe Trivulzio in Milano*. Trascritto da Luca Beltrami. Milan. Angelo della Croce, 1891.

————. Trascritto da Nando di Toni. Milan. Castello Sforzesco, 1939.

*Codice sul volo degli uccelli e varie altre materie* pubblicato da Teodoro Sabachnikoff. Paris, E. Rouveyre, 1893; ed. Jotti di Badia, Milan, Spartaco Giovene, 1946.

————. *I fogli mancanti* . . . Rome, Reale Commissione Vinciana, 1926.

*Leonardo da Vinci's Anatomical Manuscripts*. Cf. List B3.

*Feuillets Inedits de Léonard de Vinci*, Paris, E. Rouveyre, 1901. An illegal edition, printed in 100 copies. Drawings of Windsor Castle, 22 vols.; Forster Library, South Kensington Museum, 3 vols.; British Museum, 4 vols.

*Il Codice Forster nel Victoria and Albert Museum*, London. Rome. Reale Commissione Vinciana, 1930-1936. 5 vols.

*Il Codice . . . della Biblioteca di Lord Leicester* pubblicato . . . da Girolamo Calvi. Milan, L. F. Gogliati, 1909.

*I Manoscritti e i disegni di Leonardo da Vinci*, Rome, Reale Commissione Vinciana, Danesi and Libreria dello Stato, 1923 to present (1955):

*Il Codice Arundel 263, nel Museo Britannico*. 1923-1930. 4 vols.

*Il Codice Forster nel "Victoria and Albert Museum."* 1934-1936. 5 vols.

*Il Codice A (2172) nell'Istituto di Francia*, 1936. (Identical with Ms. A, Ravaisson-Mollien edition.)

*Il Codice A (2172) Complimenti*, 1938. (Identical with Ashburnham 2038, Ravaisson-Mollien edition.)

*Il Codice B (2173) nell'Istituto di Francia*. (Identical with Ms. B, Ravaisson-Mollien edition.)

*Fasicoli I-VII* and *Fascicolo unico, i disegni Geografici 1928-1952*. Elaborate reproductions of Leonardo's drawings, selected, annotated, and catalogued by Adolfo Venturi and successors.

## 2. ANTHOLOGIES. (ARRANGED CHRONOLOGICALLY.)

*The literary works* . . . compiled and edited by Jean Paul Richter. . . London, Low, Marston, Searle and Rivington, 1883. 2 vols.

*Frammenti letterari e filosofici* scelti dal Dott. Edmondo Solmi. Florence, Barbèra, Collezione diamante, 1899. Reprinted 1925.

*Der Denker, Forscher und Poet* . . . von Marie Herzfeld. Leipzig, Diederichs, 1904; Jena Diederichs, 1906.

*Frammenti e pensieri.* Con prefazione di Efisio Aitelli. Milan, Sonzogno, 1906. Biblioteca Universale.

*Thoughts on art and life* . . . translated by Maurice Baring. Boston, Merrymount Press, 1906.

*Notebooks Rendered into English* by Edward McCurdy. New York, Scribner's Sons, 1906.

*Notebooks Arranged and Rendered into English* by Edward McCurdy. London, Duckworth, 1907. Reprinted in 1908, 1910.

*Les manuscrits de Léonard de Vinci*, les xiv manuscrits de l'Institut de France. . . par Péladan. Paris, Sansot, 1910.

*Textes choisis* . . . per Péladan. Paris, Mercure de France, 1908. (Many reprint editions appeared during the following years)

*Der Denker, Forscher und Poet* . . . von Marie Herzfeld, 3. umgearbeitete Ausgabe. Jena, Diederichs, 1911.

*Scritti* con un Proemio di Luca Beltrami. Milan, Istituto editoriale italiano, 1913. Raccolta "Gli Immortali," Vol. xxii.

*Pisma Wibrane* . . . by Leopolda Staffa. Warsaw, Mortkowicza, 1913. (In Polish)

*Bilder und Gedanken ausgewaehlt* von Hektor Preconi. Munich, Kleine Delphin Kunstbuecher, 1920.

*Leonardo prosatore.* Scelta discritti . . . corredata di note, glossarietto . . . di Giuseppina Fumagalli. Milan, Albrighi e Segati, 1920.

*Kurt Zoege von Manteuffel*, Leonardo da Vinci, eine Auswahl. . . Munich, H. Schmidt, 1920.

*Notebooks arranged and rendered into English* . . . by Edward McCurdy. New York, 1923.

*Alberti, Leonardo, Michelangelo, Vasari, Cellini, Gallilei, Scritti* . . . scelti e annotato da G. R. Ceriello. Rome, Principato, 1924.

*Fiorelegio Leonardiano* con note di G. R. Ceriello. Rome, Principato, 1924.

*Leonardo da Vinci, pagine d'arte e di scienza.* Ed. Stefano de Simone. Torino, Lattes, 1925.

*Der Denker, Forscher und Poet* . . . von Marie Herzfeld. Jena, Diederichs, 1926.

*Prose*. Introduzione di Luigi Negri. Torino, Unione tipografica editrice torinese, 1928. Classici italiani.

*Scritti*, con un proemio di Luca Beltrami. Milan, Istitute editoriale italiano, 1929. Collezione Capolavori italiani.

A. Parisi e F. Laurenzi, *Scrittori d'arte. Leonardo da Vinci, Michelangelo*. . . Milan, Albrighi Segati, 1930.

*Escritos literarios y filosofocos* . . . traduccion y prologo de J. Campo Moreno. Madrid, Aguilar, 1930.

*Pagine scelte* preceduto da uno studio biografico critico. . . G. Pettorelli. Turin, 1935.

*Selected works* (in Russian). Moscow, Academia, 1935. Editors Gouber, Zoebow, and others.

*Leonardo, omo sanze lettere*. A cura di Giuseppina Fumagalli. Florence, Sansoni, 1938, reprinted 1952.

*The notebook of Leonardo da Vinci, arranged and rendered into English*. . . by Edward McCurdy. New York, Raynal and Hitchcock, 1939. Definitive edition, n.d. and reprint New York, George Braziller, 1954.

*The literary works* . . . compiled and edited from the original manuscripts. 2d ed., enlarged and revised by Jean Paul Richter and Irma A. Richter. London, New York, Oxford University Press, 1939. 2 vols.

*Tagebuecher und Aufzeichnungen* . . . uebersetzt und herausgegeben von Theodor Luecke. Leipzig, List Verlag, 1940. (German ed. after McCurdy, 1939.) Reprinted Zurich 1952.

*Les carnets de Leonardo da Vinci*, traduit . . . par Louise Servicen. Paris, Gallimard, 1942. With 5 reprint editions to 1953.

*Breviario di Leonardo da Vinci* . . . seleccion . . . de José de Espasa. . . Buenos Aires, "El Ateneo," 1943.

*L'occhio nell'universo*. A cura di G. Fumagalli. Firenze, Sansoni, 1943. Biblioteca del Leonardo, xxv.

*Aforismos*, selección de E. Garcia de Zuniga. Buenos Aires, Espasa, 1943. Collection Austral.

*Antologia Leonardesca*. Francesco Flora. Milan, Cisalpino, 1947.

*Worte Meister Leonardo's*, ausgewaehlt von Ernst Bertram. Wiesbaden, Inselbuecherei No. 446, 1950.

*Leonardo da Vinci, Kostbarkeiten aus seiner Werkstatt*, ausgewaehlt von Heinrich Ammann. Zurich, Werner Classen, 1952.

*Selections from the notebooks* . . . edited with commentaries by Irma A. Richter. London, New York, Oxford University Press, 1952. The World's Classics.

*Scritti scelti* . . . a cura di Anna Maria Brizio. Turin, Unione tipografico Torinese, 1952.

*Scritti Letterari*. Tutti gli scritti a cura di Augusto Marinoni. Milan, Rizzoli, 1952. Biblioteca Universale.

*Pensieri*. . . a cura di Vanni Scheiwiller. Milan, "Esperia," 1952. Miniature booklet.

*Léonard de Vinci par lui-meme*. Textes choisis . . . par André Chastel. Paris, Nagel, 1953.

# E. Leonardo's Life, Art, and Learning

## I. DOCUMENTS

Babinger, Franz and Heydenreich, L. H. "Vier Bauvorschlaege Leonardo da Vincis an Sultan Bajezid II. (1502-1503)" *Nachrichten der Akademie der Wissenschaften in Goettingen*, I. Phil.,-Hist. Kl. 1952, No. 1.

Beltrami, Luca. *Documenti e memorie riguardanti la vita e le opere di Leonardo da Vinci*. Milan, Treves, 1919.

Biblioteca Medicea Laurenziana, *Mostra di Disegni, manoscritti e documenti*. Quinto centenario della Nascita di Leonardo. Florence, 15 Aprile-31 Ottobre 1952. (Catalogue)

Campori, G. "Nuovi documenti per la vita di Leonardo da Vinci." *Atti e Memorie della R. Deputazione di storia patria di Modena*, 1865. pp. 43-51.

Cianchi, Renzo. *Vinci, Leonardo e la sua famiglia* (con appendice di documenti inediti). Milan, Museo della scienza e della Technica, Mostra. . . di Leonardo, No. 10, 1954.

De Beatis, Antonio. *Die Reise des Kardinald Luigo d'Aragona*. Veroeffentlicht von Ludwig Pastor. Freiburg i.B., Herder, 1905. Cf. Beltrami, *op. cit*. Doc. 238.

Gaye, Giovanni. *Carteggio inedito d'artisti dei secoli* XIV, XV, XVI. Florence, Molini, 1840.

Grammatica, Luigi. *Le memorie su Leonardo da Vinci* di Don Ambrogio Mazzenta. Milan, Alfieri e Lacroix, 1919.

Luedecke, Heinz. *Leonardo im Spiegel seiner Zeit*. Berlin, Ruetten und Loenig im Auftrage der Deutschen Akademie der Kuenste, 1952.

Milanesi, Gaetano. "Documenti inediti riguardanti Leonardo da Vinci." *Archivio storico italiano*, XVI, 219-230. Florence, 1872.

*Monumenta Hungarie Historica.* Budapest, 1877. (Letter from il Moro to Corvinus)

"La Nascita di Leonardo." (Birth certificate discovered by Emil Moeller.) *Mostra Milano.* Novara, 1940. pp. 6-7.

Pedretti, Carlo. *Documenti e memorie riguardanti Leonardo da Vinci a Bologna e in Emilia.* Bologna, Fiammenghi, 1953.

Smiraglia Scognamiglio, Nino. *Richerche e documenti sulla giovinezza di Leonardo da Vinci.* Naples, Marghieri, 1900.

Uzielli, Gustavo, *Ricerche intorno a Leonardo da Vinci.* Florence, Pellas, 1872.

————. *Ricerche intorno a Leonardo da Vinci,* serie seconda. Rome, Salviucci, 1884.

————. *Ricerche.* . . . Turin, Loescher, 1896, Serie 1. 2d ed.

## 2. EARLY RECORDS

Albertini, Francesco. *Memoriale di molte statue.* . . Florence, A. Tubini, 1510.

Anonimo Fiorentino. *Il Codice magliabechiano* xvii, 17. . . . herausgegeben von Carl Frey. Berlin, C. Grote, 1892. (Leonardo's life written between 1540-1548)

Anonimo Gaddiano. "(Cod. magliabechiano xvii, 17) nella Biblioteca Nazionale di Firenze. . . C. de Fabriczy." *Archivio storico italiano,* xii, 15-94, 275-334. Florence, 1893. Carl Frey ed. Berlin, Grote, 1892.

Bandello, Matteo. *Le Novelle.* Luca, Busdrago, 1554. (Part 1, 58, preface)

Bellincioni, Bernardo. *Rime.* . . Milan, Mantegazzi, 1493. (The first printed record of Leonardo)

Billi, Antonio. "C. de Fabriczy. Il Libro di Antonio Billi e le sue copie nella Biblioteca Nazionale di Firenze." *Archivio storico italiano,* vii, 299, 368. Florence, 1891. (The earliest source for Leonardo's life, ca. 1516)

Biondo, Michelangelo. *Della nobilissima Pittura.* . . Venice, Appolino, 1549. (The most inaccurate early record)

Castiglione, M. Sabba. *Ricordi.* Venice, P. Gerardo, 1560.

Gauricus, 1504 (cf. List B2 Perspective)

Giovio, Paolo, *Vita Leonardo Vincii,* in G. Tiraboschi, *Storia della letteratura italiana.* Venice, 1796, vii, 1641-1642, and in Richter, *The Literary Works of Leonardo da Vinci,* 1, 1939.

Giraldi Cintio, G. G. *Discorsi.* Venice, G. de Ferrari, 1554.

Lomazzo, Gio. Paolo. *Trattato del arte della pittura*. Milan, G. Pontio, 1584.

————. *Idea del tempio della pittura*. Milan, P. G. Pontio, 1590.

Pacioli, Luca. *Divina Proportione*. Venice, A. Paganius Paganinus, 1509.

Vasari, Giorgio. *Le vite.* . . Florence, 1550. 2 vols., and Florence, Giunti, 1568. 3 vols.

## 3. COLLECTED OR POLYGRAPHIC WORKS

(Arranged chronologically)

*Raccolta Vinciana*. Comune di Milano, Castello Sforzesco, i-xvii, 1905-1954.

*Leonardo da Vinci. Conferenze Fiorentine*. Milan, Fratelli Treves, 1910.

*Per il IV Centenario della Morte di Leonardo da Vinci, 2 Maggio 1919*. Istituto di Studi Vinciani in Roma. Bergamo, Istituto Italiano d'Arti Grafiche, 1919.

*Leonardo da Vinci. Edizione curata dalla Mostra di Leonardo da Vinci in Milano*. Novara, Istituto Geografico de Agostini. 1940.

*Léonard de Vinci et l'Expérience Scientifique au XVIᵉ Siècle. Paris, 4-7 juillet 1952. Colloques Internationaux*, Paris, 1952-1953.

"L'Art et la Pensée de Léonard de Vinci." Communications du Congrès International du Val de Loire (7-12 juillet 1952). Paris Alger, *Etudes d'Art*, Nos. 8, 9, 10, 1953-1954.

*Atti del Convegno di Studi Vinciani, Firenze-Pisa-Siena 15-18 gennaio, 1953*. Accademia Toscana di Scienze e Lettere "La Columbaria." Florence, Olschki, 1953.

*Leonardo. Saggi e Ricerche*, a cura del Comitato Nazionale per le Onoranze a Leonardo nel Quinto Centenario della Nascita. Rome, Istituto Poligrafico dello Stato, 1954.

## 4. STUDIES ON LEONARDO'S LIFE, PERSONALITY, AND ART

Amoretti, Carlo. *Memorie storiche su la vita, gli studi e opere.* . . Milan, Motta, 1804. Printed simultaneously as preface to *Trattato della Pittura di Leonardo da Vinci*. Milan, Classici Italiani, 1804.

Berensen, Bernhard. *The Study and Criticism of Italian Art*. London, Bell, 1916. pp. 1-37.

————. *The Drawings of the Florentine Painters*. London, Murray, 1903. 2 vols. Amplified edition, Chicago, University of Chicago Press, 1938. 3 vols.

Brion, Marcel. *Génie et destinée. Léonard de Vinci.* Paris, Albin Michel, 1952.

Calvi, Gerolamo. *Vita di Leonardo.* Brescia, Morcelliana, 1936. Reprinted 1949. Cf. above List A3.

Castelfranco, Giorgio. *Leonardo.* Milan, Aldo Martello, 1952.

————. "Introduzione a Leonardo," *Nuova Antologia* n.1816. April 1952.

Clark, Kenneth. *Leonardo da Vinci, an Account of his Development as an Artist.* Cambridge University Press, 1939. Reprinted 1952. Cf. above Lists A3 and B2.

De Rinaldis, Aldo. *Storia dell'opera pittorica di Leonardo da Vinci.* Istituto Vinciano in Roma, VI. Bologna, Zanichelli, 1926.

Douglas, R. Langton. *Leonardo da Vinci, His Life and His Pictures.* Chicago, University of Chicago Press, 1944.

*Encyclopedia italiana, Collana della.* Serie seconda I: Scritti di Enrico Carusi, Giuseppe, Favaro, Giovanni Gentile, Roberto Marcolongo, Adolfo Venturi. Rome, 1934.

Gronau, George. *Leonardo da Vinci.* London, Duckworth, 1903.

Heydenreich, Ludwig Heinrich. *Leonardo.* Berlin, Rembrandt Verlag, 1943. Reprinted with supplements: *Leonardo da Vinci,* Basel, Holbein Verlag, 1954. London, G. Allen and Unwin; New York, Macmillan Company. Cf. above Lists A3, B3 Anatomy, and below E5.

Hildebrandt, Edmund. *Leonardo da Vinci. Der Kuenstler und sein Werk.* Berlin, Grote, 1927.

Horne, Herbert P. *The Life of Leonardo da Vinci by Giorgio Vasari. . .* with a commentary. London, At the sign of the Unicorn; New York, Longmans Green, 1903.

Kikuo, Kosima. *Studien zu Leonardo da Vinci.* Tokio, Iwanami, 1952. 2 vols. (Title in German and Japanese, text in Japanese)

McCurdy, Edward. *Leonardo da Vinci, the Artist.* London, J. Cape, 1933.

Meder, Joseph. *Die Handzeichnung.* Vienna, Schroll, 1919.

Mueller-Walde, Paul. *Leonardo da Vinci. Lebensskizze und Forschungen ueber sein Verhaeltnis zur Florentiner Kunst und zu Rafael.* Munich, Hirth, 1889.

————. "Beitraege zur Kenntnis des Leonardo da Vinci." *Jahrbuch der Kgl. preussischen Kunstsammlungen,* XX. Berlin, 1899.

Muentz, Eugène. *Léonard de Vinci. L'artiste, le penseur, le savant.* Paris, Hachette, 1898-1899.

Popham, A. E. *The Drawings of Leonardo da Vinci.* New York, Reynal & Hitchcock, 1945.

Séailles, Gabriel. *Léonard de Vinci. L'artiste et le savant*. Paris, Perrin, 1892 and 1906.

————. *Léonard de Vinci, biographie critique*. Paris, Laurens, 1903.

Seidlitz, Woldemar von. *Leonardo da Vinci, der Wendepunkt der Renaissance*. Berlin, J. Bard, 1909. 2 vols.

————. *Ausgabe letzter Hand versorgt von K. Zoege von Manteuffel*. Vienna, Phaidon, 1935.

Siren, Osvald. Cf. above List A3.

Solmi, Edmondo. Leonardo. Florence, Barbera, 1900 and 1919.

————. *Scritti vinciani, raccolta di Arrigo Solmi*. Florence, "La Voce," 1924.

Suida, Wilhelm. *Leonardo und sein Kreis*. Munich, Bruckmann, 1929.

Thiis, Ragnar. *Leonardo da Vinci, I: Florentinertiden. Leonardo & Verrocchio*. Kristiania, Nordisk Forlag, 1909. English translation by Jessie Muir. London, H. Jenkins, 1914.

Valentiner, W. R. "Leonardo's early Life." Catalogue, Leonardo da Vinci Loan Exhibition. Los Angeles County Museum, June 3-July 17, 1949. Cf. List 10.

Vallentin, Antonina. *Leonardo da Vinci. The Tragic Pursuit of Perfection*. New York, Viking Press, 1938 and 1952.

————. *Léonard de Vinci*, édition revue et augmentée. Paris, Gallimard, 1950.

Venturi, Adolfo. *Leonardo da Vinci, pittore*. Istituto Vinciano in Roma, II. Bologna, Zanichelli, 1920.

————. *Leonardo e la sua scuola. Mostra Milano*, Novara, 1940.

## 5. LEONARDO'S SOURCES OF LEARNING

D'Adda, Conte Gerolamo. *Leonardo da Vinci e la sua libreria. Note di un bibliofilo*. Milan, 1873. (75 copies, privately printed)

Duhem, Pierre. *Etudes sur Léonard de Vinci. Ceux qu'il a lus et ceux qui l'ont lu*. Paris, Herman, 1906-1913. 3 vols. Reprint, Paris, De Nobele, 1955.

Johnson, M. "Pourquoi Léonard cherchait-il les manuscrits d'Archimède et comment les trouva-t-il?" *Colloques Internationaux*, Paris, 1952-1953. pp. 23-29.

Klibansky, Raymond. "Copernic et Nicolas de Cues." *Ibid*. pp. 225-235.

Marinoni, Augusto. *Le appunti grammaticali*. . . .

Santillana, G. de. "Léonard et ceux qu'il n'a pas lus." In *Colloques Internationaux*. Paris, 1952-1953.

Solmi, Edmondo. "Le fonti dei manoscritti di Leonardo da Vinci." *Giornale storico della letteratura italiana*. Turin, Loescher, 1908.

————. "Niccolo Perotti, Luigi Pulci e gli studi autodidattici di Leonardo da Vinci." *Rivista d'Italia.* Rome, March 1910.

# F. Bibliographies

Baroni, Costantino. "Saggio bibliografico." *Mostra Milano,* Novara, 1940. pp. 509-516.

(Belt) *The Elmer Belt Library of Vinciana Finding List* by Kate Trauman Steinitz and Margot Archer. Los Angeles, 1946. (Multigraphed)

————. *Manuscripts of Leonardo da Vinci, their history, with a description of the manuscript editions in facsimile.* Catalogue by Kate Trauman Steinitz and Margot Archer. Los Angeles. The Ward Ritchie Press, 1948.

————. *A descriptive catalogue of Leonardo's Treatise on Painting, manuscript copies and printed editions.* To appear 1955-1956. University of Copenhagen. Library Research Monograph.

Beltrami, Luca. *Bibliografia Vinciana di Luca Beltrami, 1885-1919.* Rome, tip. del Senato, 1919.

Heydenreich, Ludwig Heinrich. "Leonardo Bibliographie 1939-1952." *Zeitschrift fuer Kunstgeschichte,* xv (1952), 2:195-200.

Mabbott, Maureen Cobb. *Catalogue of the Lieb Memorial Collection of Vinciana.* Hoboken, Stevens Institute of Technology, 1936.

————. "A checklist of Leonardo da Vinci's works." *Bulletin of the New York Public Library,* 38:11, November 1934.

Mieli, Aldo. "Bibliografia degli scritti a stampe e delle reproduzioni dei manoscritti di Leonardo da Vinci." *Archivio di storia della scienza,* i (1919), 2:177-195.

Orlandi, Pellegrino Antonio. *Abecedario pittorico.* Bologna, Pisati, 1704, and editions to 1763.

Schlosser, Julius von. *Die Kunstliteratur.* Vienna, Anton Schroll, 1924.

*Universal Catalogue of Books on Art,* ii. London, Chapman and Hall, 1870. pp. 2067-2069.

Verga, Ettore. *Gli studi intorno a Leonardo da Vinci nell' ultimo cinquantennio 1882-1922.* Opuscoli Vinciani i. Rome, Institute di studi Vinciani, 1923.

————. *Bibliografia Vinciana, 1493-1930.* Bologna, N. Zanichelli, 1931. 2 vols. (This bibliography is an indispensable tool for Vincian studies. 2,900 publications from 1493 to 1930 are listed, summarized and annotated. Cf. all entries of our bibliography published before 1930.) Cf. also above List A3: Cicognara, Du Fresne, Firmin-Didot, Renouard, Smith, Raccolta Vinciana.

# G. Libraries

This Bibliography has been compiled from the catalogues of three great Libraries which are dedicated exclusively to Leonardo da Vinci.

1. The Raccolta Vinciana, Castello Sforzesco, Milan, the holdings of which are represented by Ettore Verga's *Bibliografia Vinciana 1493-1930*, Bologna, Zanichelli, 1931 (2,900 entries). The Raccolta Vinciana, located in the Sforza Castle where Leonardo lived and worked from 1482 to 1499, has increased its holdings since 1930. However, its growth was badly impaired during the war. Cf. *Raccolta Vinciana*, List E3.

2. The Lieb Memorial Library of Vinciana, Stevens Institute of Technology, Hoboken, N.J. Printed catalogue compiled by Maureen Cobb Mabott, 1936, with 985 entries and addenda of *ca.* 100 entries, 1954.

3. The Elmer Belt Library of Vinciana, Los Angeles, California. Finding list of 1946 and card index to date with *ca.* 8,500 entries, including the complete collections of facsimile editions, and of printed editions of the *Treatise on Painting* and of anthologies (cf. above Lists A2, C, D), a photostat archive of the manuscript copies of the *Treatise* (List A1), and a collection of the books Leonardo read in the editions he used.

There are two private libraries in the United States devoted to Leonardo da Vinci: A section of the Burndy Library in Norwalk, Connecticut and the Library of James V. Sallemi in Chicago, Illinois.

The great university libraries and public libraries in the United States have considerable holdings of Vincian editions and literature: The New York Public Library, Library of Congress, Metropolitan Museum of Art Library, Princeton University Library, Fogg Art Museum at Harvard University, Detroit Art Institute, Chicago Art Institute, and others.

# CONCORDANCE

The symbols in the third column of the Concordance refer to the following manuscripts:

A          Fragment of a manuscript, 126 p., 21 x 14 cm., written about 1492, treating on various matters, with precepts and figure drawings for the *Treatise on Painting*. Institut de France.

BN 2038   *ms* Ashburnham I, also called A (2172) Complementi, once comprised folios 65-114 of A above. 68 p., 23 x 16.5 cm., written about 1492, representing the largest and most important manuscript of Leonardo for the *Treatise on Painting*. Institut de France.

E          Notebook, in original binding marked E, 160 p., 15.4 x 9.3 cm., written 1513 and 1514, with notes on bird's flight, mechanics, gravity, plant physiology, and painting. Institut de France.

F          Notebook in original binding marked F, 192 p., 5 x 10.2 cm., written 1508-1509, on water, air, landscapes, and various other subjects. Institut de France.

G          Notebook in original binding marked G, 186 p., 14 x 10 cm., about 1510-1516, containing important parts of the *Treatise on Painting*, especially on landscapes and plants, and a description of The Deluge. Institut de France.

L          Notebook in original binding, marked L, 188 p., 10 x 7 cm., written 1497 and 1502-1503, on flight and various other subjects, also figure drawing. Institut de France.

Triv.      The Codex Trivulzianus, 102 p., 21 x 14 cm., written 1487-1490, with studies on grammar and other subjects, such as light and caricatures. Castello Sforzesco, Milan.

W          Originally one bound volume of some 600 drawings, now arranged in single sheets and 3 bound notebooks on anatomy. Various sizes and subjects, 1489-1519, containing Leonardo's most important anatomical figures, landscapes and plant drawings and descriptions, the great deluge and the world's end. Royal Library, Windsor.

# CONCORDANCE

## PART I (PARAGONE)

| McM. | Urb. | MS. | L. |
|---|---|---|---|
| 1 | 1-1v | | 1 |
| 2 | 2 | | 4 |
| 3 | 1v-2 | | 3 |
| 4 | 2 | | 5 |
| 5 | 2-2v | | 6 |
| 6 | 4v-5 | B.N. 2038 20v | 12 |
| 7 | 4 | | 9 |
| 8 | 4 | | 9 |
| 9 | 4 | | 9 |
| 10 | 4 | | 10 |
| 11 | 4v | | 11 |
| 12 | 12v-13 | | 24 |
| 13 | 7-7v | | 16 |
| 14 | 3v-4 | | 9 |
| 15 | 7v | | 17 |
| 16 | 18 | | 31c |
| 17 | 2v-3 | | 7 |
| 18 | 3-3v | | 8 |
| 19 | 19-19v | | 33 |
| 20 | 28v | | 46 |
| 21 | 1v | | 2 |
| 22 | 7v-8 | | 18 |
| 23 | 5v-6 | | 15 |
| 24 | 6v | | 15 |
| 25 | 19v-20 | | 34 |
| 26 | 17v-18 | | 31b |
| 27 | 6v-7 | | 15a |
| 28 | 14v-15-15v | | 27 |
| 29 | 9-9v-10 | | 20 |
| 30 | 8-8v-9 | B.N. 2038 19-19v | 19 |
| 31 | 5-5v | cf. W 19101-QU III, 7 | 14 |
| 32 | 14-14v | | 26 |
| 33 | 13-13v-14 | | 25 |
| 34 | 15v-16 | | 28 |
| 35 | 5 | | 13 |
| 36 | 6-6v | | 15 |

| McM. | Urb. | Ms. | L. |
|---|---|---|---|
| 75 | 36v-37 | B.N. 2038 26v | 69 |
| 76 | 35v | B.N. 2038 22v | 66 |
| 77 | 39v | | 81 |
| 78 | 34-34v-35 | | 65 |
| 79 | 38 | B.N. 2038 25 | 74 |
| 80 | 38v-39 | | 77 |
| 81 | 32v | B.N. 2038 33v | 57 |
| 82 | 34 | | 62 |
| 83 | 38 | B.N. 2038 26 | 75 |
| 84 | 35 | | 65a |
| 85 | 43v | A. 23 | 105 |
| 86 | 44-44v | | 108 |
| 87 | 44v-45 | | 109 |
| 88 | 46v | B.N. 2038 14v | 117 |
| 89 | 33v | | 59 |
| 90 | 46 | | 114 |
| 91 | 31v | G. 25 | 52 |
| 92 | 32v-33-33v | | 58 |
| 93 | 33v-34 | | 60 |
| 94 | 34 | | 61 |
| 95 | 37v-38 | B.N. 2038 25v | 73 |
| 96 | 39-39v | G. 5v | 79 |
| 97 | 39 | G. 5v | 78 |
| 98 | 49v | B.N. 2038 17v | 129 |
| 99 | 50 | | 131 |
| 100 | 50 | | 132 |
| 101 | 45v | | 111 |
| 102 | 50-50v | | 133 |
| 103 | 50v | E. 79v | 136 |
| 104 | 45v | | 113 |
| 105 | 45v | | 112 |
| 106 | 47v-48 | | 121 |
| 107 | 48-48v | B.N. 2038 1 | 124 |
| 108 | 48 | | 123 |
| 109 | 40 | E. 17 | 84a |
| 110 | 72v | | 236 |
| 111 | 48 | | 122 |
| 112 | 39v | B.N. 2038 33 | 82 |
| 113 | 43 | A. 1 | 100 |
| 114 | 40 | B.N. 2038 29 | 84 |

| McM. | Urb. | Ms. | L. |
|---|---|---|---|
| 115 | 50v | B.N. 2038 14v | 134 |
| 116 | 41 | B.N. 2038 10 | 89 |
| 117 | 39v | B.N. 2038 31v | 83 |
| 118 | 41-41v | B.N. 2038 24 | 90 |
| 119 | 42v | BN. 2038 24 | 97 |
| 120 | 43 | A. 1 | 101 |
| 121 | 41 | A. 28v | 88 |
| 122 | 42v-43 | B.N. 2038 27 | 99 |
| 123 | 43 | B.N. 2038 27 | 98 |
| 124 | 43v-44 | B.N. 2038 27 | 106 |
| 125 | 59 | A. 29 | 175 |
| 126 | 48v-49 | B.N. 2038 22v-E. 19v-20 | 125 |
| 127 | 49 | E. 20 | 126 |
| 128 | 43v | A. 23 | 104 |
| 129 | 40 | B.N. 2038 33 | 85 |
| 130 | 50v | B.N. 2038 14v | 135 |
| 131 | 43 | A. 1v | 102 |
| 132 | 41v | | 92 |
| 133 | 43-43v | A. 23 | 103 |
| 134 | 51 | B.N. 2038 20v | 138 |
| 135 | 47v | | 120 |
| 136 | 40v-41 | | 87 |
| 137 | 41v-42 | | 93 |
| 138 | 55-55v | | 155 |
| 139 | 41v | G. 19v | 91 |
| 140 | 40-40v | | 86 |
| 141 | 42 | | 94 |
| 142 | 45-45v | | 110 |
| 143 | 42 | | 95 |
| 144 | 69v | | 219 |
| 145 | 71v-72 | | 233 |
| 146 | 74 | E. 4 | 246 |
| 147 | 75-75v | | 251 |
| 148 | 71 | | 229 |
| 149 | 71v | | 232 |
| 150 | 71-71v | | 230 |
| 151 | 66v | | 204 |
| 152 | 54 | | 151 |
| 153 | 75v | | 252 |
| 154 | 71v | | 231 |

## PART III

| McM. | Urb. | Ms. | L. |
|---|---|---|---|
| 353 | 138v-139 | | 435 |
| 354 | 137 | | 430 |
| 355 | 111-111v | | 304 |
| 356 | 122 | | 354 |
| 357 | 122 | | 355 |
| 358 | 107 | | 281 |
| 359 | 104 | | 269 |
| 360 | 113v | E. 15 | 316 |
| 361 | 110v | | 301 |
| 362 | 110v | | 300 |
| 363 | 130-130v | | 402 |
| 364 | 128 | | 391 |
| 365 | 120-120v | | 349 |
| 366 | 120v-121 | | 350 |
| 367 | 122 | | 356 |
| 368 | 120 | | 348 |
| 369 | 105v | | 278 |
| 370 | 128v | | 393 |
| 371 | 128 | | 392 |
| 372 | 117v-118 | | 338 |
| 373 | 105v-106-106v | | 279 |
| 374 | 123 | B.N. 2038 29 | 362 |
| 375 | 121-121v | | 352 |
| 376 | 130 | | 401 |
| 377 | 127v-128 | | 390 |
| 378 | 127v | W. 19070 (heading) | 388 |
| 379 | 119v | | 349 |
| 380 | 119v-120 | | 346 |
| 381 | 120 | | 347 |
| 382 | 114 | B.N. 2038 29v | 319 |
| 383 | 114-114v | B.N. 2038 30 | 320 |
| 384 | 106v-107 | | 280 |
| 385 | 122-122v | | 357 |
| 386 | 114v-115 | | 321 |
| 387 | 125v | | 377 |
| 388 | 110-110v | | 299 |
| 389 | 115v | | 326 |
| 390 | 127-127v | | 386 |
| 391 | 125v-126 | | 379 |
| 392 | 127v | | 387 |

| McM. | Urb. | Ms. | L. |
|---|---|---|---|
| 433 | 133 | | 411 |
| 434 | 133-133v | | 412 |
| 435 | 133v | | 413 |
| 436 | 140v | | 439 |
| 437 | 157 | | 499 |
| 438 | 107 | | 282 |
| 439 | 131v | | 406 |
| 440 | 131v-132 | B.N. 2038 28 | 407 |
| 441 | 131-131v | | 405 |
| 442 | 130v-131 | | 404 |
| 443 | 133v-134 | B.N. 2038 33 | 414 |
| 444 | 156v-157 | | 498 |
| 445 | 154-154v | G. 32 | 488 |
| 446 | 134v-135 | B.N. 2038 31v | 419 |
| 447 | 164 | | 526 |
| 448 | 145v | E. 17 | 472 |
| 449 | 164 | | 528a |
| 450 | 136 | | 424 |
| 451 | 137-137v | | 431 |
| 452 | 135-135v-136 | | 422 |
| 453 | 140v-141 | | 440 |
| 454 | 134v | B.N. 2038 31v | 418 |
| 455 | 141 | | 441 |
| 456 | 136 | | 423 |
| 457 | 142v-143 | | 445 |
| 458 | 156v | | 497 |
| 459 | 154v | | 491 |
| 460 | 153v | | 485 |
| 461 | 141-141v | | 442 |
| 462 | 150v | | 475 |
| 463 | 137 | | 429 |
| 464 | 153 | G. 23v | 482 |
| 465 | 149v | | 471 |
| 466 | 154v-155 | | 492 |
| 467 | 153v | | 484 |
| 468 | 154 | | 487 |
| 469 | 137v-138-138v | | 433 |
| 470 | 147v | E. 3v | 464 |
| 471 | 149-149v | | 470 |
| 472 | 149 | | 468 |

| *McM.* | *Urb.* | *Ms.* | *L.* |
|---|---|---|---|
| 513 | 164 | | 526a |
| 514 | 146 | B.N. 2038 20v | 458 |
| 515 | 163v | | 524 |
| 516 | 163v | | 525 |
| 517 | 164 | | 528 |
| 518 | 145 | | 454 |
| 519 | 154v | B.N. 2038 26 | 490 |
| 520 | 150v-151 | | 475a |
| 521 | 162-162v | | 517 |
| 522 | 136v-137 | | 428 |
| 523 | 148-148v | | 466 |
| 524 | 159v-160 | | 507 |
| 525 | 160 | | 508 |
| 526 | 151 | | 476a |
| 527 | 164 | | 527 |
| 528 | 151-151v | | 477a |
| 529 | 142-142v | | 444 |
| 530 | 162v | | 518 |
| 531 | 162v-163 | | 519 |
| 532 | 144 | | 448 |
| 533 | 143-143v | | 446 |
| 534 | 147 | | 462 |
| 535 | 144v | | 451 |
| 536 | 144 | | 449 |
| 537 | 144v-145 | | 452 |
| 538 | 147v-148 | | 465 |
| 539 | 144 | | 450 |
| 540 | 145v | | 457 |
| 541 | 147-147v | | 463 |
| 542 | 163 | | 521 |
| 543 | 163 | | 522 |
| 544 | 163-163v | | 523 |
| 545 | 158v | | 505 |
| 546 | 158v-159-159v | | 506 |
| 547 | 151 | | 477 |
| 548 | 157-157v | | 501 |
| 549 | 157 | | 500 |
| 550 | 135v | B.N. 2038 31v | 420 |
| 551 | 157v | E. 6v | 502 |
| 552 | 157v-158 | | 503 |

| McM. | Urb. | Ms. | L. |
|---|---|---|---|
| 588 | 179 | | 572 |
| 589 | 176v | B.N. 248v | 557 |
| 590 | 175v | E. 32v | 553 |
| 591 | 175v-176 | E. 32v | 553a |
| 592 | 176 | | 553b |
| 593 | 176v | | 558 |
| 594 | 176v-177 | | 559 |
| 595 | 187-187v | B.N. 2038 22 | 616 |
| 596 | 183v | | 597 |
| 597 | 179 | E. 3v & G. 3v | 569 |
| 598 | 195 | G. 3v | 663 |
| 599 | 193 | | 653 |
| 600 | 188 | | 623 |
| 601 | 190v | | 638 |
| 602 | 210v | | 722 |
| 603 | 190v | | 639 |
| 604 | 194v | | 660 |
| 605 | 203v-204 | | 696 |
| 606 | 204 | | 697 |
| 607 | 203v | | 695 |
| 608 | 188 | | 624 |
| 609 | 210v-211 | | 723 |
| 610 | 211 | | 724 |
| 611 | 183v | E. 31 | 596 |
| 612 | 178v | | 566 |
| 613 | 176 | E. 32v | 553c |
| 614 | 178v | | 567 |
| 615 | 179v | | 574 |
| 616 | 181-181v | | 584 |
| 617 | 182-182v | E. 32 | 590 |
| 618 | 183v | E. 31 | 595 |
| 619 | 182 | | 588 |
| 620 | 182 | | 589 |
| 621 | 183-183v | E. 31 | 594 |
| 622 | 215v-216 | B.N. 2038 15v | 733 |
| 623 | 184 | | 600 |
| 624 | 184-184v | | 601 |
| 625 | 182v | | 591 |
| 626 | 181 | | 583 |
| 627 | 187v | | 618 |

| McM. | Urb. | Ms. | L. |
|---|---|---|---|
| 628 | 187 | B.N. 2038 29v | 615 |
| 629 | 186v | B.N. 2038 30 | 613 |
| 630 | 188-188v | | 627 |
| 631 | 186v | B.N. 2038 30 | 612 |
| 632 | 185v-186 | | 607 |
| 633 | 178v | | 565 |
| 634 | 177 | | 560 |
| 635 | 187v | | 617 |
| 636 | 140-140v | | 438a |
| 637 | 187v-188 | | 621 |
| 638 | 178v | | 568 |
| 639 | 211 | | 725 |
| 640 | 211v-212 | | 725a |
| 641 | 215v | B.N. 2038 15v | 732 |
| 642 | 214v-215 | B.N. 2038 15 | 731 |
| 643 | 212-212v | B.N. 2038 11 | 726 |
| 644 | 212v | B.N. 2038 11 | 727 |
| 645 | 199 | | 685 |
| 646 | 199-199v | | 686 |
| 647 | 199v-200 | | 687 |
| 648 | 216-216v | | 734 |
| 649 | 216v | | 735 |
| 650 | 200 | | 688 |
| 651 | 230v | G. 19v | 788 |
| 652 | 225v | | 764 |
| 653 | 225-225v | | 763 |
| 654 | 225v | | 765&a |
| 655 | 225v | | 766 |
| 656 | 208v | B.N. 2038 18v | 717 |
| 657 | 176v | B.N. 2038 9v | 555a |
| 658 | 181 | | 582 |
| 659 | 179v | | 575 |
| 660 | 179v-180 | E. 30v | 576 |
| 661 | 180 | | 577 |
| 662 | 183 | E. 30v | 593 |
| 663 | 210 | | 720 |
| 664 | 210 | | 721 |
| 665 | 238-238v | | 810 |
| 666 | 225 | | 762 |
| 667 | 233v | | 755 |

| McM. | Urb. | Ms. | L. |
|------|------|-----|-----|
| 708 | 177v-178 | | 563 |
| 709 | 178 | | 564 |
| 710 | 180v | | 581 |
| 711 | 176 | | 554 |
| 712 | 184v | | 602 |
| 713 | 184v-185 | | 603 |
| 714 | 180v | | 579 |
| 715 | 180v | | 580 |
| 716 | 185 | | 604 |
| 717 | 222-222v | | 751 |
| 718 | 198v-199 | | 683 |
| 719 | 222v | | 752 |
| 720 | 228v | | 781 |
| 721 | 228-228v | | 780 |
| 722 | 228v-229 | | 782 |
| 723 | 229-229v | | 783 |
| 724 | 204-204v-205 | | 698 |
| 725 | 202v | | 694e |
| 726 | 197 | | 677 |
| 727 | 184 | | 599 |
| 728 | 195-195v | | 666 |
| 729 | 186v-187 | B.N. 2038 30 | 614 |
| 730 | 183v-184 | | 598 |
| 731 | 180-180v | | 578 |
| 732 | 187v | | 620 |
| 733 | 238v-239 | | 810b |
| 734 | 183 | E. 30v | 592 |
| 735 | 217v | | 738 |
| 736 | 190v-191 | | 640 |
| 737 | 191 | | 642 |
| 738 | 197v-198 | | 679 |
| 739 | 205 | | 699 |
| 740 | 208 | | 713 |
| 741 | 140v | | 438b |
| 742 | 185-185v | | 605 |
| 743 | 196 | C. 12v | 670 |
| 744 | 176 | | 553e |
| 745 | 176-176v | | 555 |
| 746 | 190v | | 637 |
| 747 | 193v-194 | | 658 |

| McM. | Urb. | Ms. | L. |
|---|---|---|---|
| 748 | 194 | | 659 |
| 749 | 240 | | 817 |
| 750 | 219v-220 | B.N. 2038 32 | 745 |
| 751 | 226 | | 769 |
| 752 | 224 | | 757 |
| 753 | 188v-189 | | 628 |
| 754 | 189-189v | | 631 |
| 755 | 189v | | 632 |
| 756 | 212v-213-213v | B.N. 2038 13v | 728 |
| 757 | 213v | B.N. 2038 13v | 729 |
| 758 | 186 | | 608 |
| 759 | 179-179v | | 573 |
| 760 | 202-202v | | 694d |
| 761 | 208 | B.N. 2038 33v | 712 |
| 762 | 226 | | 768 |
| 763 | 192v-193 | | 652 |
| 764 | 207v | | 711 |
| 765 | 206v | | 706 |
| 766 | 205v-206 | | 702 |
| 767 | 190 | | 634 |
| 768 | 239v | | 815 |
| 769 | 195 | | 664 |
| 770 | 197 | | 676 |
| 771 | 197 | | 675 |
| 772 | 227v | E. 31v | 777 |
| 773 | 226-226v | | 770 |
| 774 | 227 | | 775 |
| 775 | 227 | | 773 |
| 776 | 227 | | 774 |
| 777 | 226v | | 771 |
| 778 | 226v-227 | | 772 |
| 779 | 220 | B.N. 2038 32 | 746 |
| 780 | 227-227v | E. 31v | 776 |
| 781 | 227v | E. 31v | 778 |
| 782 | 227v-228 | | 779 |
| 783 | 200v-201 | | 692 |
| 784 | 201 | | 693 |
| 785 | 206-206v | | 704 |
| 786 | 229v-230 | B.N. 2038 20 | 785 |
| 787 | 190-190v | | 636 |

| McM. | Urb. | Ms. | L. |
|---|---|---|---|
| 788 | 186 | | 609 |
| 789 | 206v-207 | | 707 |
| 790 | 205v | | 701 |
| 791 | 195v-196 | B.N. 2038 33v | 668 |
| 792 | 206v | | 705 |
| 793 | 193-193v | | 654 |
| 794 | 193v | | 655 |
| 795 | 225v-226 | | 767 |
| 796 | 189v-190 | | 633 |
| 797 | 192 | | 645 |
| 798 | 191v-192 | | 644 |
| 799 | 239v-240 | | 816 |
| 800 | 207-207v | | 709 |
| 801 | 207 | | 708 |
| 802 | 207v | | 710 |
| 803 | 206 | | 703 |
| 804 | 241-241v | | 821 |
| 805 | 218-218v | | 742 |
| 806 | 218 | | 741 |
| 807 | 217v-218 | | 740 |
| 808 | 218v | | 743 |
| 809 | 233v-234 | | 797 |
| 810 | 231-231v | | 791 |
| 811 | 189 | | 629 |
| 812 | 205 | | 698a |
| 813 | 205 | | 698b |
| 814 | 189 | | 630 |
| 815 | 205-205v | B.N. 2038 10 | 700 |
| 816 | 192 | B.N. 2038 20v | 646 |
| 817 | 200v | | 690 |
| 818 | 230-230v | | 786 |
| 819 | 230v | | 787 |
| 820 | 200v | | 691 |
| 821 | 208 | | 714 |
| 822 | 238v | | 810a |
| 823 | 233-233v | | 795 |
| 824 | 231v-232 | | 792 |
| 825 | 232 | | 793 |
| 826 | 232-232v-233 | | 794 |
| 827 | 234-234v | | 798 |

## PART VI

| McM. | Urb. | Ms. | L. |
|---|---|---|---|
| 905 | 267v | | 922 |
| 906 | 252v | | 852 |
| 907 | 252v | | 851 |
| 908 | 250v-251 | | 844 |
| 909 | 250v | | 843 |
| 910 | 251v-252 | | 848 |
| 911 | 253v-254 | | 860 |
| 912 | 257v | | 880 |
| 913 | 261 | G. 9 | 897 |
| 914 | 255v-256 | G. 12 | 869 |
| 915 | 262v | | 908 |
| 916 | 255 | | 866 |
| 917 | 255-255v | | 867 |
| 918 | 257-257v | | 879 |
| 919 | 254v | | 863 |
| 920 | 262 | G. 20v | 902 |
| 921 | 261-261v | G. 22 | 898 |
| 922 | 259 | E. 19 | 889 |
| 923 | 261v | G. 21v | 899 |
| 924 | 261v | G. 22v | 900 |
| 925 | 261v-262 | G. 21 | 901 |
| 926 | 260v-261 | G. 8v | 896 |
| 927 | 260v | G. 10v | 894 |
| 928 | 252 | | 849 |
| 929 | 257 | | 878 |
| 930 | 257 | | 876 |
| 931 | 265v | G. 21 | 916 |
| 932 | 264-264v | G. 6 | 913 |
| 933 | 258v | G. 9v | 885 |
| 934 | 266 | | 918a |
| 935 | 256 | G. 28v | 872 |
| 936 | 256v-257 | | 875 |
| 937 | 256v | G. 28v | 874 |
| 938 | 256-256v | G. 28v | 873 |
| 939 | 260-260v | G. 10-10v | 893 |
| 940 | 257 | | 877 |
| 941 | 243 | | 822 |
| 942 | 268 | | 924a |
| 943 | 262 | G. 20v | 903 |
| 944 | 267v | | 923 |

# INDEX